Murderers or Martyrs

George Skelly

Murderers or Martyrs
George Skelly

ISBN 978-1-904380-80-1 (Paperback)
ISBN 978-1-908132-06-9 (Adobe E-book)
ISBN 978-1-908132-31-1 (Kindle/ePub E-book)

Cover design © 2012 Waterside Press. Design by www.gibgob.com

Cataloguing-In-Publication Data A catalogue record for this book can be obtained on request from the British Library.

e-book *Murderers or Martyrs* is available in various ebook formats and also to subscribers of Myilibrary and Dawsonera.

Printed in the UK by CPI-Antony Rowe, Bumper's Farm, Chippenham, SN14 6LH.

UK distributor Gardners Books, 1 Whittle Drive, Eastbourne, East Sussex, BN23 6QH. Tel: +44 (0)1323 521777; sales@gardners.com; www.gardners.com

North American distributor Ingram Book Company, One Ingram Blvd, La Vergne, TN 37086, USA. (800) 937-8000, orders@ingrambook.com, ipage.ingrambook.com

Published 2012 by
Waterside Press Ltd.
Sherfield Gables
Sherfield on Loddon
Hook, Hampshire
RG27 0JG, United Kingdom

Telephone +44(0)1256 882250
E-mail enquiries@watersidepress.co.uk
Online catalogue WatersidePress.co.uk

Murderers or Martyrs

George Skelly

With a Foreword by Lord Goldsmith PC, QC

WATERSIDE PRESS

CONTENTS

ABOUT THE AUTHOR

George Skelly is a renowned writer and campaigner against miscarriages of justice, and also a novelist and short story writer. After leaving school at 15, an eleven-plus failure, he was later educated at Ruskin College Oxford and Liverpool University, obtaining joint honours in History and English. He is the author of *The Cameo Conspiracy* (Third edition, Waterside Press, 2011), which helped to exonerate the two men convicted in that historic murder case. A father of four, he lives on Merseyside.

THE AUTHOR OF THE FOREWORD

Lord Peter Henry Goldsmith, Baron Goldsmith PC, QC was Attorney General for England and Wales and Northern Ireland from 2001 to 2007, the highest law office in Britain. He now works for the USA law firm Debevoise & Plimpton as head of European litigation practice. Lord Goldsmith explains his longstanding connection with the Devlin and Burns case in the *Foreword*.

ACKNOWLEDGEMENTS

Bringing to the reader the full story of this case would not have been possible without the consistent support and practical assistance of several persons to whom I am greatly indebted. They are:

My publisher, Bryan Gibson of Waterside Press for having the courage to publish the story when bigger national publishers refused to do so.

Lord Goldsmith PC, QC for kindly reading the manuscript and providing the *Foreword*.

Mrs Joan Downing, who kindly provided a statement in 2011 about the police pressure which forced her to change her story in 1952.

Mrs Pat Jones, for the original prison letters of Devlin and Burns to her father John Ford.

Dorothy Skinner, for old street maps and photographs of Hulme and Deansgate.

Kate McNicholl of Merseyside Police for her courtesy and kind assistance.

Anne "Tejar" Carson, Marie Milne's younger sister for her statement of Superintendent Balmer's pressure on her sister and family.

Brian Jones (former police officer) for the photograph of the Lighthouse Café in 1951.

Joe Kirwan, a close friend of Devlin and Burns who helped fill in a lot of the gaps.

Jean Woolfenden, Edward Devlin's niece, for showing me around Hulme and the Barracks Flats.

Most of all there are three special people to whom I extend my deepest and most sincere gratitude. Without their unyielding loyalty and support over many years this book would never have been possible. If I were a soldier I could not have had three better comrades-in-arms. These "Three Musketeers" are:

The unassuming Mr Michael Rigby, a murder aficionado himself, who made numerous journeys down to the National Archives at Kew, London, at his own expense and obtained all or most of the files which form the basis of this book.

Mr Chris Kelly, a former Merseyside police sergeant of great compassion and a sense of justice, who—without my even asking—willingly, in his own time, and at his own expense, took photographs of locations, obtained street maps and other documents and carried out much valuable research on my behalf.

Then, last but most certainly not least, retired businessman Mr Lou Santangeli. Words cannot express my deep gratitude to him. A man with a profound sense of fairness and outrage at injustice, he was responsible for the Appeal Court's 2003 quashing of the convictions in the infamous 1950 Cameo Cinema murder case. I have been greatly honoured by Lou's friendship and his unflagging moral support and practical assistance during the past ten years.

All three men are to be greatly commended for sustaining me all these years with their faith and confidence, and for steadfastly sharing my belief in the innocence of Devlin and Burns.

Finally, my sincere thanks go to those individuals, including former prison and police staff, who shared their experiences with me and concerning whom I willingly accept their understandable wish for anonymity.

George Skelly
2012

WITNESS STATEMENTS

A selection of key statements from the case can be viewed in full, on the Waterside Press website:

www.WatersidePress.co.uk/devlinandburns

FOREWORD

As a young boy growing up in Liverpool I was close to three cousins who were the daughters of my mother's elder sister. My mother and her sister Thelma were very close and so we children were close to our cousins. Thelma's husband was Joseph Norton.

I knew him as a serious but kindly man; an outstanding and prominent solicitor with his own practice and a local politician—a former officer in the Army, a leading Conservative on the city council, an alderman and one time parliamentary candidate for a local constituency. He went on take up a judicial post in Birmingham.

I regret though that I never had the occasion that I can recall to talk to him about his earlier legal practice. This is more than a shame as this book reveals that Joseph Norton was one of the two energetic and dogged solicitors who acted for the two young men who, as George Skelly describes here, were prosecuted, convicted and executed for the brutal murder in her own home of Alice Rimmer, a Liverpool widow, in 1952.

I would have welcomed the opportunity to hear first hand from Uncle Joe his impressions of the trial, of the actions of the trial judge Finnemore J and of the competence of counsel, all of them known to me at least by reputation—Basil Nield QC, later Nield J, Rose Heilbron QC, the extraordinary woman advocate with so many firsts to her name, one of the first woman QCs. The first woman appointed recorder, first woman to sit at the Old Bailey as judge, and Sir Noel Goldie. I knew Rose Heilbron a little as she and her husband were friends of my parents.

I would also have liked to have his impressions of the other defending solicitor, Harry Livermore who went on to be Lord Mayor of Liverpool. He was another very prominent Liverpool solicitor. He had a reputation for being quick tempered, a trait this book bears out, though sorely provoked by what he saw as a seriously unfair process, according to the account given by the author of the committal proceedings.

But above all, the great interest of this book is that George Skelly has re-created in painstaking detail the different stages of this trial; the committal proceedings conducted by Norton and Livermore for the defence; the trial before judge and jury with the bulk of defence taken by Rose Heilbron for Devlin, the unsuccessful appeal before the forbidding figure of Lord Goddard and a private inquiry into new evidence by Albert Gerrard QC.

George Skelly inevitably draws strong comparisons with the miscarriage of justice which was eventually found in 2003 to have occurred with the convictions of George Kelly and Charles Connolly in connection with the murders of Leonard Thomas, manager of the Cameo Cinema in Liverpool and his assistant. In that case the role of Chief Inspector Herbert Balmer came into strong focus. Here too, Balmer was the key figure in charge in practice of the investigation, though he never gave evidence in the trial, a fact the author strongly criticises. George Skelly was very influential in the investigation which resulted in that decision by the Court of Appeal overturning those convictions as a miscarriage of justice

Here George Skelly presents a powerful case in this extremely well researched work, that the convictions of Burns and Devlin were also the result of police misconduct, the suppression of evidence and the suborning of witnesses. In the shady world of petty criminals, prostitutes and the dark underside of Liverpool life which the author skilfully and vividly recreates, the possibility that a false case was put together in order to ensure that someone answered for what was a terrible murder seems credible even if shocking. Is this what actually happened? Is it a true case? That is something that the readers of this book will have to judge for themselves, as George Skelly's application to the Criminal Cases Review Commission to refer this case to the Court of appeal was refused.

Whatever the truth, the author does an enormous service by reminding us of the imperfections of the criminal justice procedure which in the 1950s and beyond created the conditions in which miscarriages of justice—and worse—could occur.

What comes across clearly from this exceptionally clear account of the trials, the evidence given and the performance of the lawyers involved, is how many opportunities for injustice there were before the reforms of the 1990s when we had (it is to be hoped) learnt the lessons of the improprieties of police forces, such as the notorious West Midlands Serious Crime Squad. As the author shows this was not just a problem in high profile "political" cases like that of the Birmingham Six but cases like those of Burns and Devlin. Take for instance the issue of the witness statements which George Skelly believes were not disclosed to the defence: that key prosecution witness Milne had made two statements to the police and not just one; statements of two other key prosecution witnesses, McLoughlin and Bury were also not disclosed allegedly; and also a statement of the man Campbell who had pleaded guilty to the warehouse robbery, which grounded the alibi of Burns and Devlin and which the judge refused to order be shown to the defence.

If anyone ever questions modern requirements for prosecution disclosure they could do far worse than study this book to see why such disclosure is essential for justice.

The case also paints an intriguing picture of the legal profession of the time. Rose Heilbron comes across as a fine forensic practitioner. She is not saved from the sharp scalpel of criticism at points not made or complaints not aired. Though I imagine the author would be the first to acknowledge that the time he has had to study the evidence and go back over it has given him insights that counsel, in the midst of an ongoing and fast moving trial, would not have had the time to develop. Sir Noel Goldie appears as a somewhat quaint and out of touch lawyer of the older school, quoting literary allusions that may have gone over the heads of the jury but his points were nonetheless telling.

As for Joseph Norton, the reason George Skelly asked me to get involved in the first place, I am glad to have learned from this account of his tireless role to acquire the acquittal of his client. One of the final letters George Skelly quotes, written by Burns just days before his execution, says of Norton that he had done everything possible. The author himself refers to Norton as "intellectually meticulous". That is a description of my Uncle Joe that I can readily acknowledge and appreciate.

My own view of the case? There is of course one guiding principle of which we should be rightly proud in our legal system—the principle of reasonable doubt—that no one should be convicted unless the court is sure of guilt; that if there is a reasonable doubt the defendant must have the benefit of that doubt. One would think that the more serious the crime the easier it would be to apply that principle. However that is not necessarily the case in my experience. Where a truly horrific crime is involved, a brutal murder, sexual offences against children, or a shocking terrorist offence, a jury may feel pressure to convict and the more certain they may become that the police must have got the right man. So in those cases it is even more important to keep in mind that golden rule.

As the author shows here there were real difficulties with the prosecution case: the extent to which the case depended on the evidence of persons of dubious character; why nothing was taken or even disturbed from Alice Rimmer's home, though allegedly the two defendants had been waiting there for some time before she arrived home and the purpose of their venture was robbery not murder; why there was no identifiable blood on the defendants' clothing, even though according to one forensic witness called by the prosecution, there was blood spouting everywhere, "even on the walls" from the many separate wounds poor Mrs Rimmer suffered; and how the prosecution dealt with the alibi put forward by the two that they were robbing a warehouse in Manchester on the very night they were said to be committing the murder in Liverpool.

To many, indeed all of these points, there may have been an answer. Indeed that seems to be what the jury and Court of Appeal later thought. But there may not have been. That is without even considering whether there was important undisclosed evidence. The point is this, as Sir Noel Goldie said in his closing speech, quoting from George Bernard Shaw's St Joan, if the jury were left saying, "I wonder" that must indicate a reasonable doubt so they must acquit.

Having read this detailed and careful account, at the very least I am left saying, "I wonder".

Lord Goldsmith PC, QC
October 2012

For the other innocents — The widows, Alice, Amy and Nellie.

PREFACE

Over the years there have been several superficial (and sometimes erroneous) versions of the "Cranborne Road murder" by such people as crime writer Richard Whittington-Egan, "crime historian" Vincent Burke, barrister Fenton Bresler, author David Parry and a Liverpool purveyor of ghost stories and the supernatural. All have been short accounts as parts of anthologies of murder cases.

The distortions and inaccuracies have—to a greater or lesser degree—been disappointing and are likely to be due to most of them being regurgitations of newspaper and other accounts rather than resulting from original research. There has never been a fully-documented and detailed examination of the case. And none have included the abundance of suppressed evidence.

Some of the above have described Detective Chief Superintendent Herbert Balmer, who headed the investigation, in glowing terms. Indeed, Fenton Bresler—apart from giving the wrong month and year of the trial—who apparently knew Balmer personally, described him as, "The finest kind of senior police officer. Honest, hardworking, relying on his experience as much as modern forensic science". This, however, was not quite the view of Lord Justice Rix, who in the 2003 Court of Appeal Cameo Cinema case judgement condemned him for "deliberate concealment" of evidence.

In his anthology, *Liverpool Murders* (Bluecoat Press, 2009), Richard Whittington-Egan, alleged that principal Crown witnesses were violently attacked by friends of Edward Devlin and Alfred Burns after their executions, including an instance of borstal boys drawing straws to decide which of them on his release would attack a certain witness! This chapter entitled "The Frightened Witnesses" does not however cite any hospital admissions or say whether anyone was ever charged with these alleged attacks. Nor does the author mention that Balmer was an elected member of the Liverpool Press Club and often provided fictitious stories for his journalist friends.

In David Parry's account (*Merseyside Murders*, Carnegie 1973) there are innumerable errors, including wrong dates, names, etc. And the Liverpool purveyor of the supernatural even manages to introduce courtroom spiritual apparitions into his version of the case!

Most importantly, all of these accounts have failed to fully put the case for the defence. The primary purpose therefore of this book is to dispel the perpetuation of hearsay and folklore and to set the record straight.

During recent and past years there have been many armchair detectives and wild theorists, including the ghost writer—who in his chapter implies that Alice Rimmer was murdered by a secret lover and that he (the writer) was later visited by the lover's ghost whilst giving a talk at the trial venue!

Fenton Bresler (*Scales of Justice,* Wiedenfeld & Nicholson 1973), Vincent Burke (*Liverpool Murders & Trials,* History Press 2008) and Whittington-Egan (who presumably was present at the committal proceedings and trial) have all condemned Devlin and Burns for their alleged cavalier behaviour during both sets of proceedings. Yet with a little human insight it is not difficult to understand the young men's attitude—that in the certain knowledge of their innocence they found the whole process ludicrous and surreal. If their letters from prison are anything to go by, this was probably the case. The tragedy is that their belief and confidence that British justice would surely see sense and free them, was horrifically misplaced.

INTRODUCTION

Let those who have failed take courage though the enemy seems to have won.
If he be in the wrong, though his ranks are strong, the battle is not yet done.
For sure as morning follows the darkest hour of night,
No question is ever settled until it's settled right.

Ella Wheeler Wilcox (1850-1919)

On the morning of the 25th April 1952 two young Manchester men were hanged side-by-side at Liverpool's Walton Prison. Edward Francis Devlin, 22, and Alfred Burns, 21, had been convicted the previous February of the murder of Mrs Beatrice Alice Rimmer, a 52-year old widow who was found battered to death in the blood-splattered hallway of her home, 7 Cranborne Road, in the Wavertree district of Liverpool.

The murder took place on a Sunday evening, August 19th 1951, but Mrs Rimmer's body was not found until the following evening by her only child, 25-year-old Thomas, when he called at the house.

The evidence against the two men was purely circumstantial. There were no fingerprints, no murder weapon, no forensic or material evidence, no eye-witnesses and no incriminating bloodstains on the accused.

The scenario put forward by the prosecution bore a striking similarity to that in the Cameo Cinema murder case two years previously: the main Crown witnesses being a young convict with a long criminal record and two young prostitutes. In addition, the detective orchestrating the investigation was Detective Chief Superintendent Herbert Balmer, who had been promoted to Head of Liverpool CID following his "outstanding work in bringing the Cameo killer to justice". Indeed the police allegations against Devlin and Burns were almost identical to those in the Cameo case, including planted newspaper stories of intimidation and attacks on prosecution witnesses. Similarly there were police "verbals", impropriety, suppression of evidence and witness statements, and similar judicial and public prejudice against the two defendants.

Despite the official congratulations bestowed on Balmer following the Cameo convictions—including the award of the Kings Police Medal—the

Court of Appeal, 53 years later in 2003, quashed the convictions of the two accused men in that case and condemned Balmer for withholding evidence, altering witness statements and committing perjury.

From the moment of their arrests in October 1951, Edward Devlin and Alfred Burns, both admitted thieves, were portrayed by the police and the press as hardened, violent criminals. The reality, however, was quite different. Devlin had four previous convictions for petty larceny, three of them as a juvenile. His entire time spent in custody amounted to one month in a childrens remand home and six months' imprisonment as a 21-year-old for stealing a box of tomatoes. Burns had seven convictions for larceny and office breaking, of which only two were as an adult. His first juvenile conviction was for stealing four loaves from a baker's van. His custodial sentences amounted to one month in a children's detention centre and three years borstal training. Neither man had ever been convicted for any offence of violence.

The Crown case against them was that they had planned the crime weeks in advance with the complicity of two young prostitutes and a young convict — who days before the murder had been arrested, and later convicted of breaking into his own aunt's house in the same road. According to the prosecution both Devlin and Burns, although from Manchester, had detailed knowledge of the layout of Mrs Rimmer's home and her daily routine and had told the convict that she had plenty of money in the house. Yet no money or property was taken.

There had been no ransacking of drawers or wardrobes as might be expected from two housebreakers. Indeed nothing in the house was even disturbed. The police explanation for this was that the victim — who had returned that Sunday evening from visiting her son — was attacked immediately upon entering the house, which indeed she was. But contradictorily, the prosecution also alleged that the accused had been in the house for an hour-and-a-half before she arrived home. If true, it defies logic that they would immediately savagely attack her with weapons when it might have been more productive to have carried out the robbery and left the scene before she arrived.

The two accused, who vehemently protested their innocence throughout, maintained that on the evening of August 19th they were actually 30 miles away in Manchester breaking into a clothing warehouse. A female accomplice on that robbery was threatened by the police—on pain of imprisonment—to make a statement denying she was with them, which fatally damaged their alibi. Nonetheless they produced several other alibi witnesses, including a male accomplice and the owner of the warehouse. Yet the jury chose to accept the prosecution evidence of the young convict and the two prostitutes—one of whom testified that she accompanied the two men to the Rimmer home on the murder night.

The evidence of expert witnesses, pathologist George Manning and Home Office forensic scientist Dr Firth was accepted without question by the jury. This was decades before a succession of murder trials where the "evidence" of "expert witnesses" such as Sir Roy Meadows in the Sally Clarke and Angela Cannings child murder cases and forensic "expert" Dr Robin Keeley in the trial of Barry George for the Jill Dando murder, was found to be seriously flawed. Indeed, Dr Keeley finally admitted at Barry George's second, successful 2007 appeal that his evidence was wrong. Similarly it was the flawed evidence and incompetence of so-called expert witnesses in the Judith Ward, Stefan Kiszko, Birmingham Six, Guildford Four and Maguire Family cases, which ensured the quashing of all their convictions. The Devlin and Burns defence teams however, engaged on legal aid, did not have the resources to engage their own expert witnesses to adequately challenge Manning and Firth.

From the moment of their arrests on the 10th and 11th October 1951 respectively, until the morning of their executions on the 25th April 1952, the men's privacy and their legal and basic human rights were outrageously violated by the state. Every letter they wrote or received—in addition to the routine prison censorship—was diligently copied to the police, the Director of Public Prosecutions and the Home Office. These were used by Liverpool police to investigate the backgrounds—criminal or otherwise—of their friends and family and other potential defence witnesses. Also at the request of the police, every conversation during their prison visits by family and friends was diligently recorded by the Governor and relayed to the same authorities. Indeed, even consultations between the men and their lawyers during prison visits, which should have been protected by the sacred lawyer-client relationship, were supervised and recorded verbatim. Yet whenever the police visited the prison to interview the main prosecution witness and others, they were afforded complete privacy.

As for the prison's chief medical officer, Dr Brisby, they were treated by him no better than rats in an experimental laboratory. Their daily demeanour, physical and mental condition, together with their weight, was assiduously recorded in detail. Highly prejudicial and derogatory comments, before their trial, about their likely guilt were also included at regular intervals in official prison reports, variously describing one or the other as "detestable", "callous", "narcissistic", "ruthless", "manipulative", "devious" and "cocky".

Despite the paucity of even the circumstantial evidence against the two men, the all male jury took a mere 75 minutes to reach their guilty verdicts. Addressing the jury from the dock before sentence of death was passed, Burns, passionately declared

> I cannot understand how you brought a verdict of guilty. It is a most unfair verdict. We have told the truth and nothing but the truth but you have been prejudiced against us.

How indeed could a jury have come to such an unreasonable decision so readily? In the 1940s and 1950s there were some notoriously fearsome "hanging judges" such as Messrs Justice Avory, Oliver, Humphreys, Hilbery and Lord Goddard. What is less known is that there was a similar propensity among juries—at that time exclusively property owners. In this regard none were more notorious for being pro-prosecution than Liverpool juries. It was one such that convicted William Herbert Wallace in 1931 for the murder of his wife. He was later freed on appeal by reason of the jury's "perverse" verdict, which was "wholly unjustified by the evidence". It was also a 1950 Liverpool jury which convicted the executed George Kelly in the Cameo case after a mere 55 minutes deliberation—only for him to be posthumously exonerated 53 years later by the Court of Appeal.

Following the guilty verdicts, Alfred Burns concluded his address to the jury by saying, "I hope at the Appeal Court everything will come out in the true light." But he was to be tragically disappointed. The appeal, presided over by the infamous Lord Chief Justice, Lord Goddard, was a charade and a perversion of justice.

After the trial new evidence emerged that not only had one of the prostitutes admitted to three other girls that she had lied, and had named another man as the real killer, but also that another man had confessed to the murder. The Court of Appeal however—as it had in the 1947 case of Walter Rowland—refused to hear this new evidence and dismissed both appeals. But such was the public concern about a possible miscarriage of justice that the Home Secretary, Sir David Maxwell Fyfe, ordered an inquiry to be undertaken by a leading QC. This was seen by many—like the Jolly Inquiry into the Rowland case—as a sop to the public clamour for justice but with the pro-Establishment outcome a foregone conclusion.

With press and public banned, the inquiry, headed by Albert Gerrard QC, was held behind locked doors at Liverpool's Municipal Buildings and lasted five days. Like the trial and the appeal, the inquiry, insofar as justice was concerned was fatally flawed. Witnesses were not required to take the oath, the men's legal representatives were not allowed to question or cross-examine them and Devlin and Burns were not allowed to attend. Indeed at one stage it turned into a re-indictment against Devlin, based on false allegations of collusion with another prisoner to manufacture a false alibi and of allegedly admitting his guilt to a prison deputy governor. Both allegations were found to be unsubstantiated. But this did not prevent Devlin being interviewed about them at length in the condemned cell by Gerrard, a former Recorder of Salford, cruelly adding to his already agonising ordeal. This diversion moreover had nothing whatever to do with the inquiry's original terms of reference—which were: "Did the young prostitute give false evidence at the murder trial?"

Prosecution witnesses, most of them hardened criminals with convictions for robbery and violence, were accepted by the inquiry chairman as persons of truthfulness and the highest integrity. Before her appearance at the inquiry the young prostitute—who before and during the trial had been coached and bought presents by Superintendent Balmer—was threatened by him with ten years imprisonment for perjury if she persisted in now telling the truth. This forced her to retract what she had told the three girls about the alleged real killer. These factors and the inquiry chairman's obfuscation of vital issues resulted in his decision that there had been no miscarriage of justice. Short of a reprieve the two men would hang.

The outcome of the inquiry however, also raises the question—should the opinion of one lawyer, however learned, be allowed to decide whether or not two young men should be executed? This function rightly belonged to the Court of Criminal Appeal, which abdicated its responsibility.

Despite grave public disquiet, including a 6,000 name petition, letters and telegrams from all over the UK urging a reprieve, eloquent detailed petitions from Devlin and Burns themselves, and an eleventh hour lengthy memorandum from their lawyers to the Home Secretary, there were no reprieves. Two days after the close of the inquiry the terrified young men died side-by-side on the gallows at the hands of public executioner Albert Pierrepoint and his three assistants, who cruelly ignored the more humane execution procedure laid down by the Prison Commissioners. Afterwards, the legal establishment continued on its self-righteous, biased and incompetent way and the corrupt Herbert Balmer got two more scalps on his belt.

On the eve of his execution, Devlin, all hope now gone, wrote to his widowed mother,

> Don't worry Mam. We know we're innocent. If we die we will die as martyrs not murderers.

In the words of the poet, "As sure as morning follows night, no question is ever settled till it's settled right". Despite the valiant conduct of the defence — particularly Burns young solicitor Joseph Norton — the innocence or guilt of Devlin and Burns has not yet been settled right. Hopefully this book will afford them the justice they were denied at their trial, the Court of Appeal and the whitewash inquiry, and finally answer the question:

> Were they murderers or martyrs to the British state?

PROLOGUE

9 am. Friday 25th April 1951

It's a hell of a thing killing a man. You take way all he's got… and all he's ever gonna have.

Clint Eastwood, Unforgiven

These were official instructions from the Prison Commissioners on how the two "culprits", Teddy and Alfie, were to be hanged:

RE: F.74028 — E. F. DEVLIN. & B.26592 — A. BURNS.

It is observed that the above mentioned executions have been fixed for 25th April 1952.

In the event of a double execution taking place the following instructions should be observed:- Three Assistant Executioners should be employed. The Executioner should put the cap on and arrange the noose of one man and an Assistant should carry this out simultaneously with the other man. The other assistants can, in the meantime, carry out the strapping of the legs simultaneously. By this means one culprit does not stand by while the other culprit is being attended to. Please call on R L Stewart to act as third Assistant Executioner.

But Albert Pierrepoint wasn't having any of that. He felt really insulted. The bloody cheek! Those armchair hangmen weren't going to tell him how to do his job. He was a craftsman. His own procedure was tried and tested over some 600 executions. Old men, old women, young women, young men. Little weaklings like Timothy Evans or strong bull-necked bastards like Neville Heath and Josef Kramer, "The Beast of Belsen" — he'd done them all. And he'd done a few doubles too, like Smith and Brown in the "Old Gossy" case; the Alec de Antiquis killers, Geraghty and Jenkins and the two Polish would-be bank robbers, Redel and Gower. No complaints so far. Why change now?

"More humane," my arse! They were only on the trap a few seconds before the drop anyway. And why should he risk his professional reputation by putting his trust in assistants like the bungler Syd Dernley[1] or inexperienced youngsters like Smith and Stewart. He was the one who would take the rap if anything went wrong. Albert was a firm believer in, "No responsibility without power". And that's the way it was going to stay. And to hell with those white collar Prison Commission pen-pushing buggers!

And so it was that the dazed and terrified Teddy, in the nearest condemned cell, was quickly pinioned and marched the few feet through the double yellow doors to the trap. Albert wasted no time in hooding him and adjusting the noose whilst Dernley, stooping behind, strapped his legs. Although it was a bit unusual and unexpected, the sight of the trembling Teddy and the sound of his low moans from beneath the white hood didn't really bother them. It was just another occupational hazard of the job.

But where the bloody hell were those two idiots bringing Burns? They should have been well here by now. He was only in the next CC, a few yards away for Christ sake!

Noting Pierrepoint's exasperation, a solicitous Dernley muttered reassuringly, "They're coming now Albert." And so they were. But the young ambitious apprentice hangmen, Stewart and Smith, were not hurrying. They seemed to relish this power of taking a man to his doom. As they approached, with Alfie in the middle and two prison officers close in behind, the short, pug-faced Dernley stood back against the wall to let them through the yellow doors.

Like Teddy, Alfie's arms were strapped behind him but unlike his friend, he walked with head erect and a defiant expression. Indeed, amazingly the evening before, this "uneducated culprit"—who had already read Darwin's *On The Origin of Species*—had been reading William Ernest Henley's *Invictus:*

> In the fell clutch of circumstance
> I have not winced nor cried aloud.
> Under the bludgeoning of chance
> My head is bloody but unbowed.

---

1. As a Nottingham postmaster in 1954 it is alleged he was imprisoned for transmitting pornography.

But on entering the chamber his defiant expression suddenly turned to one of horror. Strangely oblivious to Pierrepoint and the hanging noose facing him, he was momentarily transfixed at the spectacle of his best friend trembling there on the trapdoors with a white hood over his head and a thick rope around his neck. Audibly gasping in disbelief, he physically recoiled for a second. And making everything even more grotesque was the sound of Teddy's quick heavy breathing coming from under the hood.

Alfie's shock at the scene only lasted a few more seconds though. He didn't really have time for the horror to turn to pity. His own legs were already being strapped as Pierrepoint quickly drew a second white hood over his head, adjusted the noose and flew to the lever. A second later the trap doors crashed down with a thunderous roar and they were both on their way to eternity. They never even got the chance to say goodbye.

The bystanders in the execution chamber, including the Under-Sheriff of Lancashire, the Governor, the medical officer Dr Brisby, the Roman Catholic Father Lane, and the Church of England Reverend Hawes — were all deadly silent. Between them, they'd seen quite a few executions, but none of them had ever witnessed a double-hanging before. It seemed to have quite taken their breath away.

In contrast to this decorous silence you would never have guessed that outside the prison gates was a noisy and angry crowd of over a thousand people, among them Teddy's tear-drenched sister Eileen, his three aunties and Alfie's mother, all kneeling in silent prayer on the pavement.

When the execution notices were posted on the main gate at 9.10 am the feeling among the crowd was, "That's it. All over!" But their grief-stricken families, struggling to remain dignified, would have been even more distressed if they had witnessed the grotesque spectacle behind the prison walls where the two bound and hooded lads were still hanging by their jawbones in the execution pit. Unaware as she was however, one of Teddy's aunties, Flo Gray from London, cried out, "Oh God, how could they do it? Why did it have to happen?!"

Alfie's mother, dressed completely in black and supported by her oldest son Henry, stumbled over to read the notices before shrieking out, "Oh God have mercy on these innocent boys!" Wailing uncontrollably, she then collapsed and had to be carried to a waiting car.

Seconds later the police arrested 35 year-old Marguerita Wise for disorderly conduct for quoting the fifth commandment at them, and then began hustling the crowd away. An hour later inside the prison, after their bodies were stripped and taken down from the gallows, Teddy and Alfie were laid out for the coroner and his jury's inspection. This was a mere formality. If anyone noticed the torn flesh on Teddy's neck they didn't say anything.[1] It was then officially recorded that they died instantaneously by means of judicial hanging.

At lunchtime they were transported in plain unvarnished coffins on two gurneys — via an underground passageway — to a corner under the east wall at the rear of the prison hospital. And there they were quickly buried without formality in the same grave simply marked "55". In life they had been together since childhood. Now in death they would be together forever.

The bitterest irony was that Teddy, during his last days in the condemned cell, so desperate to convince everyone of his and Alfie's innocence, had written a long letter setting out a theory as to how the three lying prosecution witnesses could have committed the murder themselves. To the recipient of the letter it didn't seem a bad plot in some ways... if you like fiction. But really, it was so implausible and off the mark. Why? Because the recipient knew the truth to be quite different. He knew with the utmost certainty because it was he, Detective Chief Superintendent Balmer himself, who had framed them. Poor naïve Teddy, hoping against hope, believed he was appealing to his would-be saviour when in fact it was pleading to his ruthless executioner!

Of course, they didn't do it. Balmer knew that. But what the hell: they were villains weren't they? And if they didn't kill Mrs Rimmer, then you can bet they had done other stuff almost as bad. As far as he was concerned they had it coming.

All of this though, occurred long ago in another, much harsher age — long before the liberalised culture of prisoners' radios, televisions, telephones and widespread drug-taking. Along with capital punishment it's all in the past now. Best forgotten, surely? But injustice always leaves a very bad aftertaste. Somehow you just can't get rid of it. And even today it is as if these two lads are still crying out, protesting their innocence from below the now

1.   Execution Report. Prison Commission files.

concreted-over plot they share after being hurriedly dumped there on that April morning over half a century ago. Their cries are mute now. But they are still heard by some of us.

The mental anguish and emotional torture they suffered as they languished in prison for seven long months — two of them in the condemned cells — before finally being so ignominiously despatched, can scarcely be imagined. And the terrible aftermath for their families? All that toxic pain and grief, some of it ending in alcoholism, suicides and breakdowns and deaths. All because of one policeman's messianic mission to eradicate the city of "scum".

According to his grandaughter Balmer was a kind and loving grandfather. So was he perhaps mentally unbalanced? Had his draconian zeal in hunting down criminals tipped him over the edge?[1] Or was it ambition and the glory, the plaudits and awards that propelled him onwards? Psychopathy is still not a recognised mental illness. It was certainly unknown to the city aldermen and councillors who showered him with commendations galore and even recommended him for the King's Police Medal he received from King George VI.

Some people, including former policemen, have tried to have him stripped of his honours after it was proved that he framed two other innocent men two years previously — so far without success.

---

1. In 1964 Detective Seargeant "Tank" Challinor was judged unfit to plead at the Old Bailey and committed under the Mental Health Act, after planting bricks on demonstrators at the Greek Embassy.

PART ONE

CONSPIRACY

CHAPTER ONE
THE FATEFUL JOURNEY TO LIVERPOOL

Think no more, lad; laugh, be jolly:
Why should men make haste to die?
Empty heads and tongues a-talking
Make the rough road easy walking,
And the feather pate of folly
Bears the falling sky.

A E Houseman

2 am. Thursday August 2nd 1951

Teddy was on the run from the Manchester Quarter Sessions after jumping bail and Alfie was AWOL from Portland Borstal after overstaying his home leave. The police were looking for them. It wouldn't do to hang around their usual haunts in Hulme and Deansgate—too well-known to the local law.

That was one reason they were now in Liverpool. The other was that Teddy wanted to meet up with sometime girlfriend, June Bury, who he'd spent the night with in Manchester at Whitsuntide last May. Maybe she'd be able to put them up and provide a hideout for them. Problem was, June didn't let the grass grow under her feet... or her bed for that matter. She'd probably have another fella by now. As it turned out she did. He was Stanley Rubin, a handsome, small time villain and womaniser. And she was shacked up with him in a room at 39 Canning Street, Toxteth, a large Georgian terraced house in the shadows of the majestic Anglican cathedral. June would also prove to be a pathological liar.

Teddy and Alfie had grown up within a mile of each other in the post-war slums around the bustling City Road and Stretford Road areas of Manchester's Deansgate and Hulme—Alfie in Medlock Street down by Potato Wharf and the Abattoir and Teddy in Leinster Street off City Road. Their only playgrounds were the densely packed streets and the area's numerous blitzed sites. Despite both having no fathers they were well-behaved and weren't bad lads to begin with.

Alfie's dad had been killed in action during the war. And Teddy's had died from shock in 1943 after witnessing Amy, his 18 year-old daughter and Teddy's elder sister, being run over and killed by a bus during the blackout. Alfie, who attended Atherton Street Council School, was above average intelligence. And Teddy was bright too. A pupil of St Mary's Catholic School, one of his school friends was young Anne Downey who would grow up to become the mother of Moors Murders victim Lesley Anne in the 1960s.

It all started to go wrong really when the two lads reached adolescence. By now, they could more or less do as they wished. Their mothers couldn't control them anymore, mainly because the widowed Amy Devlin and Nellie Burns, had to work long hours each day in their office-cleaning jobs in order to make ends meet and keep their families together. Leaving school at 14, their sons were no longer prepared to put up with the deprivation and poverty they had endured when they were kids during the war. They saw the black market deals, the fiddles and the robberies all around them so why shouldn't they have their share?

In the event they weren't very good at villainy. By the time they had arrived at Liverpool's Central Station that morning, they both had a few convictions under their belts, but only for petty thieving: things such as bread and cakes from delivery vans. Teddy had served two years in the British Army, including 12 months in Nigeria, and left with a good record. Alfie had also served in the Royal Signals Corps but had been kicked out with a bad character after receiving a second borstal sentence imposed when he was on leave.

Having arrived in the early hours of the morning with their mate, Tommy Nicholson, and finding Liverpool like a ghost town, they asked a man at the station where they could get a cup of tea and were directed to the all-night City Caterers coffee stall at the Pier Head, where they met some of the city's human flotsam and jetsam and a few of the local "characters".

One of these was "Eskimo Joe" aged about 22, so named for no other reason than he looked like an Eskimo. Unlike most of the others though, he wasn't scruffily dressed. More importantly, he knew June Bury. This wasn't so strange: June, a promiscuous 20-year-old part time prostitute, although a native of Manchester, was well-known down here and in the all-night cafés, like the nearby Lighthouse, the Rainbow in Islington and the Continental in Duke Street near Chinatown.

After Teddy had asked several of them, to no avail, if they knew June Bury and where she might be, Joe said he did but would only tell them if they bought him a large tea and a "Wet Nelly".

"What the fuck's a Wet Nelly?" asked a puzzled Alfie. But before he could answer, another of the down-and-outs said, "Take no fuckin' notice to him. He means a bread puddin' Nelson Cake." Joe then invited them to go with him to the Lighthouse Café on the corner of nearby Chapel Street and Lancelot's Hey, near the Mersey Tunnel Docks entrance.[1]

At the Lighthouse, Joe told them that Bury was usually in Lyons Café in Church Street every morning at about nine o'clock. Asked how he knew this and how did they know he was telling the truth, he replied, "Never mind how I know. I know everything that goes on in this town. D'yiz think I walk around all day for nothing?"

When they said they didn't know where Church Street was he offered to take them — providing they took him for a drink when the pubs opened. At this stage, Nicholson decided Liverpool wasn't to his liking and told them he was going back to Manchester.

When Alfie, Teddy and Joe arrived at Lyons Café just before nine, it was still closed so they walked around for a while. Returning half-an-hour later, it was now open but there was still no sign of June Bury. The two men then accused Joe of giving them the runaround simply to get what he could out of them. But he protested, "I'm telling yer the truth, honest t'god. I even know where she lives but she told me not to tell anyone down at the Pier Head."

Becoming increasingly exasperated, Teddy lied that he was her brother and had come from Manchester especially to see her. Alfie said that if he was having them on they would come back to the Pier Head and fill him in. But he insisted he was telling the truth and said he would take them to her address.

After they'd had breakfast the three men jumped a taxi from the rank in Williamson Square. But arriving at 39 Canning Street there was no answer at the house so they returned to town and the Dive public house near the city's Royal Court Theatre and the Queens Square wholesale fruit market.

---

1.   Closed down by the police as a "disorderly house", it re-opened in 1953 as Grays Café.

An hour later, Teddy decided to return and again jumped a taxi to June's. This time he found her alone in the bedsit and took her back down to the Dive where he introduced her to Alfie. Then, after getting rid of Eskimo Joe, all three stayed till 3 pm closing time. During this time she never mentioned she was living with Rubin. Shortly after 3 pm they grabbed something to eat in a nearby café before leaving by train for Manchester where they had a job lined up. They were going to carry out a robbery at Liverpool Road Railway Goods Station in Deansgate. As it turned out the robbery didn't materialise so they agreed to postpone it. After both men had obtained fresh clothing all three had a meal and went to the pictures. That night they all stayed at a friend's house in Stretford Road.

Very late the following evening, Friday the 3rd, they returned to Liverpool, arriving in the early hours of Saturday morning, from where June took them to the Rainbow, an all night café in Islington. Passing the imposing neo-classic St George's Hall on Lime Street, Alfie exclaimed in admiration, "Fuckin'ell what a building!" Little could he have ever imagined that in a matter of months both he and Teddy would be confined within its massive architectural splendour on trial for their very lives.

Among the petty thieves and villains hanging about downstairs in the Rainbow, was Tommy O'Toole, one of the tough O'Toole brothers from the city centre's Vauxhall Gardens tenement block, and 17-year-old Marie Milne, who was sporting the remains of a black eye. Telling Milne Teddy was her boyfriend, June asked Marie to come upstairs with them, where she introduced her to Alfie. As they chatted a young blonde girl appeared and said to Marie, "He's downstairs looking for yer," to which she replied, "He can go and fuck off!" Although slightly bemused at this exchange, Teddy and Alfie didn't comment. But later, when they were leaving, a group of young men standing outside were giving them hostile looks. Among them was O'Toole, whose older brother Austin, currently AWOL from the army, had been associating with June on and off since she was 16. Alfie whispered to Teddy to be prepared for some fisticuffs but the group made no move towards them.

Leaving the Rainbow at 4.30 am, they went down to the Lighthouse Café and stayed till 9 am. Later that morning all four strolled around town, visiting Lewis's department store, where the men bought some toothpaste, before travelling on the ferry to New Brighton in an unsuccessful attempt to obtain digs.

Things were now getting a bit complicated for June. So returning on the ferry boat, she decided to tell Teddy about Rubin and that she was scared of him but would have to go to Canning Street to get her belongings. Alfie told her not to worry as they would go with her and that if Rubin threatened her they would deal with him. When they arrived at the bedsit the two men stayed outside, walking up and down whilst June and Marie went upstairs. Alfie told Marie that if Rubin was there and got violent, to come down straight away and tell them. To June's surprise Rubin *was* there.

As she began packing her case Rubin asked, "What the fuck are you playing at? What's going on?" Without mentioning the two men waiting outside, she simply said she was leaving. Following her downstairs, he saw Teddy and Alfie. Quickly realising the situation, he asked her who she was going with — himself or Devlin? At first, with head bowed, she didn't reply. But Alfie said, "Go on tell him. Don't be scared." When Rubin again asked her she nodded towards Teddy and said, "Him." Shocked and hurt by the suddenness of it all, and hoping she might change her mind, Rubin told her to decide once and for all and to choose between him and Teddy, but she said, "Teddy". Alfie then hailed a passing taxi and as it moved away Rubin shouted after it, "Dirty poxy fuckin' whore!"

After they had deposited June's case in the Left Luggage at Central Station, Marie Milne mentioned that they could get a room around Upper Parliament Street. It was an area she frequented, the focal point being a taxi rank and the Rialto Cinema at the junction of Upper Parliament Street, Princes Road, Catherine Street and Berkeley Street.

The first floor bedsit was in Verulam Street off Upper Parliament Street. This street of Victorian bay-windowed dwellings had once housed artisans and tradesmen but was now becoming dilapidated and was home to a large coloured immigrant community. Marie introduced them to the African owner and Alfie paid him 25 shillings for the week. Both men then went for a much needed bath to Cornwallis Street Public Baths in Chinatown.

Later, whilst Alfie and Marie stayed at Verulam Street, Teddy and June went to the pictures in town. It was agreed that, in order to save money they would call back at about 9 pm and all four would share the room. But when Teddy and June returned there was no answer: Alfie and Marie were fast asleep. "Not to worry," said June, she knew a hotel in Mount Pleasant run by a friend of hers. Glad of a bed for the night, Teddy accompanied her to the cheap hotel, whose owner Dorothy Jones, was later given six months for running a brothel there. Teddy signed the register in the name of John Ford, one of his Manchester friends.

At 10 am the following morning, Sunday the 5th, when the couple called at Verulam Street, Alfie immediately took June into the hallway and told her to get rid of Marie, who the previous night had told him she frequently had intercourse with coloured men. He didn't tell Teddy this. But when they went across the main road to the Sefton pub on the corner of Bloom Street and Lowther Street, he simply told him he didn't fancy her so Teddy suggested they swap girls. After only one drink in the Sefton (known locally as "Hessions") they returned to the bedsit then all four left in a taxi for the the Dive downtown.

The Dive was a popular venue frequented mostly by prostitutes and homosexuals. Unlike a lot of city centre pubs it had a radiogram behind the bar which played all the hits of the day. It was also a favourite of local villains for the disposal of stolen goods. But, never figuring out why so many of them seemed to get caught shortly after leaving, they were unaware that the licensee, Dan English, was a great friend of many of the city's detectives — particularly Detective Sergeant John Ralphson and Detective Constable Leslie Skinner![2]

Whilst the girls waited outside because Marie was too young to be served, Teddy and Alfie met Eskimo Joe. As they were drinking at the bar, Stanley Rubin suddenly appeared with another man, telling Teddy he wanted a word with him in private. As both men went to the gents toilet, it looked like the two rivals for June Bury were about to have a "straightener". And most appropriately — with June Bury waiting outside — the powerful sound of Frankie Laine singing "Jezebel" was bellowing out of the radiogram.

In the toilet, Rubin, not expecting Teddy to be so willing to face him, had second thoughts. So, affecting concern, he said, "Listen mate, I don't give a fuck about her but you seem a genuine fella. I hope yer know she's got a fucking dose. Just thought I'd mark your card. Sort of man to man, like."

Believing it to be lies, Teddy later told Alfie that Rubin was simply jealous.

---

2.   Leslie Skinner would later arrest Devlin in Manchester.

Nevertheless, Alfie decided it was about time they got out of Liverpool, not only because of this latest incident but also the rough looking guys outside the Rainbow the previous night—one of whom he suspected had either been Bury's or Milne's boyfriend. "If we meet them again mob-handed," he said, "there could be big trouble."

Leaving the pub joined by Bury and Milne, they then walked the short distance to Central Station to catch the Manchester train. During the journey the two men were talking with Bury about the previously abortive job at the Railway Goods Depot, whilst Milne was looking disinterestedly out of the compartment window singing to herself.

Arriving at Manchester's Exchange Station at 4.30 pm, they set off for the home of their friend Norman Higgins, who lived in a flat over a shop in Stretford Road. He wasn't at home but Alfie had a key to his flat ever since he had been on the run, staying the occasional night there. After a while the two girls went out to get fish and chips. After they'd all eaten, Alfie—having agreed to swap girlfriends—took Bury out for a drink to a nearby pub, leaving Teddy and Marie in the flat where they had sex.

Returning an hour later, Alfie then went with Teddy to look in his local haunts for Higgins. Finally locating him in the Ship pub with his wife, they explained the situation but husband and wife were adamant that the girls could not stay the night. So at 11.30 pm the two men took them back to the station where they bade them farewell at the barrier, saying they would see them at Verulam Street in two or three days time, after the Bank Holiday Monday. This was the first opportunity handed to Alfie and Teddy by fate, to untangle themselves from this deadly pair. But innocently unaware of what treachery lay ahead, they would never get a second chance. The fatal die had now been cast.

At about 8.30 am on the morning of Wednesday the 8th August the two men arrived from Manchester at No. 2 Verulam Street but were surprised to find the bed-sit empty. After a few minutes, however, June Bury arrived. When asked where Milne was, she replied, "Oh her. She's floated." And when asked where she had been all night, she told them she had been on a shop-breaking job with two men the previous night and had been picked up by the police. She'd been given police bail and ordered to appear at the city magistrates' court at 10 am. But she had no intention of turning up and asked if she could go back to Manchester with them. Teddy shouted at her that he couldn't leave her alone for a moment without her fucking around with other men and this brought on some sobbing. What she did *not* tell them was that, after being seen with the two men at the Pier Head, they had run off and she had toured the area in a police car and picked them out. The men were arrested (and subsequently sent to borstal). She also did not tell them she had only been released after having sex with a detective in an empty cell at Dale Street's main bridewell.

On arrival in Manchester Teddy told her they were going to do the Liverpool Road Railway Goods Depot job that night. She asked if she could go with them. Alfie, who didn't trust her, refused, telling her to go home to her mother's in Oldham Road. But she insisted on staying with them. After Teddy had gone off to find their friend, Tommy Nicholson, to go on the job with them, Alfie took Bury to the pictures where she masturbated him as they watched the movie.

When they met up later with Teddy and Nicholson, Bury still insisted on going on the job with them. Teddy felt guilty because although he no longer fancied her he felt he had been the cause of her leaving Rubin and losing her home in Liverpool. So, wanting to give her some money out of the proceeds, he told her she could mind their gabardine macs and keep watch on the corner of Liverpool Road and Byrom Street.

After stealing a large bale of linen sheets from the goods depot, the two men told Nicholson to keep watch over it whilst they went to get transport and recover their macs from Bury. On the way, they saw a friend of theirs driving past in Deansgate but although they shouted to him he drove past without stopping. A second car then appeared, driven by another friend of theirs. He said he was in a hurry and couldn't help them but agreed to take Teddy to try and catch up with the first car.

Waiting for Teddy's return, Alfie asked Bury how she came to be nicked by the Liverpool cops and how she got out so quickly. She told him that that the two Liverpool fellows, Mickey Hadikin and Tommy O'Rourke, who were on the run from the army, had broken into a tobacconists shop in Berry Street near Chinatown and she had "kept douse". But later, at the Pier Head as they were sharing out some of the spoils — cigarettes, lighters and pipes — a cop car appeared, the two men ran away and she was arrested.

It was then that she told Alfie she had only been allowed out after agreeing to have sex with a detective. But she still didn't tell him that she had toured the area in the police car and was responsible for the men's arrests.

Once again was this a fateful portent: two men on the run, Bury, their friend, betraying them after a robbery. But how could Alfie possibly know what lay ahead?

When Teddy eventually returned with another man in a large van, they both again gave Bury their macs to mind, telling her, to wait at the corner of Deansgate and Liverpool Road whilst they loaded the van. In the event Mac, the van driver, instead of taking the bale locally to where Alfie had told him, took it to his own place miles away in Radcliffe, a Manchester suburb. Meanwhile, arriving at the street corner, they discovered Bury had disappeared, together with their raincoats.

The two men were subsequently conned out of most of the proceeds of the stolen sheets. They discovered that Mac the van driver and Nicholson had pretended to have hidden it but said that when they had returned to the hiding place it had gone.

On the 10th August, two days after the robbery, Alfie and Ted were in a pub, The Royal Brew, where they met a local man who knew Bury. He said he had been with her in the early hours of the previous morning at a coffee stall in Piccadilly, after she had left them in Deansgate. She had asked him to go with her to Exchange Station to collect her suitcase, after which he took her home. When he told them he had actually been with her again that very morning in an Oxford Road Amusement Arcade, they asked him to keep her there if she turned up the next morning and they would arrive at 9 am. When they did so they asked her for their macs, which were practically new. They were at her mother's, she said. But when all three caught a bus to the house, 470 Oldham Road, she told them to wait on a nearby street corner. Returning minutes later she said her mother had sent their raincoats to the cleaners. Just then, her mother appeared and confirmed her story. But when Alfie queried this, saying they were almost new and didn't need cleaning, she couldn't give a proper answer. It was Saturday afternoon and the cleaners were closed so they said they would call back on Monday for them. The truth, they were to subsequently discover, was that Bury and her mother had pawned their raincoats.

Returning to town with Bury, they met Mac, the van owner. After chatting for several minutes Alfie asked him to drive them to his mother's house to get a change of clothing. Giving him ten shillings, he then asked him to take Bury for a drink, saying they would meet him in half an hour. But when they arrived at the pub Mac and Bury had left. That was the last contact they had with June Bury until some three months later when she appeared in the witness box at Liverpool Magistrates' Court to give evidence against them in committal proceedings.

The following Monday Alf, Teddy and Mac drove to Bury's mother's house to collect their macs. But whilst they were talking on the doorstep a police squad car suddenly appeared and they had to run for their lives, leaving Mac talking to Bury's mother. When they saw him the following day he said the police had quizzed him and taken his address so he'd had to move the bale of sheets from his home and bury it in a nearby rubbish dump. But when the three men went to the purported dump and began digging, there was nothing there. The bale of clothing had disappeared. Mac said more rubbish must have been put there since he had buried it! Despite this however, when pressed by Alfie, he admitted that before "burying" the bale, he had taken out 12 pairs of sheets as his cut.

Mac was a big fairly tough character who always carried a cosh in his van. So anticipating trouble from him, Alfie surreptitiously slipped the cosh into his pocket then angrily said, "Fuck that! We want them and we'll call for them tomorrow."

The following day, Alfie, Teddy and Nicholson, collected the 12 pairs of sheets from Mac and took them to 38 Foster Street, the home of Fred and Joan Downing—a former girlfriend of Alfie's before she had married—for her to mind till they found a buyer.

On Friday August 17th, it was Alfie's nephew's 5th birthday. He had already posted the boy a birthday card two days earlier. But he now decided to visit his brother, Henry's house at 6 Cobden Street in Blackely. Henry was at work but his wife, Molly, introduced them to her friend, Alice Shenstone. After a cup of tea and some conversation, it was still only 4 pm so Alfie and Teddy took the child out and bought him a bow and arrow set and a few other little toys. When they returned later Henry had arrived home from work.

After enjoying an evening meal, they invited Henry out to the Old Loom, a local pub. But Molly reminded him to come back early as Friday night was her "wives night out" when she and Alice usually went for a drink. As it happened they did not return until 9.30 pm. Alfie and Teddy then left for the city centre after promising to see Henry the following night. They were going to do a job tonight and in Gianelli's Milk Bar in Stretford Road they met their friend Alan Campbell who agreed to go on the job with them. The job was at Sun Blinds Ltd at the corner of Great Jackson Street and Silver Street. But whilst they were casing the place, a man in his shirt-sleeves interrupted them so they went away for a short stroll. When they returned however, the chap was still there loitering about so they decided to leave it till Sunday night, as they had promised to go boozing tomorrow night with Henry.

At 12 o'clock the following day, Saturday 18th August, Alfie, Teddy and Alan Campbell were in Quay Street, Deansgate, where they met Alfie's brother-in-law Eddie Billingham. He asked them if they were going to the football match at Maine Road to see Manchester City play Wolves. Teddy and Campbell declined but Alfie—who had never been to a professional football match in his life—agreed to go with him simply out of curiosity. But before leaving he asked Teddy to call for him at six o'clock that evening. Leaving Campbell in Deansgate, Teddy told him they would all meet up the following night at 7 pm in the Chester Road Inn, known locally as "The Mug Shop".

When Alfie and Eddie Billingham set off for the match, all the buses were packed with the match crowds and there were no taxis about. But in Whitworth Street a friend of Eddie's was driving past in his electric milk float and gave them a lift near to the football ground.

After the match, Alfie and Eddie called at Eddie's mother's house nearby, had a cup of tea, then left after a short while. Reasoning that the police wouldn't be watching his own mother's house on a Saturday afternoon, it being a busy match day, Alfie suggested going there, where they waited until after six o'clock for Teddy to turn up as earlier arranged. But when he failed to arrive they left, only to find him walking up the road towards them.

Arriving at Henry's home, his wife Molly told them he was in the local pub. So after meeting up, they all—Alfie, brother Henry, Teddy and Eddie Billingham—went into town on a pub crawl, including the White Lion and the Ox Noble in Liverpool Road.

Travelling back to Henry's at closing time, Billingham's wife Marie, Alfie's sister, was there with her little baby, talking to Molly, They all had some tea and sandwiches. Then, at about 1.30 am Henry went out to phone for a taxi, which took Alfie, Teddy, Marie, Eddie and the baby back to Medlock Street where Marie and Eddie lived next door to Mrs Burns. On the way Alfie sat in the front talking with the driver, Bill Butler, who knew an acquaintance of his from borstal.

That night in Alfie's mother's, not wanting to be caught off guard if the police raided the house as they usually did in the early hours of the morning, both men slept fully clothed on the settee. The following morning, 19th August, they rose at about 10 am and went to Teddy's house in Leinster Street. But even though it was Sunday Alfie was taking no chances. So downing a quick cup of tea, he left for the home of Joan Fitzgerald in Cornbrook Street, where both had been staying on-and-off whilst on the run. He was annoyed with Teddy for remaining at Leinster Street and taking the time to have a full wash and change of clothes—especially with a police station only a 100 yards away at the corner of the street!

When Teddy arrived at Cornbrook Street the two men went for a drink to the White Lion and left at 2 pm. Passing the green in front of the "Barracks Flats" in Grenham Avenue, they stopped for a few moments to watch an impromptu football match between two amateur Sunday pub teams. As they did so, Alice Ford, their friend John Ford's mother, appeared asking them whether they had seen her kids because one of them had been accused of breaking a neighbour's window. Just then the kids turned up and both men went to Alice's flat on the second floor of the 1930s council flats where they had something to eat. Afterwards, Teddy decided to go down to the ground floor to his married sister Eileen's flat, to borrow some money. But when Alfie followed him half an hour later, Eileen, who had loaned her brother five shillings, said he had gone to their mother's house in Leinster Street.

Annoyed at his friend's increasingly erratic behaviour, the more cautious Alfie was worried in case he got picked up by the police. He was even more annoyed when he discovered from Teddy's mother that he had gone to the pictures. Although he followed him to the York Cinema and sat through the whole performance till the lights went up, he couldn't see Teddy anywhere.

Finally catching up with him back at his mother's in Leinster Street, Alfie told him how carelessly he was behaving, then asked why he wasn't in the cinema where he was supposed to be. Teddy said he had met Sid McDiarmid, one of the local boys on the way, who said he too was going to the cinema but that they had left halfway through the programme.

At 6.45 on that Sunday night, they both left Leinster Street to meet Alan Campbell, in "The Mug Shop" as previously arranged. When they arrived, the barman said Campbell had just left. But quickly catching up with him in Castle Street, all three then went to the Ship, where they joined their friend, John Ford and his girlfriend Anne.

Outside the pub at closing time quite a crowd had gathered as was usual. Alfie, Teddy and Campbell got chatting on the street corner to some girls they knew from the neighbourhood, including Matilda Miller, her sister Margaret and Mabel Williams. They normally would have tried to get more intimate with the girls but tonight they had more important things on their minds.

At about 11 pm they first went to Alfie's in Medlock Street, where he collected the cosh he had lifted from inside Mac's van. He had done this because Mac, who they hardly knew, was supposed to be a "hard case". During the argument over the sheets he had bragged that he often used the cosh on anyone who tried to get tough with him. So thinking he might use it on them if things got out of hand, Alfie had stolen it out of the van. But now he was going to return it because Mac had probably guessed who had stolen it. And as they wanted to use his van to transport the clothing from Sunblinds Ltd "retrieving" it would look good! He would make some excuse as to how they had found it.

Arriving at the Great Jackson Street Sunblinds warehouse at about 11.15 pm, they cased the immediate area before climbing over the fencing of the outer compound. They then climbed out of this into a little yard where Campbell held his folded raincoat against a window to deaden the sound whilst Alfie smashed it with his fist. Teddy then picked some shards out with his fingers to make room to climb in. But as they did so Alfie felt a sharp sting in his knee and felt a small rivulet of blood creeping down his leg.

The ground floor was where the best goods were so they immediately formed a three man chain and began moving quantities of gabardine raincoats and trousers out into the yard then into the compound. After climbing outside they then went looking for transport. Calling on a friend who had a big car, he refused to oblige them so they went down to the all-night lorry park in Whitworth Street to look for Mac but he wasn't there. After several further unsuccessful attempts to get transport, time was dragging on so they decided to carry bundles to the nearby Foster Street home of Joan Downing, Alfie's ex-girl friend.[3]

She returned with them on their second trip, pushing a large carriage pram into which they loaded more clothing. In the event they left a substantial amount of the clothing outside the compound—all in the open and exposed to the elements. And since they hadn't seen Mac, Alfie left the cosh at the scene in case they were caught and it was found on him.

After two trips with the loaded pram, Alfie said they had taken enough and if they were too greedy they would come unstuck because there was a night watchman, who they had seen earlier patrolling the factory next door.

The following day Alfie, Teddy and Campbell, with Joan Downing again pushing the pram, visited a local funeral parlour where the owner bought a quantity of the gabardine macs. And Campbell was given £10.

---

3.   She was later prevented by Balmer from giving evidence for the defence on pain of herself and her husband being charged as accomplices to the robbery and receiving stolen property.

CHAPTER TWO
MURDER AT NO.7 AND THE FIRST SUSPECT

9.30 pm Sunday August 19th 1951

Much Suspected, Nothing proved.

Queen Elizabeth I

Fifty-two-years-old Alice Rimmer had been at her son Thomas' home in Madryn Street[1] in the Toxteth area of Liverpool, since mid-afternoon and was now donning her coat and hat, ready to set off for her own home about two miles away in Cranborne Road, opposite Smithdown Road cemetery, where she lived alone since her husband's death two years ago. Although attending regular whist drives at the Smithdown Conservative Club and being a member of the Dovedale Ladies Bowling Club, Alice kept a dignified aloofness from her neighbours. She seemed to feel superior to the inhabitants of the other bay-windowed Victorian houses along both sides of Cranborne Road—especially those with children, whose street behaviour, she felt, brought down the tone of the neighbourhood. Her son would later tell the police that she was slightly neurotic and a bit of a hypochondriac.

As a young woman who had failed to realise her own ambitions, she had nonetheless been ambitious for her son and, together with her late husband, had made financial sacrifices to obtain for him a good education at the Liverpool Institute, whose illustrious pupils included Beatles Paul McCartney, George Harrison and TV presenter Peter Sissons. But she was very disappointed and felt let down when he failed to achieve any academic distinction. He had first become a junior clerk in the legal offices of barrister and Recorder of Liverpool Mr H I Nelson and later a constable in Liverpool City Police.

Alice, her son and daughter-in-law Marion had enjoyed Sunday tea and had afterwards played several friendly games of cards but not for money. She

---

1.   His home in Madryn St. was a few doors away from Beatle Ringo Starr's home.

was very careful about money as far as Thomas was concerned. According to her, money she had repeatedly given him "just slipped through his hands like water". So although she had five pounds in her purse, she told him she only had a few shillings to last her till her next widow's pension payday.

As she was leaving she was given a bunch of flowers and Thomas said he would accompany her to the bus stop some 300 yards away. He also wanted, he said, to test the dynamo on his bicycle which he'd been repairing that day. The bus stop was on Princes Road near the gates of Princes Park. But when the No 27 bus arrived at about 9.45 pm, the conductor, William Bentley, observed that Alice—distinctively wearing a wide-brimmed hat and carrying the bunch of flowers and an unfurled umbrella—was alone when she boarded it.

A few minutes later she alighted from the bus outside the Pavilion Theatre near the busy junction of Lodge Lane, Tunnel Road, Earle Road and Smithdown Road. To reach her home in Cranborne Road she would then either have to walk the quarter mile down Smithdown Road or catch another bus. Nobody ever discovered which of these she did.

Entering her house, she had no sooner closed the front door behind her when she was subjected to an horrific attack. Judging by her injuries—all to the left side of her head—it seemed as if the assailant had been poised on the stairs or behind the front door, lying in wait, when he pounced with such force in the dim hallway. But who was he? Who was hitting her with such fury? And why? And what was he hitting her with? Surprised and traumatised, she couldn't take any of it in. It was all happening so quickly. In severe shock all she could do was instinctively try to ward off the blows with her right hand in which the unfurled umbrella was held. But it was useless and one of her fingers got fractured.

Under this sustained maniacal assault she sank to the floor where the assailant continued bludgeoning her about the head until, with blood everywhere, she quickly sank into unconsciousness.

For such a quiet dignified lady, Alice Rimmer died an ignominious and squalid death that night; left lying like a felled beast in a pool of her own seeping blood in the hallway of her own home, whilst her attacker made his escape along the hallway, through the scullery, out into the backyard, over the wall into the rear entry between Cranborne Road and Webster Road and away into the busy Smithdown Road.

The ferocity of the attack seemed to be the spontaneous work of a mindless maniac. Or was it perhaps the calculated deed of a more calm and determined killer who had carefully planned her murder in advance?

There were several strange features about the whole horrific event: Alice's right foot was found jammed between the spindles of an upright wooden chair behind the front door and her left foot wedged underneath the wooden hall stand at the bottom of the stairs. Some locks of her hair had been cut and were lying near her bloodied head. Like any woman entering her own home at night and being suddenly confronted by a stranger, she might have been expected to scream with all her might. Yet although it was only just after 10 pm on a summer's evening, next door neighbours, the Grossman family, who were still up, didn't hear a sound. Neither did the neighbour on the other side in No.5. Was this because, rather than screaming in terror, Alice had been more surprised than shocked?

In the cosy domesticity of the home where she had always felt so safe Alice Rimmer lay dead, until 7.15 pm the following evening, when her son found her in the dim blood-spattered hall.

Thomas had arrived home from work at the Howard Ford hosiery factory in Woolton with what the police later regarded as undue haste, quickly had his tea and before glancing through the news pages of the *Liverpool Echo*, had cycled to his mother's. Although taking the shortest route, he nevertheless popped into a sweet shop in Smithdown Road — whose owner knew him — to buy two bars of chocolate.

Arriving at his mother's house, he was told by Jack Grossman, who was chatting to his friend, Ralph Rollinson on the doorstep of No 9, that his mother's bottle of delivered milk had been on the doorstep all day. Ringing the doorbell three times — as was their arrangement so she would always know it was him — he got no response. Then peering through the letterbox he saw in the dim light a crumpled bundle on the floor and said he guessed his mother must have had some sort of heart attack. She had after all been under the doctor recently for some mild heart trouble. He then called to Grossman, "She's lying in the hall. I'll have to go round the back" before racing on his bicycle round to the rear of the house and climbing over the backyard wall. There, according to Rimmer, he saw the lower right-hand window of the rear living room was broken. Trying the back kitchen door, he found it secure and could not open it. He then used a half brick lying in the yard to smash more glass out of the window in order to climb through.

Going through the rear living room into the hall, he found his mother spread-eagled on the floor in a diagonal position, her head just beyond the foot of the stairs. After "feeling her hand", he said he stepped over the body towards the front door then stepped back again, intending to return to his bike in the back entry so that he could ride to a phone box. But suddenly remembering the Grossman's had a telephone, he again stepped over the body and opened the front door. With Grossman and Rollinson outside looking anxious, Rimmer then asked Grossman to, "Come here a minute", who then said, "Shall I get the police?"

"Yes. Dial 999," he replied. The three men then went into No. 9, where Grossman phoned the police, whilst Rimmer sat in the rear living room with his head in his hands.

It was 7.25 pm when Constables Wright and Evans arrived and Grossman greeted them with the words, "I think it's murder." In the living room they noticed Rimmer still sitting in the chair but he did not speak. The officers then scaled the wall into the backyard of No 7, where they entered through the back kitchen door which had been closed but not locked. After examining the body for any signs of life, Constable Evans radioed the police information room telling them, "It looks like a murder". This message was then relayed to the CID and at 7.45 Detective Inspector Bill Lees, Detective Sergeant Armstrong and Detective Constable Nicholson arrived. Some minutes later, acting Head of CID, Detective Superintendent Hector Taylor was contacted and during the next four hours, the whole murder investigation apparatus swung into action, including the attendance of Inspector Reade's Police Forensic Team, Home Office forensic scientist Dr Firth and pathologist, Dr George Manning. At 11 pm that night Alice's body was formally identified by her son at the city mortuary, after which a post-mortem was commenced.

Interviewing Thomas Rimmer, the police were not happy with his story, mainly because they wondered why he should be in such a hurry to visit his mother so soon after she had spent the previous evening at his home. He explained that he wanted to tell her he had not received a reply to his application to re-join the police and also wanted to see if she needed any small jobs doing around the house. The police were now becoming more suspicious: why was it so imperative simply to report a negative? And why could he not have asked her the previous day whether she wanted any small jobs done? To add to their suspicions, Constables Evans and Wright had remarked upon his calmness, not even speaking to them when they entered the Grossman's home. Because of these factors he became their first suspect.

That very night, August 20th, at the Grossman home, he made a written statement—the gist of which was that he saw his mother onto the bus then immediately cycled back home. At the same time his wife, at home in Madryn Street, was also giving a statement which virtually coincided with his. His statement, describing what happened after seeing his mother's body through the letter-box, included the following:

> I cycled around to the back. *I tried the backyard door of my mother's house and found it was secure.* I put my bicycle alongside the wall by the door and used it as a step to get over the wall (Author's italics).

He later however, told the police he could not remember whether or not he had tried the backyard door.

The police meanwhile, under the direction of Superintendent Taylor, were carrying out house-to-house enquiries, extensively searching the nearby Smithdown Road Cemetery for a murder weapon and rounding-up known housebreakers and absentees from the army and navy. None of this proved successful however and the focus was switched back to Rimmer for several additional reasons.

Although the motive was first thought to be robbery, detectives were puzzled that no money or property had been stolen. Indeed nothing in the house had even been disturbed. They had however discovered a letter written by Alice Rimmer just a few weeks before her death, criticising her son as a spendthrift. In addition a forensic report by Inspector George Reade of Liverpool CID's forensic "Studio Team" and Inspector Allen of the Home Office Forensic Science Laboratory concluded after a scrupulous examination that nobody had climbed through the broken rear window. To add to this an incriminating statement by neighbour Sydney Fairbrother of No. 1

Cranborne Road — the house immediately adjacent to the wide entrance to the back entry — threw even more doubt on Rimmer's story.

Fairbrother, a lorry driver and father of five, had known the Rimmer's for several years. Indeed, he had been the first to respond to Alice Rimmer's cries for help two years earlier when her husband had collapsed in her backyard and died from a heart attack. But when he read in the *Liverpool Echo* Rimmer's account of what he did on the Monday evening, he contacted the police and made a detailed, damning statement.

According to Fairbrother, who said he was standing outside his own front door at about 7 pm, Rimmer did not cycle immediately to his mother's house but instead came racing around the corner from Smithdown Road into Cranborne Road, then immediately turned left into the wide entrance leading to the rear of the houses. He was most emphatic about this, adding that he actually said, "Hello Tommy", as he raced past and that Rimmer smiled at him and mumbled a reply which he did not hear properly.

All of this resulted in an internal police report, dated 21st August, in which Inspector Lees confirmed that Rimmer was the prime suspect.

He had been, said the report, a constable in Liverpool City Police for four years until suddenly resigning in April 1951. His reason at the time was that the pay, £8 per week, was insufficient. Yet he took a much lower-paid job, at £4 ten shillings a week, as a trainee hosiery knitter at Howard Ford's stocking factory in Woolton miles away from his home. He however re-applied to join the force on 14th August, five days before his mother's murder, but his application was subsequently rejected. Assessments made during his police career noted that, "He adopted an air of self-satisfaction and over confidence and found police discipline irksome"[2]

His late father, Thomas Rimmer senior, had worked for wholesale tobacconists Ogden's and had left his wife a works pension. After receiving a small incremental increase in the pension, Mrs Rimmer wrote to Ogden's on the 28th July 1951, less than a month before her murder, thanking them. In that letter she also confided that she was disappointed in her son — both regarding his education and in financial matters. Stating that she and her husband had always been careful with money, she complained they had gone to considerable expense to ensure a good education for their son at one of

---

2. Merseyside Police files.

Liverpool's top grammar schools, the Liverpool Institute. But according to her, he wasted the opportunity, never obtaining "any school certificate standards by the age of 17-and-a-quarter". She also complained of his profligacy with money and his constant borrowing from her. "I'm sorry to add", she wrote, "that I cannot look for any help or sympathy from my son. In confidence I tell you he has given up his police job and taken a factory job at £3.10s.0d a week less. I have not dared to tell him about this extra allowance. I have given and given but have resolved not another penny. Money slips through his hands like water and now he is realising what he has done. I do know if I passed out he would have a royal time of it for a few months".[3]

In view of his mother's account of his profligacy the police wondered why indeed Rimmer should have left the police for a much lesser paid job. But when confronted with the letter by Detective Inspector Lees, he denied he had ever borrowed money off her and said that the letter was probably her laying the ground before applying for another increase in the pension. In a later report the inspector accepted this explanation, commenting, "I'm inclined to agree with him". Yet, Lees did not seem to consider that, given the pension increases were made annually why would she be preparing an application for another increase less than a month after receiving one?

Earlier in the same internal report of 21st August 1951, Inspector Lees wrote, "Many features of the case would suggest that Thomas Henry Rimmer could have killed his mother." He began with motive, of which there seemed to be more than one. Her neighbours said Rimmer had complained that his mother was always moaning about her health and being generally cantankerous. The police also learned that she frequently complained that he never visited her for weeks at a time. And he was the beneficiary of her will to the value of some £2,000 (in 1951), which included the house at 7 Cranborne Road.

The report then dealt with opportunity. And it was in this area that Lees finally concluded that Rimmer could not have killed his mother.

In his written statement of 20th August Rimmer had stated that after seeing his mother onto the bus at about 9.45 pm he had returned home within 15 minutes. His wife, in her statement of the same date substantiated this. She was, the report went on, regarded as a truthful person, who had worked

---

3. Merseyside Police files.

for several years in the canteen of Essex Street Police Station and was well
known to numerous police officers. In addition, the police had estimated
that it would take seven minutes to cycle from Rimmer's home in Madryn
Street to his mother's in Cranborne Road and seven minutes to return. This
estimation however, did not consider Rimmer cycling to her home from
Princes Park gates via short cuts *before* his mother had boarded the bus—a
shorter distance which would have taken considerably less than seven minutes. Lees nonetheless concluded that Rimmer would not have had time
to carry out the attack. In addition, his clothes had been examined by the
Forensic Laboratory at Preston and no bloodstains were found. Although
bloodstains were found on his shoes, Lees accepted these had been caused
when stepping over his mother's body.

Forensic pathologist, Dr Manning's report stated that Mrs Rimmer had
taken some four to five hours to die and that, in his opinion, a lightweight
weapon such as a torch had caused the fatal injuries. Based on his report
(which would later be successfully challenged) Lees concluded that if Rimmer was the killer he would have used a heavier weapon to ensure she died
immediately. But was this necessarily so? If the police suspicions were valid,
Rimmer, as a former police constable would have been versed in first aid
which was a mandatory part of the two-year probationer course. Could he
therefore possibly have made sure she was dead by taking her pulse before
leaving? Indeed at the subsequent committal court hearing, Manning, under
cross-examination, changed his view twice: at first conceding that Mrs Rimmer's death could have occurred three hours "either way" of 2 am, then finally
admitting he could not say what time she actually died. But in view of the
time factor involved and Dr Manning's initial report stating death occurred
after 4/5 hours, Rimmer was finally ruled out as a suspect.

Set against this however, are many puzzling features and inconsistencies
in Rimmer's version of events, most of which are contained in the inspector's later report of August 26th following his and Chief Inspector Morris'
interrogation of Rimmer.[4] These included:

- Why, when he saw his mother's body lying in the hallway on the
  Monday evening, had he not smashed the glass panel in the door and

---

released the Yale lock catch instead of riding his bicycle around to the backyard? Rimmer said, he thought the backyard door might be open. Yet when asked if he had tried that door's handle he now said he wasn't sure. He had stood on his bike then climbed over the wall. Why did he break more glass out of the already broken window and climb through, when the two police officers, Constables Evans and Wright, stated the back kitchen door was unlocked? He replied that he had tried that door but thought it was locked, adding that it sometimes jammed. But Constables Evans and Wright stated they had no difficulty in opening it.

- Why was it so imperative to visit his mother so soon after her visit to his home the previous day? His mother, he said, had complained the previous day that he hardly visited her anymore so he had promised to visit her *every day*. But his wife stated that he only promised to visit his mother more often. He also wanted to tell her he had not yet received a reply regarding his application to re-join the police. But asked why he would be so anxious to report a non-event, he replied that he also wanted to see if she needed any wood chopping up for firewood — despite the weather that August weekend being exceptionally warm.

Rimmer had stated that on the Monday evening he had cycled from his home in Madryn Street directly to his mother's front door arriving at about 7.10 pm. But when confronted with Fairbrother's statement that he had cycled very fast into Cranborne Road *before* 7.15 and immediately turned left into the passageway leading to the rear of No. 7 and that Fairbrother had even spoken to him, he denied it. He had definitely cycled first to the front door. He did however concede he *had* seen Fairbrother standing at his front door but only *after* leaving his mother's front door.

In further replies he stated that although he used to have a front door key to the house, his mother had taken it from him when he married in 1949. He admitted that she always gave him a key whenever she went on holidays, to periodically check on the house. Next door neighbour Grossman's daughter Betty, however told the police she had seen Rimmer several times, as recently as the previous March, letting himself into the house with a key.[5] The inspec-

5.   Merseyside Police files.

tor however did not ask him if his mother had been on holiday in March.

Rimmer said that a key to the backyard door was usually kept in the rear living room on a hook but he had not seen it there for some time. When asked if he had tried the backyard door to see if it was locked, he replied, "I'm not sure. *I don't actually remember getting hold of the handle"* (Author's italics). Yet he had earlier told the police that the reason he went round to the back of the house was precisely to see if he could gain access through the backyard door. This could hardly be tested without trying the door handle. Indeed, in his statement of the 20th in the Grossman home, he specifically stated that before climbing over the wall, "I tried the backyard door". If this was true his fingerprints would be on the handle. So why was he now unsure? Was it because he did not in fact try the handle, knowing already—from the previous evening—that the door was locked? And did he suspect the police may have discovered there were no fingerprints on its handle?

Questioned about his access through the broken window, he stated that he had first tried to enlarge the hole in the window with a lavatory brush lying in the backyard but, it not being strong enough, he picked up the half brick and used that in order to be able to climb through. Yet scene of crime photographs showed there were still pieces of jagged unbroken glass remaining which would make climbing through in haste very precarious. He was therefore asked to re-enact climbing through the window on three occasions—the 25th, 26th and 27th August—with the same haste. On the first two occasions he left marks on the armchair and the window sash, but not on the third, when he was slower and more careful. Despite this however, after minute examination of the broken window, the sash, the armchair and its surroundings, Inspector George Reade and Inspector Allen of the Home Office forensic team, had emphatically stated that nobody had climbed through the window. Moreover, according to his wife, Rimmer had been wearing a Harris Tweed jacket on the Monday evening. This was of very thick material covered with visible large fibres. Yet there was no trace or evidence of fibres. Nor were there any fingerprints, footprints or indentations on the armchair or its cushions or scrapes or marks on the wooden arms of the chair. Inspector Reade's report further stated that had anyone climbed through the window, the broken pieces of glass on the armchair cushion and on the floor would have fragmented when the killer stepped onto the chair then onto the floor. This was because he would have had to clamber—as Rimmer agreed he had done—rather than climb through the window due to the different ground levels of the backyard and the room. But there was no fragmentation of the glass. Yet here is what Rimmer stated during the interrogation:-

Q. Did you notice where the broken glass was inside the house?

A. There was quite a few pieces on the chair cushion. But I only became aware of these *when I put my foot on them and broke some while getting in.* (Author's italics).

When asked how he got through the window, he said he put his right foot first, adding, "I know it touched the chair first and then onto the cushion".

Q. Were you careful going through?

A. Not really. I was more or less sitting on the bottom of the window.

With Inspector Reade's report in mind, Detective Chief Inspector Morris asked,

Q. Were you careful today?

A. Not really.

Q. Did you break any more glass going through?

A. Yes.

Q. Where were your hands then?

A. On the lower dividing sash bar.

At Inspector Morris' request Rimmer had earlier drawn a diagram of the window as it was when he first saw it. This showed two shaded sections at the top and bottom which he said he had knocked out with the brick. Referring to the broken glass on the right hand side, he wrote on the diagram, "This piece I broke with my back as I clambered in". Given that he was wearing a Harris Tweed jacket, there were, remarkably, no glass splinters on this, nor any cloth fibres on the remaining glass or any of his fingerprints on the dividing sash bar.

Apart from the police reports, there were even more puzzling features about Rimmer's story and his behaviour immediately following his mother's murder. When constables, Evans and Wright arrived at the scene, they said Rimmer was sitting in Grossman's living room with his head between his hands. He never spoke and did not seem distressed. After inspecting the scene at No.7 and returning to Grossman's, they recognised him as a former colleague and asked what he was doing there. It was only then that he told them he was the victim's son. They both said they were surprised at how calm he was. It is not known if, as a suspect, his home was ever searched for a possible murder weapon or any other incriminating evidence.

Rimmer had told police that he saw his mother onto the bus. He was never asked if he actually waited until she boarded the bus. The bus conductor William Bentley did not recall specifically seeing him at the stop. Could he therefore, like the wolf in Red Riding Hood, have left her earlier and speedily cycled to her house?

During his interrogation he'd explained that on the Monday evening he took the shortest route to his mother's. Could he have done likewise on the previous night? Riding fast, taking short-cuts, this would take considerably less than the police estimate of seven minutes. It would however still provide a very tight time frame in which to commit the murder and get back home to Madryn Street. But if this is what actually happened, would it explain Sydney Fairbrother's account, that on the Monday evening Rimmer came around the corner at breakneck speed and cycled directly to the rear of the house? And was this in order to break the rear window to create a misleading crime scene—an act involving noise and attention which he would not have had the opportunity or time to expedite the previous night?

Marion Rimmer first stated her husband was only out of the house for ten minutes but in a later statement of 26th August she changed this to 15 minutes. Rimmer stated he was back home within 15 minutes. Both however, stated that their clock was five minutes fast.

On a Summer evening when it was still quite warm at 10 pm and windows would have been open. None of Mrs Rimmer's neighbours in the closely knit terraced houses heard any screams. If she had been suddenly confronted in her hallway by two strange men, as later alleged by the police, is it not more than likely she would have immediately screamed out in shock, and even more loudly when struck with the first of those 20 crushing blows? But perhaps not so likely if she had recognised the intruder as a familiar face?

The fact that Rimmer's wife worked in a police station canteen and was known to numerous policemen seemed to unduly impress Lees and his superior, Superintendent Taylor. The fact remains however, that Rimmer solely "owned" the entire situation from 9.40 pm on the Sunday night when he left his home with his mother, to approx 7.15 pm the following night. There was only his word—and his wife's partial support for some of that time—to substantiate his account.

CHAPTER THREE
BALMER TAKES CONTROL

September 2nd 1951.

Very smooth, he looked yet grim,
Seven bloodhounds followed him.

The Mask of Anarchy, Percy Byshe Shelley.

On this fateful day, as it would turn out for Alfie and Ted, Liverpool's celebrated Detective Chief Superintendent Balmer arrived back from holiday in Ireland. Since his success in "solving" the Cameo Cinema murders of two years earlier, he had been promoted from Detective Chief Inspector and was now head of the CID.

Fellow detectives waiting to greet him at the city's Pier Head Landing Stage proudly told him they already had a suspect. Expecting a pat on the back, all they got was a dressing-down for what he regarded as incompetence. There was no concrete evidence against Rimmer and they had wasted precious time pursuing him. They should have been concentrating on more mundane matters instead of pursuing an ex-copper, one of their own. For instance, he wanted to know, had the drains surrounding Cranborne Road been dredged for the murder weapon? As it turned out they hadn't.

After reading the Riot Act, an exasperated Balmer immediately took overall control of the investigation from Hector Taylor and put Detective Inspector Lees in day-to-day charge, whilst rubber-stamping his friend, Detective Chief Inspector Jimmy Morris' inclusion and enlisting two of his protégés, Detective Sergeants Ernie Richardson, Gordon Wade and long time colleague, Inspector Jack Farragher. These were not only drinking pals but some had proved willing and capable of doing anything he required of them in order to apprehend villains—including throwing out the Rule Book if necessary. Apart from Wade, they had all done an excellent job in the Cameo case. He trusted them implicitly. If Elliot Ness had his Untouchables, these were his "Balmer Boys".

Putting Inspector Lees in nominal charge over his friend, the higher-ranked Chief Inspector Jimmy Morris, was a calculated move which ensured that Morris would not have to give evidence and therefore not be subject to cross-examination at any subsequent trial. And although he himself should have been in day-to-day control of the investigation, this same ploy ensured that he too would not have to go into the witness box. He'd had too many close shaves at the hands of defence counsel in the Cameo case to risk that! But it did not stop him from playing the major operational role behind the scenes.

One of Balmer's first acts was to contact the City Engineers Department to have all of the drains in the vicinity of Cranborne Road searched. But his journalist friends in the Liverpool Press Club were told that he and his detectives, complete with boiler suits, were carrying out the work themselves. This, he hoped, would enhance his public image even more. Never let it be said that Bert Balmer was afraid to get his men's or his own hands dirty!

Despite interviewing hundreds of suspects including army deserters and even schoolboys, the investigation was at a dead end until the breakthrough finally came a month later on September 18th. when Balmer received — via the governor of Walton Prison — information from a prisoner and local villain, Kiernan Oates, about the murder. Although his criminal record was mostly for violence, Oates, known as a "madman", was on remand for receiving stolen property. This however was not the story given out by Balmer, during drinks at the Press Club. Instead it was that the great intuitive detective had deduced, Sherlock Holmes-style, that someone serving time in Walton somehow held the key to solving the murder. So following his instinct he interviewed hundreds of prisoners until his hunch finally paid off and he had achieved the breakthrough.

The gist of Oates' information was that on exercise in the prison yard with a George McLoughlin, who was on remand for robbing his auntie's house, the latter had told him he knew who had committed the Rimmer murder. Balmer, along with Morris, was immediately on his way to Walton.

During his prison interview, Oates told the detectives McLoughlin had told him he had met a "Ginger" Dutton in the Rainbow Café in Islington and they had both "clocked" Mrs Rimmer's house. They had then robbed McLoughlin's auntie's house at the other end of Cranborne Road. But Dutton, according to McLoughlin, was eager to rob the Rimmer home first, saying the woman was loaded, lived alone and that only her son or some relative visited her occasionally. He and Dutton were due to break into her home at the weekend but he had been arrested on Friday the 17th August for robbing his auntie's so he could not go though with it. Oates added that, according to McLoughlin, Dutton, who had red hair, normally lived somewhere around Broadway in the Norris Green district and was AWOL from the army. He was still walking around Liverpool in uniform but had sewn sergeant's stripes onto his tunic. McLoughlin had further told him that Dutton was the type who wouldn't hesitate to use a knife or any other weapon if caught in a tight corner. Morris wrote down what Oates had dictated then signed it himself after noting that Oates had declined to do so.[1]

Two days later on 20th September, Balmer and Morris again visited Walton, this time to interview McLoughlin. The 19-year-old army deserter had been remanded in custody to appear at the city's Quarter Sessions for breaking into his auntie's home at 109 Cranborne Road, "between the 21st and the 28th July".[2] Even for such a young criminal McLoughlin had an astonishing record of some 40 convictions.

After first denying he had told Oates anything about the murder, he finally told Balmer that he and a man who was another army deserter had planned to rob his auntie's but that the other man had said that he also wanted to do the house at 7 Cranborne Road where an old woman lived on her own and had loads of money. They then argued about which one to do first, finally agreeing to do his auntie's first. According to an internal police report of 17th October signed by Lees and Balmer (significantly *after* false statements had been obtained from McLoughlin, June Bury and Marie Milne), McLoughlin allegedly continued at the September 20th interview,

---

1. Merseyside Police files.
2. He was subsequently sentenced to three years borstal training.

I didn't go there [the Rimmer house]. All I know is, a fellow I don't know, who I
was talking to in the *Rainbow* Café *or the Continental* Café, *wanted to do a job He
said he had a mate but he wanted three of us,* as it was a tough job (Author's italics).[3]

In view of subsequent events it will be noted how McLoughlin's original
account to Oates and the detectives was now, in the October internal report,
elaborated upon to include the Continental Café and a third participant. "I
asked what the job was," continued McLoughlin,

> … and he said, 'It's in Cranborne Road, the next road to where the Cameo is'. I
> told him that I had a job to do in the same road and if he'd come with me on my
> job I'd go with him on his. We went up Cranborne Road to 'case' the two jobs
> and he wanted to do his first. I wouldn't have it because I knew the people in the
> house I wanted to do were away because they were relatives of mine. To case the
> house he wanted to do he took me to the other end of Cranborne Road, just by
> Smithdown Road, and he said it belonged to an old woman who lived there alone,
> and who had plenty of money which she had hidden in the house somewhere.
> He also said a brother-in-law used to visit her occasionally of a night-time. I said
> my job was easier and we eventually decided to do my job right away and leave
> the other one till later. We did my job at my auntie's 109 Cranborne Road and I
> had a bit of bad luck, as I left my fingerprints behind and I was picked up by the
> jacks [police] a couple of days before we were due to do his job. The day before
> I was picked up we had arranged to do the job that weekend, but I was unlucky.

The following day Balmer again interviewed McLoughlin. Although still
refusing to sign a statement, he offered, according to the internal report,
more information. This time he told them the other man's name was indeed
Arthur Dutton, that he had "fair to gingerish hair" and was nicknamed
"Ginger". He was living rough and he (McLoughlin) had given him his own
RAOC army blouse to wear.

At this juncture however, the 17th October internal police report (com-
piled after the arrests of Devlin and Burns) simply stated that McLoughlin
then told the officers,

---

3. Merseyside Police files.

I'm no squealer. Get hold of June Bury. She knows about the job. And she's got a pal with her too. Let them do the talking, not me.

The report contained no further reference to "Ginger". Yet in late September Balmer and Morris clearly took McLoughlin's claim about "Ginger" seriously enough that in the *Liverpool Daily Post* of the 22nd of that month there appeared a news item stating that the police were looking for "Ginger" in connection with the Cranborne Road murder. Describing him as 21-years-old, five-foot-nine-inches in height, with red hair and wearing an RAOC army uniform with sergeant's chevrons, the newspaper story stated that he lived rough around the No. 14 bus route in Anfield, sometimes sleeping in old cars on derelict sites. It also gave details of his habits such as blowing smoke rings from his cigarette. It went on to state that every police station, including Scotland Yard, had been alerted and gave details of his haunts, including in London, where an aunt or other relative of his was thought to live.[4]

Unusually, the news item stated that the police had not officially issued the information but that the *Liverpool Daily Post* reporter "understood it to be correct". This was because it had been given off the record by Balmer at the Press Club—a practice he continued throughout the case and afterwards, as when planting false stories of witnesses, Bury and taxi driver Emery being threatened and attacked, in order to create prejudice against the two accused men.

All of the information about "Ginger" had come from McLoughlin himself during the initial interviews with Balmer and Morris at Walton Prison. And, although he would not sign a statement, Balmer, by informing the local press and alerting all other police forces including by using the *Police Gazette*, clearly believed he was telling the truth.

Asked who he had been consorting with and the places he had been frequenting whilst on the run from the army, McLoughlin had mentioned the Rainbow and Continental all-night cafés but never mentioned Bill's Café in Paddington. And contrary to the internal police report, he did not tell Balmer to, "Get hold of June Bury...". This was added later, when she was picked up for an entirely different reason.

4. *Liverpool Daily Post*, 22/9/52.

During his nine visits to McLoughlin at Walton, Balmer constantly threatened that, despite him being in prison on August 19th he could still be charged as an accessory to the Rimmer murder and could possibly get ten years. This strategy was employed to keep the young villain agitated and "simmering" until he decided how and when he wanted to utilise him.

Meanwhile on October 4th, June Bury was located in Manchester and interviewed — not on the so-called advice of McLoughlin but as a matter of routine after being arrested for the Berry Street shopbreaking with Hadikin and O'Rourke on the night of August 7/8th and skipping police bail.

Pathologist Dr Manning had said he thought two weapons — one sharp and one blunt — had been used in the murder, which presumably meant two attackers. Fortunately for Hadikin and O'Rourke they were in custody on August 19th, otherwise they could well have been framed for the murder. But after questioning Bury, Balmer soon had two much better candidates! She was first asked if she knew an Arthur Dutton or "Ginger", who went around wearing an army battledress and had red hair or sometimes dyed it red. No, she didn't know anyone of that *name*. She also denied knowing McLoughlin. She had been a part-time waitress at the Continental and the only information she could give was that a fellow named Kenneth McNeil, who was living rough and who occasionally cleared the tables at the Continental, sometimes dyed his hair red. Enquiries however, showed that 21 -year-old McNeil, although living rough and although an ex-soldier, was not an army deserter and had left town the day after the murder. Thus at first it was not considered that he could possibly have been "Dutton" or "Ginger". After checking all the "Arthur Dutton's" in the Liverpool area however and ruling them out, Balmer concluded that McLoughlin hadn't been so co-operative after all — Dutton was probably not his real name! Yet before McNeil was subsequently located in County Durham in a miners hostel, the search for "Ginger" was abandoned! And it was abandoned for a very good reason — Balmer realised that "Ginger Dutton" was probably Kenneth McNeil who fitted Dutton's description even down to living in Everton on the No. 14 bus route and blowing smoke rings. Also, he like McLoughlin, Bury and Milne frequented the Continental and Rainbow cafés.

Detective Constable Leslie Skinner and another officer, who knew McNeil, were keeping watch the day after the murder and had seen him at Lime Street

Railway Station. But at that time the police did not know who or where to look for the killer. Balmer, however, made a mental note to find McNeil and he was subsequently located on the 2nd November—according to the police—but the 30th October according to McNeil.

The superintendent wanted to know if Bury had any idea who might have committed the Rimmer murder. No, she didn't. But she then told him about two Manchester lads she and her friend, Marie Milne, had been "knocking around" with in early August. Giving their names, she also mentioned they had been on the run from the police. Precisely what for she didn't know. But they had asked her to act as lookout on a break-in job at a rail depot in Manchester which she had refused to do. This was most interesting to Balmer. Two villains on the run. Both desperate for money. Breaking and entering merchants. And hadn't Dr Manning stated that two weapons had been used to attack Mrs Rimmer?[5]

Armed with their names, Balmer contacted Manchester CID about Edward Devlin and Alfred Burns and was most pleased to learn that not only were they indeed on-the-run but both were also convicted shop and factory-breakers. Very good candidates indeed! Moreover, by subsequently confronting McNeil with McLoughlin's damning allegations against "Dutton" and substituting it with McNeil's, he was later able to procure false evidence from him by threatening to charge him with conspiracy to murder. A good corroborative witness against Devlin and Burns, McNeil would be a bonus—the icing on the cake!

Although Bury had said the last time Devlin and Burns were in Liverpool was about the 8th of August, Inspector Lees had learned from Manchester's Detective Constable Hancock that when arrested at Joan Fitzgerald's in the early hours of 24th September and questioned as to their whereabouts in relation to a murder in Manchester on the 11th August, Burns had said they had been in Liverpool and had been there for some three weeks afterwards.

At this good news Balmer, who had now obtained their mugshots, was becoming increasingly confident the police had got their men. All that was needed now was to build a convincing case for a jury. This would be achieved

---

5.   Balmer in his memoirs (*Liverpool Echo*, 1967) , wrongly stating the victim had wounds to both
     sides of her head, said it was he who had suggested to Dr Manning, who was a good friend,
     that two men with two different weapons had committed the murder.

primarily by alternately coaxing and coercing Bury and Milne into making false statements; bringing the "simmering" McLoughlin "to the boil" to obtain a false statement from him by activating the threat of an accessory to murder charge. And—when McNeil was finally located—getting corroboration from him of Milne's false story, by threatening him with being charged, along with McLoughlin, as an accessory before the fact or even with conspiracy to murder.

The threat against his main "witness", McLoughlin, was made even more effective when he later lied that June Bury had made a statement saying McLoughin had plotted the job with Burns and Devlin in the Continental Café. Never mind accessory, Balmer told him, he could now be charged with conspiracy to murder unless he did what he was told…and that carried a life sentence!

This was enough to force McLoughlin to co-operate. He was then shown the mugshots of Devlin and Burns, and during Balmer's further prison visits would be intensively coached in the story to be given against Devlin and Burns. This wouldn't be so difficult said Balmer. It simply meant transferring all the involvement, events and conversations between him and "Ginger Dutton" to Devlin and Burns. That way, he said reassuringly, his false evidence would be *partly* true anyway. Furthermore, his story would be easier to remember.

An important element in the tutoring of McLoughlin in addition to showing him the two men's photographs—in order to later identify them at an ID parade—was to also show him crime scene photographs which included privets in the backyard of the Rimmer home. This knowledge would lend greater authenticity to his evidence. Yet although Balmer was the architect of, and prime mover in the conspiracy he was careful to *officially* distance himself from the investigation, thus remaining largely immune to any future awkward questions.

So it was that despite his own eleven prison interviews with McLoughlin, up to the 27th October, it was Detective Inspector Farragher and Sergeant Wade who were sent to Walton on October 5th to show McLoughlin the mugshots. It would be them, not Balmer, who would have to deny it if questioned in any subsequent trial. Yet, being a victim of his own vanity, he could not resist personally taking and counter-signing Bury's and McLoughlin's respective false statements of the 8th and 9th October.

CHAPTER FOUR
THE CONSPIRACY BEGINS

October 4th 1951

It's much easier to take a suspect and a set of circumstances and make the suspect fit those circumstance, than it is to find the person… who really committed the crime.

Disgraced Commander Kenneth Drury of Scotland Yard

Like McLoughlin and McNeil, June Bury was pressurised into believing she could be charged with involvement in the murder. Indignantly she wanted to know why.

"Well," said Balmer, "we think these two Manchester fellas did this murder, and you and Marie were with them around the same time weren't you? That makes you accomplices to murder. Not only that, you'd skipped bail as well."

Not knowing anything about the law, Bury swallowed this and became even more afraid when he added, "I mean you've got form for this kind of job haven't you June? Know what I mean? The break-in at the tobacconists in Berry Street with Mickey Hadikin and Tommy O'Rourke?"

Hearing this, Bury protested that on that night she had helped the police to arrest them. "Come on June," he sneered, "Never mind helping us we both know the only reason you were let out that night was because you had sex with one of the bobbies at the bridewell. "But," he went on, "if you help me we *could* say you helped the police. But you know full well you should have turned up in court that day and instead you skipped your bail. Now apart from the break-in, that's another serious offence — absconding from bail."

At this stage Balmer was unaware of her involvement in the theft at the Manchester Rail Goods Depot and of stealing Burns' and Devlin's raincoats. This would later enable him to pressurise her even more to stick to her false evidence.

With Bury becoming increasingly panicky, Balmer, in true carrot and stick fashion, reminded her of her 18-month-old daughter Lesley Anne, who had been put in care last year. If she was sent to prison, he said, she would never see the child again. The child would probably be put up for adoption. But if she helped him he could probably manage to reunite her with her daughter. Despite these threats and promises however, she said she didn't believe Devlin and Burns could commit such a murder. They'd only been in Liverpool a few days in early-August. But truthfully for once, he told her Burns had admitted he and Devlin were in Liverpool for three weeks in August.

Although finding herself in a perilous situation, Bury nonetheless gave a truthful account of her time with Devlin and Burns, including the fact that she left Liverpool with them on the 8th of August and never went back. But Balmer wasn't interested. He had a case to make out. He wanted from her a really damning statement against the two men. The only concession she finally made was to agree with his suggestion that, on the train to Manchester, the two men had been discussing, not the Goods Depot job, but robbing an old woman's house, and that they had asked her and Marie Milne to "keep douse". That would do for now, said Balmer. But when asked to sign this statement she refused. He then threatened that unless she signed the statement he wanted, she was looking at several years in prison. Telling her to return to Liverpool where he would arrange accommodation for her in a girls hostel, he would see her again when her tutelage would begin.

Leaving Bury to her fearful trepidation for the time being, Balmer next visited Marie Milne at her parents overcrowded flat above a butcher's shop in the city centre's Great George's Place. Milne, already known to the police through frequenting the red light Rialto area, was to find Balmer over the next few weeks an unwanted and feared visitor to her home. During these visits he frequently insulted her father, an Indonesian ship's cook whose English was very poor and knowledge of the law zero. Telling him his daughter was mixed up with villains who had committed a murder, he warned him that she could be charged with a serious offence. And he and his wife could be prosecuted for child neglect and his daughter "put away" because of the life she was leading, including, "knocking around with nignogs around the Rialto". Questioning her father's nationality status, he also, suggested that he could possibly be deported as an alien.

Milne's mother, English-born Mary, whose real married name was Medali, already a mother of 16 children, was pregnant at the time but had a miscarriage, caused, she later believed, through the fear and stress they had been put through.

Milne's younger sister, Anne (known as Tejar), 13-years-old at the time, used to sit on the stairs with her brother Yousef, listening to the conversations and threats. Here's what she recollects of those visits:-

> For some time before the trial, the detective Herbert Balmer was a regular visitor to our home, which was a flat over a butchers shop in Great George's Place. In fact he was never away from the house during this period. He would often speak to Marie and my parents, sometimes to my parents alone in the living room-cum-kitchen. He used to threaten Marie with being put away in Derwent House, a secure children's home. I also know that he used to buy her presents like perfume and nylons. But she was afraid of him. And they all seemed intimidated by him. He never showed any respect to my mother or father and treated my dad, whose English wasn't too good, like dirt. During these visits to our house by Mr Balmer, there would always be two other detectives waiting in the backyard (which was the entrance to our flat) and they would usually try to fondle or grope Marie on her way into the house.[1]

Being wooed in this fashion with nylons and perfume; her father being threatened, herself threatened with a serious charge and with being put away in a detention home as "beyond her parents control" and being indecently assaulted by "Balmer's Boys", 17-year-old Marie Milne decided to run away. Detective Sergeant "Jock" Sturrock was immediately assigned to find her, which he did a few days later at a house at 164 Bedford Street about a mile from her family home.

Following Balmer's detailed instructions, she finally gave a false statement to Sturrock on 7th October. But although it corroborated Bury's story of the train conversation, in the event it wasn't good enough. But under Balmer's direction her statement cleverly included an insertion taken from taxi driver Thomas Emery's statement (later post-dated to make it appear to have been given *after* Milne's) in which he had mentioned taking Marie Milne and two men on a Sunday afternoon to Sefton General Hospital, opposite

---

1.   Anne Milne's signed statement, 16 April 2009.

Cranborne Road.

The taxi driver had truthfully stated that, although he wouldn't remember the men again, he remembered Marie whom he knew from hanging around the Rialto Cinema taxi rank. He also recalled that although the fare was two shillings one of the men had given him 2s/6d and told him to keep the change. Milne, as instructed, included this incident, stating that it occurred on Sunday the 19th, and that the two men were Devlin and Burns. They were on a reconnaissance visit to Cranborne Road and they afterwards told her to meet them in the same place at 6 pm but didn't show up. This statement of the 7th October then abruptly ended with a terse, "That's all I know".

At Lawrence Road Police Station the following day, 8th October, whilst he was coaxing a final statement from June Bury, Balmer was called away and shown Milne's incomplete statement. When he read it he was furious with both Sturrock and Milne. Severely berating the officer, he shouted,

> That's no bloody good to me! She agreed she would say she actually kept douse for them while they were doing the job, the little bitch. She's played you off against me!

Ordering Sturrock to bring her in, he entrusted Inspector Lees with getting the fuller, more incriminating statement from her that had been previously agreed.

This greatly expanded statement, dated 9th October, was much more damning. It now said that, although Burns and Devlin never showed up at 6 pm, she returned to the Rialto corner where she bumped into them. They went to the nearby Somali Café until it was dark then got a tram to Cranborne Road. She was asked to wait five minutes on the street corner until they had gone to the Rimmer home, then she was to knock on the front door, saying her mother had sent her. She was told to try and get into the hallway between the two men and Mrs Rimmer to stop her escaping. Burns also mentioned that there were two mirrors in the rear living room, one above the fireplace and one above the sideboard, also an armchair near the fireplace.

Why Burns would need to give her this irrelevant information is inexplicable—apart from it dovetailing perfectly with the police photographs of the living room—thus giving greater credibility to her story, just as

McLoughlin's description of the privets in the Rimmer backyard would accord with similar police photographs!

Armed with this fabricated statement and Bury's 8th October statement—which significantly mentioned McLoughlin being involved in the planning to rob the Rimmer home—Balmer went the same day to Walton and threatened to charge him with conspiracy to murder unless he signed a statement prepared for him, stating he had planned the Rimmer robbery with Devlin and Burns.

After obtaining the statement Balmer told him that he knew who "Ginger Dutton" really was. But he did not tell him that his allegations against "Dutton" would now be used against McNeil to also pressurise him into giving false evidence.

Balmer was a great believer in "compartmentalisation". Never let the right hand know what the left is doing, he often told his team.

Forget, Keiran Oates letter. Forget McLoughlin's interviews blaming "Ginger" Dutton.[2] Forget Thomas Rimmer's unconvincing story.[3] Forget Inspector Reade's report about nobody climbing through the rear window.[4] Forget Sydney Fairbrother's statement.[5] Even forget Bury's and Milne's original statements of the 4th and 7th of October.[6] Balmer now had three cast-iron statements against Devlin and Burns from three star witnesses—two of which he had taken personally. The case was in the bag!

---

2.   Merseyside Police files.
3.   *Ibid.*
4.   *Ibid.*
5.   *Ibid.*
6.   *Ibid.*

CHAPTER FIVE

DEVLIN AND BURNS ARRESTED AND CHARGED WITH MURDER

10th October 1951

They've all swung it on you.

Detective Sergeant Richardson

Joan Saunders was a 21-year-old feckless and promiscuous young woman whose husband John Fitzgerald had deserted her and moved to Blackpool. Her house at 3 Cornbrook Street, Old Trafford was an "ever-open-door" for all the young villains of Deansgate and Hulme.[1] Staying there, on and off, apart from Alfie and Teddy, was Joe Kirwan, a thief and friend of theirs. Indeed he did a little more than stay there. He was regularly sleeping with her. His friend and fellow thief, Victor Le Vesconte, was also staying at Fitzgerald's house although his own home was only a few doors away

In the early hours of October 10th 1951, detectives looking for Teddy, raided 3 Cornbrook Street, but he was not there. They did however arrest Kirwan and Le Vesconte for breaking into Manchester's Playhouse Theatre.

Some two weeks before that, on the 24th September, Alfie and Teddy were arrested during a three 3.00 am raid at the same house — Alfie for being AWOL from borstal and Teddy for jumping bail on a larceny charge. Taken to Bootle Street Police Station, the two men were questioned on how they had been living during their time on the run. A few hours later they were separately interviewed about a murder which had occurred in Manchester on the 11th August (where a certain Alfred Bradley was subsequently arrested, convicted and hanged on January 15th 1952 for the murder of George Camp).

When Alfie was asked where he was on that date he could not readily

---

1. On pain of being charged for harbouring, she would later give evidence for the Crown about Burns pinstriped suit left at her home. She was also jailed after the trial for child neglect.

remember but told Detective Sergeant Newton he could find out if it was important. When the detective said, "Murder is always important," Alfie became very worried. What if he couldn't prove where he was on August 11th? Since the Manchester police were regularly fitting-up innocent people he decided to elaborate on the truth. "It couldn't have been me that had anything to do with it," he said, "I was in Liverpool about the 11th of August." Asked how long he had been in Liverpool he replied,

"About three or four weeks."

"All the time?"

"Yes."

"Was Devlin with you?"

"Yes."

Teddy was asked the same questions but could not say where he was on that date. Later that day both men were removed to Strangeways Prison.

Alfie was always the careful one and Teddy the careless one. But on that occasion the roles had been reversed. Teddy had said nothing but Alfie, in his anxiety to avoid a Manchester murder rap, had unwittingly provided some of the ammunition which would subsequently be used by the Liverpool police to charge both of them with the Alice Rimmer murder.

On the 5th October Teddy was acquitted on the trumped up larceny charge. But on the 11th October, Alfie—awaiting his return to borstal—learned on the Strangeways Prison grapevine that he had been picked up the day before on a murder charge. At first he thought it was a joke. But when several other remand prisoners confirmed it he still thought it was simply a police ruse to frighten Teddy into admitting some other jobs they had committed.

That same afternoon, the 11th, the Liverpool CID came to visit Alfie. Remembering his lie to the Manchester police that he had been in Liverpool for three weeks whilst on the run, he thought they wanted to quiz him about jobs. But knowing they hadn't done any whilst in that city, he was confident they couldn't touch him. There were four of them: Chief Superintendent Balmer, Inspector Lees and Detective Sergeants Richardson and Wade. The small prison interview room was oppressive as Balmer quietly began in a friendly tone, "You know what we want you for don't you Alf?" No, he didn't. But he *was* expecting to be questioned about any thieving jobs that had been done in Liverpool.

Balmer then asked him about his movements when he was in Liverpool and he told him to the best of his knowledge. Then out of the blue Balmer told him he was charging him with a murder that occurred on August 19th. Alfie suddenly felt sick in his stomach. Even hearing the prison rumours about Teddy and a murder charge, he had never connected it with Liverpool.

"The only time I was in Liverpool," he said," I was with two girls and Teddy Devlin."

"Oh, I know that Alf," said Balmer, "I've got a statement from both of the girls." Feeling sure Marie Milne and June Bury would not be mixed up in a murder, he asked, "Then why are you charging me?" Because, said Balmer, not only had they implicated him but Teddy had too. Wise however to police techniques and their bluffing, Alfie knew this was untrue and told Balmer it was ridiculous.

After an hour or so with Balmer asking only perfunctory questions about his movements whilst in Liverpool, Inspector Lees, who had been writing down his answers, handed him a statement to sign. At that stage the detectives did not dispute what he had said regarding the dates he gave. A puzzled Alfie however noticed that Balmer didn't seem interested in his movements on the 19th August when the murder was supposed to have been committed. Nor did he give any details about it. But unknown to Alfie an account of his true movements on the 19th was irrelevant and unnecessary: Balmer had already scripted them!

When he pleaded that he was in Manchester on the night of the murder, Richardson said, "You can bring half of Manchester up as witnesses but it won't do you any good." Alfie knew Balmer was lying when he said Teddy had implicated him because they had not committed any offences, much less, murder, during their stay in Liverpool. What he didn't know was the circumstances surrounding Teddy's arrest the previous evening.

This had occurred at 8 pm when Teddy and another friend had entered Granelli's Milk Bar on Stretford Road. He had just ordered two coffees when Detective Constable Skinner of Liverpool CID and Detective Constable Lynch of the Manchester force—who had been tailing them—grabbed him. All he was told was that he was under arrest. Nothing about a murder was mentioned. And when Lynch asked him where he had been the night before and in the early morning, he thought it was in connection with the break-in he had been involved in with John Ford and Joe Kirwan at the Play-house Theatre. Indeed, in the early morning of that same day the Manchester police had raided Joan Fitzgerald's house in Cornbrook Street looking for him. Not finding him there, they had arrested his friends Kirwan, Vic Le Vesconte and John Ford for the theatre break-in. Ford later walked out of the police station without being charged. Vesconte wasn't involved in the break-in but evidence was planted on him and Kirwan, who were both later given respectively sentences of 12 months and two years

After his acquittal on the larceny charge Teddy had been at liberty for only five days. He was now back in custody and would never be free again. Taken first to Ormond Street Police Station then to the Police HQ at Bootle Street he was confronted by Balmer, Morris, Lees, Richardson, Sturrock and Wade. After questioning him for over an hour, Balmer told Richardson and Wade to go to 26 Leinster Street and "turn over" his home, where they collected his fawn suit and other items including a glass-cutter. The following day they would also retrieve Burns' clothing from his brother-in-law, Eddie Billingham's home.

When Richardson and Wade returned the questioning continued. A bemused Devlin asked, "What am I being charged with?" to which Richardson replied, "Murder."

"You're kidding aren't you?" he said incredulously, then, turning to Lees, he said, "He's not serious is he?"

"You'll soon find out whether he's serious or not", replied Lees.

Devlin then asked nobody in particular, "Who's supposed to have been murdered?"

"Don't give us that," said Wade, "there's been a murder in Liverpool and you know all about it."

"There was no murder while I was there," said a puzzled Devlin.

Again without cautioning him, Lees said, "Look we're taking you to Liverpool now and charging you with the murder of Mrs Alice Beatrice Rimmer of 7 Cranborne Road on the 19th to the 20th of August. That's enough for now."

At the wheel of the police car travelling down the East Lancashire Road was Detective Sergeant Wade, with Inspector Lees sitting next to him. In the back seat the handcuffed Teddy was sandwiched between Richardson and Sturrock. Balmer and Morris had made their own way back in another car. There were dense foggy patches on the road which caused the car to frequently alternate between a fast and a crawling pace. During the journey Richardson, playing the good cop, tried to get Devlin to talk and hopefully incriminate himself.

"You know what," he opened conversationally, "Marie's not a bad girl but I don't care much for Bury." When Devlin didn't reply, he continued persuadingly,

> Look, if you don't tell us what you know to clear yourself you're going to end up getting topped. We know all about you and Burns and Bury and the Chinese bit. They've all swung it on you so why don't you tell us what you know?

"As God's my judge," he replied, "I don't know anything about it." Realising he was getting nowhere, Richardson suddenly abandoned the good cop act and angrily retorted, "Well, God's not your fucking judge!" And when Devlin asked for a cigarette and complained that the handcuffs were hurting he was told to "Fucking shut up."

Arriving at Liverpool's Allerton Police Station, Lees formally charged him with the murder but again failed to caution him. Balmer, who had arrived ahead of them, immediately took charge of the questioning whilst Lees sat noting down the answers on a statement form

"When you were in Liverpool how did you get back to Manchester?" asked Balmer.

"We got the train from Central Station, I think."

"When you were in Liverpool where did you go?"

"We were in several cafés around the Pier Head and a Chinese café by a washing baths. Me and Alfie went there for a bath."

"Do you mean Cornwallis Street Baths?"

"I don't know the name."

"There's an all night café near there in Duke Street called the Continental. You were probably in there as well, weren't you?"

When Devlin said he didn't know the names of the cafés, Balmer said, "Well the one you met Marie in was in Islington. That's the Rainbow."

"Yes, we were in the Rainbow and a Chinese café."

"And the Continental?"

Assuming the Lighthouse Café near the Pier Head, whose name he did not know, to be the Continental, he replied, "Yes."

Continuing, Balmer asked when were they last in Liverpool, to which he replied about the 8th or 9th of August.

"Have you ever given June Bury anything to mind for you?"

"When we were in Manchester we gave her our macs to mind."

Asked if he was sure he had not been in Liverpool after the 9th August, he said he was sure (in his signed statement this appeared as, "I am quite *definite* I have not been in Liverpool since the 9th of August" — a favourite Balmer word).

"What clothes were you wearing when you were in Liverpool?"

"My fawn gabardine suit," said Devlin, "and the shirt I'm wearing now" (in his statement this was altered to, "When in Liverpool I wore a fawn gabardine suit and the shirt I am wearing now, which is salmon colour with a Scotch plaid collar and cuffs"). The question arises here however, that since he was wearing the shirt at this interview, which all the detectives could see for themselves, why would Devlin need to describe it in such detail? This is indicative that these expositional comments, which he did not utter, were inserted into the statement. Thus what was a question and answer session emerged as a statement which, "dictated by the prisoner", was signed by Devlin and countersigned by Lees and Balmer!

During the entire period from his arrest, particularly before the "statement" was extracted and signed, Devlin did not have the advantage of any legal advice nor was he advised to seek any.

Having already retrieved his fawn suit from his home, Lees now told him they were going to take possession of the brown suit he was wearing. "Well", he said, "there are no bloodstains on that. But what will I wear if you take it?" Lees told him that they would leave him with his trousers for the time being.

After being processed and despatched in a Black Maria down to the main bridewell at Cheapside, the detectives congratulated themselves on a good night's work. The following day they would be off to Manchester to complete their mission — the arrest of Burns.

CHAPTER SIX
THE COMMITTAL PROCEEDINGS COMMENCE

Friday November 2nd 1951

A fucking kangaroo court.

Alfred Burns

The committal hearing opened at Dale Street Magistrates' Court No 3. This was the forum where the prosecution would present their case in order for a single magistrate to decide whether or not there was a *prima facie* case for the accused to answer at the Assizes. During this procedure, although defence solicitors could cross-examine Crown witnesses, only the prosecution allegations and their witnesses would be heard. Murder cases were rarely thrown out at the committal court. Defence solicitors therefore usually reserved their defence in the knowledge that a full trial had to be heard before a jury anyway. These proceedings however, often included unproven, sensational and lurid allegations which were reported nightly in the local evening newspapers and often in the national press. This was highly prejudicial to the accused before their trials proper and doubtless influenced juries against the accused.

The case against Devlin and Burns would be no different. It would also prove to be a marathon of pig-headed obstruction and disregard for proper procedure by the examining magistrate; an appalling example of petty pedantry and obstruction by prosecuting solicitor, J R Bishop—a fellow freemason of Balmer's—and a flagrant abuse of office by clerk of the court, Henry Harris.

Each day's proceedings would be extensively reported, almost verbatim, in the city's two evening newspapers—the *Liverpool Echo* and the *Evening Express*—with lurid headlines such as, "Waitress Alleges Knife Threat" and "I Was To Be Robbery Decoy Alleges Girl"—thus ensuring widespread prejudice against the two accused men among the public and potential jurors. To add to this, Balmer, an elected member of the Liverpool Press Club, was periodically planting false stories of prosecution witnesses being attacked.

All of this, together with three unexplained lengthy postponements, would result in an appalling breach of justice to both men. In total, the staggered hearing would last from the 2nd to the 23rd November, when they were finally committed for trial at the Assizes.

As early as October 17th, the defence lawyers had told the police that their defence would be an alibi; that at around eleven pm on August 19th, their clients had been breaking into Sunblinds Ltd, and to prove it, they had taken the stolen gabardines to the nearby Foster Street home of Joan Downing, who had helped to remove the goods in a pram. Hearing this, Balmer determined something had to be done to silence Downing. This was achieved on the 27th October by arresting her husband, Frederick, detaining him for 24 hours at Bootle Street Police Station, and taking a statement from him to the effect that Devlin and Burns and his wife Joan had brought the stolen goods to his house on the 19th August. This statement was then used as leverage against his wife to force her to sign a statement denying that she had been with Devlin and Burns that night. If she co-operated, she was told, neither she nor her husband would be charged. But if she refused her husband would probably go to prison for ten years and herself for 15 years. Subsequently, in true Balmer "carrot and stick" fashion, he paid her £20 for two of the three days he ordered her to attend the trial, "just in case you are called by the prosecution."[1]

A compliant Joan Downing felt she was hopelessly trapped in Balmer's web. But this was no more than a daring bluff. For had the 23-year-old not been so terrified and naïve, she would have realised that the police would not dare charge her or her husband. For to do so would have meant the police in effect admitting the truth of the accused men's alibi of the Sunblinds break-in and thus disproving their own false case against them for murder.

After the first day of the committal, which included Bishop's opening speech and the testimony of the three main Crown witnesses, George McLoughlin, June Bury and Marie Milne, the hearing was unaccountably adjourned for ten days. It had ended with Milne giving her evidence-in-chief. Her cross-examination by the defence would have to wait for over week. This would give Balmer plenty of time to have a comprehensive rehearsal

---

1.   Author's interview with Joan Downing, June 2011.

with Milne and the others of their false evidence.

From the outset it was obvious that the magistrate, Mr C G S Gordon, was going to be as unhelpful as possible to the defence solicitors, Harry Livermore and Joseph Norton. It was felt by many that his hostile attitude was not only because he was a Tory alderman on the City Council's Watch (Police) Committee and therefore pro-police, but also that he harboured anti-semitic prejudice against the two Jewish lawyers.[2] Had there been any justice, the case against the accused would have got no further than this court and been thrown out. That it wasn't was due to the legal obfuscations, confusion, misinterpretation of the law, persistent hostility to the defence and the wilful lying which took place.

In his opening speech, containing numerous inaccuracies, Bishop, with a total disregard for the rules of evidence, referred to an alleged taxi ride to Cranborne Road on the afternoon of the murder, unequivocally stating that Milne, was accompanied by Devlin and Burns, and that evidence would be called to verify this. In the event no independent evidence was called to substantiate it. The taxi driver, Thomas James Emery, later gave evidence stating that he did not, and still could not, recognise the two men with Milne. He could not even say for certain that the taxi trip was on the 19th of August. Indeed he admitted, under cross-examination, that it was the police who suggested to him that it must have been the 19th. Surprisingly however neither Livermore nor Norton — otherwise so punctilious throughout the hearing — failed to object to Bishop's unfounded and prejudicial statement, which subsequently went into the official transcript.

When 19-year-old George McLoughlin was called, he entered the witness box wearing an apprehensive expression. Bishop, anticipating later defence requests, immediately announced, "I won't be asking this witness his address."

The story McLoughlin had to tell caused many expressions of incredulity in the crowded courtroom with some onlookers quietly shaking their heads in disbelief. And as his story progressed it would have been laughable had it not been so fatally damaging to the accused. The American, H L Mencken's, witty observation about a court case he had witnessed — "The penalty for laughing in court is six months in jail. If it were not, the jury would never

---

2.   As explained in the Foreword, Norton, who had served as a Lieutenant Colonel in the British army was the uncle of Lord Goldsmith QC, Attorney General (2001-2007).

hear the evidence"—was most fitting!

According to McLoughlin, he first met Devlin on the morning of the 27th July in Bill's Café at the top of Paddington near Wavertree Road. The defence however, were unaware that his undisclosed signed statement to Balmer of the 9th October stated that he *first met* both Devlin and Burns "eight or nine days before the murder", which would make it the 10th of August. And not in Bill's but in the Continental all-night café several miles away.

The dark, steamy, smoke-filled, Bill's Transport Café was frequented daily by the area's numerous coal lorry drivers due to its close proximity to the coalyards at Crown Street and Edge Hill railway sidings. It was usually filled with jokes, banter and raucous laughter among its hard-working customers. It was not the sort of place for secretive hole-in-the corner discussions about serious crime. But McLoughlin stated that, upon meeting Devlin, a complete stranger, he told him he was going to burgle his auntie's house in Cranborne Road about a mile away. The Mancunian Devlin then said, "That's funny, I've got a job there and all".

When it was going dark, continued the witness, he and Devlin went to No. 7 Cranborne Road at the far end from his auntie's at No. 109, and went around the back entry to "case the joint". He gave Devlin a leg-up, and then he "took a look over" himself. He observed there was a light on in the house and there were privets in the backyard. Neither defence lawyer thought to ask him that if Devlin had required a leg-up, how had he himself managed to scale the wall unaided and with enough time to observe so much detail. His observation of the privets in the backyard would, however, give his evidence greater authenticity, fitting in nicely as it did with the police photographs of the backyard!

Before the defence began their cross-examination of McLoughlin, Burns' solicitor had to request the bench to order the removal of witnesses from the courtroom until they were called. This request, regarding such a serious breach of procedure, would have been unnecessary to any competent magistrate. But this was merely the beginning of Mr Gordon's egocentric courtroom management.

The first clash came when Harry Livermore, for Devlin, requested a short adjournment in order for him to consult with his client in private. Or, he suggested, he could do this during the lunch adjournment. Reluctantly telling him he could have a few minutes, Gordon added, "It would not happen at a higher court". Livermore, who could be quite short-tempered, immediately retorted, "I don't understand that. This evidence is flung at me. I cannot start cross-examining before I get instructions. What would apply at a higher court does not apply here, and I am rather surprised at your worship saying that." Ignoring these comments, the magistrate told Norton he too could see his client in the cells for a few minutes.

When the two lawyers returned, Livermore said to McLoughlin, "I did not get your address," to which the prosecuting solicitor smugly remarked, "He did not give it." Ignoring him, Livermore asked McLoughlin if he would like to write it down. Gordon then pronounced, "I don't think the address of the witness at the moment has anything to do with the case and I really think it is not necessary."

"Are you saying I am not entitled to the addresses of any of the prosecution witnesses?" asked Livermore. "Their present address, yes," he replied.

Livermore then commented on the serious wrongness of his decision, adding that Gordon knew perfectly well why he was asking for McLoughlin's present address. But Gordon simply confirmed that it was not necessary. Unwilling to drop the matter, Livermore said, "I cannot help feeling your worship is being a little unfair about that."

"I am not being unfair at all," he concluded.

Unknown to onlookers in the public seats, who may have been puzzled at this testy exchange between the bench and the defence, there was a subtext here: namely that Livermore, Norton, Bishop and the magistrate knew McLoughlin's present address was HM Prison Walton. But whilst Livermore wanted it revealed in order to cast doubt on McLoughlin's character and evidence, Gordon—in order to help the prosecution and in violation of his neutral role—wanted it kept concealed. And he would persist in this unethical obstruction when later in the proceedings other prosecution witnesses, including detectives, would be asked similar questions, such as where McLoughlin was interviewed by the police.

Continuing his cross examination of McLoughlin, Livermore exposed several inconsistencies in his evidence. After first expressing doubt about the conversation in Bill's Café between him and Devlin, a complete stranger to him, and the extraordinary coincidence of him having a burglary lined up in the very same road as McLoughlin's, he elicited from the witness that he "went to" his aunt's the next day (28th July) with Devlin.

Although tutored by Balmer, McLoughlin was now departing from the script, "ad-libbing" and in the process possibly digging a deeper hole for himself. Livermore pounced on this.

"You never told us about that, did you?" he asked, to which McLoughlin deftly replied, "I was not asked." This was a reference to McLoughlin's earlier evidence when he had stated to Bishop that after casing 7 Cranborne Road with Devlin, he had not met him again until a week later in the Continental Café in the company of Burns. Yet despite this clear contradiction the magistrate in an attempt to help McLoughlin square what he was now saying with what he had previously stated, suggested, "Did you go alone?" Rejecting this "lifeline", however, he replied, "No, with Devlin." He then commented to Livermore, "I told the police that in my statement."

"I am not interested in what you told the police," he retorted, "I am interested in your evidence here today."

When Livermore read out his earlier evidence about not seeing Devlin until the following Thursday, McLoughlin simply replied, "If I said that, yes. But I saw him the next day." As the hearing progressed, "the old woman" was frequently referred to. But, although the officious clerk of the court, Henry Harris, would be quick to exceed his relatively minor role, regularly making inappropriate comments, he could nonetheless be quite obtuse, unable as he now was to differentiate between McLoughlin's aunt and Mrs Rimmer the 52-year-old murder victim, asking him which "old woman" he was talking about.

When Livermore, who knew McLoughlin had been charged with burgling his auntie's, suddenly asked, "Did you ever get round to robbing your auntie's house?" Bishop was immediately on his feet: "Are you going to attack this witness' character?" Keeping a straight face Livermore, replied that he was not! But ready to contest almost every question asked by Livermore, Bishop said, "Aren't you asking him to incriminate himself?" This comment ignored the fact that McLoughlin had already incriminated himself by pleading guilty to robbing his auntie's, for which he was now in prison awaiting sentence.

The magistrate, again siding with Bishop, commented, "On this night, all this talk had to do certainly not with his auntie's house 109, but with the house two or three doors up from the alleyway, which was apparently number seven." He went on, quite wrongly, "There is no question, as far as I know, of ever going near his auntie's house. What he did or did not do at his auntie's house has nothing to do with this case." This perverse pronouncement effectively silenced Livermore. But it flew in the face of what had earlier transpired when McLoughlin, in his changed evidence, had replied to the magistrate's own question that he had gone with Devlin to his auntie's house on July 28th, the day after their first meeting. If it had "nothing to do with this case", then it could be reasonably asked, why had the magistrate asked him the question?

Continuing, Livermore asked when he was interviewed by the police and whether he had approached them or had been approached by them. He said they had approached him about six weeks ago, about the end of September. In a surreptitious attempt to obtain his address and thereby expose him as a prison inmate, Livermore then asked *where* the police had seen him. But Bishop was again on his feet objecting, unless Livermore could prove the question was relevant. Once again Gordon came to the aid of the prosecution, pronouncing, "I uphold that objection." When Livermore pleaded, "Cannot we know even whether it was in Liverpool or Manchester?" Gordon responded that it did not matter where McLoughlin was seen by the police and repeated that he was upholding Bishop's objection. "Your worship is being singularly unhelpful to me," he complained. But Gordon refuted this, telling him, "I am going on the lines I took the very first time you asked the question you are asking this man now." Livermore protested it was the first time he had asked the question. But an increasingly rattled Gordon, his face becoming flushed, retorted, "Excuse me, it is not! You were anxious to know about where he was and where he is, etc., etc. It is practically the same question."

There then followed an extraordinary episode—akin to the Theatre of the Absurd—of petty squabbling among these legal figures -- who seemed oblivious to the deep anxiety felt by the two accused young men in the dock and their families watching from the public seats.

Hoping this titbit would satisfy Livermore, Harris the clerk, said there could be no objection to him being told only whether it was in Liverpool that McLoughlin was seen by the police. But he was not going to be so easily mollified. "His worship has ruled against me. He won't have it," he petulantly proclaimed. "He says I'm not entitled to know. I've never known such an unfair attitude to take."

Responding to the clerk's advice, Bishop declared that he would withdraw his objection if the only question was whether McLoughlin had been *interviewed* in Liverpool. The magistrate then asked Devlin's solicitor, "Do you want to know the town?", to which he emphatically replied, "No!".

Disregarding this unequivocal response, the clerk asked McLoughlin, "Was it in Liverpool?" Yes it was, he said. But this was not good enough for the indefatigable Livermore, who said, "I want to know *where* it was in Liverpool." When Bishop repeated his objection Gordon, once again, ignoring the defence protest, repeated that he would uphold his objection. A by now thoroughly exasperated Livermore then stated, "I am not going to cross-examine this witness any further. This is a very serious matter. And I am being obstructed all along the line by your worship,"

Now appearing to adopt a more accommodating mode, Bishop said, "If he can show me it is relevant I will withdraw my objection." But this was merely an academic exercise in order to cover himself. It was not incumbent on Livermore to "show" his opponent the relevance of his question. It was the magistrate's responsibility to decide the relevance—which he failed to exercise. In the event however, Livermore ignored the invitation and sat down in disgust. It was indeed a serious matter. Devlin, his life in the balance, may now be wrongly sent for trial because his solicitor was not allowed to fully cross-examine the main prosecution witness and therefore, possibly, submit, at the conclusion that there was not a *prima-facie* case for his client to answer.

Before Burns' lawyer, Joseph Norton, rose to cross-examine McLoughlin, Burns, sitting impassively in the dock, was observed muttering something to Devlin to which his friend responded with a smile. Only those sitting closest heard Burns comment. But they may well have agreed that it was indeed a "fucking kangaroo court".

Despite the earlier objections and rulings against Livermore, Norton defiantly but quietly asked McLoughlin his current address. His purpose like Livermore's, was to make public the fact that McLoughlin was a prisoner at Walton, knowing it would be reported in that evening's newspapers.

Gordon, however also ruled him out of order but said the address where he was living *at the time of the offence* could be asked. Norton's response to this however, albeit more restrained, went even further than Livermore's as he argued that McLoughlin's present address was of the utmost relevance and that the magistrate's ruling amounted to obstruction of the defence's right to communicate with him, which they were entitled to do. Surprisingly, in an apparent reversal of attitude, Gordon replied that Norton knew perfectly well he only had to ask to interview (in private) this witness for his address, and every facility would be afforded to him. "But," he went on, "at this moment the address is not essential." Gordon however was fully aware that a private interview would not get into the newspapers!

At this ostensible *volte-face* all those present in court, including the two accused, silently gave thanks that the unseemly squabbling had now ended. But this respite was short-lived. For when Norton asked if the witness could write down his address and hand it to him so that it was not communicated to the public, Gordon snapped, "No!". Harris, the self-important clerk then commented, "Of course you would not seek to interview any witness, on behalf of the accused, without reference first to the prosecution, would you?" When Norton replied that he would be entitled to do so, Harris warned, "It might be open to criticism", with Bishop adding that he would take strong exception to it.

Bishop's position, which he correctly surmised would be supported by the magistrate, displayed either an ignorance of, or a wilful disregard for, the law. For, in arguing the point, Norton stated that the legitimacy of his submission — that witnesses are not the witnesses of any particular party but are witnesses of fact — had been endorsed by the Council of the Law Society, with the approval of the Lord Chief Justice. Astonishingly, Harris, the clerk of the court (also a solicitor) then began to question the judgement of his own professional body and the highest judge in the land.

"As a general proposition that is true," he said, "but whether it goes so far as having an *interview before trial* unless it is arranged with the prosecution, I have my doubts" (Author's italics).

Apart from a lowly clerk of a provincial magistrates court pompously challenging such lofty legal rulings, his arrogant comment about an "interview" — like the magistrate's earlier comment — demonstrated that both had either missed or wilfully ignored the fact that Norton had not requested an interview but simply McLoughlin's address, and that theoretically he was entitled to "communicate" with him. Harris moreover, was being very presumptuous by mentioning "before trial". The outcome of the proceedings had not yet been determined. For all Harris knew, the magistrate could well rule at their conclusion that there was no case to answer, in which case there would not be a trial.

What the clerk of the court did not know was that there had been considerable correspondence on this very crucial matter between Norton and the Law Society. He had written to them on the 27th October in anticipation of this very obstruction, asking for guidance because he did not want to act improperly. The reply he received on the 29th October included the following:-

> The Council [of the Law Society] have always held the view, and held it very strongly, that there is no property in witnesses. And so long as there is no question of tampering with a witness or seeking to persuade a witness to change his story, it is open for a solicitor for either party in criminal proceedings to interview and take a statement from any witness or prospective witness at any stage of the proceedings, whether or not that witness has been interviewed or indeed called as a witness by the other party. That statement was published in January 1944 and before publication it received the approval of the then Lord Chief Justice.

The letter ended with, "This is not widely known."

Norton had been courteous enough to send a copy of this reply to Bishop who, rather than thanking him, wrote to the Deputy Director of Public Prosecutions, Mr Paling—after the proceedings were adjourned on November 2nd. In his letter he complained about the Law Society's advice to Norton. Then, after stating that, "Milne's evidence-in-chief was word perfect with her proof," and that, "McLoughlin and Bury were not shaken and had also come up to proof", he boasted that, "As arranged at our recent conference" he had withheld the three witnesses addresses. He then referred to the "outbursts" in court of the two defence solicitors and attached a copy of the letter to Norton from the Law Society.

Paling's reply stated there was "no unanimity on the point" and referred to Mr Justice Avory in 1922 and Mr Justice Humphreys in 1934, stating that it was improper for the defence to be in communication with witnesses who have, or are about to give evidence in the magistrates' court. Yet despite admitting that these judges were only dealing with the circumstances of two particular cases, Paling's letter advised that, "The DPP is bound to pay heed to these judicial (Avory's and Humphrey's) remarks and is satisfied you were right in refusing". It did not seem to matter that not only had the Lord Chief Justice's 1944 endorsement of the Law Society's view superseded the earlier rulings of these two hanging judges, but that he was also the most senior judge in the land.

Whether Gordon, a lay magistrate, was aware of this correspondence or not, siding with the prosecution, he again refused Norton's request, adding he would not allow it to go on the depositions. Unlike the hot-headed Livermore, however, the cool Norton quietly told him he would renew his protest elsewhere.

Replying to Norton during his continued cross-examination, McLoughlin said he did not know, nor had ever heard of Stanley Rubin. This was despite both him and Rubin regularly frequenting the all-night Continental Café, where Rubin had first met — and from where McLoughlin had known — June Bury.

Norton then asked that Rubin be called into court. But Bishop, again in obstructive mode, said he was not due to be called until later in the proceedings. In further replies to Norton, McLoughlin stated that Devlin had told him he would, "take care of the old woman if she gave any trouble" — the precise words he had told Balmer in September that Ginger Dutton had used.

"What did you understand Devlin to mean by that?" asked Norton.

"To shut her up or give her a hiding or something."

He was then asked if he was prepared to stand by if violence was used on Mrs Rimmer and do nothing about it, to which he unabashedly replied, "Yes."

When Norton asked why the break-in had been postponed from the 2nd August (when he said he had met Devlin with Burns in the Continental) for a fortnight, McLoughlin could not give a satisfactory answer.

"But you were one of the party," said Norton. "You must know why it was put off?"

"I don't know what is in other people's minds," he replied. But, he surely must have enquired why it was being put off for so long? "I never gave it a thought" was his implausible response.

Given that McLoughlin at the time was on the run from the army and admitted he was desperate to get money, the inexplicable lengthy postponement by the two accused, of what was supposed to be a very lucrative "job"—and his acceptance of this without question—was quite contrary to the *modus operandi* of most housebreakers and quite unbelievable.

In a further significant reply, regarding Devlin introducing him to Burns on August the 2nd, he said he had never seen Burns after that date. He had apparently forgotten the short written statement Balmer had concocted for him, dated 9th October, 1951, which began,

> All I know is about 8 or 9 days before the murder (10th or 11th August) I saw a man named Alf Burns, and Ted Devlin in the Rainbow Café, Islington and the Continental Café, Duke Street. They wanted to do a job and said they had a good one specked out in Cranborne Road off Smithdown Road. I told them I had one ready for doing there. It was a relative's house, 109 Cranborne Road.

Unfortunately the existence of this statement was not known to Livermore or Norton. Nor were the internal police reports in which Kiernan Oates and McLoughlin had first named Arthur "Ginger" Dutton as his intended partner in the burglary of the Rimmer home. Had they known of these documents, even the antagonistic magistrate and obdurate prosecutor would have had to agree, however reluctantly, to throw the case out of court. In the event however, the legal squabbling, the lies, the chaos, confusion and the hostility towards the defence would continue unabated throughout the hearing.

CHAPTER SEVEN

THE HEARING IS POSTPONED

A lie which is all a lie may be met and fought with outright.
But a lie which is part a truth is a harder matter to fight.

Alfred Lord Tennyson

After outlining the evidence the two women would be giving, Bishop stated that, "From the discovery of the crime onwards Superintendent Balmer and his officers carried out a vigorous inquiry." This was yet another inaccuracy, minor perhaps but symptomatic of the prosecution's distorted presentation of the facts. Balmer — a friend of Bishop's — had been in Ireland at the "discovery of the crime" and had not taken over from Superintendent Taylor until 2nd September.

Bishop then called blonde-haired, 20 year-old June Bury. She was well-known to almost all the small time villains, drunks and down-and-outs who frequented the Lime Street bars and all night cafés at the Pier Head and Chinatown. She was also a minor gangsters' moll of the O'Toole's — a tough trio of three brothers in their 20s — and had been the sexual partner in turn of two of them. Virtually an unpaid prostitute, she was also a police informer.

Bury told the court she had first met Devlin in Manchester at Whitsuntide last May and had spent about a week in his company, before leaving for Liverpool, where she went to live with Stanley Rubin in a bedsit at 39 Canning Street in Liverpool city centre. She next saw Devlin on the morning of August the 2nd when he arrived at Canning Street in a taxi, and took her downtown to a pub called the Dive near the Royal Court Theatre. There, she was introduced to Burns. All three stayed in the Dive till 3 pm and from there went to the Rainbow Café in Islington, remaining there until the early evening when they went on to the all night Continental Café. It was here she heard part of a conversation between McLoughlin, Devlin and Burns. But she then moved away from the table and did not hear the rest of it.

To Balmer, sitting behind the solicitors' bench, so far so good. It was his belief, he would often tell his colleagues, that the best lies were those that contained a nucleus of truth—always much more convincing. But his self-satisfaction was to be short-lived, for at this stage in Bury's evidence small flaws began to appear in his carefully woven "embroidery". Like McLoughlin earlier, Bury had either forgotten her lines or suddenly decided to depart from the script and ad-lib. For she then told the court that at about 3.30 am in the Continental, the two accused, "spoke to a man named *McLoughlin, who mentioned* a place where there was an old woman who lived on her own (Author's italics). He said there was a good deal of money and it was in a back place near a main road". Nobody registered any surprise at this revelation, yet here was a prosecution witness undoing the prosecution case, stating that it was McLoughlin, their main witness, not Devlin or Burns, who had suggested breaking into the "old woman's" house! To an exasperated Balmer, Bury was obviously hopeless at learning her lines!

As her evidence continued, Devlin and Burns, sitting impotently in the dock, were relieved to see that she was at least trying to mitigate her lying evidence. Their relief however was short-lived: Balmer's "embroidery" would soon reappear in her testimony.

Meanwhile, Bishop was so pleased with her corroboration of the alleged meeting between the three men that he too completely missed Bury's contradiction of McLoughlin's evidence. Instead, he simply asked McLoughlin—who was still in court—to stand up so that she could identify him as the same man who was in the Continental Café—which she did.

When the Continental closed, she continued, they went down to the Lighthouse Café near the Pier Head, staying there until 9 am. That evening all three re-visited the Rainbow where Burns asked her if she could find him a girl. She called Marie Milne upstairs who then partnered Burns. They remained at the Rainbow till 4.30 am then went again to the Pier Head.

Later that morning she went with Milne, Devlin and Burns to 39 Canning Street, where she was confronted by Rubin as she was leaving with her suitcase. There was an altercation outside the house, when Rubin asked her to choose between him and Devlin. She decided to go off with Devlin, accompanied by Burns and Milne.

After putting her case in Central Station's left luggage office, all four "walked around". They then went to 2 Verulam Street, off Upper Parliament Street, where Burns obtained a room for himself and Milne. That night she stayed with Devlin. Exactly where, she was not asked. Later however replying to Livermore, she said, "In the cafés, the Rainbow and the Continental". Perhaps she did not tell the truth because she did not want to put the spotlight on the seedy hotel in Mount Pleasant where she and Devlin stayed because it was run by a middle-aged female acquaintance who was later given six months for running a brothel there.

The following day, a Sunday, she and Devlin met Burns and Milne at Verulam Street and all four went by train to Manchester. On the journey they had a compartment to themselves and Burns mentioned a job in Liverpool which "was connected with the old lady and that she had plenty of money."

Despite the slang word among Manchester villains for keeping watch being "crow", Bury went on to state that one of them asked her if she would "keep douse"—a Liverpool expression. She refused but when Milne was asked, she said, "I don't know." Contradicting herself, Bury then said she couldn't remember if either of the accused had said what kind of job it was.

When Bishop asked if either man had shown her anything from his pocket, she vaguely replied, "No, but I had seen a glass cutter, I think, in Manchester." This, also contained in her statement of 8th October, neatly fitted in with the police discovery of a glass cutter at Devlin's home!

On arrival in Manchester, she continued, they all went to the house of a friend of Devlin and Burns. But they couldn't stay there. And because they could not get any suitable accommodation, Devlin and Burns put her and Milne on a train back to Liverpool that evening, telling them they would see them at Verulam Street in a few days time. On Wednesday August 8th, the two men returned to Verulam street. By that time Milne had "floated" and she went back to Manchester with them.

She did *not* tell the court that before meeting them at Verulam Street that day she had, in the early hours of August 8th, been shopbreaking with the two Liverpool men, Hadikin and O'Rourke and had later toured the streets in a police car and picked them out. And that this favour to the police, for which she was told she would not be charged, was followed by a further favour—allowing a police officer at Cheapside Bridewell to have sexual intercourse with her. Nor did she tell the court that late that evening

in Manchester, she acted as lookout, while Devlin and Burns stole a bale of
sheets from the Goods Depot at Liverpool Road Railway Yard. And that she
minded their macs for them, which her mother later pawned.

Continuing, she said she obtained employment in Manchester on August
16th, and saw the two accused on the 17th August, when they said they were
going to Liverpool as they had some important business with a man and a
woman. And that was the last time she saw them.

What was also unknown both to the defence and prosecution and kept
secret by the Liverpool police until 1953, was Bury's third statement of 17th
October 1951, to Manchester police, stating that in Woolworths Café in
Market Street *a red-haired man wearing a bloodstained army battledress blouse*,
had admitted to her that very day that he had killed Mrs Rimmer. She had
told the man that the police were looking for a red-haired man wearing an
army battledress and she had advised him to get away.[1]

After several mundane questions about minor matters from Livermore,
Norton asked her about the night of August 8th and managed to elicit from
her that she had minded their macs for them, arranging to meet them later
at a coffee stall. This line of questioning however wasn't pursued by Norton.
Had he done so he may have discovered what really happened that night
and revealed her not only as an accomplice in the robbery but as also stealing the men's raincoats—and that this was one of the reasons why Balmer
was able to pressurise her to give false evidence.

Under Norton's forensic questioning, Bury stated she had been to Manchester twice with Devlin and Burns. The significance of this was however
lost on the defence lawyer. Had he asked when the first occasion was it
would have been revealed that it was the 2nd August, the same night she and
McLoughlin had falsely stated they were all together in the Continental.

After her evidence was read over to her and she had signed the deposition,
Bury was about to leave the witness box when the magistrate told her that
she would be notified when, "*she would be required for the trial at the Assizes*"
(Author's italics). He then almost inaudibly, advised her, "Meanwhile if anyone approaches you and wants you to start talking to them about the case,
just you refuse to talk to them by yourself. And if anyone goes on molesting
you, go to the first policeman and he will tell you what to do."

---

1.   Merseyside Police files.

Unable to hear him properly, Norton asked Gordon to repeat what he had said. "I simply warned her," he replied, "that she must not talk to people about the case, and if anyone approached her and tried to force her to talk about it she should refuse and go to the police for advice."

Despite these crass imputations against his own and Livermore's professional integrity, Norton, cool as ever, said he hardly felt such advice would apply to defence counsel. "It applies to everyone," he retorted. "But it does not apply to the legal advisers for the defence?" asked a shocked Norton. Gordon however was adamant.

"It applies to everyone."

"But that is not the law of this country," protested Norton.

Although fully aware of the correspondence about witnesses between the defence and the Law Society, Bishop commented, "I don't agree." Admirably maintaining his composure in this increasingly heated atmosphere, Norton courteously and rationally argued that the magistrate was not obliged to prevent her being in touch with the defence, and that if they wished to be in contact they were entitled to. Livermore, however, could not contain himself so readily, telling Gordon that he strongly resented the innuendo in his remarks. When the magistrate denied any innuendo, he snapped back, "Yes there is!" There was no question of any threat being made to Bury or any other witness, he said, and it was gratuitous for a magistrate to say that to a witness in open court. He told Gordon, "We have had a very definite ruling from the Law Society about that position. And I am prepared to accept their ruling and not your worship's." But this remonstration against his plainly unjust conduct did not perturb Gordon in the least. Ignoring Livermore's rectitude, he simply looked down to the clerk and said, "Let's have the next witness, Mr Harris."

Indignant at Gordon's more controversial comments, both defence lawyers had overlooked the equally significant remark to Bury about being notified "before the trial at the Assizes". The purpose of committal proceedings was to ascertain *if* there was a *prima-facie* case to go to the higher court. Cases *had* been thrown out at committal on the grounds that the accused had "no case to answer". The magistrate was therefore not only showing strong bias against the accused men but, like Harris earlier, was also being grossly presumptuous. They would not however have been so presumptuous and the case would probably have ended there, had they known about Bury's 17th October signed statement to Manchester police, that David Coyne, the man she had met that day in Woolworths Café, was the murderer. And that Liverpool's Detective Sergeant Wade had been immediately despatched to Manchester to get her to retract her statement.[2]

When the 17-year-old, half-Malaysian Marie Milne stepped into the witness box wearing a haughty expression, Burns again turned to Devlin and muttered with contempt, "Chinky cunt. Hope she fuckin' chokes on her chopsticks." At this utterance Devlin broke into laughter with Burns grinning at him. Given the gravity of the charge against them, those in the packed court who witnessed this behaviour were appalled at the apparent levity of the pair.

Milne was streetwise and sexually experienced beyond her years. Even as a schoolgirl at St. James School in the shadows of the Anglican Cathedral, she was known as a "sure thing". Well-known around the Rialto area amongst the Jamaican and African club owners and taxi drivers from the nearby rank, she was also a regular in Berkeley Street's Man Yow Café, where she would often perform sexual acts in the toilet for as little as a meal. This knowledge was one of the levers Balmer had used to make her comply with his instructions. With only the occasional slip-up during her evidence, she would prove to be Balmer's most able pupil and—as Inspector Lees had earlier predicted in an internal report to the Director of Public Prosecutions—she made "an excellent witness".[3]

Embarking at the request of Bishop on an uninterrupted narrative of what allegedly happened, she said that on Friday evening/the early morning of August 3rd/4th she was introduced by June Bury to Devlin and Burns in the Rainbow Café. It was assumed she was to be Burns' girl. They stayed there till 4.30 am, which was closing time, and then went down to the coffee stall at the Pier Head, where they stayed till about 6 am before moving to the nearby Lighthouse Café till 7 am. They then strolled around town. Although she said they did some shopping, she omitted the visits to New Brighton to look for digs and Lewis's department store where the men bought toothpaste.

---

2.   Merseyside Police files. Not revealed until 1953 when David Coyne complained that he was being blamed for the murder.
3.   Merseyside Police files.

Later, she said, they got a taxi to Canning Street where Bury lived. She then
confirmed the confrontation between Devlin and Rubin, adding that she
and Burns stayed that night at 2 Verulam Street.

On Sunday, the 5th August, all four went by train to Manchester. During
the journey the conversation turned to jobs the two men were going to do in
Liverpool. Burns asked her to go on a job but she refused. That night she and
Bury returned to Liverpool. But before leaving from Manchester's Exchange
Station, *Burns took her aside and, out of the earshot of Devlin and Bury, told
her he would see her on Friday, the 17th August in Liverpool.* She subsequently
met both Devlin and Burns on that date outside the Rialto Cinema in Upper
Parliament Street. All three then went for something to eat at the Golden
Dragon Chinese Restaurant in Leece Street. As they were eating, Devlin,
complaining about his knife being blunt, pulled out a red-handled knife
with a spring blade to cut his meat with and Burns started talking about a
job they were going to do at an old woman's house off Smithdown Road.
He said her name was Rimmer and she lived alone at No.7, four doors away
from the back entry.

They then went down to Central Station where they met a man in a merchant navy uniform outside Lewis's store, who she now knew to be Kenneth
McNeil. She then left them. But before doing so she agreed to meet Devlin
and Burns the following afternoon. This was because Devlin had threatened
her with the knife.

Continuing, Milne said she met the two men the next day, Saturday the
18th, by Lewis's at about 4 pm and they went again to the Golden Dragon.
She asked where Bury was and was told she would be returning from Manchester over the weekend. In the café both men asked her if she was afraid
of going on the job with them and she replied, "Yes."

Interjecting at this point, Bishop asked her if they had mentioned the
time the "job" was going to be done. "No", she replied, "they just said when
it get's dark on Sunday the 19th".

Before leaving the men, Burns told her to meet them the following day
at 1 pm by the Rialto. And when they met the next day Burns told her they
wanted to show her where the old woman lived, so they got a taxi, "to a point
near Smithdown Road Hospital." The fare was two shillings but Burns gave
the driver two shillings and sixpence. This detail had already been told to

Balmer by Emery the taxi driver. But neither Livermore nor Norton asked how *she* could remember such a detail.

Burns then showed her a tram stop near a street further up from the hospital, where he said he wanted her to wait for them at six o'clock that night. He then pointed out the road where the old woman lived, telling her it was the next road to Webster Road where the Cameo Cinema was. They then got a bus back downtown to the Golden Dragon. Burns gave her ten shillings and told her to go to the pictures, and that they would see her as arranged at 6 pm.

She subsequently returned to the tram stop at the appointed hour but after waiting till 7.30 pm they hadn't shown up so she got a bus back to the Rialto. As she alighted from the bus she saw the two men on the opposite side of the road. She asked why they hadn't kept the appointment. "Burns said he did not want me with them on the job." She then complained that, instead of leaving the cinema early to meet them, she could have stayed and watched the whole programme. Burns then apparently changed his mind and asked if she would come on the job and "keep douse" for them.

Continuing, she said they went to the Somali Café until it got dark. Then at 9 pm they jumped a tram back to Cranborne Road, although she didn't know the name of it at the time. Burns told her to wait on the street corner for five minutes to give them time to go around to the back of the house. She was then to knock on the front door and if the old woman answered, she was to say her mother sent her. She was to try and follow the old lady into the hallway so that she was between her and the front door to prevent her from leaving. In arguably the most damning part of her testimony, Milne then stated, "Burns described the inside of the house and said there were two mirrors on the kitchen walls, one on top of the sideboard, and that Mrs Rimmer always sat in an armchair by the fire." This once again just happened to coincide with the police crime scene photographs of the Rimmer living room in which the two mirrors and armchair could be clearly seen!

In the event, she said, she did not carry out Burns instructions to go to the house. But she *did* wait on the corner for one and a half hours till 10.30 pm, then decided to go back to the Rialto because she had to meet her brother in nearby Wilkie's Club. But alighting from the bus, she again saw the two men on the opposite side of the road. After them calling her over she went across and asked had they done the job and Burns said, "No, we didn't do it."

"They appeared excited and frightened. And as we were walking along they were discussing the job. Not very loud but I could hear what they were saying. Devlin said that they should not have come through the park as he had mud on his shoes and that I might suspect something". When Bishop asked if she had noticed their shoes, she cryptically replied, "They were muddy but I couldn't see properly because it was dark."

Continuing down Parliament Street, she said Devlin asked Burns, "Will the old woman live?" and Burns replied, "To hell with the old woman. We will be out of Liverpool before long and we'll take Marie, the little bitch, with us." She noticed that Devlin had a handkerchief on his hand which was stained. Burns then asked him where his knife was and he said he had lost it coming through the park. She also noticed wet stains on Burns coat, *"just by the buttonholes"* (Author's italics). When she asked him what they were, he told her to, "Mind your own fucking business. They're beer stains." There were also stains, she said, on Devlin's shirt, *"near the buttons"* (Author's italics). These comments tallied, of course, precisely with forensic scientist Dr Firth's report, of which Balmer had received a report two months previously!

Reaching the bottom of Parliament Street, she suggested that they go for a meal to a Chinese café near Great George's Place (where unknown to them she lived). But Burns said they were in a hurry to get back to Manchester. The two men then walked towards town and that was the last she saw of them. That concluded her evidence-in-chief and she was allowed to stand down.

Unfortunately the defence and the court were totally unaware of Milne's second signed statement of 9th October, taken by Inspector Lees, in which she had stated that after meeting them at 10.30 she actually took Devlin and Burns to the *South China* Café at the corner of Great George Street and Upper Frederick Street. It was closed but after knocking on the front door, all three were let in by the Chinese female owner, whom she knew, and they had a meal of corned beef and chips. And it was *there* that she overheard the conversation and saw muddy shoes and stains on their clothes.

In her previously signed statement of 7th October however (taken by Detective Sergeant Sturrock), of which the court was also unaware, none of this ever happened. In that shorter statement—which ended, "That's all I know"—she said she did not see them again after 7.30 pm on the Sunday by the Rialto when they told her they didn't want her on the job after all.

The reason Milne's eventual testimony varied from these statements was because Balmer realised that, since her second statement mentioned the café and its owner by name, the defence could easily disprove the veracity of this by interviewing the owner and showing her photos of the two accused men.

Similarly, both in her first and second statements she had stated—as did Bury in her statement of October 8th—that she first met Devlin and Burns on Friday, the 10th August, "after the Bank Holiday". This false date was dictated by Balmer in order to move all of the true events a week forward because he realised that the unduly long interval between the planning and actual robbery was not plausible. Having second thoughts however, he decided to simplify matters by inventing the phoney conversation between Burns and Milne at the Manchester Railway Station on the 5th August, when Burns allegedly told Milne (out of earshot of Bury and Devlin) that he would see her again not in a few days but on the 17th by the Rialto.

Had the defence been allowed sight of the women's three statements, which contradicted each other and their testimony under oath, the case would doubtless have come to a halt there and then.

Despite Balmer's clever tutelage—and apart from her undisclosed statements—there was however still much in Milne's evidence to be seriously challenged. But the defence solicitors would now have to wait ten days to cross-examine her. For the magistrate, without giving any reason or explanation, announced the proceedings would be adjourned to the 9th November for a formal remand of the accused, and then properly resume on the 12th.

This adjournment was to be most fortuitous both for Milne and Balmer. It gave him plenty of time to reappraise her "performance", iron out any problems and provide further coaching.

It was most unusual for ongoing committal proceedings like this to be adjourned for such a long period. And although it was of obvious benefit to the police, it extended the ordeals of Devlin and Burns, who would now unnecessarily have to spend an additional ten days in the bleak prison "hospital" segregated from each other and locked up for 23 hours a day.

CHAPTER EIGHT

THE COMMITTAL HEARING CONTINUES

Is't not enough thou hast suborned these women
To accuse this worthy man, but, in foul mouth
And in the witness of his proper ear,
To call him villain?

Shakespeare, Measure for Measure

After the two co-accuseds' nominal court appearance on the 9th November the committal proceeding were resumed on the 12th November, the court again packed to capacity with police officers, reporters and the general public. As Marie Milne again entered the witness box she smiled at Mr Bishop the prosecutor. But when Harry Livermore rose her expression changed to one of hostility before he had even spoken.

Devlin's solicitor then proceeded to ask her a series of apparently irrelevant questions, such as did she know where the Cameo Cinema was, a reference to the location of the double murder two years earlier in the next road to Cranborne Road. Asked by the clerk, Harris, what the relevance was, Livermore cryptically replied that it should be obvious to him so he was not going to explain it. Those in the packed court however, including the two accused, were also puzzled by the raising of an irrelevancy and then not pursuing it. But this was a peculiar feature of Livermore's style, which usually caused irritation and confusion among fellow lawyers and his clients alike.

When did she first hear of the murder? he wanted to know?

"On the Tuesday in the café," she replied. And when was she seen by the police?

"Just after it happened."

"How long after it happened?"

"About four weeks."

Did she think four weeks was "just after it happened" asked a sarcastic Livermore.

"It was just after it happened," she repeated, rolling her eyes with impatience.

"Now look, Miss Milne," he snapped back, "don't start pulling faces and behaving like that. Just answer my question. You don't call four weeks, 'just after it happened?'" to which she wearily conceded, "No."

Replying further, she said she had not been seen *first* at a police station but at her parents' home where she had been living since the 19th August. She did not tell him however, *how many times* she had been seen at her parents home and at Lawrence Road Police Station, by Chief Superintendent Balmer. And he didn't ask.

Stating that she went to Manchester with Devlin, Burns and Bury on August 5th because her parents were looking for her, she denied being told by a girl that her parents would kill her if they got hold of her. She also denied that when leaving the two accused in Manchester on the night of August 5th it was arranged for them to meet at Verulam Street in two or three days. Instead, she insisted — in accordance with Balmer's script — that Burns, out of the earshot of the other two had arranged to see her on Friday the 17th.[1] She went back to her parents' home on Monday the 6th. But she also did not tell him she ran away from home to a house, 164 Bedford Street, during October to escape Balmer's threatening visits.

Livermore suggested that, since she had earlier agreed that neither Burns nor Devlin knew her address, if she had wanted nothing further to do with them she could have ended her involvement before August19th or even the 17th, to which she simply replied, "Yes."

Re-examining, Bishop, producing a brown paper, partly opened parcel, asked her if she would recognise the suit Burns was wearing on the murder night. But Livermore, immediately objecting to this, argued that she should be shown the suit along with other similar suits. "Otherwise," he claimed, "she would obviously not say 'No' to the question." Milne simply turned up the suit's collar then pushed it away, ready to answer the next question.

---

1.   She never in fact met Devlin and Burns after being seen on to the train on August 5th. Her undisclosed statement (and Bury's and McLoughlin's) said they first met them on Friday 10th August. To Balmer this would rule out the lengthy period between the planning and commission of the robbery/murder. But realising the landlords at 36 Canning St. and No.2 Verulam St, would contradict this if they read it in the papers or were contacted by the defence, he reverted to the true time frame but still made it plausible by having Milne say that Burns had made an arrangement with her alone to meet on the 17th.

At this, Burns muttered to his friend in the dock, "By the time they're finished with it the fuckin' thing won't even be fit to be pawned." At which they both again began giggling.

With mock sympathy the magistrate told Livermore, "I'm afraid before we could stop it, it has been put in." But Milne hadn't yet answered the question, said Livermore. Nevertheless Bishop said he was going to ask her to answer it. When Livermore complained that the suit should have been put to Milne in her evidence-in-chief, the clerk, officiously intervening once again, said that it was being properly brought up now because Milne at the earlier hearing had been asked to identify the suit Burns was wearing when he had been asked to stand up in the dock. At this point, Burns' solicitor, Norton, apparently irritated at Harris' petty interference, corrected him by reminding the court that Burns was asked to stand up for a totally different reason. This injection of a little commonsense into the proceedings saw Bishop retreating, simply saying he would prove the point later.

In subsequent answers to Livermore's questions, Milne again denied the arrangement to see the accused in two or three days time at Verulam Street. She insisted Burns told her the 17th August. And when she did meet them at about 4 pm on the 17th she was later threatened with a knife by Devlin. "Where did you think of that little bit?" asked a sarcastic Livermore. But Bishop, protested, "I don't think that is a proper question to put to her." Livermore then simply asked her *where* she was threatened. Despite stating at the previous hearing that it was at Central Station, she replied, "At the Golden Dragon in Leece Street." This was another departure from Balmer's script. But Livermore didn't seem to notice it. It was only because she had been threatened, she said, that she agreed to go on the job the following Sunday. But why, Livermore wanted to know, if she was so afraid did she turn up at the meeting at 3.30 the following day, the Saturday? She didn't think they were going to do the job, she said. "I thought they were just going to see me." But, immediately contradicting herself she then said she kept the appointment because she was, "scared that they might come looking for me." But, asked if they did come looking for her, she replied, "No, I went to meet them." Although, looking quite impassive, Balmer was becoming increasingly anxious: his star witness was falling apart before his eyes!

Livermore told her that, since she had admitted the accused did not know

where she lived, they would not know where to look for her, adding that
there had never been any threats. And, to demonstrate her changing version
of events, he asked if he could have the deposition read out. But the clerk of
the court told him he was just wasting time, to which he angrily retorted,
"Don't be childish Mr Harris. If I want it read I will have it read. And I am
not wasting time."

Returning to Milne, he asked, if, being so afraid, did she go to the police
before the Saturday meeting? No she didn't. Then, referring to Sunday after
she had been to the pictures and kept the rendezvous with the accused at six
o'clock, he cynically asked, "I suppose you were so scared that you waited
for them for an hour and a half?"

"Yes."

"And you were so scared that when they didn't turn up you went back to
the Rialto to look for them? And you saw them?"

"Yes". But she didn't know they would be there.

"So it was pure luck that you bumped into them?"

"Yes."

When she repeated Burns alleged instruction to her about getting into the
house and preventing the woman from getting out, Livermore suggested that
her role was quite a lot more than merely "keeping douse" but she replied
that she simply waited till but 10.30 and didn't go to the house.

"Was that", he asked, "because you were scared to go or scared to stay?"

"I was scared to go."

"You were so scared that you could not even run away or even walk away
and get a passing tram or bus?"

"Yes. I thought they would come back"

Listening to her absurd replies, Balmer was silently fuming inside. The
whole bloody case was in imminent danger of collapsing!

In a final reply, Milne stated that once again it was pure coincidence that
she met the two men after the murder outside the Rialto. She finally left
them at the bottom of Parliament Street at 11.15 pm.

Resuming Milne's cross-examination on behalf of Burns, Joseph Norton
was further able to demonstrate her selectivity, inconsistency and down-
right lying. This was exemplified by a series of questions about what name
Burns had given her. She said she did not know his name until June Bury

told her when they arrived back in Liverpool on 6th August. She called him Fred because he had told her that was his name. She did not believe Bury and thought she had told her a false name until the police told her he was Alfred Burns. At this reply Balmer visibly winced.

In that case, asked Norton, "Why did you tell us at the hearing on November 2nd that from the very start Burns told you his name was Rimmer?"

"I didn't know you wanted to know his last name. You asked me his first name."

"But," said Norton, "You told us a few moments ago that the *only* name he ever gave you was Fred."

"Yes."

When Norton put it to her that it was utterly untrue that Burns had ever given her the name Rimmer, she sheepishly almost whispered, "It was true sir."

In later replies, Milne admitted that although she was so ill on the 3rd August that she was unable to go to work, she nevertheless spent that night with Bury, Devlin and Burns at the Rainbow until 4.30 am and then went on to the all night Pier Head cafés.

Later, when she reiterated being threatened with the knife by Devlin in the Golden Dragon, Norton, unlike Livermore earlier, spotted the discrepancy. "At the last hearing," he said, "you told the court that it was only after you had left the café and gone down to Central station that you were threatened with the knife." When she denied she had said this, Norton asked for the deposition to be read, and the magistrate, for once, agreed with Norton. The clerk then read out.

> After leaving the café we went to Central Station. They asked me again if I would go on the job and I still said no. Then Devlin threatened me with the knife and told me what he would do to me if I would not go. So I said 'Yes'.

Thanking Harris, Norton asked Milne, "What do you say now?" But she still insisted she was threatened in the Golden Dragon. So, he suggested, when she said it had occurred at the station that was either untrue or a mistake? It was a mistake, she said, and agreed with Norton that her allegation of being threatened with a knife was of tremendous importance. "And," he suggested, "if you are mistaken about *that* you may be mistaken about other parts of your evidence?" to which she firmly replied, "I am not."

When Norton later said it was clear to Milne that force would be used to prevent Mrs Rimmer from summoning assistance and that she did not see fit to go to the police, she replied, "I was too scared. I don't know what they were going to do to the old woman."

"Didn't you realise that the police would have fully protected you?"

Replying softly with an innocent expression, she said, "I did not know. I was just too scared to go to the police."

Coming to her evidence of going to the cinema on the Sunday afternoon, Milne said she could not remember what the film was. "But," said Norton, "you have remembered with remarkable accuracy events and times which occurred further back than August 19th. Yet you cannot remember the film you saw that day. Is that what you are telling the court?"

"Yes."

Considering she could not remember the film she saw on the 19th August, Milne was nevertheless most observant about more minute details on that same day. For instance she had no problem remembering that the fare on the taxi clock was two shillings and that Burns gave the taxi driver two shillings and sixpence. Neither Norton nor Livermore thought to ask how she had come to notice this detail. Nonetheless, this part of her testimony satisfied Balmer, dovetailing perfectly as it did with taxi driver Emery's statement.

Milne stated that she was relieved Devlin and Burns did not turn up at six o'clock, despite waiting until 7.30 for them, and denied that she went back to the Rialto at 7.30 to try and find them. She only went past that point because it was on her way home, she said, maintaining there was no other way. In order to ascertain if this was true, Norton asked where she lived at the time, to which the magistrate immediately objected. But Norton insisted the question was of the utmost relevance since he may be able to show that she could have got home by another route without passing the Rialto. In total contradiction to his own objection, Gordon then asked Milne where she lived, to which she replied, "29a Great George's Place."

"If you had really been so apprehensive," asked Norton, "couldn't you have walked home by a roundabout way without passing the Rialto?" Milne replied that she did not know the Smithdown Road area except for the hospital. This of course avoided the question, the Rialto being an altogether different location.

Surprisingly, Liverpool-born Norton did not suggest or demonstrate alternative routes from Smithdown Road to Milne's home in Great George's Place. Yet a mere glance at a Street A-Z map could have shown that to avoid the Rialto altogether she could have left the bus one stop before the Rialto then walked home via Bedford Street South, Huskisson Street, Hope Street and (Lower) Parliament Street. Or via Mulgrave Street, Selborne Street, Stanhope Street, Windsor Street and (Lower) Parliament Street.

Continuing his cross-examination, Norton asked Milne that, since she had carried out her part of the arrangement by turning up at the appointed six o'clock and the accused had failed to do so, why she didn't drop out of the conspiracy there and then?

"That is what I was going to do," she replied.

"So you did not go back to the Rialto because you were scared of them?"

Agreeing there was no longer any threat and that the reason she did not go straight home was not because they had prevented her from doing so, she said she pretended to be annoyed with them for not showing up, "but in my heart I wasn't." In further replies she stated that although she couldn't remember what type of shirt Burns was wearing, she was able to state that the stain on it near the buttonhole and the stain on his coat was about half an inch and that both stains were wet. Balmer was relieved she had at least remembered this telling detail correctly!

Although agreeing with Norton that when she met them at 11 pm the pair had obviously done something wrong and that she was desperately afraid of them, she nonetheless had suggested that they accompany her to the *South China* Café for a meal. She also agreed that it was quite possible she had invented everything she said had happened between her and the accused, and that she was annoyed with Burns because he had been, "indifferent to her charms."

"I put it to you," said Norton, "that if you say what happened on the 17th, 18th and 19th of August did in fact happen then it was not with the accused but with two other men?" But defiant to the end, Milne replied, "No, the two men who are sitting in the court now."

The second of that day's three witnesses was the diminutive Stanley Rubin who, although an unemployed labourer, told the court that he was currently working as a charge-hand ship's scaler. He stated that after Bury had left 39 Canning Street with Devlin and Burns on August 4th he just walked away. He never saw Devlin and Burns again until a fortnight later on Saturday the 18th August in the Dive public house. He said he had been "knocking about" with Bury for about four weeks and admitted he was "pretty sore" about the August 4th incident. But when Harry Livermore suggested he did not feel friendly disposed towards Devlin, he replied, "I wouldn't say that."

"But he was pinching your girl, wasn't he?" He didn't blame Devlin, he said. It was Bury's fault rather than Devlin's.

When challenged by Norton about dates, Rubin said he was first seen by the police "about six weeks ago, about the end of September." Then, after first stating he had no difficulty remembering the date when Bury had left Canning Street with Devlin, Burns and Milne—and that the police had not helped him to fix it—he then agreed that the police had to remind him the date was August 4th. But when it was suggested it was the following day, Sunday the 5th that he met Devlin in the Dive and told him Bury had a venereal disease, Rubin emphatically stated that he had no difficulty remembering it was not the next day the 5th but Saturday the 18th August, a fortnight later. He was certain of this, he said, because it was whilst the Festival of Britain fireworks display on the River Mersey was on.[2]

Because no witness statements had been disclosed to the defence there was no time or opportunity to challenge Rubin's damning assertion which wrongly placed Devlin and Burns in Liverpool the day before the murder. Had there been they would have discovered that there were only three fireworks displays—Thursday 26th July, Wednesday 8th August and the final one ended Friday 10th of August, eight days before Rubin said it was while the "fireworks were on."

To test his memory, Norton suddenly asked Rubin, "Where were you on Sunday September 30th?" But appealing to the magistrate, he asked, "Do I have to answer that?" Rather than telling him to answer, Gordon told him, "If you do not know, just say so." Rubin then replied, "I don't know."

"I make a most strong protest," said Norton, "that that answer should be put into this man's mouth." But his protest was once again ignored.

---

2. It would emerge at the trial that the police had actually suggested the 18th August to Rubin.

Addressing Rubin, Norton then said, "You can't tell me where you were five or six weeks ago, yet you can remember the precise date weeks prior to that when you met Devlin in the Dive?" Rubin did not reply. Nonetheless, before he left the witness box Norton managed to obtain his admission that the police had *helped* him to fix the date as the 18th.

When middle-aged taxi driver Thomas Emery was called it was apparent that here was a basically decent and honest man who found being involved in these criminal proceedings quite alienating. Trying to be truthful but nonetheless under the pernicious influence of Balmer, he was clearly out of his depth with all eyes on him in this packed courtroom. Mindful however of Balmer's implied threats that he could lose his Hackney carriage licence if he didn't co-operate, he was also most anxious to give the "right" answers. Despite this pressure however, he genuinely could not recall the two men who were with Marie Milne on the journey to Smithdown Road. And although shown by the police photographs of Devlin and Burns and being told they were the two men, he had still refused to identify them He was asked, he said, to describe the two men but was never asked to attend an identity parade because he had told the police he could not remember who they were or what they looked like.

Emery stated that on Sunday August the 19th at about 2-30pm he had picked up Marie Milne, whom he knew from around the Rialto area, and two young men and had taken them to Smithdown Road "near the hospital". The fare was two shillings but one of the men gave him 2s.6d — a sixpenny tip. He was not asked anything further by Bishop.

Under Livermore's cross-examination Emery stated he had first spoken to the police about it when they called at his home in Pine Street, Liverpool 7 on a Friday night some five or six weeks after the murder on Sunday August 19th. Now even six weeks would make that date 2nd October. But in order for him to appear to be corroborating Milne's false story rather than her "corroborating" his truthful account, Balmer arranged for his signed statement to be dated 14th October, five days after Milne's concocted statement of 9th October. Neither defence lawyer was able however to query this discrepancy, simply because — on the advice of a Mr G Paling, Deputy Director of Public Prosecutions — they had been refused copies of his, and other prosecution witnesses, statements, including that of Rimmer's neighbour,

Sydney Fairbrother.

Replying to further questions Emery stated that the two men were not *described* to him by the police but then appeared to slip up by stating that he was then asked to *identify* them He could only have "identified" them by being shown their photographs, as was done with the photograph of Marie Milne. But both defence solicitors failed to note this discrepancy.

Asked again by Livermore, if the location he took the three persons to (as opposed to the hospital) was suggested by police, he denied this.

When Burns solicitor, Norton, suggested that Emery—who could not even remember what the two men looked like—could not possibly remember which Sunday he had taken this particular fare, he vaguely replied he was guessing the 19th because he had had his taxi clock repaired a few weeks earlier. Seizing on this totally unconnected reply, Norton asked how he was even certain it was a Sunday, "It might just as easily have been a Monday or a Tuesday?" he suggested. Emery's reply was again irrelevant: "I'm going by the lady (Milne) I picked up. It was a Sunday afternoon."

The taxi driver's inability to directly address specific questions was becoming increasingly evident by his response to Norton's next question: "How can you pick up a lady on a Sunday afternoon but not on a Tuesday afternoon?"

"Because I have never had the lady since."

These illogical replies were gradually losing him all credibility. And when asked, even if it were a Sunday in August, how he could be so certain it was the 19th, he feebly conceded, "To tell the truth I cannot be sure." So why at the outset had he been so certain about the date, asked Norton, to which he finally admitted, *"The police suggested that date to me"* (Author's italics).

Balmer was now looking quite despondent. Yet another of his witnesses was departing from his script!

Attempting to expose the suspected police collusion with this witness, Norton then asked if, when he was interviewed by the police, he was asked and had immediately remembered where he had taken the fare to, he clearly replied, "To Smithdown Road Hospital." This was the truth: Sunday afternoons were the regular and busiest visiting times for hospitals. And it was obvious that Emery's passengers, whoever they were, were visiting somebody at the hospital. He had also said in his signed statement: "They got out at the hospital entrance... all three walked towards the hospital".

Altering the date and the true destination of the taxi journey into subsequent "corroboration" of Milne's false evidence — namely that they alighted *near* the hospital — Balmer did not want Emery's statement about the trio's true destination to be known (whoever they were). The defence might start enquiring as to whether Milne was actually visiting at the hospital on August 19th, and with *whom*! And if these enquiries revealed she was indeed visiting a patient, her false story about being taken to Cranborne Road that day to reconnoitre the proposed target house would have been exposed. Was this why Emery's signed statement was also withheld from the defence?

Assuming Emery's testimony was correct, whoever the three passengers were it was obvious they were in fact visiting the hospital on that or another Sunday afternoon in August, which was 200 yards past Cranborne Road on the opposite side of Smithdown Road. In any event it seems both illogical and inexplicable that Devlin and Burns would need or want to travel in a taxi at 1.30 or 2.30 in the afternoon to the scene of a crime they had decided to commit that evening when it was dark. And then — according to Milne — arrange to go again at 6 pm before returning at 9 pm. It is even more improbable since, as Milne had testified, they already knew so much about Mrs Rimmer and the location and details of her home, even down to how many mirrors she had in her living room.

At the conclusion of Emery's testimony the defence solicitors would have been justified in arguing that it did not corroborate Milne's testimony about the taxi ride, and thereby submitting that there was no case to answer. But perhaps because they knew they had no chance of success in Alderman Gordon's "kangaroo court", they didn't even try. The court was then adjourned to the 19th November. No reason was given by the magistrate for this latest lengthy adjournment but it *would* give more time for Superintendent Balmer to further coach his witnesses!

CHAPTER NINE
MORE DAMNING PROSECUTION EVIDENCE

November 19th 1951

Was there ever seen such Villainy, so neatly plotted and so well performed?

Christopher Marlowe (1564—1593).

At the resumed hearing, the first witnesses to be called were Thomas Rimmer and Henry Francis Bentley, the conductor of the No.27 bus on which Alice Rimmer had made her last journey.

Rimmer gave his evidence without any sign of emotion, his testimony basically the same as the statement he had made. Prosecuting solicitor Bishop did not ask about his police interviews. Nor was the statement of Sydney Fairbrother, his mother's neighbour, contradicting his account, mentioned. The defence solicitors had no knowledge of Rimmer's interrogation as a suspect. Nor were they aware of Fairbrother's statement. It was therefore not surprising that they decided not to cross-examine him.

When asked by Bishop how long it took when he had made journeys to his mother's, Rimmer obliquely replied, "Ten to 15 minutes walking from the bus stop." This reply left many in court puzzled as to why he had specifically said, "walking" and "from the bus stop". Firstly, he usually cycled to his mother's and had not been asked if he had walked. Moreover when he made journeys to his mother's it would be from his home in Madryn Street not from any bus stop.

It emerged that Rimmer had taken his mother's pulse on discovering her body—although whether purposely or not, he put it less professionally and with less certainty: "I touched my mother's wrist," he said, "and she appeared to be dead."

After describing the lady who boarded his bus, it was clear that the conductor, Bentley, was describing Alice Rimmer, including as he did, her attire and the flowers and umbrella she was carrying. Although he stated that she was on her own when she got on his bus, he too was not questioned by Norton or Livermore.

Next came a most important and controversial witness, 21-year-old Kenneth McNeil of Towson Street in the Everton district of Liverpool. He was a friend of the O'Toole brothers and had lodged in July and August at their home, 4b Vauxhall Gardens, a city centre tenement block. Although he was described as a ship's steward, and sometimes wore a ragged merchant navy uniform, unknown to the court he was not a merchant seaman and had never possessed a seaman's book. As a drifter who would frequent Lewis's department store cafeteria to pass the time, he was finally given a casual job there as a porter. He commenced the job on the 16th August and left both the job and Liverpool on the 21st, two days after the murder.

At an identity parade on November 2nd — despite alleging he had seen them several times in the Continental and Lewis's cafeteria and had been in their company on the 17th August for several hours — he had failed to pick out either Devlin or Burns but had instead picked out two non-involved and thus completely innocent men.

Replying to Bishop he stated that, "Some time in August" he was in the Continental all-night café where he met Devlin, Burns and June Bury.

When Harris the clerk asked, "You do know them do you?", excluding Bury whom he also knew, he replied, "I know Devlin and Burns."

"Are they here today?" asked Bishop. But before he could answer Livermore immediately objected. McNeil however repeated that he saw two men, one named Devlin, the other Burns. "That is all we want to know," said a smug Harris who then asked Livermore, "Is that all right?" No, it wasn't said Devlin's solicitor. He didn't know whether it was evidence or not, adding, "He attended an identity parade and failed to pick out my client." Bishop reminded him that he could cross-examine the witness later. But he asked, "Does this become evidence if he fails to identify my client? He could be talking about anybody." Bishop then asked McNeil if at the time he knew their names. "I did not at that time by name," he replied, "but I knew them a few days afterwards when they appeared again in the Continental."

Although McLoughlin and Bury had stated Devlin and Burns had been in the Continental — and even then on only one occasion — neither had ever said McNeill was present. Inexplicably however, Norton and Livermore failed to question him on this point.

When Bishop again asked Livermore if McNeil's explanation was all right, sarcastically mimicking him he retorted, "'Is that all right?' No it isn't all right. My point is he is going to say he met a man called Devlin." Yet, he continued, McNeil failed to pick out his client at an identity parade on November 2nd. Indeed, he picked out an entirely innocent man.

"That being so," he said, "If he cannot identify my client does his statement that he met a man called Devlin become evidence? He is not identifying my client at all. It could be anybody. He might be a man he knew as Devlin but who was not Devlin, and it was not fair to introduce that evidence."

After more convoluted argument and without any guidance from the bench, Bishop said, "I am going to have it my way if I may." He then asked McNeil if he had met the three people on a second occasion in the Continental, to which he agreed.

"What were their names?"

"Devlin and Burns and I was introduced to them by June Bury." But once again the defence solicitors did not point out that neither McLoughlin nor Bury had stated that McNeil was ever present in the café.

Attempting to resolve the matter, the clerk said that all anyone could say was that on a date in August McNeill met two men and a girl in the Continental Café. He did not know their names. Four days later he saw, "the same two men *and the girl*" (Author's italics).

"Is that right?" he asked McNeill, who replied, "Correct." But it was not correct. He was forgetting his lines! The "girl" he allegedly saw them with on the later occasion (outside Lewis's) was not Bury but Marie Milne.

Harris then stated, "And he understood their names were Devlin and Burns". But this clever attempt to overcome Livermore's important point did not go un-noticed.

"If you don't prove my client was there," he told Harris, "how are you going to give evidence of that? He can only give evidence of conversations. By saying the witness 'understood' the name was Devlin you are only getting in by the back door what should not be allowed to come in." But Bishop stated that — despite him being unable to identify either man at the ID parades — because McNeill had now given the names of the two men then it must be admissible evidence. Harris the clerk then said the magistrate had ruled that McNeil's identification would go down on the depositions. A frustrated Livermore once again asked that his objection be formally noted.

Coming to the identity parades, McNeil admitted to picking out two men whom he knew were not Devlin and Burns and were not the men he had earlier referred to in his evidence. "I saw them but I didn't pick them out because I was a bit nervous," he said. Then, rather than the magistrate ruling as inadmissible at least this part of McNeil's evidence, he remained silent whilst Bishop asked, "Do you see them here today?" to which, pointing to the dock, he said, "There they are there sir."

Having been given a second opportunity to identify the accused, McNeil's courtroom identification was most unfair and devoid of any of the safeguards of a proper identity parade.[1] Earlier in his evidence McNeill told the court he had worked at Lewis's department store as a porter from the 16th to the 21st August and had seen Devlin and Burns some time in August in the cafeteria there. Whilst working there he wore an old merchant navy uniform because he had no other clothes. He had previously been away to sea and had joined the merchant navy in 1947. In truth he had never been in the merchant navy.[2]

Replying to Joseph Norton, for Burns, he said he saw the accused men with a girl outside Lewis's store and Central Station on Friday 17th August. The girl then left them.[3] He did not know her then but now knew that she was Marie Milne. The court however was unaware that he had been a casual table-clearer at the Continental where Milne was a regular habitué.

Continuing, McNeill said that after meeting Devlin and Burns on the 17th he went with them to Tracey's pub in nearby Hanover Street, then to the National Milk Bar in Lime Street, leaving them at 1 am on Saturday the 18th. If this was true it begs the question, since it was too late to return to Manchester where Devlin and Burns stayed that night? There was no evidence that they stayed in Liverpool but the defence did not raise the point.

---

1.   Quashing the 50-year-old conviction of executed Mahmood Mattan, the Court of Appeal in 1998 severely criticised "dock" identification, stating it would not now be allowed.
2.   Merseyside Police files.
3.   McNeil's false story was designed by Balmer in order to corroborate Milne's evidence of Burns meeting her on the 17th as allegedly arranged with her before she and Bury left for Liverpool by train on the night of Sunday August 5th.

Nor, since it was his witness' contention, did Bishop attempt to explain this.

When McNeill said he did not pick out the accused men at the identity parades because he was nervous, Norton asked why he was now identifying the men in the dock when he had failed to do so whilst surrounded by police officers on that occasion. "I've just given you the reason, nervousness," he replied. When Norton pressed the point, he replied, "Well I've just got enough courage to do it today." That phrase, with its connotation of implied threats against him, made the headlines that night in the *Liverpool Echo* and the *Evening Express*, just as Milne's "knife threat" allegation had done on November 12th.

Asked by Norton what happened after the abortive identity parades, McNeill said he went into the CID office where there were several detectives. But, he said, there was no conversation between him and them. Neither Norton nor Livermore asked *why* in that case had he gone into the CID office. Without being asked he then spontaneously volunteered, "I wasn't shown any photographs." If that was true—which it wasn't—then to a certain extent it was irrelevant: you don't need photographs when the two suspects are obviously those sitting in the dock!

When Home Office pathologist, Dr George Manning[4] was called by the prosecution it was obvious by his replies to questions that he was not going to concede anything favourable to the defence. For example, despite stating that Mrs Rimmer had received some 20 blows, including 15 wounds to the head, had suffered two fractures of the skull and had been subject to a brutal and violent assault, he disagreed with Norton's suggestion that it was the work of a madman! Stating that she would not have died immediately from the "probable 20 to 30 blows", he then described in detail the wounds to the victim's head which he said ran in various directions. Some were very straight, some were curved, some were stellate (star-shaped), some were clean-cut and others jagged. And an area of the skull two inches in diameter was exposed.

When he stated the victim had lived for several hours after the attack and had died at two am the following morning, Norton suggested, in view of the terrible injuries, that this was surely a matter of conjecture? But he disagreed and went on to state that despite the horrific injuries, she would *not* have died almost immediately. He was not asked how he had arrived at

4. Manning, according to Balmer's 1967 *Liverpool Echo* memoirs, was a good friend of his.

this conclusion. But pressed further by Norton he said she could have died three or four hours either side of 10 pm, until he finally agreed that he did not know what time she had died. This admission was a minor victory for the defence which was never fully exploited at the trial.

In relation to Manning's evidence about the different shaped wounds, his report on which his evidence was based had been in the hands of Balmer for over two months. Was this why the police alleged two men had carried out the attack with two different weapons?[5]

Stating that Mrs Rimmer's right hand was bruised and the index finger fractured, Dr Manning said this would seem to indicate she had tried to ward off the blows with this hand, around which the umbrella was still attached. Or perhaps even an attempt to strike her assailant.

Next to give evidence was the Director of the Home Office Laboratory at Preston, forensic scientist Dr J B Firth. It was quickly ascertained from him that the bloodstains on Devlin's fawn gabardine jacket and trousers, and similar stains on Burns brown pin-striped trousers, were minute and not of the same blood group as Mrs Rimmer's. Yet replying to Livermore, he then contradictorily stated that because there was insufficient blood but some tests showed presumptive, he could not be certain they were not hers! On October 15th and 16th (two months after the murder) he had examined the accused men's clothing and found on Devlin's fawn jacket small bloodstains on the left front under the lapel and the left sleeve. They were so small he could not group them. He also discovered presumptive small bloodstains which, while not visible to the naked eye, he insisted were human blood. Visible and invisible bloodstains were also found on the fawn trousers. On Burns' trousers, he stated he found a small visible blood smear on one leg and the lining on the *inside* right pocket. These were Group B although Mrs Rimmer's was Group A. There was also a small stain on the inside of the left leg. On the pinstriped jacket of the suit no visible bloodstains were found but presumptive tests on some areas gave an indication of blood.

The barely distinguishable stains he described on the accuseds' clothing were in exactly the positions Marie Milne had earlier testified to. It was no coincidence that Superintendent Balmer had studied Dr Firth's report weeks

---

5.   Balmer said in his 1967 memoirs, that it was he who had suggested to Manning that two men carried out the attack.

before interviewing her!

The scientific findings from inconclusive presumptive blood tests are not difficult to argue against. Precisely because they are presumptive they could come from anyone or any blood group. As such, they are not evidence against an accused person. Nonetheless the defence did not call their own forensic expert to contest Dr Firth's evidence. Nor did they request the court to rule this particular evidence inadmissible.

In further replies, Dr Firth stated that, judging by the direction of blood spatter on the hallway walls and the inside of the front door, he estimated that most of the blows had been delivered whilst the victim was lying on the floor. There was a large pool of blood under Mrs Rimmer's head. And her coat, hat, yellow floral frock, umbrella and white net gloves, which she was still wearing, were all "heavily bloodstained." He then dramatically stated that he had found three locks of hair near the victim's head which appeared to have been cut with a very sharp instrument. Although there now appeared to be a ritual aspect to this murder rather than a botched housebreaking, the defence did not pursue the matter.

Replying to Harry Livermore, Dr Firth agreed that he could not ascertain the age of the bloodstains on the accused men's clothing. In other words they could have been acquired before or since August 19th. He also maintained that the absence of substantial bloodstains on an assailant's clothing did *not* mean he had not been in close proximity to the body. This assertion was not challenged by the defence. But other forensic experts have before and since stated that an assailant would in fact be heavily bloodstained. The nearest Norton got to this was to ask Firth if blood recently splashed on the wearer would be noticeable as he walked the streets, to which he agreed. He further agreed that the positive presumptive tests were not infallible and that the minute bloodstains on Burns' clothing (which he was wearing on August 19th) did not come from the victim. Asked if ordinary cleaning processes would remove bloodstains, Dr Firth said if organic solvents were used they would not. He then reiterated he could not tell whether or not the stains had been acquired at varying times, and further admitted that there were no traces of blood, either visible or presumptive, on Burns shoes apart from a presumption underneath the toe, which even then he could not say was human blood. Interested observers in the court wondered why he had mentioned this non-evidence about the shoes, other than to exaggerate the paucity—without any proof—of blood evidence against the accused men.

In relation to the absence of Mrs Rimmer's blood on either Devlin or Burns clothing: during the trial of Walter Rowland five years earlier for the murder of a prostitute on a bombed site, Firth, after first stating there would not necessarily be blood on the attacker, had to eventually agree that because the victim had suffered hammer blows to the head from which blood had spurted everywhere, together with the crime scene being heavily blood-stained, it was "not improbable" that Rowland would have had substantial bloodstains on his clothing and shoes. Yet there was not a trace of blood on Rowland's clothing. And in the 1934 "Brighton Trunk murder case" in which Toni Mancini was acquitted, defence counsel, Norman Birkett KC success-fully challenged another "expert witness", the renowned forensic pathologist Sir Bernard Spilsbury—who had first stated that the victim's head wounds had been caused by the small end of a hammer, then later that it had been caused by the large end. He also asked Spilsbury how he *knew* the victim had died within three minutes, to which he remained speechless!

Addressing the jury in that case, Birkett said, "I am not attacking the good faith of Sir Bernard Spilsbury... Men may have names and reputa-tions, degrees, distinctions; but high and low, famous and obscure, known and unknown, men are all human and fallible." [6]

Apparently, however, Livermore and Norton were unaware of these two similarly significant murder cases where expert opinion had been success-fully challenged.

Next in the witness box on this last day of the committal proceedings was the staff manager of Lewis's department store, Frederick Richardson. After stating that McNeil had worked there as a porter from the 16th to the 21st August, he told Norton he knew McNeil because although his assistant manager had engaged him, he himself had accepted his notice when he left.

What followed was a lengthy exchange over what most onlookers regarded as trivial if not totally irrelevant, but which yet again illustrated the pettiness and obduracy of Bishop and the magistrate, Alderman Gordon. Joseph Nor-ton wanted to know if it was the policy of Lewis's to allow their employees

---

6. *The Life Of Lord Birkett of Ulverston*, H Montgomery Hyde (Hamish Hamilton, 1965). See also *Chapter 34* which deals with expert evidence.

to wear torn merchant navy uniforms on duty. If he was a porter, replied Richardson, it might well be the case, although they usually wore khaki drill dustcoats. "I am asking you would you allow a man to wear a merchant navy uniform while working for Lewis's?"

"You have had the answer once haven't you?" piped up Bishop.

"No I have not," said Norton, "I would have thought a firm of the repute of Lewis's would have certain standards."

Richardson said that Lewis's did indeed have standards, then repeated that a porter would normally be given a dust coat to wear over his suit. But Norton again asked if a dust coat was not or could not be provided, would he allow a porter to work on the premises wearing a torn uniform? Yes or no? The magistrate then chimed in, "He cannot answer the question, yes or no," to which Norton retorted, "I think he can. He is the staff manager. I have asked him a direct question which he is obviously trying to evade."

"You cannot say that," declared Gordon.

After the manager had given the same imprecise answer for the third time a quietly determined Norton said, "I am going to repeat the question. Would you allow a member of your staff to wear a torn merchant navy uniform whilst on duty? Would you permit it or not?" Either deliberately procrastinating or unable to answer a simple question, the staff manager said he might allow it and that it depended on the job the man was doing. With a sigh of resignation Norton lamented, "Then I regret to say I have been mistaken about the high standards of your firm."

That really should have been the end of this minor peripheral issue. But Bishop, acting more like Lewis's PR representative rather than a prosecutor in a murder case said, "That is a most improper comment to make, if I may say so. And I wish to say so publicly." Knowing the obvious answer, and despite McNeil stating he wore the uniform on duty, he then asked Richardson if the firm had any control over what their employees wore *off duty*. Norton protested, "That does not arise out of the cross-examination. I object to that going down." But, predictably, Gordon told the clerk, "Put that down."

Thus ended another absurd chapter in this catalogue of semantics, pedantry and petty point scoring, which had hardly anything to do with the grave issue of murder. Indeed, what had emerged as apparently more important than anything else, was the revelation that such a prestigious department store as Lewis's would allow a staff member to carry out his duties dressed as a scarecrow!

CHAPTER TEN
POLICE GIVE THEIR EVIDENCE

Half the truth is often a greater lie.

Benjamin Franklin

On the final day of the committal proceedings it was the turn of "Balmer's Boys" to give evidence. But Balmer himself was conspicuous by his absence from the witness box. His close friends, Chief Inspector Morris and Inspector Farragher would also take no part in the proceedings—either here or at the trial proper. Morris had been with him on all the prison visits to procure McLoughlin's false statement. And it was Farragher and Sergeant Wade who had shown McLoughlin the mugshots of Devlin and Burns. By keeping himself and his two friends out of it, Balmer made sure those two crucial aspects of the case would not be questioned or even mentioned.

Detective Constable Skinner gave evidence of arresting Devlin in Manchester and Inspector Lees, Detective Sergeants Richardson, Wade and Sturrock, all corroborated each other's version of events in the Bootle Street Police Station and the car journey from Manchester to Liverpool. They all denied that there was any conversation with Devlin in the car, other than him asking them had they seen the girls, what did they say, asking for cigarettes and complaining his handcuffs were too tight. Likewise they all agreed that they did not speak to Devlin or even each other.

They denied that both men's statements were taken down in response to questions from Superintendent Balmer. And despite their admissions that Balmer was in charge of the investigation and that he had been present when the statements were taken, the defence solicitors never asked for him to be called. This was even more peculiar, particularly since they had alleged several times that the statements were obtained by way of answers to direct questions. If however they had known that Balmer had personally taken and countersigned the statements of McLoughlin and Bury perhaps they *would* have called him!

Detective Constable Leslie Skinner had a reputation for ruthlessness among Liverpool villains, who claimed he wouldn't hesitate to put self-incriminating words into the mouths of suspects. A handsome womaniser, tall and slim with Errol Flynn looks, he was popular with the licensees of most of the city centre pubs — particularly those around the Queen Square district, like the Old Royal, the Dart, the Duck House and the Dive — where he and his partner Detective Sergeant John Ralphson would often enjoy after-hours drinks and get information about any villainy going on — especially from Dan English, the licensee of the Dive.

In the witness box, Skinner was questioned by the defence solicitors about the night of October 10th when he and the Manchester detective, Lynch, arrested Devlin in Stretford Road. It was in Granelli's Milk Bar and when he got hold of him, Devlin said, "What's all this about?" He then admitted that Constable Lynch did ask Devlin where he had been the night before, which was a reference to a robbery the previous night at The Playhouse Theatre. But he could not remember what Devlin's reply was. They first walked Devlin to the nearest police station in Ormond Street, said Skinner and later they took him by car to Bootle Street HQ.

Livermore wanted to know why in his evidence-in-chief, Skinner had omitted to say that he had not cautioned Devlin after he had told him he was being detained in connection with the murder of Mrs Rimmer? Skinner readily agreed he should have done so. The real reason however was that neither Skinner nor Lynch had in fact mentioned the Rimmer murder. They had questioned him about the *Playhouse Theatre* break-in — hence there was no need for a caution. But rather than admit to that he took Livermore's censure on the chin! When Livermore suggested that was not a fair way to give his evidence, Harris, the clerk, said that was a matter for the court, stating, "He has given certain evidence. It is not for him to say whether it is fair or not." Ignoring Harris, Livermore again asked Skinner if he agreed that it was unfair to the accused man, for him to give his evidence-in-chief in that way, to which he replied, "No."

Replying to further defence questions, Skinner agreed that when they got out of the car with Devlin at Bootle Street Police HQ there were some flashes, which he, "gathered were made by photographers".

Skinner's assumed naïveté disguised that he knew the newspaper photographers presence was the result of Balmer's handiwork (who was already inside the police station). He had tipped off his journalist friends in the Press Club that an arrest in Manchester was imminent. This picture of a startled, handcuffed Devlin being frogmarched into Bootle Street police station by Lees, Skinner and Richardson, was soon afterwards to feature in most of the newspapers including the *Manchester Evening News*, the *Liverpool Echo* and the *Sunday Express*—as did another of him being driven away to Liverpool. Their publication would, as intended, create prejudice against Devlin. And despite seriously compromising the integrity of any future identification evidence, as far as Balmer was concerned, they would provide more up-to-date images for the benefit of his "witnesses" McLoughlin and McNeil!

Entering the witness box Detective Inspector William Lees began to read out Devlin's statement but Livermore said there was a part of it he did not want to be disclosed. This was Devlin's self-incriminating remark at the end of his statement, that he was "probably screwing gaffs all through August." Bishop, in his first friendly gesture to the defence, agreed that, " It might be something which may prejudice the prisoner." But questioning the exclusion, Harris, the clerk again commented, "Would it be prejudicial to the prisoners *at their trial*?" (Author's italics).

These frequent Freudian slips from both the magistrate and the clerk of the court about the impending "trial" seemed to indicate their confidence that the outcome of these proceedings was cut and dried and appeared to totally discount the alternative eventuality of there being no case to answer.

Despite Harris' intervention, the magistrate finally agreed that part of Devlin's statement could be left out of the depositions. But as Lee's read out the rest of the statement it was obvious that it had been made by question and answer and that the wording had been tailored to incriminate both Devlin and Burns. For example:

"When in Liverpool" (official phraseology). Not, "When I or we was in Liverpool."

"I am quite *definite* I have not been in Liverpool since the 9ᵗʰ of August." ("Definite" Balmer's trademark word).

And, "While you are going around Liverpool it saves time to get taxis and we took *two or three*" (Author's italics).

In addition to Devlin's admitted single journey on August 2nd and the second and third journey with Burns to and from 39 Canning Street on August 4th, this would fit Marie Milne's and Emery's evidence of the alleged Sunday afternoon taxi ride to Cranborne Road. It also had the double advantage of contradicting Burns statement— "We only went once in a taxi and that was from the Pier Head to Verulam Street."

By putting in Devlin's statement, "How could I get them [bloodstains] *I haven't been in a fight* or anything" this effectively nullified Devlin previously telling the police that he *had* been in a fight with Irishmen in Manchester. (Author's italics),

Lees then read out Burns statement in which he was alleged to have added, without any prompting, "I would like to put in that from the day we first met the girls and for the next two or three weeks I was with Devlin *all the time*" (Author's italics). This was agreement to a pointed question from Balmer rather than the words of Burns. But it cleverly made impossible any potential "cut-throat defence" by either man at their trial, i.e. blaming each other by denying they were together on the night of the murder.

Although Lees read out the men's full statements, he did not mention, much less read out, Kiernan Oates letter from prison nor the subsequent interviews with McLoughlin in which both had named "Ginger" Dutton. Nor did he mention Thomas Rimmer's and Sydney Fairbrother's statements or Inspector Reade's report about the broken window. And he certainly did not mention the undisclosed statement of Frederick Downing, who on 27th October, had told the police his wife Joan had been on the Sunblinds job at 11.30 pm on August 19th. But even if he Lees had mentioned Downing's statement—of which the defence knew nothing—there would have been no problem: there was no danger of him giving evidence—not after he and his wife being threatened with imprisonment!.

When Livermore asked Lees where George McLoughlin had been interviewed, the magistrate once again upheld Bishop's objection, saying it was irrelevant. The well-worn upholding of that particular objection by the magistrate really should have been predictable to Livermore. Whether he knew it or not, he was flogging a dead horse. It may have been more illuminating and productive to have asked the inspector precisely *who* had interviewed McLoughlin. And if he had truthfully replied, that would have entitled the defence to call Superintendent Balmer for cross-examination. Instead, by way of a farcical elimination contest with Inspector Lees—who admitted he knew where McLoughlin was interviewed—Livermore embarked on a final attempt to elicit the information.

"Was it at CID HQ?"

"No."

"Was it at his home?"

"No."

"Was it in the street?"

"No."

After Bishop had smugly commented that, "There will be a long process of elimination," Livermore said to Lees, "I won't make this any more ridiculous. I now ask where *was* he interviewed. Will you please tell me?"

"No," retorted the magistrate angrily. "I am telling you it is not relevant and I have told you so before!"

Notwithstanding the wrongness of the decision it nevertheless seemed that the stubborn Livermore simply could not take no for an answer. And before this charade inconclusively ended, it apparently never occurred to this rather pompous lawyer—who already knew the answer he was seeking—to simply ask, "Was it at Walton Prison?" Had he done so the inspector would have had to answer yes or no.

During further cross-examination, Inspector Lees, quite apart from being obstructive, actually began lying. Firstly about Devlin's clothing being on a table at the police station and his (Devlin's) alleged remarks about his suit. Also that there was no conversation with Devlin in the police car, and then about the dates of the prosecution witnesses statements. Replying to Livermore, he said Bury was interviewed on 4th October, Milne on October 7th and Emery "about 14th October". Neither Livermore nor Norton could challenge this because their earlier requests for copies of all the statements had been refused on the authority of the Director of Public Prosecutions. Thus, they were not aware of Bury's incriminating signed statement of the 8th October or of Milne's even more damaging false statement of 9th October—taken respectively by Balmer and Lees.

When the red-handled knife was mentioned, with which Devlin had allegedly threatened Milne, the inspector admitted (despite Milne's allegedly overhearing Devlin telling Burns he must have lost it in the park) that no police appeal was made in the local press for its recovery nor for anyone who had found it to come forward. The reason of course was that there never was a red-handled knife.

Asked about the signed statements made by the accused men, Lees stated that both were taken down in the presence of Superintendent Balmer but they were in his (Lees) own handwriting. They were dictated to him by Devlin and Burns and were not in response to any questions asked by Balmer. In fact, he reiterated, no questions were asked by anyone. At this Devlin in the dock gave a look of astonishment, and Burns muttered, "Lying bastard."

On this Friday afternoon of 23rd November, after fairness, justice, legal propriety and the Rule of Law had been severely strained by the stubbornness and arrogance of the prosecution and the prejudicial, bombastic "Tammany Hall"-type behaviour of the bench, the committal proceedings finally closed and the accused men were sent for trial at the next Liverpool Assizes. They would be confined in Walton Prison's Hospital Wing for the next nine weeks, kept apart and not even allowed to exercise together. Apart from two half hour periods they would continue to be locked up for 23 hours a day.

Alfred Burns in particular, would be treated most inhumanely because the governor of Walton Prison now decided that since he had been arrested on 24th September as a borstal absconder (before being charged with murder on the 11th October) he would be treated as a convicted prisoner. As such, in addition to being confined to his cell 23 hours each day, he would not be allowed daily visits or to have food, newspapers or tobacco sent in. It was also decided that he would be kept isolated from Devlin and the other prisoners and would exercise alone.

CHAPTER ELEVEN
A MEETING IN THE CELLS WITH THE HATCHET MAN

Birds of a feather flock together.

Proverbs

In the large, packed holding cell below the court in the Cheapside Bridewell, Devlin and Burns met ex-seaman, Jimmy Tucker, who resembled the veteran Hollywood actor Joseph Cotton. But there, because of his numerous facial scars, the resemblance with the handsome movie star ended. Jimmy, an alcoholic from Toxteth, was a recidivist and a Liverpool "character". He was also nicknamed the"Hatchet Man" and had just been given seven days for being drunk and disorderly.

Some years earlier during a seamen's strike, he had punched a scab for crossing the picket line and because he had numerous previous convictions for assault he got ten years. Whilst in prison, a member of the notorious "Swallow Gang" had been having an affair with his wife. On his release he got drunk and, armed with a small hatchet tracked the man down to Wilkie's Club in Upper Parliament Street, where he was drinking with other gang members. After attacking him with the hatchet and with the victim writhing on the floor covered in blood, Tucker pulled down the man's trousers telling him, "You fucked my wife, now I'm gonna fuck you!" He then simulated buggery on him which brought raucous laughter from the man's "friends".

But sober, as he was now, Tucker was a different character: a raconteur and purveyor of homespun philosophy, he was witty and funny, yet possessed a wide knowledge of literature and history.

Alfie and Teddy didn't have a particular liking for Scousers, it was after all three Liverpudlians who had just sworn their lives away. But the two young men sensed that Tucker hated the police and would therefore be on their side. Realising from their accents that they were Mancunians, he asked if they were the ones accused of the Rimmer murder. Agreeing they were, Teddy told him they were being framed and were innocent and when he

asked if he knew Balmer, Tucker cried, "Oh no, not that prick." He then
began in his gruff voice to quote Caesar's observation on the conspirators
in Shakespeare's Roman play.

Yond Cassius has a lean and hungry look.
He thinks too much. Such men are dangerous.

Although Alfie recognised the quote, a bemused Teddy asked, "What's
that got to do with us?"

"Fuckin' Balmer! That's what it's got to do with yiz," he replied. "And for
fuck's sake don't tell me yiz made statements." When they said they had, he
cried, "God help yiz, yer poor fuckers. Yer never ever make statements to
the bizzies—especially Balmer. He's fuckin' notorious. 'Aven't yiz heard of
the Cameo case. Same prick set up Kelly and Connolly last year. You fuckin'
pair of mugs. There's nothin' down for you'se two now."

Then, pretending to pile on the danger they were in of being hanged, he
made up a tale of a moonlit walk one night in the cemetery when he was
drunk. Staggering along, he said he came across a gravestone which said:

Dear friend as you pass by,
As you are now so once was I.
As I am now so you shall be
So be prepared to follow me.

This stark reminder of their horrendous situation didn't endear them to
Tucker. But they hadn't noticed the twinkle in his eye when he added that,
as he passed by, he mumbled to himself:

Dear friend to follow you I am content,
But I'm fucked if I know which way you went.

At this Alfie and Teddy and all the other prisoners in the cell burst into
laughter.

He then pretended to be more serious, asking the two Manchester men
if they thought Strangeways was, "a better Nick than Walton?" When they

nodded agreement, he said, "It's fuckin not yer know. You'd never get a song like this about Strangeways", and then began to sing in his gravelly voice, a parody of an old Irish folk song.

> In Liverpool city there are some hotels,
> That give board and lodging to all the big swells
> But the best place I know of is now in full swing
> It's a place up in Walton that's run by the King.
> We left the Assizes we left in the bus,
> And while in the bus we kicked up a fuss.
> We rode through the streets like the Lord Mayor in State,
> And the screws all bowed down as we entered the gate.
> We entered the Reception and they asked me my name.
> They asked my address and the reason I came.
> And when that was over the screw pressed the bell,
> And I took my first bath in the Walton Hotel.

Once again they all laughed and broke into spontaneous applause. When calm was restored, Alfie mentioned the witnesses against them and asked Tucker if he knew any of them. He only knew Stanley Rubin and told them he was a stool pigeon and a ponce.

After more entertainment from the "Hatchet Man" it was nearing 6 pm when they were all finally shipped up to Walton. In the Black Maria, Tucker began singing Bing Crosby's *Pistol Packin' Momma* to the tune of *Onward Christian Soldiers.*

> Lay that pistol moh-oh-oh omma,
> Lay that pistol down.
> Pistol packin' Momma lay that pistol down,
> Drinkin' beer in the cabaret was we having fun,
> Till one night, she caught me right and now I'm on the run.
> Oh, pistol packin' Moh-oh–oh-omma, lay that pistol down.
> Pistol Packin' Mo-oh oh-omma, lay that pistol down.

On arrival at Walton the "screws (did not) all bow down as they entered the gate", but shunted them through Reception as quickly as possible like sheep going to slaughter. After Alfie and Teddy had the regulation bath in two inches of lukewarm water in the rust-stained bath tub, Alfie went to put on his clothes but was abruptly stopped by a principal officer.

"Hey Manc, what they fuck do yer think you're doin' ?" he shouted.

"Getting dressed sir," he replied.

"Not in my fuckin' nick you're not, me Laddo. You're a borstal absconder. You're in grey now. Governor's orders."

Alfie was now being treated as a convicted prisoner and would have to wear the drab prison grey uniform. Tucker, who was watching, told the officer it wasn't fair and that it was," bad enough the lad being on a murder charge." But he was told, "Got fuck all to do with you Jimmy. Your only here on a fucking dog watch anyway."

That prison officer never knew how lucky he was that Jimmy Tucker was sober!

CHAPTER TWELVE
THE PRISON LETTERS
(OR HOME THOUGHTS FROM ABROAD)

We think caged birds sing, when indeed they cry.

John Webster 1580 –1625.

Although the penurious widowed mothers of both men had been refused financial assistance by the authorities to help with their travelling expenses between Manchester and Liverpool, the unremitting State also refused the men's petitions to be transferred to Strangeways.[1] Both families and friends therefore had to bear the financial strain of regular train visits to Liverpool for the next three months and thereafter for another two months.

Several days after the committal proceedings ended both men began a voluminous correspondence with family and friends, which would continue to the very eve of their executions. Considering they left primary school at 14, their grammar, vocabulary, punctuation and spelling were remarkable. Whilst Devlin possessed immaculate handwriting and very good expression in English, it was Burns who proved to be the more interesting correspondent. He was also — unusually for a small time villain — exceptionally well read, whilst demonstrating in his letters — particularly to their friend John Ford — a grim humour. Whether he was a true cynic or was simply whistling in the dark, considering the ordeal he underwent for almost seven months — there was no doubt that he possessed a certain *sang-froid* and an indomitable character.

The following (edited) letters sent by the two men mainly to John Ford and their mothers, were all written before, during and after the committal proceedings but before their February 1952 trial at the Assizes. The letters are noticeable for the contrasting tone of youthful bravado when corresponding with their contemporaries and their barely disguised vulnerability when

---

1. Prison Commission files.

writing so poignantly to their widowed mothers.

Number 5749. Burns. A. 13.10.51

Dear Mam,

…you remember the girl I fetched home one night? Her name is Mary Tierney. What do you think of her Mam? You see she has been writing to me while I have been in prison. Anyway I'll explain it all some other time.

Well dear, when you send me the tobacco, etc. would you send me the last few days papers. I would like to find out what they think of it all. I'm sorry about my photograph being in them… About the solicitor to defend me; I hope it is the same one Teddy has. What I don't know is how long I will get when Ted and I tell them about the sheets and gabs. It will most likely be C.T. [Corrective Training] for both of us. Not only that, but we shall have to implicate other people beside Alan [Campbell]. Still, it is better than being on a charge we know nothing about…

I will close now Mam.
Look after yourself,
Your loving son, Alf.

PS: please excuse the writing.

Copying this letter, the prison governor attached a note saying the police would be "most interested" in the contents.

The "sheets and gabs" referred to the proceeds of two robberies — at the Liverpool Road Railway Goods Yard on the night of 8/9th August and the Sunblinds warehouse on the 19th August. It also proves that there was no collusion between the two men and Alan Campbell to procure a false alibi after Campbell pleaded guilty and was convicted in November 1951 — as would be subsequently alleged at the Gerrard Inquiry.

Number 5749. Burns. A. 6/11/51.

Dear John

Sorry for the delay in answering your letter. I suppose you realise the reason. Your letter didn't reach me till 4 days after you had written. Well John I suppose you have read or heard what went on in (committal) court. How they expect to get away with such lies I don't know. At first, I thought McLoughlan [sic] had done it and was trying to frame us. But it seems he was picked up two days before it happened. It is amusing to watch their actions when they are giving their "evidence". It will be more amusing when I am watching them get weighed off for perjury though…. In the cells waiting to go up to the court Teddy was singing such hit songs of the day as, "Give My Regards To Mother" and "It's The Ring My Mother Wore."… I heard a rumour about Walter Rowland. I hope it doesn't take a couple of years to find the truth about <u>our</u> business. Still, as Ted tells me — Sudden death, sudden mercy… When I met Ted at the court. I said, 'I think your hair is nice'. He admired my teeth, I his shoes, he my coat. After a few minutes 'they' just shook their heads as if to say, 'too bad'.

Look after yourself.
Your old Pal Alf.

Number 5749. Burns A. 10/11/51

Dear John…

Ted and I are up at court again on Monday. We will then be remanded to the 19th… You didn't tell me about the Rowland business… Did you get the letter I sent on the 6th? All letters I get here arrive about two days after they were posted. It's certainly a terrible service between Manchester and Liverpool… John, if the law try chatting to you tell them nothing at all. In my opinion, after looking over everything, I think it's the law whose trying to frame us. They framed Walter (Rowland) well enough didn't they?

... I'm afraid I haven't written such a good letter. I never was a good letter writer but I think this one is worse than usual...Give my regards to Anne and everybody else who wants them.

Your old pal, Alf.

Although he knew prisoners letters were censored, Burns was unaware that the reason for the delay in sending and receiving his mail was because the prison governor, at the request of the police, was having all of his and Devlin's correspondence, typed out and copied to the police, the Home Office and the Director of Public Prosecutions. Walter Rowland was hanged in 1947 for the murder of a Manchester prostitute on a bombed site in Deansgate. He vehemently protested his innocence but the Court of Appeal refused to hear the evidence of another man who had confessed to the murder.

Number 5736. Devlin. A. 16/11/51

Dear John

just a line to let you know I am in the best of health hoping that this letter finds you the same. I never thought John, that I would be writing to you in the position that I am in now. It's funny the way one's life turns out. Who in the world would have thought that afternoon when we were having a drink in Totties that at the night time I would be in Liverpool on a murder charge that I know absolutely nothing about. It makes one frightened to think what will happen next.

John remember me telling you about the only girl I ever liked?... all the time I used to go with the lads, and you know how well I liked being with the boys,, if she would have raised her little finger and said 'Come' I would have crawled to her like a lap dog... Well I lowered myself the other week and wrote her a letter telling her how much I cared, and do you know what John, the horrible creature did not have the decency to say she had received my letter...People say there is plenty of fish in the sea, so when I come home you can come fishing with me!

I am up in court on Monday so if you can get off work you and Cammie can come to see us being tried. But if you don't come I'll know why, so I won't be disappointed… Well John, I will have to draw to a close for now, so Goodnight + Godbless.

Hoping to be hearing from you pretty soon.
From your old pal Ted.

"Cammie" was Alan Campbell who later in November received 18 months for the Sunblinds break-in.

Number 5736. Devlin.E. 26/11/51.

Dear John and Anne (Ford)

… well John as you already know, the Pantomime of the Rimmer Murder has ended for the time being. And I must admit that I am very surprised at the British Film Industry for not signing on the witnesses for the Prosecution for their next picture. But I guess the scouts for J. Arthur Rank have not been sleeping, so I can imagine that in the next few weeks the film studios will be sorting the very best actors out of the whole bunch of them and giving them contracts, because, myself, I should say they definitely deserve the chance of being film stars for their superb acting in my case… Well John and Anne I'll close now, hope to hear from you both very soon. Cheerio for now.

From your old pal Ted.

Number5749. Burns. A. 28/11/51

Dear John,

Just a few lines to let you know everything is ok. Well by the time you get this letter you'll have done it. I have written to Anne wishing her all the best, etc. I hope you had a good time afterwards. I'd like to have been there, it would have been — happily married one moment, miserable and penniless the next… Have you noticed my spelling is getting worse? I put it down to the letters you send me!… I was talking to a man, a psychiatrist this morning. The talk was ok but what

on earth he sent me that box of paints and toy drum around for, I don't know…
There is a fellow in here who's about 60. Well they came to take him on exercise
the other day; he'd been walking around for 20 minutes before they found they
had taken Teddy by mistake…still he looks a young 60!

I will close now John. Don't forget to write back soon.
Have a good time New Year's Eve,

Your old pal Alf.

This was a reference to John Ford's marriage to Anne Fitzgerald.

Number 5636 .Devlin.E. 1.12.51

Dear Mam,

Just a couple of lines to let you know I am in the best of health, hoping this letter
finds you and all at home the same. Well Mam… I will be tried at the end of
January or beginning of Feb. And I want you to know no matter how the case
goes I am Innocent and some day, whether I am here or not, my Innocence will
be proved. I have done a lot of thinking while I have been in here and I reckon
this has been done for a purpose, because as you know I was getting a bit swelled
headed as to what I could do… so if there is such a thing as God, I think he has
put me in here as a warning, making me realise that the way I was heading, I
might have finished doing something like what I am charged with.. So perhaps it's
for the best he has allowed me to be charged with something I know absolutely
nothing about. That's why I am confident everythink (sic) will turn out alright.
Well Mam I have not much more to say… so I will close now, goodnight and
God bless all at home.

From your ever-loving son Ted. xxxxxx

PS. Thanks for the jerkin.

Number 5749. Burns. A. 3/12/51

Dear John,

Sorry for the delay in writing… How is this business of mine and Teddy affecting everyone? I should imagine (as Ted says) they have their doubts… Teddy wanted to jump from one roof to the other. I told him I didn't have a flying licence… He wanted to know what I thought he would do when this is over with. I said you'll be "hanging around as usual." It's pretty cold in here and I told Ted it was simply "topping weather." He doesn't like my sense of humour.

Well John I want you to do a little thing for me — take my place! But seriously, will you find out what the date was when "Kiss Tomorrow Goodbye" was on at the Dominion. You see it was a Sunday and I want to make a check up from then… If you go down to my house tell Eddie (Brother-in-law Edward Billingham) the books I want are the Hank Jansen types.

I will close now John…
Your old pal Alf.

The roof jumping referred to the 24th September when both men were arrested at the Cornbrook Street home of Joan Fitzgerald.

Number 5749. Burns. A. 9/12/51

Dear John,

…I am doing ok at the moment. So is Ted I think. The only time I see him is when he goes on exercise. I am never able to speak to him. They think he'll get me into trouble I suppose!

Those books you gave her (his mother) for me, she didn't read them you see I'm still the baby of the family! You know how it is… I expect we will have Rose Hildebrande defending one or both of us. She is an exceptional woman you know. Well Christmas will soon be here. It will be a choker for Ted. I am resigned to spending Christmas's inside. This will be my third… The silly things that happen in here; why should they measure me from head to toe and ask what size collar I take?! As you know the food in nick is in short supply. It's so short those two boils I showed you have died from malnutrition... I think if I kept a diary it would be unique. For instance Monday 23 hours in cell, 1 hour exercise on my own. Tuesday—ditto, Wednesday—ditto, Thursday-ditto. See what I mean?

...I will close now. I only wish I had more paper. Give my love to Anne.

Your old Pal Alf.

The books referred to were the soft porn "Hank Janson types". Rose "Hildebrande" was Rose Heilbron QC.

Number 5749.Burns. A. 12/12/51.

Dear John,

I wrote to you on the 4th but haven't yet had an answer. I was just wondering. John will you go down to my house and tell my mam I haven't had anything sent in yet. Tell her I have not had a smoke for 2 days... There hasn't been any answer to my petition about Strangeways yet: though I don't suppose I will get a transfer. Ted has got Rose Hildebrande defending him, so it's not bad at all is it. I was hoping one of us would get her. It doesn't matter who... Every night I try and get into contact with Cammie and Vic—mental telepathy, you know. All I get is strange looks off people passing my cell! By the way, I heard from (?) that that taxi fellow who is on the other team got filled in. You can see what's going to happen now can't you? Do you know that certain types of wood are edible? I do. I'm just finishing my table!

Well John, I will close now. Give my regards to Anne.
Your old pal Alf.

PS; Write back soon.

"Cammie" and "Vic" are references to friends Alan Campbell and Victor

Le Vesconte, both in prison respectively for the Sunblinds and Playhouse break-ins. The "taxi fellow" is Crown witness, Thomas Emery who was allegedly attacked—a newspaper story planted by Balmer. Burns rightly suspected his family or associates would be blamed for this.

14/12/51 From John Ford to Devlin.

Dear Ted,

Just a few lines to let you know I received your welcome letter and was glad to hear you are okay. Well Ted you say you are doing your nut but you don't want to worry. Just think of the good times you will be able to have when you come out. I know it's a sickener being in there for Christmas but Christmas isn't everything you know... Well Ted I can't think of anymore at present. So I will say Goodbye for now and Cheer up.

Your old Pal John.

Number 5736. Devlin. E. 15/12/51.

Dear John,

Just a line or two hoping you are ok and wondering whether you received my last letter. You see John, I have been having a lot of trouble lately about my mail because the letters I have written previously don't seem to be reaching their destination. Well John, I don't know about Cammie being sick about doing bird, but if he feels half as bad as me he has my sympathy because I am sick to death of it. I can tell you this, when I come home, you might laugh at me for saying this, I am going to get a job and settle down. Being in here for something I have not done has made me realise only mugs go to prison. The wide ones are outside earning a weekly wage. Just remember this John, freedom is not valued until it's taken from you. John, don't think I'm preaching to you but I know you will understand how I feel. I can tell you this, I am dead choked...

From your old Pal Ted.

PS: I have just heard Cockell got murdered the other night by Slade. Another British hope finished.

This was a reference to British Heavyweight Champion Don Cockell's defeat against American Jimmy Slade.

Number 5736. Devlin. E. 17/12/51.

Dear John,

I received your most welcome letter… I am rather surprised but very pleased about you and Anne… I sincerely wish you and Anne the best of luck and I hope that the New Year is a successful and happy one for you both…. Well it's Christmas again John. I don't think I will, in fact I know I won't, be having a good time. But it won't make much difference to me because if you look back over the last five years, I have always been unlucky at Christmas. So I am not really bothered about it…John let me know the date you get this letter. I have had so much trouble with my mail…so I have decided to check the dates I hand them in and the date they reach their destination — that is if they reach it… Well John can't think of anything else to say at the moment so I will close, hoping to hear from you very soon.

From your old Pal, Ted.

By the way, wish your Mam, Dad and Bernard a Merry Xmas and a Happy New Year for me.

Number 5749. Burns. A. 17/12/51.

Dear John,

I wrote a letter to you last Friday but I was not allowed to send it. So I am re-writing it. ("There I was waiting at the Church."). It will be a good thing for you. Make an Alf, sorry a man, of you. Sorry for the mistake, it's just my ego-tistical mind at work again…On my life, these pens in here do more to lower a bloke's morale than anything else I can think of. Well John Christmas is near. I have written to Santa Claus and asked him for a couple of files, box of dynamite and a long distance jet plane. Not that I expect all three things, the dynamite and plane would do…

I will close now John. Give my regards to Anne.
Your old pal Alf.

Burns comment about the pens was because the nib was broken and he kept running out of ink.

Number 5749. Burns. A. 22, 12.1951..

Dear Mam,

Just a few lines to let you know I am in the best of health; hoping you are the same. Thanks for the (Christmas) parcel. I received it on Wednesday.

John Ford sent a letter, and he told me that my mail was not reaching him until several days after I post it. Does the same happen with my letters to you? He tells me, also, that a few of the letters have had a London postmark on the envelope. I just can't understand it. John will be coming up tomorrow; I told him to call at the house before coming, to get the necessary shirt, socks and hat. Has anybody seen about my Gab yet? I hope those people haven't sold it. I don't know whether I asked you in my last letter or not, but do you know if we are getting tried in January or February? Last Saturday I told Eddie to phone Norton and tell him I wanted to see him; well Norton hasn't been up. It just shows that I would be better off in Strangeways; there is no need for me here. Well dear, it's almost Christmas, I expected to be out for it. Still, I will get the pleasure of seeing those mendacious people spending the next few years inside for perjury, if not for something worse. I'll have to get Ted singing carols on Monday night!

I will close now Mam, Look after yourself.

Your Loving Son, Alf.

Gab — his gaberdine suit. Norton — Solicitor Joseph Norton. Eddy — Edward Billingham brother-in-law.

Number5736. Devlin. E. 1/.1.52.

Letter to Miss Pat Farren.

Dear Pat,

Just a few lines to let you know I am in the best of health, hoping that this letter finds you and your mother the same. I am sorry for my delay in writing but since I have been in here I have been so fed up I have not had the heart to do anything, so please forgive me. No doubt you have read my case in the papers but don't take any notice of them. What they say is a load of tripe. I can honestly say we are Innocent and in time I hope to prove it.. But if we are found guilty all I can say is a grave injustice will have been committed. Remember that day when I left your café, little did I think that within a couple of hours I would be arrested and charged with a murder I had never even heard of let alone supposed to have helped to do. In fact I think it is ridiculous, as I told the police. But apparently they think different. Well Pat I would like to thank you and your mother for the cigarettes you sent me. I can tell you I really appreciated your kindness… I guess I'll have to close now. I can't seem to think of anything else to say at the moment. But before I do I would like to wish you and your mam a very happy New Year, so cheerio for now.

Yours sincerely, Ted.

P.S. Pat, if you have any spare time would you write these songs out and send them to me.

I'm Sitting On Top Of The World,
Tut-Tut-Tootsie Don't Cry (sic),
Maybe Someone Else Will Be There When I'm Gone,
Baby Face.

These were all Al Jolson songs, who was enjoying a revival in 1951 with films like *The Jolson Story*. The full title of the third song was Irving Berlin's poignant ballad, *Someone Else May Be There While I'm Gone*.

Number 5749. Burns. A. 2.1.52

Dear John,

I suppose you realise by now what you have let yourself in for. Do yourself a favour. get a divorce before it is too late! Well John. I don't blame you. It's not your fault that you are weak willed. Do you think Anne will let you come and visit me this Saturday? That is if you have time after doing the housework. Did you enjoy yourselves on New Year's Eve? Ted and I thought we might get in lumber if we went out so we decided to stay in and listen to the wireless... By the way, how did the wedding go? Who was there? What kind of a party did you have? Now to get down to what <u>everyone</u> is interested in — I am doing ok.

You know when Rose Hildebrand was on the Kelly case, well her partner was Basil Neill (sic) — I think I've got the name right — Well this Basil Neill is prosecuting us. I'm looking forward to it; it should be quite a battle of wits. Can you see the papers, "The Liverpool Case" co-starring Alf and Ted? How did you like that word I used "prosecuting"? Bigger than marmalade isn't it?

There are seven blokes in here on capital charges so they don't call it the Hospital; It's now known as "Madame Tussauds."

Well I'll close now John. Give my regards to the missus.
Your old pal, Alf.

PS: See you Saturday.

"The Kelly case" was a reference to the Cameo Cinema murder trial a year previously.

Number 5749. Burns.A. 2.1.1952.

Dear Mam,

When I saw you yesterday I told you I had just sent a letter off that morning. Well that letter was stopped. I'm afraid my vocabulary has let me down, words have a different meaning nowadays! So never again take notice of a dictionary—they're all wrong! Well dear I was very pleased to see you yesterday. As I told you, I just get depressed on occasions, which is really only to be expected considering.

John was telling me that some of my letters had a London postmark on the envelope. Obvious isn't it? If it had my handwriting on the envelope it means that those letters have been sent in another envelope for other reasons. I find it quite amusing. By the way Mam, it was a very nice card. I rather liked the verse. Still, you always did pick the card on verse value. At the moment I feel fine. It only needed getting Christmas and the old year over; the time will pass pretty quickly now. Tell Marie and Eddie that I will be writing to them either today or tomorrow. How is young Brian getting on? He certainly is a lovely baby isn't he?

Well dear, I will close now. Look after yourself.

Your Loving Son, Alf.

Marie—his married sister, Marion Billingham. Brian—his young nephew.

Number 5736. E. Devlin. 6.1.52

To elder brother Leonard Devlin.

Dear Len

Just to let you know I received your most welcome letter... The reason I wrote to Pat Cavanagh is because I've had a crush on her ever since I came out of the army. And why I never made a play for her is because she is apt to be conceited. If I, with being so handsome, in fact a woman's dream, had shown any attention towards her she would have got it into her mind that she was irresistible and there is nothing worse than a swelled headed woman. Now it is her turn to break the ice before it is too late because... some Mother's lucky daughter will be putting a ring on my finger, I am getting exhausted of refusing my many woman admirers. When you see Bill Casey tell him to leave Manchester... he ought to be a spiritualist... or give up dreaming. To think he foresaw all this, no one would have believed it. On Saturday the eleventh of August I borrowed eight shillings and sixpence off Mrs Cavanagh. Tell her I'm sorry for the delay in paying it back but when I come out I will attend to it straight away. Well Len, can't think of anything more to say except you Annie & Pat wants to stop being misers and come up to see me. After all if things go the wrong way at my trial it might be the last time you will be able to see me in one piece. So cheerio for now. Hoping to see you soon.

From your Loving Brother Ted.

PS. Give Annie my Regards and both of you write back.

Annie Devlin — Leonard's wife.

Number 5376. E. Devlin. 11.1.52

Dear John,

I received your most welcome letters and I am very sorry I have been so long in answering them, but you can rest assure (sic) I am not entirely to blame, this is my second attempt. The first letter I wrote was stopped by the Governor because I wrote what appears to be the truth. I cannot explain any more than that because I fear if I do, this one will be stopped.

I appreciate John... getting Pat Cavanagh to write, but I'm afraid it's pretty obvious to me she does not want to, besides I have asked Mary Bibby to marry me and she said she would any time I want. Matter of fact she is coming tomorrow to discuss a possible date. But I think I have been a little hasty don't you? But I reckon I can put that right tomorrow by making no definite date until I have been home for a bit. You see, I still think a lot about Pat Cavanagh and I know in my own mind that if I could take her out a couple of times I could make her think a lot about me. So I think it is only fair to Mary that I take Pat out and then I will be able to judge properly which one I want. How is everyone at home. I hope everything is O.K.. Give Anne and your Mam and family my regards… for a happy and prosperous New Year.

Well John, can't seem to think of anything else to say except to hope everything is going right for you, so I will close. Hoping to hear from you soon

From your Old Pal, Ted

Number 5749. A. Burns. 14.1.52

Dear John,

…say John I was sat here in my peter reading and I saw a cartoon which instantly reminded me of you and Anne (enclosed). I hope you got home safe after you left me. Do you still have that electric treatment for your nerves? I'll never forget that day you had that screaming fit when that mouse ran over your foot. It must have been terrible for a man in your condition. Ted's solicitor came up yesterday. They were together for hours. The way Ted and I feel we will get a verdict fetched in of Not Guilty…but Insane! I see the Home Secretary is having Walter's (Rowland) case investigated after all. Do you still go to the Ship? I think you would have a better time if you were to buy a crate of beer and drink it in a cemetery. At least you would feel some emotion. I believe a bloke died in the Ship one night and he was there three weeks before they tumbled it!

Well John, all good things come to an end so I will close. Don't forget to come up on Saturday the 19th.

Give my regards to Anne,
Your old pal, Alf.

This minor infraction of attempting to enclose a harmless cartoon from a magazine was the subject of grave correspondence between the governor and Home Office officials!

Number. 5749.A.Burns. 21.1.52

Dear John,

I must be settling down now; for the last few days I have been in a contented frame of mind. There is one thing I must tell you. In future I am dispensing with humour in case it is taken the wrong way. So you will have to put up with dreary letters. This will only be for 2 or 3 weeks until after the trial, then I hope to be home, if I can get my borstal sentence quashed altogether. One good thing about this Assizes business is that we shall have their team in the witness box again before we perform. I am looking forward to the trial. It will have some amusing effects which are unexpected at the moment. And, when it is quite finished, I am going to have quite a statement to make concerning various happenings since I was charged with this business. If you can make it I will expect to see you at the trial, though I suppose you will be grafting… Well John just before I close I will tell you where to find 3 smashing pubs: all near each other. The place is Pendleton, and the pubs are, The Woolpack, the Maypole and the Horseshoe. Just try them and let me know what you think.

Give my regards to Anne,

Your old pal, Alf.

PS: Write soon.

At the same time as the two friends were writing these letters, the prison authorities, particularly the medical officer, were keeping a daily log on both men, recording their weight and mental states but also making the most inappropriate, prejudicial and derogatory personal comments which were of course copied to the police and Home Office. For example here are excerpts from the medical log on Devlin, commencing on the 11th October 1951, the very first day he was received into Walton Prison.

Height 5ft.7 and a quarter. Weight 151lbs. Been in prison before. Recently been awaiting trial at Manchester. Found not guilty. Was on the run. A callous type of 'tough guy'. Knows nothing about any murder His surprise that he has been charged with murder does not ring true. No previous disease. He had touch of Malaria in West Africa 1948/49. Sacked from work for refusing to obey an order. Talking about his movements. Thinks he is making a statement. He is clearly looking around wildly for an alibi—which is none of my business. Of good intelligence and sound mind. No memory defect. Quite unscrupulous. No suggestion of any mental disorder past or present.

14/10/51.
Cut on his hand. Said he had a fight with two Irishmen on 24th September. Clearly trying in advance to clear up the matter of bloodstains.

18/10/51.
A hard boiled cunning type of man. I should think quite ruthless. His mood varies between fear and aggrieved innocence. Says the police are fixing it on him. Quite unscrupulous. Weight 152lbs.

24/11/51.
Committed Liverpool Assizes. Not so cocky now.

15/1/52.
Mind more subdued now.. Repeatedly makes efforts to get a change of room (cell) Complains of cold, obviously in order to get near Burns. Weight 155lbs.

1/2/52
Not nearly so confident, though still stressing his innocence. Complains police have always been against him. Says he was innocent of his last three convictions—which clearly he was not!—but the police framed him.[2]

27/2/52.
Sentenced to death.

---

2. It is not clear, apart from prejudice, why the officer should assume Devlin "clearly" was not innocent. He had been acquitted of the previous offence of stealing tomatoes from the fruit market—for which he received six months—and he had also asserted his innocence in court.

28/2/52.

20 cigarettes daily. Beer I pint daily.

30/3/52.

At Wandsworth, for Appeal.

The daily log concluded on 25/4/52 with one word — "Hanged."[3]

---

3.   This would only be surpassed by the cold-hearted clinical post-execution report stating, "Some tearing of soft tissue of neck".

CHAPTER THIRTEEN
MORE BALMER-PLANTED PRESS STORIES

Those who prepare and conduct prosecutions owe a duty...
to ensure that all relevant evidence of help to an accused is
either led by them or made available to the defence.

Lord Justice Lawton, 1979.

During the long bleak winter months between the end of the committal and their trial, the isolation of the two men continued. Despite being remanded in custody on a charge of murder, Burns had been treated as a convicted prisoner because he had not returned to borstal in July whilst serving a sentence. As he had already served 19 months, he sent a forthright and cogent petition to the Home Secretary on the 10th December 1951 requesting that his borstal sentence be terminated. In it he wrote:

Dear sir,

I will try and be as concise as possible so as not to take up your time too much.

I want my discharge from borstal.

1. I am being held on a murder charge I know nothing about.

2. Being on this murder charge I am being treated somewhat worse than an ordinary convicted prisoner, being in my cell 23 hours a day and the other hour spent exercising on my own.

3. I am not allowed to have anything sent in, such as tobacco, etc.

4. As you probably know, a borstal sentence is from 9 months to three years. I have already done 19 months of this one and, only for this charge I might have been going out soon.

5. I consider if the police are confident enough to charge anyone with such a terrible crime, they should have the decency to quash any present sentence the person might be serving.

I hope you see my point and grant my request.

I remain sir,
Your obedient servant. A. Burns.[1]

This caught the Home Office off guard because there was no precedent for Burns' application. His petition also threw up an even more serious issue. It was a long standing rule that an adult convicted prisoner who had escaped or absconded and was charged with a second offence whilst on the run would, pending trial, be treated as a convicted prisoner with the substantial loss of privileges that status entailed. Unknown to Burns however, a lengthy correspondence ensued, following his petition, between no less than eight senior Home Office officials until they finally had to consult a legal specialist.

The matter was finally settled when it was decided that the rule only applied to persons serving a term of *imprisonment,* and that since Burns had been a borstal trainee and not an adult prisoner when he absconded, it did not apply to him. But fearing that if this news got out a precedent would be set, followed by numerous copy-cat claims from others in the same situation, it was decided not to formally issue the ruling to all prisons and borstals. Instead, Burns' petition was returned to the Governor two weeks later with a handwritten note on the file that Burns must be immediately treated as an unconvicted prisoner with all the normal privileges of a remand prisoner. No written acknowledgement was sent to Burns himself.

Although delighted with this unexpected outcome, Burns never knew just how big a victory he had achieved against such a massive Kafkaesque

---

1. Prison Commission files.

bureaucracy—or what headaches and panic he had caused them!

He had waged his campaign without the help of his lawyer and was justifiably quite proud of himself. But despite the victory, which now allowed him, like his friend, to have daily visits, food, tobacco and newspapers sent in, the policy of isolation was not relaxed. Both men were still unable to exercise or associate with each other and were still locked up 23 hours a day. To make matters worse, since Devlin was Catholic and Burns Church of England, there was no respite from this deprivation, even on Sundays, when other prisoners of the same denomination mixed freely at chapel or church.

Burns had earlier applied for a transfer to Strangeways Prison and smuggled a note to Devlin to do likewise. This was on the grounds that both their widowed mothers had been fired from their cleaning jobs because of the publicity surrounding the case and were finding it difficult to afford the frequent visits to Walton. Both applications were however refused—the Governor stating that "they cannot be transferred for various reasons" (which were never given). Instead it was suggested the Prisoners Aid charity should be contacted to see if they could help with the women's fares. In the event they either couldn't or wouldn't help.

If the accused men were being treated with contempt by the police and prison authorities then, their solicitors were being treated, if not with the same contempt, certainly with disdain and obstruction by the police and the Director of Public Prosecutions by refusing them, for example, information, including witness statements, etc. And to add to their clients' difficulties, Balmer had been planting prejudicial stories in the newspapers via his Press Club drinking companions.

On November 29th and December 6th stories appeared in the *Daily Express,* that Bury had been attacked in Manchester's Piccadilly and taxi driver Emery had been attacked in Liverpool. The Emery story headline was, POLICE PROBE ATTACK ON TAXI DRIVER. It ran thus:

Superintendent Herbert Balmer, Liverpool CID Chief, said last night that police were enquiring into an attack on a taxi driver, Thomas James Emery who gave evidence for the prosecution at the committal proceedings....[2]

---

2.   Home Office files.

The newspaper report regarding Bury — who was alleged to have been attacked in Manchester in broad daylight by a woman wielding an umbrella — said she had previously told the police she was afraid she would be attacked for giving evidence and had returned to Manchester to lessen this risk.

Worried about the prejudicial effect of these stories, the defence lawyers, immediately wrote to the chief constable requesting details of the attacks, including the extent of their injuries,which hospitals Bury and Emery were treated at, and asking if those responsible had been arrested. The chief constable simply replied that the police were not responsible for the press reports, had not arrested anyone but had merely "confirmed them following press enquiries". He advised the lawyers to contact the newspapers concerned for any further information. Maybe the police were not *officially* responsible but — unknown to the defence — Superintendent Balmer certainly was!

After considerable correspondence backwards and forwards, it was established that the alleged attack on Emery had occurred *before* the committal proceedings had commenced on November 2nd. So why, the solicitors wanted to know, was this information released to the press *after* those proceedings which had been widely reported in the press? They made the point that nobody could have known at that time that Emery and Bury were going to be prosecution witnesses, therefore the attacks, *if indeed they were true,* could not possibly be connected to the two accused, their families or friends. The intention could only have been to create prejudice among the public and potential jurors after the reporting of the committal.

By 20th December Livermore, increasingly exasperated by the police refusal to properly address the matter, wrote again to the chief constable,

> It is a matter of grave concern that your Criminal Investigation Department
> released information about this attack after the committal proceedings and
> in such circumstances that the innuendo against the defence was obvious.

He went on to request a police press release that the attacks, if indeed they had occurred, had nothing to do with the case. Norton made a similar request, pointing out that, "These press reports have further aggravated the already difficult situation of ensuring a fair trial for these men at the next

Liverpool Assizes". He went on to express the hope that a public statement by the police would "counteract, if this may now be possible, the unfortunate publicity and consequent misconstruction which has now resulted".

After almost three weeks of procrastination Assistant Chief Constable Fothergill finally wrote on 24th December to the defence solicitors,

> I wish to make clear that information regarding the alleged attack on Mr Emery was not released to the press by the police, who merely confirmed a press inquiry that Mr Emery had reported an attack on him prior to his giving evidence.

This disingenuous reply ended, "So far as I am aware there is no connection between these matters and the prosecution of your clients and I am not aware that any such has been suggested." Then came the final insult: "If you feel the press reports embarrass the defence perhaps you will take the matter up with the newspaper concerned".[3]

The police never did answer the questions about the alleged attacks. Nor why the news of them was released after the nightly news reports of the murder allegations against the two men at the committal court. And they never issued a public statement of refutation to the press.

In addition to this blatant example of Balmer's chicanery, the official police obstruction of the defence continued apace. Running parallel with the December correspondence regarding the alleged attacks, there were—on the advice from defence counsel—repeated written requests by the two solicitors for details of the Liverpool Road Goods Depot robbery by Devlin and Burns and Bury on the night of August 8th and, among other things, the criminal records of Devlin and Burns and prosecution witnesses, McLoughlin, Bury, Milne, Rubin and McNeil. Regarding the Goods Depot robbery, the police—via Manchester police—denied there had ever been such a robbery, thus again sabotaging the defence case. And although initially refusing the request for the criminal records, the chief constable was so unsure of his own action he wrote to Bishop the prosecuting solicitor seeking advice.

Over a week later Assistant Chief Constable Fothergill sent the criminal records of Devlin and Burns but refused the others, telling both lawyers to apply to the Director of Public Prosecutions. Protesting against this refusal,

3. Merseyside Police files.

Livermore reminded Fothergill that the Crown witnesses' convictions had
been requested by defence counsel, Rose Heilbron and Sir Noel Goldie,
as essential to preparing a defence and that as recently as the 6th December the Home Secretary in the House of Commons, replying to former
Attorney-General, Sir Hartley Shawcross, stated the prosecution must make
known to the defence *any* information which is relevant to a case. Yet despite
the Home Secretary's comments, Deputy Director of Public Prosecutions
Paling—who had refused even the prosecution witnesses addresses at the
committal—wrote to Norton and Livermore also refusing the requested
records.

This saga of stubbornness and obstruction had now gone into the New
Year, when on 2nd January Livermore wrote directly to the Home Secretary,
reminding him of his own statement to the former Attorney General and
requesting from the DPP a copy of a statement made to the police by Alan
Campbell who was a potential defence witness. Astonishingly, the written
response, from a legal secretary in the current Attorney General's office (to
whom the letter had been passed) again refused the records, stating that,

> The Director of Public Prosecutions does not ask for the convictions of every
> witness called by the prosecution. Were it to do so it would place *an intolerable*
> *burden* on the police and the Criminal Records Office (Author's italics).

The letter went on to state,

> In any event, unless the alleged convictions are put to the witness, and he admits
> them, the Director has no means of identification, and he certainly could not take
> the risk of giving the wrong information on a matter of this kind.

In other words, despite their existence at the Criminal Records Office, a
person had to admit that he actually did have those convictions!

This absurdly disingenuous reply not only disregarded the Home Secretary's parliamentary reply to Hartley Shawcross but also ignored the fact that
obtaining a simple criminal record from police files was not by any stretch
of the imagination "an intolerable burden".

As for the Campbell statement: the letter continued that it was *the first time* the legal secretary had heard of Campbell but that the Manchester police were being contacted.[4] "And if he [Campbell] had indeed given a statement containing material evidence, the prosecution will call him as a witness or make him available to the defence". But, he went on they are not under any duty to provide the defence with his statement". When Livermore replied, stating that in the Cameo murder trial two years previously (in which he was involved) a list of the prosecution witnesses previous convictions *had* been provided, the matter was referred to the Attorney General's Private Secretary, who finally conceded that the requested list of convictions would be provided to defence counsel.

This letter—contradicting the junior civil servant who had said he'd never heard of Alan Campbell—also revealed that Campbell *had* been interviewed by the police. The writer then added he understood Campbell had also been interviewed by Livermore and by Burns' mother *before* the police interviewed him. Therefore, he concluded, there was no problem about the defence having access to Campbell. That Livermore was requesting Campbell's *statement to the police* was quietly ignored, as was the fact that Campbell had made two statements—one to Manchester police and another the same day to Detective Sergeant Richardson. Nor did it reveal that Richardson and Wade had improperly taken a statement from Burns' mother in a police car when she was returning home after a hard day at her cleaning job at the Employment Exchange.

Campbell's so-called "interview" by Burns mother consisted of her meeting him in the street and suggesting to him that he was with her son and Devlin at the Sunblinds break-in on August 19th.

Despite these prolonged efforts by Livermore and Norton, the two statements of Alan Campbell were never shown to the defence—an omission which would prove fatal at Devlin and Burns' trial. Moreover, despite Campbell's statements implicating Joan and Frederick Downing in the Sunblinds robbery and subsequent signed statements taken from the Downings themselves, these were never disclosed to the defence.

After Campbell's two statements of 27th October, Frederick Downing had been taken into custody the same day and shown them. Threatened

---

4. This indicates Campbell's two statements to Manchester and Liverpool police were not even shown to the DPP.

with ten years for receiving the stolen goods, he then made a statement which, although admitting his wife's part, said he had not been involved. This enabled Balmer to then threaten his wife with being charged unless she retracted her first statement and signed a second denying she was involved in the robbery—which she did, thus denying the men their alibi. She was then told by Balmer to attend the trial for three days in case she was called, and on two of those days was paid £20 per day.

Meanwhile, a joyless, uneventful Christmas came and went for Devlin and Burns, the only bright spots in their existence being the voluminous correspondence between them their family and friends.

Burns' letter to his mother following her New Year's Day visit (2nd January 1952) showed that he had finally realised their letters were being copy-typed and sent to the police and the Home Office. He was then determined to let the authorities know he was not dispirited and that he was taking everything in his stride. On the 15th January, Burns wrote to his married sister, Marie Billingham, as follows:

Dear Marie,

Just a few lines hoping they find all at home in the best of health... How is young Brian? I was glad to see him. He gets more cheerful as he gets older; in fact I don't think even young Harry (his brother Henry's son) had his—Brian's –disposition at his age, and that is really saying something.

It was not much of a visit for you and Eddie was it? I was so browned off. In fact it was only the kid (Brian) who made me feel a bit brighter. Anyway, I am feeling ok now.

Only another 3 weeks or so and we shall be right. Ted had his solicitor to see him on Sunday, so I suppose everything is ready as far as he is concerned so it only leaves it for Norton to visit me. I am writing to him today....

You remember those spots and tiny pimples? Well they are nearly all gone now. They have left tiny marks but hardly noticeable. I know now it must have been something at Portland that caused them. The trouble the people at that place have caused me. If it hadn't been for them I would not have overstayed my leave: I would not have had to lie in Bootle Street and therefore I would not now be in here. Still I suppose Rowland's felt the same.

I will close this dreary letter. Tell Ed I was asking about him.

Your Loving brother Alf.

Bootle Street Police Station and Portland Borstal referred to his arrest on 24th September when he lied that he had been in Liverpool for three weeks, in order to avoid being framed for the August 11th Manchester murder.

The significance of this letter however—of which Balmer as usual received a typewritten copy—is the mention of "The Kid", his nephew Brian. Following his fabricated press stories of the alleged attacks on Emery and Bury, this gave the CID chief a further opportunity to plunge the dagger of prejudice once again into the two men. This time he manufactured a crude threatening letter sent to Marie Milne. It was allegedly from "The Razino Gang", written in a combination of small printed letters and handwriting and composed in disguised form exactly as follows:

The Razino Gang

Hello Sister,

We've been checking up on your movements and everybody you associate with and we've come to the conclusion that you're a (lousy squealer) so the best thing for you to do is to forget all about it because if these fellows go down you and your family will pay, We know that you have got a brother who is an ex [borstal boy] who done Hollasley Bay a sister older than yourself and a younger sister and you wouldn't like to see them and your mother getting chivved to pieces by some nice steel razors [HA HA, HA HA]. We know all the dives you go to its no use running away you are getting watched night and day we even know that you used to knock around with a gunman who is now inside but even he won't be able to stop us for what we are going to do. Because if you don't forget about it they will find you getting washed up in

the Mersey with your face battered in. This is your last warning SO WATCH
YOURSELF BECAUSE THIS GANG [HA HA HA] IS ORGANISED."

Tony Razino

Tony Lacy And The Kid."[5]

The envelope, bearing a Yorkshire postmark was posted on 5th February.
The trial actually began on the 12th but it was originally intended to start on
the 11th. Balmer hoped publication of the letter would provide a sensational
and suitably prejudicial opening to the trial.

Although the author wrongly spelled George as "Gorge" in Milne's address,
29a Great George's Place, the correct spelling of words in the letter such as
"conclusion", the sentence structure, despite the lack of punctuation, and
the correct capitalisation of nouns like Hollasley Bay (notwithstanding the
deliberate mis-spelling of Hollesley) clearly indicate the writer was not uneducated, as it was intended to convey. Moreover, given the persistent refusals
at the committal hearing to divulge any of the witnesses' addresses, it is clear
that only the police had Milne's address.

As Balmer knew she would, Milne handed him the letter. On this occasion
however, instead of acting arbitrarily he suggested to his immediate superior,
Assistant Chief Constable, Fothergill, issuing the letter to the press. Balmer's
methods being well-known among his colleagues, however, Fothergill rejected
the suggestion, stating it was far too inflammatory and would so enrage the
defence they would demand a full investigation. "Best to let sleeping dogs lie
Bert," he told him. This was most disappointing to Balmer and his friends
in the Press Club. What a scoop it would have been on the opening day of
the trial! There was one consolation however: if nothing else the letter would
serve to create *genuine* hostility from Milne towards the accused men and
make her a more effective witness!

The only means of communication for Devlin and Burns was via a cleaner,
who would carry messages and other items such as tobacco between them.
This was a regular practice among segregated prisoners. But early in January when a particularly eagle-eyed hospital officer saw Burns slipping some

---

5.   Merseyside Police files.

contraband to a cleaner, he immediately confiscated it and made a written report to the Governor. This "contraband" consisted of a note written in faded ink on a piece of toilet paper, half an ounce of tobacco and a cheap paperback. But judging by the over-reaction of the authorities to this minor infringement, anyone would have thought a massive escape plan had been uncovered. It was wrongly stated by the Governor that Burns had been trying to smuggle a letter out of the prison. In truth his note was simply asking his friend why he never answered questions he'd asked him in previous smuggled messages. This relatively innocuous episode however, was magnified out of all proportion, with numerous reports, memos and letters flying between the Prison Commissioners, the Director of Public Prosecutions, the Home Office and Liverpool Police.[6]

The intense supervision of the men was originally requested by Liverpool City Police, and meant that every move they made, every visit they received was scrupulously observed and reported on, and every letter they wrote or received diligently copied and typed. In this desolate, stifling atmosphere, Devlin was told on the 24th January that he had a visitor named "Miss Thomas". He did not know anyone of that name. But glad of anything to break the tortuous tedium of isolation he willingly agreed to see her. Peering inquisitively through the wire-strengthened glass window in the visiting box, he was amazed to see that "Miss Thomas" was none other than June Bury!

Full of apologies, Bury told him she had given a false name and address at the prison gate in order to see him. As a sort of peace offering she had brought him 30 cigarettes. During their conversation, according to William Bradshaw the supervising prison officer, Devlin told her that he had nothing to do with the murder and was amazed when he was charged with it. She rather cryptically replied that "Marie had seen Joan and got the truth out of her and that Marie was going to tell the truth at the trial". When the visit ended and he was escorting her to the gate, she said to Bradshaw, "Why could I have not kissed him? After all it is my birthday and I am the mother of his child, 18 months old."[7]

What was *not* contained in the officer's report was Bury telling Devlin that she did not even know McLoughlin; that she was sorry she had put him

---

6. Prison Commission files.
7. Prison Commission files.

in prison for the past four months; that she had given false evidence at the committal hearing because Milne had told her she had to back her up and that she herself would tell the truth at the Assizes. This was reported back to Balmer which was why and how he was able to threaten her with ten years for perjury if she changed her evidence.

Apart from of how Bury was able to obtain 30 cigarettes—on ration at the time—when she was only receiving a weekly National Assistance allowance, it is curious how she, as a prosecution witness in a murder case, was able to give a false name and address and freely visit a man charged with that murder against whom she had already given evidence.

During the same visit another officer, Mr Murphy, on duty at the prison gate also made a written report. In this he stated that as Bury was leaving, Detective Sergeant Young and Detective Constable Wright were standing just inside the prison gate. They recognised Bury and she recognised them. "And she was obviously very surprised." The officers asked him who she had been visiting but according to Murphy he told them it was confidential. Bury and the two detectives chatted for awhile and, "before leaving they told me her name was June Bury and she was a prosecution witness in an important case. I later checked and found that the young lady had given the name of Thomas and her address as 4 Pearson Street, Newton Heath, Manchester." [8]

Was the presence of the two detectives—who reported back to Balmer—merely coincidental? If this visit was instigated by Balmer and, at his request, Bury's false details were overlooked by the Governor, it had several advantages:

1. Devlin may incriminate himself or threaten Bury, both of which could be used against him at the forthcoming trial.

2. By threatening her with possible charges of deception and perverting the course of justice by giving false particulars and visiting the accused in a capital case, he could ensure she did not deviate from her false evidence.

3. The visit could validate the truth of Bury's false evidence by asserting that, far from bearing Devlin any enmity, she was friendly and

8. Prison Commission files.

sympathetic towards him even a few weeks before the trial (The latter advantage was actually used by the prosecution and the judge at the trial).

And was the presence of the two detectives to ensure that she did indeed visit Devlin and would be able to testify to that if she later tried to deny it? Conversely, if the visit was *not* instigated by Balmer, he was still able to threaten her with visiting the accused under false pretences, giving a false name and address and possibly perverting the course of justice.

It is significant that in a police report of September 1953, Detective Sergeant Wade recalled a statement Bury had made to Manchester police on 17th October 1951 naming a David Coyne as the murderer In the report he stated,

> Her attitude from the time of making her first statement on 8th October until the committal stages *and indeed until the trial itself,* caused us considerable anxiety as to whether she would give her evidence truthfully (Author's italics).

The "considerable anxiety" was clearly this — undisclosed — statement which would have wrecked the case against Devlin and Burns. Wades' report went on, "She was however a truthful witness not only at the committal but also at the trial".[9] She was not a "truthful witness" but an obedient one. Because, informed of this statement Balmer immediately drove to Manchester and renewed his threats against her, which resulted in her retracting it. "Truthful" was no more than code language for her maintaining the false testimony fabricated by Balmer?

At the end of January 1952 Kenneth McNeil — via the Birmingham Police — was summoned to an interview with Balmer

After the committal proceedings Balmer, liaising with the Birmingham Police, had arranged for McNeil to obtain a job as a kitchen porter at that city's Grand Hotel and be provided with accommodation at the Salvation Army Hostel. This was because he needed to ensure that pending the trial his "witness" would not be subject to any threats or defence attempts to get him to tell the truth. To ensure he did not go missing, Birmingham Police were asked to keep him under observation. Believing the trial would commence on Monday February 11[th,] Balmer had a telegram sent to Birmingham

---

9. Merseyside Police files.

Police on February 1st, asking them to instruct McNeill to "be warned" to
attend Liverpool's Cheapside Bridewell on Sunday 10th February to be interviewed by him. A reply was duly sent stating that McNeill had been seen
and would attend as ordered.[10]

Despite intimidating McNeil with the legal phrase "be warned" which was
only used on court calenders, there was no legitimate reason why Balmer,
rather than prosecuting counsel, should be interviewing a Crown witness
the day before the trial. The reason however was he needed to go over his
false story with him in a final "dress rehearsal" in order for him to be word
perfect when giving evidence.

As with the December false reports of the alleged attacks on Emery and
Bury, it was around this time that Balmer unsuccessfully tried to drum up
more prejudice against the accused men by having the phoney threatening
letter sent to Marie Milne from the non-existent "Razino Gang".

---

10. Merseyside Police files.

PART TWO

DAMNATION

CHAPTER FOURTEEN

THE TRIAL BEGINS

Can this, in your judgements my Lords, seem likely to be true?

Sir Thomas More. Executed 1535

The trial opened before Mr Justice Finnemore at 10.30 on the morning of Tuesday the 12th February 1952 in No. 1 Court at the city's vast, neo-classical St Georges Hall. A crowd of 1,000 had been waiting outside the Lime Street edifice since 7 am to gain admittance and hundreds were left waiting outside on St George's Plateau.

This was the same massive, glass-domed Victorian courtroom which had seen some of the nation's most notorious and dramatic trials including those in 1889 of the 26 year-old Florence Maybrick, Herbert Wallace in 1931 and a mere two years ago those of George Kelly and Charles Connolly for the Cameo Cinema murders.

Both Maybrick's, and Kelly's second trial, at which they were sentenced to death, had been marred by biased judges and juries. As far as juries were concerned, even before trials commenced, the accused — regardless of the evidence — were probably guilty. The prevalent thinking was that the police didn't charge innocent people. The trial of Devlin and Burns would be no different.

Leading for the prosecution was Basil Neild QC who had prosecuted Walter Rowland in 1947 and defended Connolly in the first Cameo trial. He was assisted by Mr A R Baucher. For the defence, Rose Heilbron QC represented Devlin and led Mr Jack Tarsh. Burns was defended by Sir Noel Goldie QC and his junior, Mr Frank Nance. All the defence counsel had been engaged on legal aid.

The short, tubby, ineffectual 70-year-old Liverpool-born Goldie, although a junior judge himself, would prove to be linguistically eccentric, long-winded, unduly deferential to the prosecution witnesses and overly obsequious towards the judge—all to the detriment of his client. Indeed, when presiding at the Manchester Quarter Sessions, he was nick-named "Roly-Poly Goldie" by local villains and his court was bizarrely known as "Goldie's Follies!" He was of the old school of theatrical performers who may have been more suited to the stage. It was no accident that his idol was the flamboyant Sir Edward Marshall Hall. Sadly however, he did not possess that famous advocate's courtroom artistry or skills.

The proceedings, which had been due to start the previous day had been postponed because the judge was unwell. In the well of the crowded court, waiting for the trial to open, Counsel could be seen making last minute arrangements, with Goldie, clumsily gathering up his dropped papers and ruby-lipped Rose Heilbron adjusting her wig whilst hurriedly holding a last minute briefing with Devlin's solicitor, Harry Livermore.

The judge, 63-year-old Sir Donald Finnemore was a bachelor, a religious non-conformist and a teetotaller. Alcohol was forbidden in his Birmingham chambers, so much so that they became jokingly known as "Cocoa Chambers". In addition, young barristers were encouraged to take up officer positions in the Boys Brigade if they wanted to progress in his practice.

The Boys Brigade was Finnemore's main extra-curricular interest, an active involvement he continued up till his death in 1974. As the founder of the very first Birmingham Company of the Boys Brigade in 1913 and later national vice-president, he had even published a book in 1924 entitled, *Boys!: A Complete Manual for Workers With Boys.*[1] Among his contemporaries he was known for "sometimes being warm-hearted" but his natural disposition was described as "icily-cold" and known as " a stern judge who would stand no nonsense".[2]

At the March 1951 trial of William Watkins for the murder of his newly born baby, despite his counsel pleading not to admit in evidence a refuted so-called confession by the stone deaf, mentally-ill father of eleven, Finnemore ruled it admissible and the next day sentenced him to death. Although regarded primarily as a prosecuting barrister, he had represented Alfred Arthur Rouse in the infamous 1931 "Blazing Car" murder case, in which the jury had returned a guilty verdict after only 15 minutes!

---

1.   Coincidentally, Detective Chief Superintendent Balmer was in 1966 President of the Liver-
     pool Boys Brigade.

2.   *Execution: One Man's Life and Death,* John Mervyn Pugh (Waterside Press, 2005).

Appointed a High Court judge in 1947, Finnemore's career had so far been undistinguished. This case would remedy that (although for the wrong reasons) as would the Old Bailey trial a year later of Rillington Place serial killer John Halliday Christie, at which he would also preside. But in his long career his main distinction, of which he was so proud, was in becoming the national Vice-President of the Boys Brigade. Yet despite his dedication to the welfare of boys it was clear, as the trial unfolded, that he wasn't going to be too worried about the welfare of these two particular boys!

After the 12-member all male jury had been sworn in, the angular, aquiline-nosed Finnemore entered in his resplendent red robe and short wig. Wearing an aloof expression, he did not look at anyone in particular, as if he were somehow above the rest of mere humanity.

When the clerk of the court, Ian Macauley, announced, "Bring up Edward Francis Devlin and Alfred Burns" the two smartly-dressed young men emerged from the cells and entered the dock escorted by two prison officers—Devlin was dressed in a dark blue suit, blue shirt and cream tie and Burns in a light blue suit, blue shirt and blue and silver-striped tie. When the charge was read out to them, both replied in soft but clear voices, "Not guilty."

They had earlier arrived at the northern end of St George's Hall, not as Jimmy Tucker's song romantically described, "like the Lord Mayor in State" but in a nondescript small grey prison van.

Below, in the whitewashed, dungeon-like cells, both men were instructed by their counsel to give brief yes and no replies when in the witness box; not to be demonstrative, not to elaborate on their answers and most definitely not to volunteer any information. Basil Neild, they were told, was very skilful at twisting witnesses' testimonies to give them the meaning he wanted. To Burns, who could be quite articulate, this would subsequently prove to be a disadvantage: he instinctively wanted to expand on his replies in order to convince the jury of their innocence. But since he and Devlin intended to be truthful—even to the point of incriminating themselves over the Sunblinds robbery—neither appreciated the inherent pitfalls of cross-examination… even when you are telling the truth!

Before Basil Neild opened for the Crown, Sir Noel Goldie asked that all witnesses should leave the court until called to give evidence. Somewhat unsure about this until reminded that this was the normal practice, the judge then ordered all witnesses to leave. As Superintendent Balmer would not be giving evidence, however, he was allowed to remain, which he did throughout the trial. This would prove invaluable to the smooth execution of his conspiracy, allowing him to follow the evidence and to advise and manipulate his witnesses accordingly as each day's proceedings unfolded.

Outlining the case for the prosecution, Neild first dealt with the details of the murder: the location of the Rimmer home and other background information, showing in the process, street maps, photographs of the exterior of the house and the murder scene inside it. Asking the jury to pay particular attention to the privets in the backyard and the interior of the rear living room, he pointed out the armchair and the two mirrors — the materiality of all of which, he said, would become apparent as the trial progressed.

When describing Thomas Rimmer's visit to his mother's home at 7.10 pm on the 20th August, Neild pre-fixed it with, "As was his custom." But according to his wife's and neighbour Jack Grossman's undisclosed statements it was *not* his custom. Indeed his mother had actually complained that he hardly ever visited her.

Recounting how Rimmer discovered his mother's body in the hallway, Neild stated, "He then went around to the rear of the house *and tried the back door* leading to the yard" (Author's italics). This was speculation rather than evidence. It will be remembered that in his statement Rimmer said he had tried the door but in his interview said he wasn't sure whether or not he had tried that door.

Coming to Rimmer's access into the house, Neild stated that although the rear living room window was already broken, he had to knock more glass out with a brick in order to climb through. If that was true, a valid question during cross-examination would be: "How therefore could the accused men get through that before more glass was removed?" But that question was never put by the defence.

Continuing, Neild then began to narrate the events leading up to the murder, starting with the alleged meeting between McLoughlin and Devlin in Bill's Café in Paddington, on the morning of 27th July, 24 days before the murder, which he called, "The first chapter in this grim story."

Devlin, who was alone got into conversation with George McLoughlin, who told him he was going to "screw" his auntie's house in Cranborne Road. "That's funny," said Devlin, "I've got a job there as well." That same *day,* continued Neild, "these two men made their way to, 'case the job up'" A few moments later, seemingly mindless of what he had just said, Neild went on, "There they were in *the evening* of 27th July at 7 Cranborne Road where Beatrice Alice Rimmer lived alone" (Author's italics).

From the outset Basil Neild, a man of the utmost integrity, had unknowingly been provided by the duplicitous Liverpool CID and the office of the Director of Public Prosecutions with a completely false prospectus to put before the jury. He was unaware, for example, of McLoughlin's signed statement to Balmer of 9th October which never mentioned Bill's Café but stated he met both Devlin and Burns in the *Rainbow* and *Continental* cafés eight or nine days before the murder (approx 10th August). He was also apparently unaware, as was the court, of McLoughlin originally naming "Ginger" Dutton; of McLoughlin's numerous interviews with Balmer at Walton Prison and being shown photographs of Devlin and Burns by detectives Farragher and Wade. But Balmer — sitting in court listening attentively — wasn't too bothered about this. He was just glad he had instilled into McLoughlin, and Milne such details as the privets in the backyard and the armchair and the mirrors in the Rimmer living room, until they were word perfect. It was even more pleasing to now hear an eminent QC unwittingly validating these lies.

Recounting Alice Rimmer's journey to the No. 27 bus stop, Neild stated that her son "saw her to the bus stop". Yet this was pure supposition based solely on Rimmer's word. There was no objective evidence — as there likewise would not be for many of his assertions throughout the trial. And since the judge was otherwise so punctilious, he did not reproach Crown counsel for presenting such assumptions as fact.

When it came to the medical evidence, after dramatically recounting in detail the way "this defenceless woman was set upon with brutal savagery" — clearly intended to inflame the jury — Neild again appeared to be misinformed when stating the medical opinion was that Mrs Rimmer had taken three or four hours to die. On the contrary, pathologist Dr Manning had finally admitted under cross-examination at the committal court that he did not know how long she had lived.[3]

---

3. See *Chapter 34* which deals with expert evidence.

During this lengthy opening speech Neild went into great detail about the accused men's alleged journey after the murder, through Princes Park to the Rialto area, the obvious implication being that they didn't want to be seen by anyone in their bloodstained state. But if forensic scientist Dr Firth's committal court evidence was correct they would have had no visible bloodstains on them—thus making such a lengthy detour totally unnecessary. Moreover, when describing the meeting with Milne, after the murder, and the trio's walk from the Rialto down Parliament Street when—despite the dim, discolouring tungsten street lighting—Milne observed the stains on the men's clothes and their muddy shoes, Neild was clearly unaware of her signed statement of 9th October in which she said she observed all of this inside the South China Chinese Café where they had a meal of corned beef and chips.

According to Neild, after waiting on the corner of Cranborne Road from 9 pm till 10.30, Milne decided to jump a bus down to the Rialto for a pre-arranged meeting with her brother at nearby Wilkie's Club. She then happened to see the accused on the other side of the road and they called her over. When she asked if they had done the job Burns said, "No."

"They appeared," he went on, "to be excited but also nervous and frightened." Devlin had a stained handkerchief over his hand. Then for emphasis in case the jury missed the connection, he said, "You will remember *how* the back living room window was broken" (Author's italics).

This comment was indicative of the sort of prejudicial innuendo masquerading as evidence, from both the prosecution and the judge, which would recur throughout the trial. For this was not evidence: there was no connection between an alleged bandage on Devlin's hand and the broken window. Thomas Rimmer had said *he* had broken it further with a brick. The jury would not "remember" because not they nor anybody else knew how the window had *originally* been broken. Moreover, according to Inspector Reade and Mr Allen of the Home Office, nobody had climbed through it! But then, their reports had also been suppressed.

As they walked along, said Neild, Milne overheard Devlin say to Burns, "We should not have come through the park. We have mud on our shoes, she may suspect something." And Milne saw that their shoes were indeed muddy. Burns asked Devlin where his knife was and he said he had lost it coming through the park. Milne then noticed wet "marks and stains" on their clothing and asked Burns about these, to which he told her to mind her own fucking business and that it was beer. At the corner of Great George Street Milne suggested going to the *South China* Café but they declined, saying they were in a hurry to get back to Manchester. They then walked quickly away in the direction of the city centre and she never saw them again.

Suddenly remembering, Neild then added, "Also, members of the jury, Milne heard something she wasn't supposed to hear. Devlin asked Burns, 'Will the old woman live?' to which Burns replied, 'To hell with the old woman. We will be out of Liverpool before long and we will take Marie, the little bitch, with us'." Again, this uncorroborated story was not evidence. But it did provide more prejudice and helped considerably towards the character assassination for which it was intended.

Given the ruthless picture he had painted of Burns, Neild never explained why, in the event they didn't take "the little bitch" with them. Nor did he explain why she had completely forgotten about the intended meeting with her brother in Wilkie's Club! (her excuse for returning to the Rialto area).

Narrating how the crime was committed, Neild again repeated his contradiction: "These two men, the prisoner Devlin and McLoughlin, on the 27th July in the evening, made their way to the back of No.7. McLoughlin gave Devlin a leg up on to the wall and he himself looked over into the yard where they saw a light in the living room." He did not offer any explanation as to how McLoughlin was able to get on the wall and see everything, including the privets, without himself getting a leg-up! Nor did anyone ask.

It was just going dark said Neild, and because of the light in the house McLoughlin said they had better "beat it" as they did not want to be seen around there.

Then the prisoner, Devlin, said to McLoughlin—and I am paraphrasing members of the jury—'There is only an old woman living there. I think there should be a lot of dough in the house. An occasional bloke goes in and out and I think it must be a relative'.

He then added the obvious point, "You will not have failed to observe that this woman in her fifties *did* live alone and *was* visited from time-to-time by a man, and he was a relative, her own son."

Neild then related how Devlin explained how this "screwing job" was to be done. "He said he would grab the old woman and put her on the bed, and if she started messing about he would see to her."

It is very doubtful if this Queens Counsel, this man of integrity, was aware that these were the exact words McLoughlin had originally told the police "Ginger" Dutton had used. So according to his brief, prepared by Balmer and Bishop the Crown solicitor, he told the jury in good faith that they would notice a very important point here: that there was apparently no hesitation on Devlin's part to use violence and force if need be. This damning conclusion however—although given authority from such an illustrious personage—was again not, strictly speaking, evidence but simply the uncorroborated word of a lying convict. Neither was it evidence when he related the role of witness Emery, the taxi driver.

Neild first told the jury that at or about 1 pm on the 19th August,

The two prisoners hired a taxi and drove with Marie Milne to Smithdown Road.
Mr Emery knows Marie Milne and you will hear his evidence (Author's italics).

But contradicting himself, he then stated, "He drives Marie Milne and *two young men whom he did not know and cannot identify*. And that was the party" (Author's italics). This was not only self-contradictory but also a classic piece of non-evidence. Firstly, Neild omitted to mention that the journey was *to the hospital*, as admitted by Emery at the lower court, and therefore could have been a different journey on a different Sunday. Secondly, he made an unequivocal statement of fact that the "two prisoners" made the journey with Marie Milne. Then, whilst admitting that Emery did not know the two men and could not identify them, he nonetheless concludes with, "And that was the party" as if it were proven fact. Unfortunately, neither defence counsel objected to this as inadmissible. Nor did the judge correct him as he regularly did whenever defence counsel strayed.

Before concluding his opening speech, Basil Neild paid lip service to fairness by warning the jury about accepting the evidence of "accomplices" McLoughlin, Milne and Bury, without corroboration but immediately nullified this stricture by stating that if they believed their uncorroborated evidence, they could accept it.

One of the first witnesses called by the Crown was Jean Hunt, a draughts-woman employed by Liverpool Corporation. She was briefly questioned on the street maps she had produced from the Ordnance Survey map of the area, together with all the relevant locations and distances marked in red ink. The Crown had called her simply as a "technical witness" and junior Crown counsel Mr Baucher's formal examination had only lasted a few minutes. The defence however were going to question her in much more detail since Devlin and Burns protested they had never been in Cranborne Road or gone through any park.

Cross-examining, Rose Heilbron, with Milne in mind, managed to elicit from the witness that it was quite possible for someone to walk or get a bus up Smithdown Road, then at Lodge Lane a No. 26 circular bus—which did not go near the Rialto—and which would take her to Great George's Place (where Milne lived)—the obvious implication being there was no need for Milne to have gone anywhere near the Rialto area. Balmer had however anticipated this logic, which was why his script involved Milne having a pre-arranged meeting with her brother at Wilkie's Club which was next door to the Rialto Cinema.

Later, Sir Noel Goldie, during his cross-examination, wrongly described the location of the Rialto Cinema as being at the junction of Princes Street (not Road), Upper Parliament Street and Windsor Street, whereupon Milne had to correct him! Considering, however, that both Crown and defence counsel, and the judge, all had street maps of the area in front of them, no one else bothered to correct him.

Later, after establishing that Mrs Rimmer's home was approximately one and a half miles from the Rialto, Goldie was trying to demonstrate that the accused men, leaving Cranborne Road after the murder, would have been going far out of their way to get to the Rialto via Princes Park. Unfortunately however, his questions to the witness were based on going in the opposite direction! Yet although this confused her she nonetheless agreed with him.

The next witness was 19-year-old George McLoughlin who had been brought from borstal—via Stafford Prison. It was considered by the authorities too dangerous to house him even temporarily in Walton Prison.

Unusually smartly dressed in a brown double-breasted suit, cream shirt

and light blue tie, the giraffe-necked convict entered the witness box wearing a sullen expression, avoiding looking at either the jury or the accused
men in the dock. Before his cross-examination by defence counsel began,
McLoughlin was putting his foot in it even under the benign questioning
of the friendly Basil Neild.

Launching into his account at Neild's request, his story would become
so riddled with improbabilities and inconsistencies it would have been risi-
ble had it not been so gravely damaging. Nonetheless, bearing in mind the
jury's unawareness of his eleven sessions of extended tuition by Balmer, his
original claim that Ginger Dutton was the killer and his earlier evidence at
the magistrates' court, his testimony seemed quite plausible… up to a point.
Adhering to Balmer's script, he initially acquitted himself quite well, as he
told of meeting Devlin in Bill's Café when he told him he was thinking of
breaking into his auntie's house in Cranborne Road and Devlin saying he
had a job planned in the same road. Devlin told him an old woman lived
there and she had plenty of money. They then went round to the rear of the
house to have a look at Devlin's job, which was, "three or four houses down
from Smithdown Road on the left hand side." But contrary to his committal evidence, he now said that this first meeting was on "Thursday the 28th
of July." He never mentioned, as in the lower court, meeting Devlin the
next day when they went to his auntie's house. He also changed his story
about meeting both Devlin and Burns six days later. Instead, he now said he
met them in the evening of the same day at the Continental Café where all
three discussed the robbery. As for his committal evidence of giving Devlin
a leg-up on the back wall, he now simply said, "We got on top of the wall
together, like." And when the judge asked him if he had said "I" or "We",
he replied, "Me and Devlin sir."

This minor alteration by Balmer to the "leg-up" incident, corrected
McLoughlin's earlier evidence which would have prompted the question
of how he himself got onto the wall. But this evidence was most important
because when shown exterior photographs of the backyard and the privets,
he was able to agree that was the view he had described—notwithstanding
that, unknown to Neild, he had previously been shown those photographs
by the police.

McLoughlin said there was a light on in the Rimmer home because, he said, that though it was mid-morning it was going dull. Again, quite different from his earlier evidence when he said it was going dark. He then said Devlin told him a bloke usually called at the house now and again. When Neild, mistakenly giving the wrong date, said, "And that was on this same day, the 18th July?" McLoughlin agreed without hesitation! It was noticeable that the judge, though subsequently correcting the defence over trivial errors, let this pass without comment. Nor did either defence counsel spot the error. Insignificant in itself, it nonetheless showed that McLoughlin was willing to agree with anything Crown counsel said.

When Neild asked what Devlin said he would do when he got into the house, McLoughlin replied, "He said he would just grab hold of the woman like. I said, 'what if she starts screaming?' and he said, 'We will see to her.'"

For emphasis the judge then asked, "You said if she starts screaming. Is that right?" When McLoughlin agreed, he again asked, "What did he say then?" to which McLoughlin repeated, "We will see to her."

This unnecessary intervention one of many throughout the trial—obviously intended to inflame the jury—made it clear that, like the committal proceedings magistrate Alderman Gordon, Mr Justice Finnemore was not going to be of any assistance to the accused men! Almost vicariously, he then asked, "Did he give you any more details of what he would do?"

"He was going to have a girl or something round to the front of the house," he replied, "and we were to get in the back way while she was talking at the front door."

Despite McLoughlin stating that he met Devlin that same night by arrangement in the Continental where Burns was present, Neild asked him if the next time he met Devlin had been a week later. This confusion was due to Balmer "tuning-up" and modifying the false evidence of his witnesses so that even prosecution counsel's effectiveness was sometimes compromised.

Agreeing the job was discussed in the Continental, McLoughlin said there was a girl at the table who moved away soon after he arrived. He had to ask Devlin and Burns who she was and they said she might be one of the girls going on the job with them. When Neild asked who she was, McLoughlin immediately replied, "June Bury."

Continuing, he said the job was going to be done in a few weeks time over a weekend. Burns said they would get in through the back door or by slipping the catch on the window. The girl would keep the old woman talking at the front whilst they got in the house. He was going to get them over the wall then go inside with them.

After leaving the Continental that night at about midnight, he said, the three of them went to the Pier Head coffee stall and later to the nearby Lighthouse Café. They arranged to meet a fortnight later to do the job that weekend. There was apparently no definite time or place arranged for the meeting. Replying to Neild, McLoughlin said, "I was going to see them in the Golden Dragon or see them round the Continental or the Rainbow." He was arrested for the robbery at his auntie's a few days before he could meet them and had been in custody since.

Most of the conversations were alleged to have taken place either before arriving at the Rimmer house or whilst he and Devlin were looking over the back wall before he met Burns. But under cross-examination it was to change radically, with McLoughlin attributing some of these damaging remarks to Burns in the Continental Café. These blatant contradictions however were ignored by the judge and apparently went completely un-noticed by the jury.

If, as McLoughlin said, this was the plan, it must have been the most cock-eyed, implausible burglary ever contemplated by so-called professional thieves. Several questions needed to be posed which neither defence counsel ever raised.

- Why should a straightforward housebreaking be postponed for two weeks?

- If the two accused had, as alleged by the Crown, so much detailed knowledge of Mrs Rimmer and her routine, wouldn't they know she would be at home at 10 pm, thereby making matters much more fraught with danger? So why purposely decide to burgle her house whilst she was at home when it would have been much easier when she was absent?

- Why would the plan need to be complicated by having a decoy at the front door? If they broke in when Mrs Rimmer was at her son's they would not need any such decoy And, in relation to the even more fantastical alleged strategy, why would they assume that Mrs Rimmer—a

lady known to be reserved and not very sociable even with her neighbours — would readily invite a young female stranger into her rear living
room late at night?

The only validity this bizarre scenario could claim was insofar as it allowed
Superintendent Balmer's script to explain the time gap between the planning
and the execution of the robbery; to validate Marie Milne's damning allegation of Burns describing the interior of the Rimmer home to her — which
could be confirmed with crime scene photographs. And to show that these
were violent men hell bent on more than simple burglary. The only problem
with this rationale however is that he had overlooked his script for Marie
Milne stating the men had been in the house for one and a half hours when
it had been empty!

Sitting in the well of the court, Balmer had been quite satisfied with
McLoughlin's performance. But once Rose Heilbron's gruelling cross-examination commenced, he began to seriously have second thoughts. And
by the time she had finished with him — despite the judge's frequent interventions to protect him — McLoughlin had been exposed as a devious and
incompetent liar. In any other court at any other time his total loss of credibility would have been as clear as daylight and may have even resulted in
the judge stopping the trial. But Mr Justice Finnemore allowed the charade
to run its ruinous course.

After suggesting to McLoughlin that he did not know Devlin, had never
met him and that his evidence and his whole story was untrue, Heilbron
began her demolition job with a simple fact. He had stated to Neild that he
first met Devlin on the 28th July (despite stating the 27th at the lower court)
and was sure it was a Thursday. But when she pointed out that the 28th was
a Saturday, he simply replied that it must have been before then, adding. "I
know it was a Thursday."

"You know you are giving evidence on oath, do you not?" she asked. "You
realise the importance of being truthful?"

"Yes."

"Do you remember in the police court saying that that meeting was the
27th?" Becoming flustered, McLoughlin's sullen expression changed for the
first time when, glancing imploringly at Basil Neild, he replied,

I do not remember. You get mixed up with all these dates. They were firing
questions at you left and right. You don't know what you're doing half the time.

Assuring him she would not fire questions at him and would go slowly,
Heilbron, referring to his evidence at the committal, reminded him that he
had signed a deposition to the effect that it was the truth.

"And was it true?"

"Yes."

Then why, she wanted to know, did he say he had not seen Devlin until
a week after the first occasion and was now saying he met him, with Burns,
in the Continental Café the same night? Unable to give an explanation he
simply repeated that he met Devlin twice: on the Thursday morning and
the same night with Burns.

"Are we now agreed on that?" she asked.

"Yes." So, she asked, his evidence under oath at the magistrates court was
completely different from the evidence he was now giving? Adopting her legal
phraseology he mockingly replied, "Well, it must be different, must it not?"

Asked again if he was telling the truth on the earlier occasion, he replied,
"I do not know. I must have been mixed up with the dates, that's all." But
Heilbron would not let him off the hook, telling him it was difficult to get
confused between an interval of six days and the same day.

Again looking around the court for support, he said, "I don't see how
you expect me to remember all that when it was months ago." Reminding
him that it was his evidence which differed from itself, she asked if he could
really remember *anything* that happened?

"I can remember what I told you already," he replied.

"But you have told us two different things. Which is right?"

In an attempt to bale him out, the judge wrongly stated, "What he said
is that he cannot remember the dates."

McLoughlin of course had said much more than that. He had admitted
telling two different stories under oath in two different courts. But Heilbron,
seemingly intimidated by his Lordship, said, "Yes my Lord. I will not pin
him down to dates because it is a little difficult to remember dates so far
back." But Finnemore's satisfied expression quickly disappeared when the
shrewd QC said, "I will ask him about *occasions* instead."

Pressed on the discrepancy in his evidence, he could only offer that he must have got mixed up when they were mentioning dates and that he was, "Just a bit panicky when I was down at the other court."

Watching his pupil's performance from the well of the court, Balmer, although remaining outwardly calm, was now silently raging at this idiot! In another context, had he been a football manager on the sidelines watching such a disastrous performance from one of his players, his rage would doubtless have been expressed in foul and abusive four-letter expletives.

Asked how they would gain access, McLoughlin said, either through the back kitchen door or by slipping the latch on the window, after which they would, "grab the old woman". In later replies McLoughlin said he left the Continental at about midnight with Devlin and Burns and all three went down to the Pier Head to a coffee stall then to the Lighthouse Café. He at first said June Bury was not with them. But then he agreed that a girl was following them and finally agreed that it was June Bury. He left them, he said, because he was tired and "bevvied". But when Heilbron suggested his memory might be faulty because he was drunk, he quickly retorted, "I wasn't *that* drunk!"

Before splitting up, they agreed to do the job a fortnight later at the weekend. But unfortunately on the 17th August he was arrested for his auntie's robbery and couldn't keep the appointment. When Heilbron expressed curiosity as to why the job had been postponed for a fortnight. He replied that Devlin wanted to be seen around Manchester and not Liverpool pending the robbery. What possible advantage this could have been to Devlin — a man who was known to, and actually a fugitive from, the Manchester Police — he could not say.

During further questioning, McLoughlin made another departure from his earlier evidence. He now said that he broke into his auntie's house on two separate occasions.

The exchange began with Heilbron asking when he had broken into her house. He said it was a few days before his Thursday meeting with Devlin but could not remember which day. Funny, said Heilbron, that he had remembered so much detail about everything else but couldn't remember that date. After being pressed by defence counsel and the judge, he said he thought it was the 26th July. Seizing on this, she said "Do you mean a day or two days before you met Devlin?"

"Yes".

Suddenly realising his false story was crumbling beneath him, he said he had broken into his auntie's twice, then quickly added that he did not steal anything, "I only got into the house and come right out again." Then back-tracking once again, he said he *had* stolen "some stuff."

"I thought you said you took nothing," said Heilbron.

"I only took a flat iron and some other stuff."

Pressed further, he said he also robbed the cash in the gas meter and admitted that the first occasion was the main burglary. So why was he discussing robbing the same house with Devlin when he had already done it? He replied that he had left the latch off the window and on the second occasion only broke in to iron his suit.

As McLoughlin's evidence became increasingly absurd, Balmer remained tight-lipped but fuming inside.

When Heilbron suggested that when he looked over the back wall, if he did look over it, it was not with Devlin but either alone or with somebody else, he spontaneously replied, "Yes, with somebody else."

"And not with Devlin?" But quickly correcting himself, he said, "Yes, with Devlin." Asked what he saw, he remembered to mention the privets, which were of course on the police photographs. There was, he said, a light on in the living room but he couldn't see what was on the walls. The latter question was asked by Heilbron to explore the possibility of him having provided Marie Milne's description of the Rimmer living room. But she was not to know that Milne's accurate description had been obtained from crime scene photographs repeatedly shown to her by Balmer.

Once again Heilbron had McLoughlin on the ropes as she again exposed his lies in relation to Thursday 26th July. He said Devlin had spoken — *before* they visited 7 Cranborne Road — about the "old woman", the money she supposedly had and the involvement of a girl to distract her. Previously, however, he had said Devlin had mentioned the old woman and her money later when they were on the back wall. She not only quoted his committal court evidence but also the testimony he had earlier given to Basil Neild, when he had said the entire conversation took place with Devlin in the morning of the 26th July after which they agreed to meet that night in the

Continental. Ignoring her comments however, McLoughlin was now saying that dealing with the "old woman" and the part "the girl" would play were mentioned by *Burns* that Thursday *evening* in the Continental. Avoiding the truth of this, he irrelevantly repeated that *Devlin* was with him on the first occasion. But when Heilbron again reminded him he had first stated it was Devlin who had made all these comments, he replied, "I told you that because I knew what was going to happen already and I just thought you was writing it down." Telling him it didn't matter what *she* might be writing down, Heilbron reminded him he was giving evidence under oath to the jury and his Lordship.

Satisfied that both McLoughlin's integrity and veracity had been discredited, Heilbron summarised by stating he had sworn he and Devlin had "cased the joint" when it was going dark but was now saying it was on a dull morning. And further, that Devlin had made all these comments when they first met in Bill's Café but was now saying Burns made them at night in the Continental. Emphasising his unreliability for the jury's benefit, she then confidently concluded, "Therefore, what you said is wrong." But unexpectedly, he said, "No, it is right. It must be right."

"But it did not happen when you say it did? And he never said it?"

"He never said it. No."

If Heilbron had destroyed McLoughlin's credibility, exposing him as an unreliable witness at best and an outright liar at worst, then Sir Noel Goldie, for Burns, could not have done a better job, if he had intended, of restoring it, as McLoughlin, constantly out-witted him with sharp clear answers, often revealing counsel's eccentric manner and careless approach.

Wrongly assuming that because McLoughlin was a Liverpudlian he would have been absent from the Liverpool Kings Regiment, Goldie was immediately corrected by the witness who told him he had served in the Royal Army Ordnance Corps. That was the first of several exchanges which would show the poorly educated, streetwise 19-year-old as more mentally alert and quick-witted than this experienced Queens Counsel.

After McLoughlin had said he had been living rough before his arrest, Goldie superfluously asked, "Do you mean that night after night you were sleeping out?" He then suggested that, "one must have a certain amount of money to be going to these all night cafés", so where did McLoughlin get his from?

"By doing odd bits of deals," he replied, adding that he got some money off his father. To everyone's irritation, Goldie, oblivious of the evidence given so far, then commented, "I know nothing about these cafés in Liverpool. Are they open all night?"

Goldie had earlier spent the best part of half an hour laboriously going through McLoughlin's 40 previous convictions—most of which were as a juvenile—only to elicit that he had never been convicted of violence He then went over the witness' changed evidence about meeting Devlin which had already been thoroughly ventilated by Heilbron. These repetitive and pointless questions, accompanied by hopelessly irrelevant comments such as, "I hope I am not saying anything I ought not to: they are a pretty peculiar crowd in there, there are plenty of ladies in there of a kind, and girls, are there not?" and "Do the people who go to these cafés gradually get to know one another?" were answered succinctly with untutored directness by McLoughlin: "Yes they do. They are all crooks."

When Goldie made a similarly absurd comment—"A sort of thieves kitchen? All those people rather on the seamy side know one another. Did it not occur to you that it was a most dangerous thing to discuss with a stranger that you were going to break into your auntie's house?"—McLoughlin once again shot him down with a short answer which would have been obvious to a five-year-old child: "Not among crooks." Yet despite this logical reply, Goldie insisted, "But you never know who you might get in there?" People, he replied, just got talking to each other in the café, which drew another frivolous question obviously intended to be witty: "About what has won the 3.30 or what is the closing cricket score, even in the Continental where you say they are all crooks?" Growing more confident by the minute at this absurd questioning, McLoughlin once again corrected him, "He never came over to me in the Continental. It was in Bill's."

"Then in the other place then, Bill's Café?"

Bill's was of course a daytime transport café not frequented by crooks, of which Goldie was seemingly unaware.

To all intents and purposes it was game set and match for McLoughlin when the following exchange occurred:

"Are you really asking my Lord and the jury to accept that Burns, a total

stranger who had not been with you and Devlin on the earlier reconnaissance told you what they were going to do to the old lady at No 7 Cranborne
Road?"

"You seem to forget that Burns was on the run from borstal."

When Goldie asked yet again if he had told Devlin he was going to rob
his auntie's house, there were visible expressions of exasperation by the judge
and others in the court.

The two accused men in the dock may have been strangers to florid speech
and grammatical terms and unaware of where Goldie was going with this
line of questioning but wherever it was, to Burns it was taking an awfully
long time to get there as he whispered to Devlin, "Fucking bumbling idiot."
At this, Devlin, despite himself, began giggling, whereupon Burns playfully
elbowed him in his side, which appalled court onlookers at their apparent
irreverence for the gravity of the occasion.

Succinctness was certainly not one of Goldie's attributes. He seemed to
be more interested in displaying a sort of whimsical eccentricity rather than
getting to the heart of the matter and scoring points as effectively as possible. This approach would increasingly reveal him as rather lackadaisical
and seemingly more concerned with indulging in quaint, flowery oratorical
irrelevancies rather than following up Heilbron's concise, piercing cross-examination of Crown witnesses. Indeed, compared to Heilbron's directness
and lucidity, his conduct could well have been summarised by the Duke of
York in Shakespeare's Richard II, thus:

As in a theatre, the eyes of men,
After a well graced actor leaves the stage,
Are idly bent on him that enters next,
Thinking his prattle to be tedious.

CHAPTER FIFTEEN

THE CASE FOR THE CROWN

I am sorrier for your perjury than for my own peril.

Sir Thomas More to his accuser Richard Rich

When June Bury was called she walked gracefully, under Balmer's scrutiny, across the well of the court to the witness box. The straggly-haired, unkempt figure usually seen around Lime Street and the all-night cafés had been completely transformed under his direction. Wearing full make-up, a black Tam O' Shanter and a grey plaid loose-fitting coat and black silk scarf, she looked more like a respectable secretary. This sober image was complemented by her newly permed hair, new nylon stockings and high-heeled black shoes. But despite this outer air of sophistication, when junior Crown counsel, Mr Baucher rose to examine her, she could not hide her apprehension and inner nervousness.

Asked her occupation, she immediately began lying, saying she was currently working as a showgirl at Manchester's Belle Vue Amusement Park. Her second lie, which would be one of many, was that she spent a week with Devlin after meeting him in Manchester at Whitsuntide last May, when in fact they had only spent one night together. Her third lie was that when she moved to Liverpool she had not lived anywhere else but 39 Canning Street. In truth, she first lived for a few weeks in Mulgrave Street, Toxteth with a West Indian before moving in with Stanley Rubin.

Neild opened by asking for her account of what happened when Devlin called at Canning Street on August 2nd and took her to the Dive to meet Burns. Leaning across the dock rail Devlin was listening intently. This was it, he thought excitedly. June would now make good her promise to tell the truth made during the prison visit. But to his disappointment and anger, she began to tell a completely false story.

According to her they didn't go back to Manchester later that day but went to a café near Lime Street Station then later to the Rainbow, where they stayed until the early hours before going to the Continental and meeting McLoughlin. At this stage however, she began to depart from Balmer's script, stating that after the Continental, only she, Marie Milne and the two men went to the Pier Head. But unknown to her, McLoughlin, whom she said she only knew by sight until that night, had earlier testified that he had gone with them. Moreover he had not mentioned Milne being present!

Asked by Baucher if they went to the Rainbow that *day* then if she also went that *night*, an indication of her lying was that she answered, "Yes" to both questions. In further replies she said she stayed at the Continental with the two men till about 4 am. When asked if she met someone else whilst they were there (meaning McLoughlin) she replied, "Yes." A confident Baucher then asked, "What was *his* name?" to which she confusingly replied, "I did not meet any man."

"Did you not meet someone else there?"

"No."

With Balmer seething at her performance, Sir Noel Goldie objected that Crown counsel should not be allowed to press her because she had already given a definite answer. Both the judge and Crown counsel however, quietly ignored his objection. Baucher insisted, "Just think about it will you?" to which she replied, "I did not meet any man. I met Marie Milne. That is all."

Replying to the judge she said McLoughlin was already in the café when she entered with Devlin and Burns. But several minutes later, when asked if she had sat down at a table, she replied, "I was on my own at the time." Her inconsistent story prompted Baucher to *tell* rather than *ask* her, "You went there with Devlin and Burns. Did you sit at a table with them?"

Contradicting herself yet again she replied, "Yes." After which the judge asked, "Did you remain at the table with them all the time or did you move?" Suddenly remembering her lines, she replied that she sat with them. When she said she couldn't remember the two men talking, the judge again helped her by suggesting: "This is the first *day* you had met Burns' (Author's italics). You remember the occasion do you?"

Apart from him wrongly stating the day rather than the night, this prompting by Mr Justice Finnemore was quite wrong, for she would later admit under Rose Heilbron's cross-examination that she was *not* in the Continental with Devlin and Burns that night. Under further pressure, however, from Baucher, she then said that she could hear them talking about doing a job, *not anything in particular*, just a job in Liverpool. Yet, once again contradicting herself, when asked what kind of job, she said specifically it was a house and it was an old woman.

"Did they say anything about who lived at the house?"

"No."

But immediately after being asked by the judge the same question, she replied, "They said the old woman lived alone." It was now becoming quite obvious that she was a very reluctant witness and a very poor student of Balmer's.

In further replies, despite originally stating that no job in particular was mentioned, Bury, now back into her stride and under the combined questioning of both Crown counsel and the judge, further elaborated, stating the two men had said the old woman had got some money and said it was a house near a main road a few doors away from a back entry. Stating that she saw McLoughlin and the accused men in conversation, she then said that she didn't hear the conversation, which totally contradicted what she had previously said.

Leaving the Continental about 4 am, she said she, Milne, Devlin and Burns went down to the Pier Head. This was of course was completely different to McLoughlin's earlier testimony that he went with them and "a girl" (Bury) was following them.

Replying to the judge, Bury then recounted the journey to 39 Canning Street with the two accused and Marie Milne and the ensuing incident with Stanley Rubin. This had of course occurred. But she again lied, saying that on Saturday, the 4th August, they had come straight from the Lighthouse Café to Canning Street, omitting to mention first walking around town, going through Lewis's department store then over to New Brighton to look for digs.

After obtaining the room at Verulam Street later that day (August 4th), she stated that she didn't know which day it was but the following day all four went to Manchester. On the train Devlin and Burns were talking about the Liverpool job and wanted one of the girls to go on it with them. She refused but, when Milne was asked, she didn't know what answer she gave. Taken to a flat above a shop in Manchester, she said she and Milne went out and brought back some food. The two men then went out but they both stayed in the flat. Later that Sunday night they were taken to the station and put on the train back to Liverpool. The men said they would see them in Liverpool in two or three days. Responding to a question from the judge, she said that three days later (8th August) the men turned up at Verulam Street. She told them Marie had "floated" and she returned to Manchester with them that day.

At this stage the hopes of the Devlin and Burns, listening anxiously in the dock, were raised at this nugget of truth. Her reply clearly contradicted Milne's version at the committal, who had said Burns took her aside at the station telling her he would see her again on the 17th August. But her reply conveniently omitted the incident of herself, Hadikin and O'Rourke being arrested in the early hours of the 8th for the tobacconists shop break-in and having sex with a policeman at Cheapside before being released on bail. She also failed to mention that, on their return to Manchester the same night, she had accompanied them on the theft of the bale of sheets from the Liverpool Road Goods Depot.

After that night she never saw them again until 16th or 17th August, when they said they were going back to Liverpool on some important business. It was clear that, although giving false evidence because of Balmer's threats, Bury was nonetheless trying to limit the damage against the two men. Although she was not asked about her undisclosed statement of October 8th, she could for example have gone much further in her condemnation of Devlin and Burns had she repeated the following lies which she had been forced to sign in her statement of 8th October:

> Burns said he knew where a woman lived who had plenty of money hidden away in the house under a mattress. They said they would do it the back way. They spoke about the entry being near the main road. And while I was listening they chased me away. The next day (I think it was the next day) me and Ted and Alf and Marie went to Manchester. We were the only ones in the carriage. Alf Burns said to Ted, 'There's that job with the old woman.' Ted said, 'No good. It came unstuck once.' Alf said 'I think it's worth trying again. It's easy and the old woman has plenty of money.' He then said to me, 'We'll want someone to keep douse. What about

you, you're an old hand.' I said, 'No dice.' He then asked Marie... Alf said, 'It's an easy job to do and if the old woman makes trouble I can easily handle her.'[1]

But fortunately for the two accused, since that damaging statement had not been disclosed even to prosecuting counsel, she was spared any questioning on it.

Under Rose Heilbron's cross-examination Bury now agreed that she had only spent one night with Devlin at Whitsuntide in Manchester. Why then had she said they had spent a week together? Brushing this off, she said she must have been mistaken. This was to be the first of many "mistakes" uncovered during her time in the witness box. Bury said she came to Liverpool alone and first went to live in Canning Street, But when asked if she'd first lived in Mulgrave Street, she readily agreed.

"So," commented a sarcastic Heilbron, "you were *mistaken* again when you said you went straight to Canning Street?"

"Yes."

When it was suggested that Devlin first met her at Canning Sreet on the 2nd August, before she could answer Mr Justice Finnemore made another of his many interventions: "Do you know the date or not?"

"No."

She then confirmed that she had "no idea" what day it was. Yet in her 8th October statement she had specifically stated she first met Devlin in Liverpool on the 10th August. Again, fortunately for her, that statement, along with those of Milne and McLoughlin — which had also stated the 10th — had been suppressed. But knowing Rose Heilbron's forensically analytical skills, Balmer knew his witness was going to emerge from her cross-examination greatly damaged if not totally discredited.

Later, Heilbron tried to nail the lie about Bury going to the Continental with Devlin and Burns. Despite her undisclosed statement about the 10th, Bury agreed that on that first day, August 2nd, when she met up with Devlin and was introduced to Burns in the Dive, she was "positive" the three of them did not go back to Manchester. "I did *not* go back to Manchester," she emphatically stated. The three of them, she said, went for lunch to a café in Lime Street, then to the Rainbow then in the night time to the Continental.

---

1.   Merseyside Police files.

As if to emphasise for the jury's benefit, the judge once again intervened, asking her, "So far as you can remember did you go back (to Manchester) that day or not?"

"No," she repeated. When Heilbron asserted she *did* go back on that day with the two men and they stayed at a house in Stretford Road, the judge asked Bury, "Do you remember anything about that?"

"No."

Put to her by Heilbron that they came back in the early hours of Saturday morning the 4th and went to the Rainbow Café where she introduced Burns to Marie Milne, she replied, "Yes I did. I remember now."

Heilbron: "Then it is right. You *did* go to Manchester on that day, as I said?"

"Yes."

Bury had not only lied to defence counsel but also to the judge. But Mr Justice Finnemore apparently did not think this warranted one of his frequent interventions or admonishments!

Told by Heilbron that if she had gone to Manchester on August 2nd and stayed there that night, she could not have gone, as she had testified, that same night to the Continental or any other Liverpool café, Bury meekly replied that it was either that day or the day after. Once again the judge did not comment on this blatantly dishonest testimony.

The logical conclusion of Bury's gradual admissions clearly showed that there was no available night from the 2nd to the 8th August (the last time the accused were in Liverpool) when she could possibly have been with them and McLoughlin in the Continental. Yet, having clearly established this fact by her skilful cross-examination, Heilbron failed in her closing speech to sufficiently stress its importance to the jury. In relation however to the alleged comments in the Continental about the job and "the old woman", Heilbron — in order to impress it on the jury — reminded Bury that she had sworn at the committal court and again a few minutes ago that these were made the night Devlin and Burns had first arrived in Liverpool but she had now agreed she was in Manchester with them that night.

Quickly following up with a related question, she asked who had made the comments about the old woman who had plenty of money, to which Bury replied, "Burns I think." But, reminded Heilbron, she had sworn at the committal that it was McLoughlin. "Do you still say that McLoughlin made the conversation about the old woman?"

"I am not certain."

"Do you say that you went to the Continental *after* you returned from Manchester?"

"Yes."

"Then what you said today, that you went the same night, cannot be true?"

Agreeing with Heilbron, a thoroughly confused Bury admitted almost in a whisper, "We did not go the same night."

When Heilbron again tripped her up by observing that she could not, as she had testified, have been with Devlin and Burns in the Continental even late on the Friday night/Saturday morning of August 3rd and 4th, when she had already stated that was the night she had introduced the two men to Milne in the Rainbow, Bury finally admitted, "I do not know *what* day it was." Heilbron was slowly but surely exposing Bury as either a liar or an entirely incompetent witness, as almost every question was now answered with, "I don't know," "I can't be certain" or "I think."

In an attempt to rescue her from any further exposure, Basil Neild told the judge, "I don't think the witness is very well." But when Finnemore asked if she wanted to sit down, she replied with a mournful expression, "No, I am all right."

After several further questions about herself, Milne, Devlin and Burns leaving Rubin in Canning Street, going for lunch in a Chinese café then over to New Brighton before obtaining the room in Verulam Street and going to Manchester the next day, Heilbron asked Bury about the occasion when she and Milne were returning to Liverpool on the Sunday night. Bury said all four were together at the station when the two men said they would see them in Liverpool in two or three days' time. That reply differed from Milne's version, who would later testify that Burns had taken her to one side and said he would next see her on the 17th. Unfortunately, although Heilbron had Milne's deposition from the earlier hearing showing her conflicting version, she did not put this to Bury.

When the court resumed after the lunch adjournment the clerk of the court announced the cancellation of the rest of the day's proceedings due to the judge becoming ill. As had happened at the committal court, the trial on this second day was then postponed for almost a week to the 18th February.

In the large holding cell in the bowels of St Georges Hall, waiting to be transported back to Walton Prison, Devlin asked one of the prison officers how he thought the trial was going. "You'll get chucked, both of you," he confidently replied. "McLoughlin and that young whore are bloody-well lying through their teeth. It's as plain as a pikestaff." Heartened by this apparent support, Devlin innocently asked the officer, "What's a pikestaff?" But before he could reply Burns said, "Something I'm gonna fuckin' shove up the arses of those lying bastards when we get chucked."

CHAPTER SIXTEEN
MORE LIES

The Villainy you teach me I shall execute.

Shakespeare, The Merchant of Venice

At the resumption of the trial on the Monday morning of 18ᵗʰ February when June Bury was recalled to the witness box, Mr Justice Finnemore, said to Heilbron, "According to my note you were just reaching Sunday when she said they went to Manchester."

Heilbron then embarked on a series of questions to Bury regarding peripheral matters such as whether they had breakfast, whether Devlin and Burns went for a drink then came back to Verulam Street, whether all four had gone into town and then to Manchester. Readily agreeing with all of this and that a girl *had* approached Milne at Central Station, she then denied the girl had said Milne's parents were looking for her and were going to kill her. But the most important and contentious issue occurring that day, Sunday 5ᵗʰ August, was whether the two men, as they said, had gone into the Dive where they met Rubin (when he told Devlin Bury had VD). Bury agreed that they did, "go off for a drink." Heilbron hoped this reply would help to considerably dent Milne's and Rubin's subsequent evidence that that particular meeting took place on Saturday the 18ᵗʰ August.

To further illustrate the inconsistency of Bury's own evidence, Heilbron reminded her that, when the men did indeed return to Verulam Street three days later and took her back to Manchester, she had earlier said she did not tell them she had been out all night. Yet she was now saying she *had* told them. She was also exposed as a liar over the issue of the men's mackintoshes, when she admitted they had not, as she had told them, been sent to the cleaners (they had in fact been pawned by her mother).

When Heilbron pointed out that she had been untruthful and had even told Devlin during the January prison visit that she would tell the truth at the Assizes in January, the judge intervened once again saying: "She didn't say that." But Heilbron, who was not so easily intimidated as Goldie, told him, "Well I don't want to be misunderstood." Then to Bury, "Have you told someone that the evidence you gave before was untrue?"

Bury: "Only you." Finnemore, who seemed to be minimising Bury's obvious lying, said, "That was over the cleaning of the macs, was it?"

"No, my Lord. I am talking about the whole of her evidence in the police [committal] court." But the judge, determined to protect this lying witness, and much to the watching Balmer's delight, sternly told Heilbron, "She has not told you that. On the contrary she has said it is true *but with some qualifications…*" (Author's italics)

To some onlookers this was a most biased and even contradictory comment, "some qualifications" appearing to be a euphemism for lying.

Responding to Heilbron's further questions Bury agreed she had told Devlin that Marie Milne had asked her to back up her story and further agreed that she had told him she didn't know McLoughlin. When she admitted taking him 30 cigarettes, Heilbron did not ask where she, a girl on a weekly Public Assistance handout, was able to afford 30 cigarettes — especially since they were on ration. And Balmer was greatly relieved she hadn't!

Bury again lied about her employment. Stating that she had been working full time in Manchester from August 16th to Christmas 1951, it was later revealed that during October and November she was living, under Balmer's instructions, at the Morningside Girls Hostel in Upper Duke Street, near her old bedsit in Canning Street.

Quizzed about Kenneth McNeil, Bury's replies were similarly contradictory. Although stating she did not know McLoughlin, she admitted knowing McNeil for a long time. She went out with him, "once or twice last year when he came home from the merchant navy."[1] Although she said those occasions were before the murder, McNeill would later testify that he never went out with her until *after* the murder. Milne, she said, also knew McNeill and that Milne had spoken to him whilst in her company. This was another important admission elicited from her, for McNeill would later state that he did not know Milne.

Asked when she had first been seen by the police specifically in connection

---

1. It was stated in Merseyside Police files that Mc Neil was never in the merchant navy.

with the murder investigation she stated it was a week after she had started work on the 16th August. But that could not possibly have been true, since McLoughlin, who allegedly had mentioned her to Balmer, was not interviewed until the 20th September. And the Crown evidence was that she was first seen by the police in Manchester on October 4th. Yet this reply passed without comment by either defence counsel or the judge. Heilbron, however, reminded her that she had been seen by the police before then in relation to *herself*—presumably meaning the shop break-in with Hadikin and O'Rourke on the night of 7th/8th August. But raising her voice for the first time, Bury angrily retorted, "That has nothing to do with this case." Telling her that was a matter for the judge and the jury, Heilbron asked, "You have been in trouble before have you not?" to which she agreed. Whether Heilbron was fully aware or not of Bury's involvement in the tobacconist's robbery—which would have shown her as a willing accomplice—she did not pursue it any further.

That exchange ended Heilbron's cross-examination, which, to many people in court, had been a very competent demolition of this reluctant lying witness.

When the ultra-courteous, almost reverential Sir Noel Goldie rose to cross-examine, Bury must have been greatly relieved after her rough ride at the hands of Heilbron.

For the most part his opening was about matters which had already been aired and agreed by Bury. But his gentlemanly disarming demeanour—which often led witnesses into a false sense of security—could at times cloak a shrewd brain. This was most evident when, apparently in passing, he got Bury to admit that she and Milne had indeed met in Lawrence Road Police Station. And that it was the occasion when Marie Milne had said she had to back her up. This was despite Inspector Lees in later evidence denying this, and both he and Balmer at the subsequent inquiry insisting the two girls never met.

Goldie's cross-examination however would be marred by such superfluous prefaces as, "Just let me get this quite right." "Correct me if I am getting this wrong." And, "I don't wish to be unkind." This excessive civility and misplaced courtesy to hardened prosecution witnesses gave an impression of weakness and not being in command of his brief, which McLoughlin had already exploited and which Bury and Milne would likewise take advantage of.

In this vein his opening remark was, "Now Miss Bury, I do not for a moment wish to pry into your private affairs. You are a Manchester girl and your home is in Manchester?" Yet the question itself was totally unnecessary, that fact had been stated repeatedly both here and in the committal court. This was followed by similar time-wasting questions and statements such as, "Had she met Devlin in Manchester … not known Burns before being introduced to him", etc. In addition he asked her no less than three times in his brief cross-examination if she had ever met Burns before that occasion!

During Goldie's cross-examination the judge made a detrimental mis-interpretation of Bury's evidence. This occurred over the events of the 2nd August when, after being introduced in the Dive to Burns, she had travelled to Manchester with Burns and Devlin on the first occasion. When Goldie was taking her through her story he asked, "Correct me if I am getting this wrong but you said you stayed in the Dive till until (afternoon) closing time, then went to a café in Lime Street. You went to the Rainbow Café that night and early the next morning went on to the Continental. Is that right?"

"No."

"Where did you go after the Rainbow Café then?"

"That is the day they arrived and I went to Manchester with them."

Mr Justice Finnemore: "She went to Manchester and came back again. *That was in cross-examination*" (Author's italics). But the judge was quite wrong. Goldie had correctly quoted her evidence. It was only when Heilbron pressed her that she had "remembered" going to Manchester that day. But instead of sticking to his guns Goldie typically caved in, simply responding with, "Yes, that is quite right my Lord." The judge had deftly skipped Bury first telling Heilbron in "cross-examination" that she Devlin and Burns did *not* go to Manchester on that first occasion (August 2nd) but had gone to the Rainbow and the Continental where they had met McLoughlin and the conversation about robbing the "old woman" occurred.

All of Bury's lies and "mistakes," including her "amended" version of what happened on the 2nd of August—that she *did* go to Manchester with the accused men, stayed at Stretford Road, returned to Liverpool in the early hours of Saturday the 4th and went straight to the *Rainbow* where they met

Milne—showed beyond doubt the impossibility of her and the two men being in the Continental with McLoughlin. Moreover, notwithstanding her reply to Heilbron that, "It must have been the next night" when they all went to the Continental (Friday August 3rd), that also could not have been true because that was the night/early morning that all four left the Rainbow at 4 am for the Pier Head and the Lighthouse Café. And it certainly wasn't the Saturday night when, by her own admission, Burns and Milne were at Verulam Street and she and Devlin at the Mount Pleasant hotel. And of course all four were in Manchester on the Sunday.

The basic impossibility of Bury's story—exposed but not emphasised by Rose Heilbron—should have totally discredited *all* of her testimony. Yet, in his summing-up, Mr Justice Finnemore failed to point this out to the jury, which was exceptionally fortunate for Balmer. But that was why he had programmed in an alternative scenario, which did not include Bury. This was Milne's, tutored story about Burns taking her to one side when the two girls were leaving Manchester and telling her he would see her again on the 17th August. Apart from this story telescoping the long interval between the planning and the execution of the Rimmer robbery, as stated by McLoughlin, it also provided independent evidence against the two men regardless of what Bury might say or however much she slipped up. Moreover, it did not require Bury's or McLoughlin's corroboration, who were respectively in Manchester and Walton Prison on the 17th August.

This alternative version however, even in its own right, was extremely implausible, given that Burns did *not* wait till the 17th but returned three days later on 8th August with Devlin as they said they would and as Bury testified. Moreover, why would Burns make a private appointment with Milne for almost two weeks hence when he and Devlin intended to return in only three days time? It is not as if Bury would have been unwilling to "keep douse" at the Rimmer break-in, either alone or with Milne. She had after all, quite willingly kept watch for them on the night of August 8th during the Liverpool Road Goods Depot robbery when she had stolen their macs. Burns moreover had only paid one week's rent at Verulam Street. How could he be sure Milne would still be there on the 17th?

As Basil Neild rose to re-examine Bury, Burns, thoroughly fed up with the lies he had heard and desperately needing a smoke, passed a note to Goldie pretending he urgently wanted to urinate. Goldie then told the judge his client needed to leave the dock for a few moments. Down below in the cells, the same prison officer offered him a cigarette and lit up himself, saying he didn't blame him for making the excuse but that he had better use the toilet just in case.

On Burns return to the dock, Basil Neild, attempting to regain some ground for the prosecution, began by reminding Bury of what she had allegedly said about Milne asking her to back her up. He then asked, "Was it you or was it Milne who first made a statement to the police?"

"I did," she replied.

"And, in the magistrates' court did you give your evidence before Marie Milne or after?"

"Before."

These two questions were designed to refute the evidence about Milne asking her to "back her up". But what Neild nor the jury knew was that Bury had signed a written statement on 8th October the day *after* Milne's first signed statement of 7th October—which the latter elaborated upon in a second statement on the 9th October. The truth about the sequence of their statements therefore made Neild's second point about which of them gave evidence first at the committal court, immaterial and irrelevant.

As for Goldie asking Bury, why when she was asked on the train to take part in the robbery she didn't go home and never see the men again, Neild asked, "In fact when you were asked to take part in the robbery you said No, did you not?"

"Yes."

"And you did 'float' to use the language quoted, did you not?"

"Yes."

"And took no further part?"

"No."

As Bury left the witness box without even a glance at the two men in the dock, Balmer was moderately pleased, despite her many slip-ups, with her performance. But how much worse would she have come across to the jury if he hadn't arranged her makeover!

Passing each other in the well of the court June Bury and Marie Milne avoided making eye contact. It was as if one was ashamed of what she had just done and the other did not wish to be reminded of what she was about to do.

Milne's appearance in the witness box was in complete contrast to Bury's. Wearing flat-heeled shoes, a plain beige costume and devoid of any make-up or jewellery, this was the image Balmer wanted to convey to the jury — a very young working girl, hardly above school age, who, if sordid details about her did emerge during the trial, her appearance would help to dispel.

If the lying Bury had at times unwittingly helped the accused men or purposely tried to ameliorate her damaging false evidence, then her 17-year-old less vulnerable friend had no such compunction. Enthusiastically taking to the role assigned to her like a duck to water, Balmer's star witness was even prefacing her references to Devlin and Burns most professionally with the term "the accused".

The first part of Milne's evidence generally concurred with Bury's and the statements of the accused men. Balmer's script however soon took over — as it did at the committal — when it came to when they were leaving Manchester's Exchange Station at midnight on Sunday 5th August. It was then, she said, that Burns took her aside telling her he would next see her in Liverpool between 4 and 5 pm on the 17th. Since Balmer had realised that Burns would not have arranged to see her at Verulam Street after the week's rent had expired, her story was that he arranged to see her outside the Rialto Cinema at about 4.30 pm.

Although she said she accordingly met both Burns and Devlin on that day, Neild, in view of Bury's evidence, felt the need to emphasise this to the jury — thus retaining some credibility for her story. Milne then began to repeat almost verbatim her evidence given at the committal court in November. But now, after continued rehearsals by Balmer in the intervening months, she was almost word perfect.

At one stage there was a disgraceful episode where Neild was blatantly leading the witness, which neither the judge or defence counsel did anything to stop.

Neild: When he [Burns] said you were to keep the woman talking did he say anything else about whether you should go in or stay out?

Milne: Yes, he told me to try and get the woman to invite me into the house.

Neild: And if she did so?

Milne: I was to follow her so that I could get between her and the front door.

Neild: Did he say anything about the kitchen [rear living room]?

Milne: He said there were two mirrors there.

Neild: Did he say where they were?

Milne: Yes, one on top of the sideboard and one over the mantlepiece.

Neild: And did he say anything about the furniture?

Milne: He said she usually sat in the armchair.

These gravely damaging answers, as intended, neatly dovetailed with the police crime scene photographs where the living room mirrors and armchair could be clearly seen.

From the Rialto, said Milne, they went to the Golden Dragon then she took the men down to Central Station, where they asked her again to go on the job and she said no. But Devlin threatened, "To cut her up in little pieces" if she did not go. This dramatic phrase was too good for Neild to miss, as he repeated it for the jury's benefit: "When he threatened to cut you up in little pieces what did you do?"

"I said, 'All right. I will go.'"

Shortly afterwards, between Central Station and Lewis's department store, she said, they met a man named McNeil wearing a uniform, whom she did not know at the time. And after arranging to meet Devlin and Burns the following day at 3.30 outside Lewis's, she left them with him. At this juncture, at Neild's request and the judge's agreement, Kenneth McNeil was brought into court for Milne to identify him. Why this was necessary, as opposed to her identifying him on a normal identity parade, was not questioned by the defence. But it did produce a direct connection and tangibility to her testimony, which would hopefully make a deep impression on the jury.

Edward Devlin with Detective Sergeant Sturrock
following arrest (left) and Alfred Burns (right)

Alice Rimmer as a young woman

Thomas Rimmer climbing through
his mother's broken window at police
request (kept from the jury)
© Merseyside Police

The three "star" crown witnesses: June Bury, George McLouglin and Marie Milne

Rose Heilbron QC

Joseph Norton (Alfred Burns' solicitor)

Mr Justice Finnemore in his Boys Brigade uniform
© Birmingham Post

Mr Justice Finnemore at the opening of the Assizes
© Birmingham Post

Prosecuting solicitor Mr J R Bishop (far left) with the murder squad — left-right: DS Richardson, DI Lees, DS Balmer, DCI Morris, DI Farragher and DS Wade — following the committal hearing © Liverpool Echo

Basil Neild QC

Harry Livermore

Examining Magistrate CJS Gordon

Home Secretary David Maxwell Fyfe

The "Child" (Lord Goddard's description) 15-year-old Elizabeth Rooke being escorted into the Gerrard Inquiry by police Inspector Ivy Woods © Liverpool Echo

Mrs Rimmer's garden including the privet hedge shown to
George McLoughlin by DS Balmer © Merseyside Police

Mrs Alice Rimmer's rear living room at No.7 Cranborne Road with
the two mirrors shown to Marie Milne © Merseyside Police

Murder squad celebrating after the guilty verdict, left-right: DS Balmer, DI
Lees, DI Farrager, DCI Morris, DS Sturrock, DS Wade © Merseyside Police

The renamed Lighthouse Café, 1953

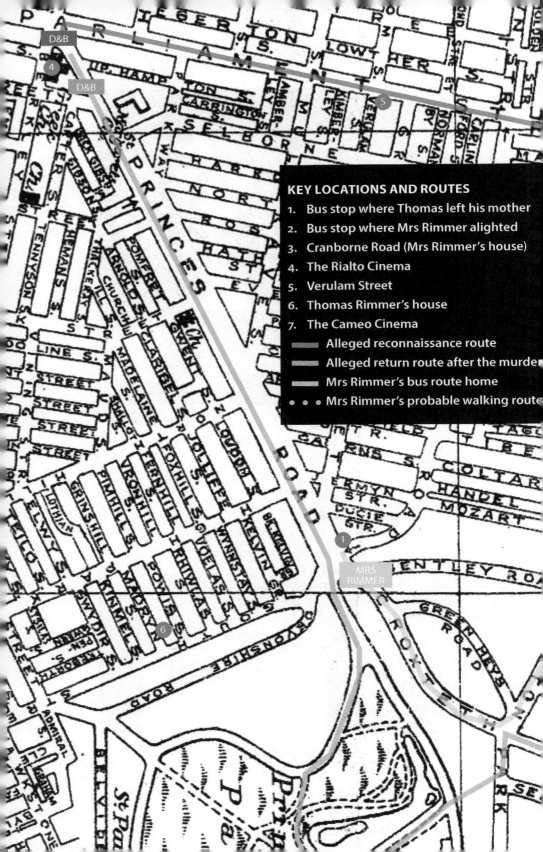

KEY LOCATIONS AND ROUTES

1. Bus stop where Thomas left his mother
2. Bus stop where Mrs Rimmer alighted
3. Cranborne Road (Mrs Rimmer's house)
4. The Rialto Cinema
5. Verulam Street
6. Thomas Rimmer's house
7. The Cameo Cinema

── Alleged reconnaissance route
── Alleged return route after the murder
── Mrs Rimmer's bus route home
••• Mrs Rimmer's probable walking route

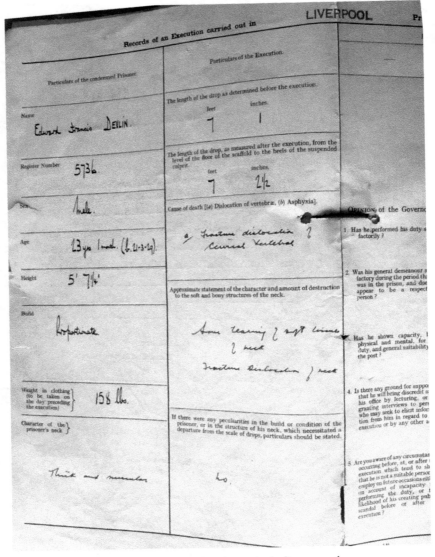

Devlin's Execution Report — including remark
about "tearing of soft tissue of neck"

CHAPTER SEVENTEEN

MARIE MILNE IN THE WITNESS BOX

I am satisfied Marie will make an excellent witness.

Detective Inspector William Lees

It was now the turn of Rose Heilbron KC. In the face of her rigorous cross-examination, Milne proved — as Inspector Lees had predicted — to be a very good witness, her attitude to defence counsel being one of non-cooperation and quiet hostility. Nonetheless, despite Finnemore's frequent interventions on her behalf, Heilbron was gradually exposing Milne's contradictions, if not outright lies, in her evidence. But her main armoury against Heilbron's forensically clinical questioning was, as instructed by Balmer, short answers and her own determination and sarcasm. It was only in the later stages that the edifice of her carefully constructed story began to crumble.

Asked her occupation, she said she was a waitress but was currently unemployed. Was she working between August and November last year, Heilbron wanted to know. Yes, she lied, she had been working at Butlins Holiday Camp.

"For that whole period?"

"Yes," she replied with a straight face!

The scripted lines came easily to the facile liar, for this was the period when she was staying out all night or at home being tutored by Balmer whilst her parents were being threatened, or at Lawrence Road Police Station making her false statements of 7th and 9th October. But since her prolonged tutelage was unknown to the defence and her statements had not been disclosed, Heilbron, bereft of any counter argument, had to accept her word.

In further replies Milne stated she had previously worked as a waitress at the Corn Exchange Café but had left on her pay day, Friday 3rd August. Yet despite being on her feet all day, she still had the stamina to have been in the Rainbow that night and the early hours of the following morning when

Devlin, Burns and Bury arrived with Bury!

Asked if Burns was the first man she had ever slept with, she replied, "He is the first white man I have been with," adding that the Saturday night at Verulam Street with Burns was the first time she had ever stayed out all night. This again was a lie. She had been out all night on several occasions, which was why the girl at Central Station had said her parents were looking for her and were going to kill her.

During an exchange about the meal in the Golden Dragon Milne said Devlin took out a red-handled knife to cut the sausages with and threatened to knife her. When Heilbron commented, "Is it not a complete fabrication — this story about a knife?" Basil Neild was immediately on his feet, objecting that it was a matter for the jury to decide. But when she explained she was not referring to all of Milne's evidence, just the issue of the knife, the judge intervened and told Neild she was entitled to ask a witness, "Is not that untrue?" Heilbron's gratitude however at Finnemore's first favourable intervention was short-lived, for he then admonished, "Fabrication is not the right way of putting it Miss Heilbron."

"Perhaps the word 'fabrication' is not a happy one my Lord," she said. "I am simply suggesting she was not there at all and that the knife story is not true."

The irony was, if the judge and Neild had known the truth they would have seen that "fabrication" was indeed the most appropriate description — but it was Balmer not Milne who was the weaver!

Despite being shown the evidence contained in her deposition, about the alleged knife threats, Milne still maintained she was threatened in the Golden Dragon. It was only when the judge pointed out that she had previously said it had been on the way to Central Station and asked, "Where do you say it happened?" she then replied, "I can remember now where it happened."

"Where," he asked, "in the café or on the way to the station?"

"It happened twice — in the café and on the way to the station."

Balmer, who was becoming worried, was nonetheless relieved to see how quick-witted his witness was. Not so Heilbron, who asked disparagingly, "Are you really seriously suggesting that? Are you really asking my Lord and the jury to believe that is the truth?" But convincingly hitting back with affected indignation, she declared, "I am asking them to believe me because

I am telling the truth and nothing but the truth." When Heilbron pointed out that even the judge had exposed her lies, she brazenly retorted, "I am going to stick to my evidence."

Asked if she had been threatened twice in such a short period why she hadn't gone to the police, she said she was too scared. When they met McNeil at Central Station she said she did not know him then and still did not know him. If Bury said she knew him, asked Heilbron, would that be untrue?

"What June has to say and what I have to say," she arrogantly replied, "are two different things altogether." To which Heilbron sardonically rejoined, "The jury have probably realised that by now." Even when she was told that Bury had testified she, McNeil and Milne had been together and that Milne had actually conversed with him, she insisted, "I still say I don't know McNeil and did not know him."

Moving on, there ensued an unnecessary trivial debate, instigated by the judge, as to whether Milne had earlier said they got the taxi at 1.30 on the Sunday afternoon or had said "After dinner". Wasting considerable time—even searching through the committal court depositions—he finally decided it didn't matter. But Heilbron, determined to expose Milne's lack of credibility, pursued the matter, finally getting her to agree that, once again, she had said something different to what she was now saying.

After the afternoon taxi ride, said Milne, and being shown Cranborne Road and arrangements made for her to meet them at 6 pm on the corner of Cranborne Road, they went to the Golden Dragon for a meal. Burns then gave her ten shillings and she went to the Forum Picture House on Lime Street. Leaving without seeing the full programme she turned up at 6 pm and waited till 7.30. But when they didn't show up, she jumped a tram down to the Rialto area, where she met them. Referring to her arrival at Cranborne Road, Heilbron asked, "Then it was just after six was it?" to which she dismissively replied, "Leave it like that." Somewhat taken aback, Heilbron said, "I don't want to leave it like that. I want to get your evidence." Undermining Heilbron's role, without censuring Milne, Finnemore asked the witness, "It was just before or just after six?" To which she replied, "Yes."

When Heilbron asked why she went back to the Rialto to meet two men who she was afraid of, Milne gave the same weak excuse she had given at the lower court: there was no other way to reach her home in Great George's Place.

"And just by coincidence you saw the two men there?" mocked Heilbron.

"Just by luck," she replied.

"It was bad luck for you, was it not?"

"It was very bad luck," replied the wise 17-year-old.

Asked if she was sure she was not referring to two *other* men, she replied, "I am sure."

Agreeing she was in this trouble "up to the hilt" she denied she was shifting the blame onto the men in the dock. "I am not shifting the blame onto the accused," she said, "I like them very much." Amid incredulous expressions and murmurs from the public gallery, Devlin whispered to Burns, "Funny fuckin' way of showing it!"

Devlin's comment aside, if it was true that she still liked the two men, then Heilbron missed the perfect opportunity to expose her to the jury either as a liar or a most amoral woman. Otherwise, why would she still "like very much" two men who threatened to cut her up in pieces and had battered a woman to death?

When Milne first said she was not annoyed at the two men for not turning up at six o'clock, then said she was annoyed, Heilbron asked, "You showed annoyance that they didn't turn up?"

"I think any girl would," she replied.

"Any girl would show annoyance?" asked an astonished Heilbron, "if a man had not turned up to do a robbery with her?"

"No, for a date with her."

But, she said she did not let them see she was annoyed.

"So these two men you were scared of," continued Heilbron, "who were going to cut you up into little bits, did not turn up? And you were *annoyed*? Did you not heave a sigh of relief?"

"Yes, I did."

But when reminded of what she had just said about them not turning up, she quickly added, "I was not annoyed in my own heart but I showed them I was annoyed." This admission was a typical example of her capacity for duplicity but whether the jury of 12 men noticed is doubtful.

Referring to the meeting after the murder, Heilbron said she supposed Milne was delighted when Burns said they would take her back to Manchester. No, she wasn't: "I was not delighted at all." Then, although the Crown had never alleged she was being detained against her will, she prejudicially added, "I thought they were not going to let me go home."

When reminded that the No. 26 bus to Great George's Place could be caught in Lodge Lane at the top of Smithdown Road without going near the Rialto, Milne said she did not know where Lodge Lane was. At this there was an audible collective sigh of disbelief from the public gallery. And, when Devlin and Burns in the dock turned to each other slowly shaking their heads, they were rebuked by the judge for "making gestures". Pressed further, Milne said, although she was born in Liverpool, she did not know it very well. She admitted the No 26/27 circular bus went past her house but she didn't know where the stop was. She also admitted she had visited the *Pavilion Theatre* on several occasions, which was opposite the bus stop in Lodge Lane.

Asked about keeping watch for the two men, Milne said she was told to wait on the corner of Cranborne Road for five minutes before knocking on the front door. In the event she said she waited from 9 pm to about 10.30. After that, she returned to the Rialto area, where once again she saw the two men standing on the corner. Earlier, Milne remained silent when Heilbron recounted even though the men did not know where she lived, she was so scared of them that she showed up for the meeting; that she knew they were going to do a job and that she did not go to the police for protection.

Moving to the pub conversation between Devlin and Rubin, Heilbron suggested that it really took place on Sunday 5th August before the four went to Manchester. Denying this, Milne said they had not seen Rubin on the 5th, adding, "I do not think the accused saw him then because they were with us."

"If June Bury says they went off for a drink on the 5th is that also untrue?" asked Heilbron.

"I do not know whether she is making a mistake or not."

Deciding on an attack from the flank, Heilbron asked her to assume they *did* go off for a drink on the 5th without her knowing about it and suggested they came back and told her about the conversation with Rubin, she unexpectedly replied, "Yes; that is right."

Staring at Milne in the witness box, Balmer was fearful she had made a horrible slip-up. But he need not have worried. For when a confident Heilbron followed up with, "And it happened not on the day you suggest it happened? Milne firmly replied, "No."

When counsel reverted to the question of the knife and embarked on a lengthy recitation of what she had told defence solicitor Norton in the lower court, Milne, aware she was going to be exposed as a liar, began tut-tutting, rolling her eyes and giving out small sighs of exasperation. This prompted Heilbron to tell her, "Do not look like that Miss Milne. I am afraid you have to answer my questions." In order to maintain the dignity of the court this was the proper function of the judge. But having previously rebuked the two accused for simply shaking their heads, he predictably failed to reprimand her.

Dealing with the final trip to Cranborne Road, Milne admitted she clearly knew what her role was to be, but she did not follow the instructions. She was reminded that—according to the Crown—she was only expected to wait for five minutes after the men had gone down the back entry to the Rimmer home, so why had she waited one and a half hours? "Because I was scared." she replied. "And then you went back to the Rialto" said Heilbron, "and by pure coincidence you say you saw these men again?"

"Yes, just by luck."

"And according to you they practically admitted committing a very, very grave crime but you nonetheless invited them to go to the South China Café?"

"Yes."

"You thought a cup of tea would make you feel better, did you?"

"No," she sullenly replied, "I did not think that."

Well said Heilbron, according to her evidence they were not as anxious to stay with her as she was with them, to which there was no reply. She then expressed doubt about Milne's assertion that the men had not complained about her not playing her agreed part in the crime , and that she had over-heard a very damaging conversation which the men did not want her to overhear. To these observations, Milne still remained mute. It was as if even she was realising just how unbelievable her story actually was.

When asked did she know McLoughlin and McNeil, she firmly said she did not. So, continued Heilbron, if McLoughlin said he had met her on occasion he would be wrong? "Yes."

Here again, the judge intervened, stating that McLoughlin had said he did not know Milne and had never spoken to her. But Heilbron reminded him that McLoughlin did in fact mention she was at the Continental. She would not however press the witness. But determined to side with the prosecution, Finnemore, repeated that McLoughlin did not know her. An equally determined, Heilbron then quoted McLoughlin's evidence:

Q: Did you know Marie Milne?

A: I had seen her but did not know her. She was one of the girls.

Q: Was she there that night?

A: I do not know, she could have been.

With a self satisfied Finnemore concluding that that was consistent with what Milne was now saying, Heilbron moved on.

When Milne said she was too scared to go to the police, Heilbron reminded her that when she was asked if she would "keep douse", on the train to Manchester with Bury and the accused men, she had no reason to be afraid of the police. Similarly, on the 17th when she was threatened with being knifed, she had not yet done anything wrong, so why be scared to go to the police? Milne agreed there was no reason.

Then came the matter of her telling Bury she had to back her story up. Denying any such thing, she said, "I did not see June Bury until after I had made my statement. We never talked about the statement at all." Asked if Bury was lying, she once again said she may have made a mistake. Milne's careful choice of words (for which she had been prepared by Balmer) was picked up by the judge, who once again attempting to torpedo Heilbron, asked, "She [Bury] did not say 'statement' did she Miss Heilbron?" "Yes, she did, during Goldie's cross-examination", said Heilbron.

Making once again a big issue of a matter which should have been readily accepted, Finnemore stated, "I have not got that. I have got, 'Marie Milne at some police station said I have to back her up'. Then Mr Neild asked in re-examination if June Bury had already made her statement."

But Heilbron — who was becoming increasingly irritated at his frequent interventions — corrected him: "My Lord," she said purposefully, "at the end of my learned friend's cross-examination Bury said, 'Marie said for me to give the same *statement* as she had given'." To which Finnemore finally conceded, "Yes, that is right at the end. I see now."

When Heilbron then suggested that Bury was speaking the truth, a defiant Milne still maintained her denial, declaring, "It is not right."

If the court had known the truth, it was a purely academic point anyway because Milne had made two statements: one before and one after Bury's statement.

At the conclusion of her cross-examination of Milne, Devlin's counsel managed to extract an important admission from her, which was that the two women had indeed met each other at Lawrence Road Police Station at the time they were making their statements. This was something the police had always denied in order to avoid the charge of collusion—which Balmer would continue to deny at the subsequent Gerrard Inquiry.

When Sir Noel Goldie rose to cross-examine, it was obvious he was so pre-occupied with giving a theatrical performance that he had lamentably failed to master his brief and was hopelessly out of his depth. Because of this fundamental failing, together with his undue deference towards the judge and the witness, he had unwittingly handed the psychological advantage to Milne from the very outset. One seasoned Liverpool lawyer described it as like watching a boxing match where the gentleman boxer was strictly adhering to the Queensbury Rules whilst being hopelessly outfought by a sharp, quick-witted street fighter with no regard for the rules. As a result, Goldie's cross-examination was in the main, farcical and disastrous for Burns. Indeed, at one stage Devlin, in an aside to Burns quietly remarked, "I told you it would be a fuckin' pantomime."

"Yeah," replied the other, "a pantomime of fuckin' lies."

Goldie's first question was to ask Milne if she was sure she wasn't mistaken. About precisely what he didn't say! Nonetheless, in negative mode, she automatically replied, "I'm quite sure." And when he prefaced his next question with, "Forgive me Miss Milne if I have got this wrong..." She instinctively sensed that, unlike the fearful Heilbron, he had no aura of authority about him and she was going to have an easy ride.

Reminding her of the accused men's alibi, and the evidence he would call to support it, Goldie said, if that was true, she would indeed be mistaken. But he was immediately censured by the judge telling him it wasn't right to put it like that to the witness. Goldie then dutifully begged the judge's pardon, adding, "We will pass on."

His next question, referring to June Bury, was, "I think you said she was one of the girls." But, fully aware of the pejorative meaning of the phrase, she quickly rebuffed him: "I didn't say 'one of the girls'. I said 'An ordinary girl like myself'".

When she disagreed she knew Bury quite well, he then asked her what sort of life she herself was leading and whether she was a regular habitué of the all-night cafés. If he was expecting her to agree, he received instead a predictable and very indignant, "No, I am not!" The night of August 3rd was the first time she had been in an all-night café, she said. Not content with leaving it at that however, Goldie then unnecessarily asked her again if it was the first time. This was an irritating repetitive and time wasting practice of Goldie's which would recur throughout his cross-examination of witnesses.

Moving on to when Burns obtained the room in Verulam Street, Goldie said, "Please do not think I want to ask you anything I need not but did I understand you to tell Miss Heilbron that was the first time you had ever been with a man?"

"Yes."

"With this man Burns? Or any man?"

"Yes."

He had obviously forgotten, or had not even heard, Milne earlier telling Heilbron that Burns was the first *white* man she had been with.

His next question — was the compartment door on the train open or shut? — had everyone in court puzzled, wondering what possible relevance this could have. Nonetheless, a bemused Milne replied that it was in fact closed.

Referring to the knife she was allegedly threatened with, Goldie wanted to know whether it was a boy scout's knife or a pocket one, to which she replied, "A nice tidy little thing like you sharpen pencils with." Putting words into her mouth, he suggested she must have been frightened, to which she readily agreed. "Let us get this quite clear," he said, "when a knife was produced and a man threatened you, did you not say to yourself, 'My word, this is going a bit too far'?" Since he was providing her answers, she again readily agreed!

"Why did you not say, 'Goodnight' and clear out?" he asked.

"I was still scared in case they came round looking for me."

Stating that she knew very well they did not know where she lived, Goldie then said, "Now let us come to the *next day*, that is the Sunday" (Author's italics). Again the judge had to intervene, asking him, "What about Saturday the 18th, *when she met them* at Lewis's?" (Author's italics). Quite implausibly, to save himself from embarrassment, he replied, "I left that to Miss Heilbron, my Lord."

Aside from Goldie's inexcusable omission of the very important events of the 18th, it was noticeable that when reminding him of "when she met them at Lewis's", Finnemore not only stated the wrong day but also failed to prefix his comment with "allegedly" or "she says" but instead stated it as if fact.

When Goldie erroneously stated that Milne's alleged conversation with Devlin outside the Dive about Bury's "disease" was on the 17th, she automatically agreed. But Rubin had stated in the lower court and would re-state later that it was definitely Saturday the 18th.

Replying to further questions, Milne said the only thing Burns mentioned on the train about the job was that it was "breaking-in." This was an opportunity for Goldie to once again exercise his colourful vocabulary: "Did you not say to Burns in ordinary everyday language, 'Look here, this sort of thing is a bit too hot for me'. What *did* you say?" An increasingly confident Milne replied, "I did not say anything." Like many of her other lies, Goldie was quite willing to let this one pass but the judge, apparently doing his job for him, said, "She went on to say they wanted her to keep douse." Minimising his own ineptitude, he commented, "I am much obliged my Lord. That was going to be my next question." Then addressing Milne, "Miss Heilbron has just reminded me that you said you didn't know what they were talking about on the train. Do you remember saying that?" Readily agreeing, Milne did not appear to be at all worried about the contradiction. Nor did the judge.

When Milne said she had been asked to keep douse in the Golden Dragon and not the train, the judge—who seconds before had intervened on her behalf—interposed again, this time addressing her directly: "You said it was *in the train before*," adding, "And you went on, 'I said No, and then I said I'd think about it'" (Author's italics).

Seemingly unembarrassed by the judge making his points for him, Goldie again minimised his helpful intervention with a passing acknowledgement of, "Yes my Lord." Then turning to Milne, and totally ignoring the judge's accurate observation, again absurdly asked the question she had already answered: "Did they say that to you in the Golden Dragon or in the train. Or, as I put it to you, not at all?" This was not a crucial issue, yet even these matters of limited importance, of which Goldie still should have been aware, the judge and Heilbron had had to remind him about. As for Milne: despite the judge directly reminding her from his notes of what she had actually said, she still insisted that it was said in the Golden Dragon. And he surprisingly allowed this clear contradiction of his own correct observation to pass without further comment.

Onlookers in court wondered whether it was ineptitude or plain laziness which was causing Goldie's embarrassing performance. But worse was to come, both regarding his misplaced civility to such an obviously un-cooperative witness and his own failure to maintain an accurate narrative. Several glaring examples of the latter were when he confidently, but wrongly, stated that, according to Milne, the knife episode in the Golden Dragon occurred on *Sunday the 7th August*. He had of course, got the wrong date and the wrong day. But following Balmer's instructions not to venture any more information than necessary, Milne simply replied, "No."

Undeterred, he then compounded the error: "I'm sorry Miss Milne, August 5th?"

At this the judge once again had to jog his memory, asking, "Is that right Sir Noel?" In the event it was Milne the liar (who could at least remember her lines) who contemptuously corrected him saying, "It was Friday the 17th."

A further gaffe occurred when he again confidently pronounced, "We all know where the Rialto is: on the corner of Windsor Street, Upper Parliament Street and Princes Street. That is right is it not?" But once again he was shot down by Milne who correctly replied, "No. Upper Parliament Street, Catherine Street, Princes Road and Berkeley Street."

As if the matter of whether the Sunday afternoon taxi ride was at 1.30 or "after dinner" had not earlier been thoroughly exhausted, the 70-years-old Goldie decided to cross-examine Milne again, taking up a great deal of time in the process and gaining nothing of any value to the defence. "What time did you get back to the Rialto?" he then asked. But once again she outscored him: "Not the Rialto. The Golden Dragon."

When Goldie asked what she was *doing* between 6 and 7-30 pm whilst waiting for the men to show up, her estimation of him had apparently sunk so low she did not even bother replying. And when asked the purpose of the meeting, she again avoided answering by dismissively reiterating, "I was supposed to see them at six and they didn't show up." Goldie apparently decided not press her further on what she was actually *doing* for the one and a half hours!

Further questioned, she said she got a bus back to the Rialto where she saw the two men. She did ask them why they hadn't shown up but, Burns just told her she should have stayed in the pictures, adding, "We don't want you any more."

The clearest indication yet that Goldie was out of his depth and had no idea of the Sunday timetable, was when he then asked, "Was that the occasion when he told you they had not done the job?" When Milne said it wasn't, he then reverted to superfluously quoting verbatim, the very words she had just quoted of Burns and the pictures, asking, "Is that right?"

If the following exchange is anything to go by, the court was becoming increasingly confused about the order of events. It was becoming a case of the blind leading the blind. Here is Goldie on Milne's movements after leaving Cranborne Road alone at 7.30:

"Accordingly, you went to tea and then you walked, did you not, to Upper Parliament Street?"

"Yes" (She had never previously stated this).

"Then according to you, you caught a No. 8 bus to Smithdown Road hospital?" (She had never previously mentioned a bus number. There was a No. 8 tram but no bus).

"Yes."

"And you got off there. When you reached the corner five minutes later you were told to wait five minutes to let them get in the back way. Is that right?" (This was in relation to the later alleged visit at 9 pm).

"Yes."

"And after you say you left them there—I am putting to you that it was not Devlin—you never saw them again until much later in the evening did you?" (She did not meet them at 6 pm. This is a combination of the 6 pm and 9 pm visits to Cranborne Road).

"No."

"Then again you had another long wait?"

She was then asked if she knew Hartington Road which was off Smith-down Road and led to Croxteth Road where access could be gained to both Sefton and Princes Parks?

"No."

Despite Milne not knowing any of the parks or routes, Goldie persisted, "Would there be *any* park at all through which men going from Smithdown Road to the Rialto would go unless they went out of their way?" With Milne repeating she did not know and the situation worsening by the minute, Burns instructing solicitor Joseph Norton, clearly frustrated at Goldie's dire performance, could be seen leaning over the lawyers benches whispering animatedly to Heilbron. If solicitors had then been allowed to appear as advocates in the higher courts, the intellectually meticulous Norton would undoubtedly have been much more effective than the hapless Goldie.

Whatever was said between Rose Heilbron and Norton, she decided to break the deadlock of Goldie's completely unproductive line of questioning. "My Lord," she said, "I wonder if I might clear up the answer which came up about four questions ago? I have got down when the witness was talking about boots: 'I could not see them, but they looked muddy.' It sounded nonsense my Lord." Obsessed apparently with the local geography, this was something Goldie had completely missed. But despite the matter ending "four questions ago", Goldie, once again blustering his way through, said, "I was going to deal with that." He then again asked the witness if it was really true that the men's boots were muddy. To which she again contradictorily said she couldn't see but they, "looked dirty-looking on top." Asked whether the men's conversation about losing the knife, and her asking them had they done the job, were also true, she again said it was.

Despite Milne already telling Crown counsel and Rose Heilbron what was said by the two men, Goldie asked, "Are you really telling my Lord that after Burns said they hadn't done the job, he said, 'To hell with the old lady, we shall be out of Liverpool before there is any trouble', or something like that?" To which she gave the obvious reply — "Yes."

Referring to the stains she said she saw on their clothing, Goldie asked if they might have been beer stains, despite her stating earlier that that was what Burns had said. Seemingly bored by now with his repetitive questions, she simply replied, "It might have been beer stains. I do not know."

Finally, after saying she left the men near her home in Great George Street and they just walked away towards town and did not run, Goldie instead of leaving it there, asked, "Did they walk straight along the main road or go darting down side streets?" Despite him foolishly putting ideas into this accomplished liar's head, she said she didn't watch them but just went home. But when he persisted in asking whether they were just walking unhurriedly, she spontaneously embellished her reply. Now they weren't just walking away anymore! "They were walking fast as if in a hurry." This senior Queens Counsel had virtually invited these most damaging words against his client who was on trial for his very life.

When Goldie, with a flourish of his gown, finally sat down and Basil Neild rose to re-examine, a disgusted Burns muttered to Devlin, "Our fuckin' budgie could've done a better job!" Milne, meanwhile, could be seen exhaling a deep sigh of relief.

During Neild's brief re-examination it seemed irrelevancy was contagious and had become the order of the day. Asking Milne the precise size of the red-handled knife Devlin had allegedly threatened her with, Milne, demonstrating with her hands, indicated it had become much bigger than she had earlier told Goldie! Agreeing she was scared of Devlin and Burns, she said that although they did not know her address they knew she always hung around the Rialto area and would have no difficulty in finding her. When Neild asked if she had seen either man between August 5th when she and Bury left Manchester, and August 17th when she again met the men in Liverpool she firmly replied, "No."

As Milne finally left the witness box Balmer had a little holiday in his heart. Against the bumbling Goldie, she had exceeded all of his expectations!

But again, if the defence had been in possession of her two statements of 7th and 9th October, not to mention Bury's of October 8th and McLoughlin's of the 9th October—all of which contradicted their testimony under oath—the trial would have ended there and then.

During the whole of McLoughlin's Bury's and Milne's detailed evidence it was never alleged by the prosecution that Burns or Devlin ever wore gloves or any protective hand covering—particularly on the night of the murder. Neither did the defence or the judge ask any of the witnesses if they did so. Similarly the important fact had not been addressed by anyone, that if Thomas Rimmer, as he had testified, had to break *more* glass in order to climb through the window, how did Devlin and Burns manage to get through before him? Given that the men's fingerprints were not found anywhere in the Rimmer home, it might have been more productive if Heilbron and Goldie had pursued these crucial issues rather than some of the more innocuous—and in Goldie's case—absolutely absurd matters.

After lunch on this second day of the trial, it was adjourned a second time because the judge had a heavy cold. It would not be resumed until the following Monday, the 18th, adding considerably to the weight of the Sword of Damocles hanging over the heads of Devlin and Burns for the past four months.

CHAPTER EIGHTEEN

MORE CROWN WITNESSES IN THE BOX

Monday February 18th.

A fuckin' pantomime of lies.

Alfred Burns

The next witness in the box on this the third day of the trial was wide boy Stanley Rubin, who gave his occupation as a "charge hand ship's scaler" and said he was working on the weekend of August 3rd and 4th. He was in fact an unemployed labourer and had been for some time. It always impressed a jury however to say you were gainfully employed, preferably with some rank—and nobody knew this better than Balmer!

Asked by junior Crown counsel Mr Baucher, Rubin—given his shaky memory at the committal hearing—was now able to unhesitatingly reply that it was on the 4th August that Bury had left Canning Street with Devlin and Burns. Yet later when wrong dates were put to him he also immediately agreed!

With some slight variations his evidence was essentially that which he gave at the lower court, coinciding with Bury's and Milne's testimony about the Canning Street incident. But when asked if he saw Devlin after the 4th, when he had walked away arm-in-arm with Bury, yes he had.

"About a fortnight later or just over."

"What day?"

Again, he knew exactly the day and the time: "Saturday in the Dive public house at about one o'clock."

What did he say to Devlin? "I said, 'I do not know how true it is but I was told June Bury has a disease'."

This sanitised version of what he had actually said wasn't lost on Devlin who, listening intently in the dock, said under his breath, "Fuckin' liar."

Under Heilbron's cross-examination however he first said he didn't know if it was true about Bury's disease, saying, "No, she could not have done." But pressed, he said she had told him she was going to the hospital with it."

"For treatment for that disease?"

"Yes."

The tone of Heilbron's next statement seemed to suggest to the jury that Rubin was in fact Bury's pimp. "I am just wondering", she said, "under what sort of arrangement you were living. You were able to go into this house and take over for the night. This young woman is not living with you but you visited her on four or five occasions. Was there an arrangement you could go and sleep there when you liked? You were a casual visitor were you?"

"Yes, a casual visitor."

Questioned further about his feelings towards Devlin, he repeated he held no animosity, said he wasn't even annoyed with him and denied he was "pretty sore" about it. But she reminded him of his evidence in the lower court when he had admitted he *was* pretty sore.

Continuing, Heilbron said Bury was the girl whose flat he could visit whenever he wanted and sleep there even when she was not there, a girl he had been on intimate terms with. "Are you really saying you did not feel at all aggrieved?"

"No."

Heilbron was insinuating that not only was Rubin's ego severely dented but also possible loss of income by losing Bury, which gave him even more reason to hate Devlin.

In addition to his many interventions in favour of the Crown, the judge had a habit of prompting their witnesses, telling them, "If you don't know, say so." By so doing it could be construed as putting words into the witnesses mouths—something the two defence solicitors had attacked the committal magistrate for doing. But neither Heilbron nor Goldie ever complained. The following sequence was a classic example of this. It was when Heilbron had almost shaken Rubin on his lie about the day he had seen Devlin and Burns in the Dive. Rightly assuming he had not seen them on the 18th, she framed her question as if it were a given; "When you saw Devlin the *next day* (August 5th), you had a conversation about June Bury's disease?" (Author's italics). Missing the implicit assumption, Rubin automatically answered, "Yes." But she now indulged in overkill as she had earlier when cross-examining Marie Milne on the same issue. He had already implicitly made an important admission which she would be able to capitalise on in her closing speech to the jury. But she could not resist clarifying his reply by expressly stating, "I am going to suggest that that conversation took place on the Sunday morning, the 5th," by which time he had regained his focus and said, "No." But even losing the momentum, she nonetheless ploughed on and still managed to show how uncertain he still was. "You are not very certain when that conversation took place are you?" she asked. And despite him emphatically stating it was not on the 5th, he replied, "No, I am not." When she had almost won the argument by adding, "And if Devlin said it was on the 5th you would not disagree with him?" the judge yet again intervened, asking him, "Would you?" Affecting confusion to give himself time to think, Rubin said, "I did not catch it." This gave Finnemore the opportunity to make things much clearer for the jury's benefit: "You say it was on the Saturday a fortnight later. It is suggested it was not then. It was really the day after—the 5th. What do you say it was, a fortnight later or the next day. Or do you not know?" When Rubin again said it was not the next day, Heilbron, now clutching at straws, asked if it was perhaps a few days later. But the moment had passed, he now firmly stated, "No, it was a fortnight later."

The judge, by commandeering the questioning, had rescued Rubin and helped him to become more certain! Despite this setback however Heilbron wasn't quite finished as she reminded him of what he'd said at the committal court. He admitted that when first seen by the police six weeks after the murder he could not remember the date of the Canning Street incident. So perhaps, she suggested, he equally might not be able to remember when he saw Devlin in the Dive? But he disagreed. Undeterred, she continued, "When you were asked about the date in the lower court, the reason you said you knew was because the [Festival of Britain] fireworks were taking place. Is that right?"

"On the Friday before. Yes."

Heilbron then told him that if she said the fireworks had in fact taken place not a week but a fortnight before, "that would shake your recollection a little, would it not?" When he nodded in response, she asked, "Does that mean "Yes"?"

"Yes."

This admission clearly indicated he wasn't sure. But surprisingly Heilbron did not press the issue further. And although getting a half hearted admission of uncertainty from Rubin, she failed to make the much more telling point that he had admitted at the lower court that the police had "helped" him to fix the date as the 18th.

Heilbron had actually been bluffing. In truth, there were three nights of fireworks displays on the River Mersey—Thursday 26th July, Wednesday August 8th and Friday 10th August. Rubin had been correct. Balmer, his tutor, had at least done his homework!

Sir Noel Goldie's cross-examination of Rubin lasted a mere four minutes, predictably covering old ground already agreed by all the parties and producing nothing of any value to either his client or Devlin.

The next witness was Kenneth McNeil. Entering the witness box dressed in a smart suit, shirt and tie, the 21 year-old was unrecognisable as the itinerant scruffy part-time table-clearer and hanger-on at the Continental Café. He had been kept under wraps by Balmer since the committal, at Birmingham's Grand Hotel, where he had been provided with a kitchen porter's job and accommodation in the Salvation Army Hostel. A few days before the trial started, a message was sent to the Birmingham Police asking them to tell McNeil to "be warned" by Superintendent Balmer to come to Liverpool's Dale Street main bridewell on the 10th February to be interviewed before the trial commenced the following day[1] (due to the judge's indisposition it was actually postponed until Tuesday the 12th)

To "be warned" was a legal phrase used by High Court staff compiling the court calendar, which Balmer had appropriated for himself. But McNeil being putty in his hands, kept the appointment at which he was further tutored about the false evidence he was to give.

Lying that he was currently unemployed, he agreed with Basil Neild that at the time of these events he had been a steward in the merchant navy. That was also a lie—the second of many uttered during his testimony. Although Balmer of course knew he was lying, it is doubtful if Neild did so.[2]

When asked if he recalled meeting anyone in the Continental Café in the

---

1. Merseyside Police files.
2. Internal report. Merseyside Police files.

early part of August, it was clear he was going to be very careful about his answers in order not to make any slip-ups.

"What would you call early?" he asked.

"The 1st, 2nd, 3rd or 4th of August."

"Not in the early days, No."

All he would concede was that it was in August, when he met Devlin, Burns and June Bury. But when asked how often he had met them, he said he hadn't actually met them but just saw them there. Repeating his committal court evidence, he said he also met the two men outside Lewis's on the 17th August and was introduced to Marie Milne, who then left them. Asked if he was a porter in Lewis's cafeteria, no he wasn't, he was employed all over the department store. But he agreed he had seen the accused men on two occasions in the cafeteria. Asked when he last saw them, he said it was about 7.30 on the 18th and that it was a Friday. This was his first slip up when Neild had to remind him that Friday was the 17th. But he was not asked why he just happened to be standing outside his place of work at 7.30pm, two hours after the store had closed!

When he said he knew the two girls as Milne and Bury, at Neild's request he identified them sitting in the court. Asked how he was dressed when he met the accused men on the 17th, he said, "A merchant navy *uniform*, without a cap" (Author's italics). Whether Neild or anyone else knew it, even if McNeil *had* served in the merchant navy, ship's stewards were not officers and thus did not have, and were not entitled to wear uniform—even ashore.

Continuing, McNeil said that after Milne left them outside Lewis's on the Friday, he went with Devlin and Burns to "Dick Tracey's pub in Hanover Street", stayed there till 10 pm then went to milk bars in Church Street and Lime Street till about 10.30/10.45. Departing from his committal evidence, he then added that all three went to the *Continental*, with him leaving the two men at 1 am.

When being primed by Balmer and told to say he had gone with Devlin and Burns to a pub, the detective had only mentioned the word "Tracey's" which the Empire public house was informally known as after its landlord, Harry Tracey. Not knowing this however, McNeil had wrongly assumed it was named after the comic book detective, Dick Tracy. If he had actually been there, either with Devlin or Burns or on previous occasions, he would have known this. But since judge and counsel were unaware of the nicknames of Liverpool pubs, he was allowed to get away with this minor piece of fiction.

Replying to Neild, when McNeil said he picked out two innocent men at the ID parade because he didn't want to get mixed up in the trial. Sir Noel Goldie objected, saying he was not entitled to give reasons why he picked out the wrong men. It was vital to the defence that he had picked out other men. And, "I submit you cannot go on to say, 'Why did you make the mistake you made?'"

Telling Neild the question could be put in a slightly different form, the judge helpfully suggested, "The proper question to put might be, 'Did you recognise these two men on the parade?'" When Neild, following the judge's advice, asked McNeil this, he replied that he had picked out two different men.

"We know that," said the judge", But did you see these two men who are in the dock?" Saying he did so, he agreed he still picked out two strangers.

Rose Heilbron began her cross-examination by suggesting to McNeil that he did not see the accused men either in Lewis's or at Central Station and the Continental on the 17th August. She then dealt in detail with the ID parades, in order to emphasise to the jury that McNeil's conduct could have resulted in two blameless men being charged with murder. When she suggested therefore that McNeil could not expect the jury to put much reliance on his evidence, Neild objected to her putting that type of question. The judge agreed, telling her it was not for McNeil to answer. Ignoring the reprimand, she asked McNeil when he was first seen by the police, to which he replied early August then apologised saying he thought it was October. Seizing on this, she suggested his memory wasn't very good, to which he did not reply.

Later, Heilbron asked how long he had known Devlin and Burns and he replied about seven months She then questioned him at length about the various jobs he had had which were all for short periods, the last being at Lewis's until the 21st August when he left the job and left Liverpool. After some prevarication by McNeil, he finally remembered that immediately before the Lewis's job he had worked, as a labourer for the Pier Head Company for five days but could not remember which day he left *that* job. By contrasting his clear memory of the Lewis's employment with his vagueness about a job immediately preceding it, Heilbron was clearly hinting at collusion.

Denying he had got the dates wrong in the lower court, he agreed when the judge reminded him he had said he started at Lewis's on the 15th instead of the 16th. But when Heilbron, again hinting at colluded revision of his evidence, asked, "You have learned since then when you actually started?" he indignantly replied, "I have not learned since then."

McNeil said he did not eat in Lewis's cafeteria or the staff canteen, he usually went to the Lime Street Milk Bar at lunchtime. But when Heilbron put to him that he had earlier said, "I used the canteen", he said there was a staff canteen and a cafeteria for customers, adding that he worked in the canteen. Apart from this last remark contradicting what he had earlier told Basil Neild, i.e. "I worked all over the store," he was evading Heilbron's question. "That may well be," she said, but reminded him he had just said he never ate in the canteen and now he said he did. She wanted an explanation. He now said that he *had* used the canteen but *generally* went over to the milk bar. Yet by her persistence in asking him if he had eaten in the staff canteen, she was hoist by her own petard when he agreed he had also eaten in the cafeteria—the very location he said he had seen Devlin and Burns! This of course did not alter the fact he was lying: manual workers in Lewis's such as porters, drivers, etc. were prohibited from dining in the customers basement cafeteria.

Continuing, Heilbron suggested that if he did see the accused in the cafeteria it was before the 16th of August, but he was adamant that it was during the five days he worked there. Reminded that in his evidence at the committal court he had not mentioned going from the milk bar with Devlin and Burns to the Continental, he insisted that he had and that the deposition must be wrong. When she asked if perhaps the deposition was a mistake, the judge, once again coming to the rescue of a Crown witness, said McNeil had said in the depositions that he was with the men until about 1 am. But Heilbron insisted that he had not mentioned the Continental. Not as obsequious as Goldie, she nonetheless trod carefully and conceded there may have been a mistake, that it was not a very big point and that she would move on.

Asked about his relationship with June Bury, McNeil denied he was "quite friendly" with her and had ever been out with her. But when told about Bury's evidence, he agreed he *had* been out with her but only since the court case began. He also denied knowing Marie Milne, saying the first time he met

her was on the 17th August outside Lewis's with Devlin and Burns. When
Heilbron suggested that was untrue and that he knew Milne previously, he
replied, "I say that is wrong." And, Heilbron went on, he had met her in
company with June Bury. Not knowing what Heilbron had up her sleeve,
he then admitted he had *seen* her but had never spoken to her. So how did
he know it was Milne if he had never spoken to her, she wanted to know.
When he said he saw her photograph in the newspaper when she was leaving the court, Heilbron reminded him she was referring to August 17th, long
before Milne was ever in the newspapers. But again he had a ready answer:
"I did not know it was Marie Milne at that time."

Suggesting he had seen both Marie Milne and June Bury at the police
station before the identification parade, he agreed with Heilbron but denied
he had *spoken* to them. Replying to the judge, he said police officers were
present but the girls were not together when he had spoken to them. He
also denied he had said to Milne at the station, "Oh I have seen you before.
I have known you for some time."

The truth was that McNeil and Milne—both habitués of the Continental—had known each other for several months before the murder. That is
how and why—apart from the other pressures on them—Balmer was able
to invent and synchronise their false stories to result in the supposed meeting
outside Lewis's with Devlin and Burns on the 17th August—which of course
provided independent corroboration for "accomplice" Milne's evidence.

Reverting to June Bury, Heilbron asked if McNeil was sure he had never
been out with her? Forgetting his earlier admission, he replied, "I am positive
I have not." But surprisingly, Heilbron did not exploit this clear contradiction.

There then followed a curious exchange which demonstrated that if
McNeil was not genuinely confused, he was a very poor liar:

Heilbron: "Is this not right? June Bury has said in evidence, 'I went out
with him when he came home on leave last year'?"

"I was not even in the forces last year so it is an impossibility."

"When were you in the forces?"

"I was in the forces in 1949."

"Were you in the merchant navy?"

"I was."

"Were you home on leave from the merchant navy?"

"I never came home on leave from the merchant navy. I was in the army at the time."

When a confused Heilbron said she didn't follow, his explanation became even more abstruse. Asked if he was "serving in 1950?" he said, "I was an absentee from the army and I joined the merchant navy abroad."

When was that, she wanted to know.

"That was in 1947." Realising she was losing her grip through McNeil's increasingly confusing replies, Heilbron said, "We are going back rather a long time. Can you get nearer to last year, 1951?" Yet despite their exchanges becoming more confusing, she herself then went back, asking him if he was abroad between 1947 and 1951, to which he again confusingly replied, "1947 and 1949 I was abroad, yes." Although this was still not a proper answer to her question, Heilbron did not help the situation by now asking him to come nearer to 1950, to which he replied "I was not in the forces in 1950."

"Were you ever in the merchant navy?" she again asked. Agreeing he was, he again stated he never came home on leave when he was in the merchant navy.

"Were you in the merchant navy in 1951?"

"No."

"What were you doing in 1951?"

"I was a civilian."

It had taken Heilbron this long tortuous and confusing route to get absolutely nowhere with this surprisingly clever and devious witness. As with the other Crown witnesses, Balmer had instructed him not to offer any gratuitous comments or exposition but to keep his replies short and sweet. The truth of the matter however was that although McNeil had never been in the British merchant navy, he had done one or two trips on a Norwegian ship—for which one had minimal employment protection and did not require a Seaman's Book or any training. The Norwegian "pool" recruited mostly those British seamen who could not get a British ship, through either bad reports or for "backing out" in foreign ports.

After further questioning, McNeil repeated his admission of only going out with June Bury in January 1952. With a disdainful expression Heilbron sarcastically asked, "You have suddenly become friendly with her and been out with her?" He had only taken her to the pictures, he said, to the *Majestic*

Cinema, on or about the 20th of January. "That is a bit of a difference," said Heilbron. "Are you really saying that that is true and that you never took her out at all in 1951?"

"Yes."

Not too worried about the ineffectual Goldie's imminent cross-examination, Balmer was very pleased with McNeil's performance so far. He had considerably exceeded the superintendent's modest expectations and had come through Heilbron's inquisition almost unscathed. Later to a colleague, he scored the verbal contest between Heilbron and his protégé, a draw!

Sir Noel Goldie's questioning consisted mainly of going into detail about the mechanics and sequence of the identity parades, asking, for example, if there were two separate parades when it had previously been fully explained that Devlin and Burns had appeared separately! The most significant aspect was when McNeil repeated he had picked out the wrong men because he didn't want to be involved in the case and the judge once more sided with a prosecution witness during the following exchange:

> **Goldie:** In other words, what you did in a murder case, was you deliberately said to the police (on each parade), 'That is the man', knowing perfectly well that the man had nothing to do with it?

Although McNeil unequivocally replied, "That is quite correct." the judge interjected, "No Sir Noel. He was not asked to pick out a murderer. He was asked if he recognised one man or two men he met at Central Station" (Lewis's). But Goldie, who had been misquoted, was quite right for once and stood his ground, telling Finnemore, "I am sorry my Lord. I thought I had carefully prefaced my question by saying: 'Were you informed it was an *enquiry into* murder?'" Then turning to the witness he asked, "Is this right. You said at the lower court 'I knew this case related to a murder charge. I was asked to identify two men in connection with this murder charge'?"

> **McNeil:** That is quite correct.

Correctly challenged, for a change, Mr Justice Finnemore was silent. Reiterating his committal court evidence, the Lewis's staff manager,

Frederick Richardson confirmed that McNeil had indeed been casually employed as a porter between the 16th and 21st August, when he suddenly left. Nobody asked Richardson why he had suddenly left. Or why he had left two days after the murder of Mrs Rimmer.

Next in the witness box was the middle-aged taxi driver Thomas Emery—arguably the only honest prosecution witness. Repeating his lower court evidence, he stated he could not recognise the two men with Milne on Sunday 19th August. His only value to Balmer was the telling incident of being given 2s.6d for the fare when it was only two shillings. Regardless of the fact—unknown to the court—that he had told the police this *before* Milne's 9th October statement, it nicely confirmed her testimony, giving it a degree of restored credibility in the minds of the jury.

Asked by Heilbron about Marie Milne, he said he knew her quite well as someone always hanging around the Rialto taxi rank. He had taken her several times to Great George Street and Verulam Street last year, mostly in the afternoon between three and four pm. Then, in a departure from his committal evidence there was no equivocation about the passengers' true destination. It was now admitted by Emery and accepted by the court that the three passengers were dropped off on Sunday the 19th August at Sefton General, informally known as Smithdown Road Hospital. This admission didn't unduly worry Balmer, who reckoned that after six months, even if the defence did make enquiries, memories would be so vague that nobody at the hospital would remember Milne and the two men or who they had been visiting.

Asked if he had any idea who the two men were, Emery replied, "I haven't the slightest." Agreeing with Heilbron that Sunday was visiting day, he added he was very busy taking fares to and from the hospital. When she therefore suggested he could not be sure it was Sunday the 19th, he conceded, "To tell the truth I would not be sure." And when she said, "I think actually the date was suggested to you by the police?" he readily agreed that was true.

When Heilbron suggested he could have been mistaken about Milne, he volunteered that the police had shown him Milne's photograph. In any case he couldn't have been mistaken: "Not about Marie", he said. "I knew her. She used to pass up and down Berkeley Street in the mornings and evenings and pass the time of day with us on the rank."

"Was she there often?" asked Heilbron. "Very often." he replied.

"Just hanging around there?"

"Yes. She used to go in the Man Yow Café in Berkley Street."

Despite Emery's ostensible certainty, both he and Rubin had now openly admitted the police had suggested crucially specific dates to them. As for Emery being shown Milne's photograph, what the defence still did not know was that McLoughlin, before he had identified Devlin and Burns, had also been shown their photographs.

CHAPTER NINETEEN

THOMAS RIMMER'S VERSION

Tuesday 19th February 1951. ?

Thomas Rimmer could not have killed his mother.

Detective Inspector William Lees

On this fourth day of the trial, Mrs Rimmer's son Thomas, was the first into the witness box. The former policeman's evidence-in-chief was given in a clear, crisp authoritative manner. Shown crime scene photographs of his mother's body lying in the blood-splattered hallway, he answered Basil Neild's questions without showing any emotion. But when Rose Heilbron rose to cross-examine, despite the sympathetic atmosphere surrounding him she was not prepared to routinely take on trust everything he said—even though she did not know about him being interrogated as the first suspect or Sydney Fairbrother's statement to the police!

Replying to her about arriving at his mother's house on the Monday evening, he said he had tried the backyard door but found it locked. Given that he must have tried the handle to know it was locked, that reply was more definite than that given during his police interrogation on August 20th when he said he wasn't sure—of which she was also unaware. After this length of time there would now of course be no fingerprints to prove or disprove his assertion.

Stating he then "tried" the back kitchen door and assumed it was locked, he now agreed that it wasn't locked. And although, he said he had to knock more glass out of the broken window to gain access, he nonetheless asserted it would previously have been large enough for someone smaller to climb through. But pressed on this he admitted it would have been very difficult and there would be a great risk of cutting oneself. Unaware however of the forensic reports that nobody had climbed through the window, Heilbron was unable to ask him why *he* did not cut himself or leave any fingerprints or fibres after climbing through.

In later replies Rimmer said he, "saw his mother to the bus stop" but did not say he saw her onto the bus. Indeed the following witness, bus conducter, Henry Bentley, would testify that *he* helped her onto the bus and that she was unaccompanied. A convoluted exchange then developed between Heilbron and Rimmer about the times and distances involved, during which he seemed to be disingenuously obfuscating the issue. Replying to Crown counsel earlier he had said it would take between ten and 15 minutes to walk from the bus stop at the corner of Granby Street and Princes Avenue to Cranborne Road. But when Heilbron queried this, reminding him of the distance involved, he said he meant by getting a bus part of the way to the *Pavilion* in Lodge Lane. When it was agreed that his ten minutes journey time involved getting off the bus then walking down Smithdown Road to his mother's home, Heilbron — reminding him that his mother was older and would have been slower than him — said, "That's cutting it a bit fine isn't it?" to which he reluctantly agreed but added that the walk was downhill to Cranborne Road. Given that he had taken his mother to the bus stop, near Princes Park gates, wheeling his bicycle, and travelled to her home the following night by the same means, he was not asked how long it would take him to *cycle* from there to Cranborne Road.

To further questions he stated that his mother visited him every Sunday at about the same time and had only missed doing so about four or five times in the last six months. But Heilbron was not aware of his wife's statement contradicting this. A vital question however, which was not asked, would have been why he had felt compelled to visit his mother so soon after spending time with her the previous day and night?

Goldie's cross-examination of Rimmer — conducted in his by now familiar eccentric manner and picturesque language — was predictably quite brief, most of his questions being either irrelevant or meaningless. The next witness, bus conductor Henry Bentley's appearance was also brief, centring mainly around the times his bus would take to get from Princes Park gates bus stop to the *Pavilion* where Mrs Rimmer had alighted. Replying to Rose Heilbron, he first stated that there was somebody at the stop with Mrs Rimmer. Unfortunately he was not asked whether it was a male or female nor to describe this person. But he did say she was alone. Asked again, he repeated she was not accompanied by anyone and that he had helped her onto the bus. Goldie's threadbare cross-examination consisted of suggesting to the bus conductor that the shortest *walking* route from the Park gates to the Pavilion bus stop would be up Bentley Road then along Lodge Lane. Given that Bentley was the guard of a *driven* vehicle who lived miles away in the Low Hill district, his valueless reply was, "I presume so."

When Constables Evans and Wright were called they simply reiterated their evidence in the committal court about being first on the scene after responding to Grossman's 999 call. They had both made written statements describing Thomas Rimmer's demeanour and attitude, how surprised they were at how calm he appeared and that they had found it quite easy to open the back kitchen door which he had said was locked. Unfortunately these statements had also not been disclosed to the defence so cross-examination would be limited. But unaware as she was of the officer's statements and Inspector Reade's report on the broken window, it was nevertheless clear Heilbron had not been convinced by Rimmer's story. An indication of this was to ask Constable Wright if the catch on the inside of the window was on or off? When he replied that it was screwed down, she asked if it was screwed firmly? The clear implication was, if it was able to be opened why would Rimmer, or indeed Devlin and Burns, have had cause to break the window?

Heilbron had no questions for the next witness, Mrs Rimmer's next-door neighbour Jack Grossman. The only value to be derived from his evidence was in a series of replies to Sir Noel Goldie—albeit asked in that counsel's own peculiar fashion.

"Were you at home on the evening of the previous day—on the Sunday. Can you remember?"

"I arrived home at 20 minutes to ten on Sunday night."

"Now can you help us with this? Did you hear a disturbance at all in the next house?"

"In my house do you mean?

"No, in the house next door."

"No."

"You did not hear the sound of breaking glass or anything?"

"No. I had the wireless on."

"I must not ask you whether it is a well-built house or not. About what time did you go to bed? Do you remember?"

"About ten past eleven."

"And from 20 to ten you did not hear any disturbance next door?"

"No, I cannot say I did."

Notwithstanding Grossman having the wireless on, neither he nor his daughter—who was, according to her undisclosed statement, upstairs in her bedroom *not* listening to the wireless—had ever indicated, even in their statements, that they heard any disturbance. This would tend to suggest that the window was not smashed on the night of August 19th. Did it support the theory that Mrs Rimmer knew her killer? And that it was perhaps smashed *after* her murder? Was Goldie, like Heilbron earlier, also implicitly casting doubt on Thomas Rimmer's evidence?

When pathologist Dr George Manning took the oath, he verified that he had carried out the post-mortem on Mrs Rimmer, enumerating the wounds she had suffered and repeating his evidence given in the lower court. The nature of the cuts to her head, he said, was consistent with two weapons being used—one sharp, one blunt—or one weapon with both a sharp and blunt edge. The cause of death was shock, haemorrhage and fractures of the skull. He also indicated that the force of the blows had knocked the lower set of dentures from her mouth. In further replies to Basil Neild he said he had taken blood and hair samples and handed them to forensic scientist Dr. Firth. Categorically stating the time of death as 2am on Monday 20th August, he added, "I think the deceased probably lived for a few hours after receiving the injuries." He was not reminded of his evidence in the lower court when he had finally admitted to Burns solicitor that he did not know what time she had died. Replying to the judge, he described the five incised and ten ragged star-shaped wounds to the head, adding that the former were probably caused by a sharp edge such as a knife or the sharp corner of another instrument and the latter by some flat or round object.

Under Heilbron's cross-examination Manning said that the cuts—the deepest being a quarter of an inch—went down to the skull but did not penetrate it. Considering he had earlier stated the cause of death included two fractures of the skull, she did not question this apparent contradiction. But mindful of the Crown's claims of Devlin possessing a knife, she did obtain his agreement that there was no injury in the nature of a stab wound. He however disagreed that bruising of the scalp around the wounds indicated that it could only have been caused by a blunt instrument but then conceded that such bruising is *mainly* from a blunt instrument.

It had seemed from these opening exchanges that defence counsel was going to be engaged in a long etymological battle with this expert Crown witness. But despite his medical terminology Heilbron—whose husband was a surgeon—kept her questions short and strictly to the point.

In further replies Manning disagreed that it was unusual to find an attack on the skull with a sharp instrument as opposed to an attack on the soft tissues of the body. Ignoring this logical point of Heilbron's, the judge then decided to make the pathologist's evidence lead more clearly to *two* attackers. "Does that mean," he asked, "that two weapons were used on the head?"

"Either two weapons or different parts of one weapon," he replied. But discounting the possibility of one weapon and thus one assailant, Finnemore's next appallingly leading question was precisely in keeping with the prosecution case. "It would be consistent would it, with someone using a knife and someone using a blunt instrument?"

"Yes."

Cross-examined by Goldie, Manning, despite earlier stating the wounds had been as deep as a quarter of an inch, and that the force of the blows had caused two skull fractures and had even dislodged the victim's dentures, said he didn't think the amount of force had been excessive. And when Goldie mentioned the "appalling brutality" and that the number of blows must have been caused by a homicidal maniac, the doctor disagreed.[1] He did agree however that, in Goldie's words, there, "would have been blood all over the place." This answer would be used to challenge the later evidence of James Brierley Firth, the Home Office forensic scientist.

The next Crown witness was Lily White, manageress of the Silver Knight Dry-cleaners in Upper Jackson Street, Hulme. Mrs Wilson agreed with Basil Neild that on 23rd August a fawn tweed jacket and a gabardine suit had been brought in by two young girls, the first item in the name of A Cavanagh and the second in the name of Devlin. The address on both receipts

---

1.   The defence lacked the resources to call their own expert witness to challenge Dr Manning's evidence.

(Exhibits 22 and 23) was 26 Leinster Street. Handed a fawn suit (Exhibit 26) by Neild, she identified it as the same one, adding that the jacket was creased and crumpled when she received it and looked as if it had been roughly washed. At this juncture Heilbron asked that Devlin—who had a urinary infection—be temporarily excused from the dock. Whilst he was gone, she asked the judge for permission to recall Thomas Rimmer to put a question she had earlier forgotten to ask. Agreeing, he said she should finish with the present witness first.

On Devlin's return Heilbron ascertained from Mrs Wilson that the garments had been cleaned under the six-hour express process and were returned to the branch from the firm's factory the same day. She then embarked on a lengthy questioning as to how the woman could recognise the suit, given that she had said hundreds of similar suits were received for cleaning during the month of August, and how she could remember the jacket had been washed. The witness had to agree that she was only guessing it was the same suit. This last question was however unnecessary. Mrs Wilson had already agreed that garments submitted for express cleaning had to be fairly clean—particularly gabardine. It was therefore quite reasonable for the jacket to have been sponged beforehand by Mrs Devlin to try and remove stains and dirt to make it acceptable for the express process.

When Thomas Rimmer re-entered the witness box, Heilbron said she wanted to ask him a few more questions about the broken window. Although still unaware of the forensic reports relating to this, she nonetheless had her own view of Rimmer's story and began by asking if there was glass on the inside. Yes, he said there was.

"What was the size of the opening you saw?" she asked.

"About three quarters of the whole window."

"That was *before* you broke it, was it?" (Author's italics).

"Yes."

Once again the judge intervened. He was so used to doing this, with an obvious bias towards the Crown, that he did not realise he was falling in line with what would be Heilbron's as yet unspoken thesis.

"That was before you broke it, was it not?" he prompted. "You broke it almost completely did you not?"

"Yes, that was before."

"About three-quarters of the window was broken before you finished it off?"
"Yes." [2]

Heilbron then asked, "You broke it practically completely?" When Rimmer agreed, she said, "Would you be good enough to look at the photographs?"

Realising his overzealousness had been misplaced, Finnemore then resumed his role of neutrality by asking the jury to look at the photographs of the broken window taken *after* Rimmer said he had climbed through. Addressing Rimmer Heilbron said, "You see, there is a sort of small circle [of glass] at the top and a wider piece at the bottom. Do you see that?"

"Yes."

"Can you remember what it was like before you broke it?"

"Well, there was a jagged piece at the side — the left-hand side of the photo — and a small narrow piece right the way down on the other side, and a small piece was sticking up *which broke as I got in*" (Author's italics).

"Did you think that it was not possible for you to get through unless you broke some more glass?"

"I thought it was possible but not easy."

"Do you think you would have cut yourself?"

"Yes."

Here there are two vital considerations: When Rimmer said a piece of glass "broke as I got in", had Heilbron the benefit of Inspector Reade's report, she could have asked to devastating effect, how was it that no fibres were found from his clothing on the glass? Moreover — notwithstanding her unawareness of the categorical forensic report — Heilbron dismally failed in her closing speech to point out to the jury that if Rimmer had to break almost all of the glass in order to climb through, how could Devlin or Burns have earlier gained access through the same window?

Heilbron was however not finished with Rimmer. Turning to the matter of the back kitchen door she reminded him that he had said when he tried that door that it appeared to be locked. But, she said quite pointedly, "We have since heard from constables Evans and Wright that it opened quite easily," to which he again agreed.

"Do you still say that it appeared locked?" she asked.

---

2.   Crime scene photographs show that the opening was still only three quarters of the window after Rimmer's alleged climb through.

"Yes."

"Did you try it?"

"Yes."

"And you could not get in that way?"

His reply, that he gave it "a quick try" but when it did not open he assumed that it was locked, drew expressions of mild puzzlement from several members of the jury.

"And of course, you then went to the window," concluded Heilbron, as she sat down barely disguising her disbelief.

CHAPTER TWENTY
THE "EXPERT" WITNESS TESTIFIES

Expert witness testimony in many cases creates more confusion than it alleviates.

Criminologist, Dr. Sandra Lean

When the court resumed after the lunch adjournment, James Brierley Firth, Director of the Home Office Forensic Laboratory at Preston was called. He was a seasoned witness, having testified in numerous murder trials, always for the prosecution.

As far as the blood evidence was concerned he would prove reluctant to agree with any explanation made by the defence for the minute bloodstains on the clothing of Devlin and Burns.[1] And for a forensic scientist, he was far from precise in his answers but seeming to agree with almost anything asked by prosecuting counsel, even to the point of occasionally contradicting himself. For example, after first stating there were "three angular *cuts*" on the back of the victim's coat and three corresponding ones on her frock, he then agreed with Neild that they were "holes".

When Firth was handling Mrs Rimmer's heavily bloodstained hat in the witness box, the judge addressing the jurors sitting immediately behind the witness, said "Do you see that members of the jury," as Firth obligingly turned to show them it. This prejudicial invitation to the jury was not evidence against the accused, no more than was Lord Goddard's showing of a knuckleduster to the jury at the Craig and Bentley trial a year later. It seemed that Finnemore's only purpose was to once again inflame the jury against the accused.

Stating that the blood on all of her garments were Mrs Rimmer's and were of Group A, Dr Firth added that, judging by the direction of the blood spatter on the walls and the inside of the front door, most of the blows had been delivered when she was on the floor. Replying to the judge, he insisted

---

1. See *Chapter 34* which deals with expert evidence.

that several locks of hair, which were "in the vicinity of the head", had been severed with a very sharp instrument and not as a result of the blows.[2] Finnemore asked him three times to repeat this. His intention was clearly to make the connection to the jury between this and Milne's allegation of Devlin having a sharp knife. There was however an even more sinister aspect to this bizarre revelation, that there might be a ritualistic element to the killing. For apart from the locks of hair, photographs of the victim's body showed one foot caught in the spindle of an upright chair to the right of the front door and the left foot in the same position in the spindle of a hall stand at the bottom of the stairs. It was as though they had been deliberately placed there. Yet it is hardly likely that housebreakers would take the trouble to do this. But when these photographs were taken the crime scene had been already compromised, Thomas Rimmer and the two police constables had already contaminated it by traversing the hallway.

Questioned about bloodstains on the jacket of Devlin's fawn suit, Dr Firth told Crown counsel that there were two—a small one on the left front of the lapel and one on the left sleeve—but they were of insufficient amount to be grouped. He was then asked about invisible bloodstains and said these showed presumptive reactions—"two spots on the front of the coat", one at the bottom and another on the left side near the bottom. The two coat buttons also gave presumptive reactions. The trousers, he said, showed no visible stains, "But human blood invisible to the naked eye was found on the outside front of the left leg." After stating that the area between the knee and bottom of the trousers was *generally stained* with this *invisible* blood, he then said he could not tell what blood group they were because the area was not "sufficiently concentrated" (Author's italics). The term, "generally stained" was most misleading, for as would be elicited later in his evidence, it did not refer to a large area of actual bloodstains but a tiny spot enlarged by dilution with water during his forensic tests. It was also erroneous to state that there was human blood *invisible* to the naked eye. If it was invisible and could not be grouped then it was surely a mere presumption that it was human blood or even blood at all? Indeed this part of Firth's testimony would seem to be a contradiction in terms and, even by scientific standards,

---

2. He was not reminded that, as earlier testified by pathologist Manning, he had been handed samples of the victim's hair.

was pure conjecture, proving nothing against the accused—and it should not have been admissible. But neither Heilbron nor Goldie objected. Yet judging by the thoughtful expressions on the faces of some jurors, they were clearly impressed with this damning "evidence!"

Coming to Burns brown pin-striped suit, handed to Firth, he stated there were visible signs of human blood inside the right hand pocket of the trousers and it was Group S. there was also a "faint smear" on the outside of the left leg near the knee and near the turn-up on the same leg. There was a presumptive reaction on the lower front of the right leg. Regarding the jacket, he first stated no visible bloodstains were found but that, "considerable areas gave strong presumptive tests for blood, particularly on the left side."

Some of the locations of blood spots on the men's clothing tallied of course with what Milne said she witnessed when she allegedly met the accused men outside the Rialto after the murder. Balmer, her tutor, had after all been in possession of Firth and Manning's reports since a few days after the murder! And in the case of Manning's report—that the victim did not die till two a.m.—Balmer's "verbals" in the mouth of Devlin via Milne—"Will the old woman live?" fitted nicely!

Continuing his examination, Neild asked Firth to give a detailed explanation of the analytical procedures he employed. This was so technical that it must have left the jury totally befuddled but nevertheless, impressed, as it was intended to do.

At this point the judge decided that he and the jury required a lesson about the difference between a positive and a presumptive reaction to human blood. Firth explained that it was a matter of concentration of blood. Basically it meant that if you dilute blood with water up to a certain concentration it will give you a human blood test, which is called a precipitation test. "But if you further dilute it the dilution is so great that it will not answer to that test but will answer to what we call a presumptive test, which will operate to one in 20,000."

"So," asked the judge, "if you have what you call a presumptive test, it means that it looks like human blood but you are not absolutely sure?" to which Firth agreed.

Mr Justice Finnemore was not so naïve as he wished to appear. The purpose of his question was to instil into the jury that the non-evidence about the presumptive tests *could* still be evidence against the accused.

Because no visible bloodstains were found on Burns jacket, Neild asked if it appeared to have been cleaned, to which Firth replied, "That is the impression I got." Once again—notwithstanding his status as an "expert witness"—this was not scientific evidence but purely a matter of opinion, which should not have been admissible. Yet again no objection was made by the defence.

Moving on to the matter of Burns' shoes, Firth said there was a presumptive test on the toe of one shoe. "What about the soles?" asked the judge, apparently taking on the role of prosecution counsel. "Nothing on the soles," he replied.

Rising to cross-examine, Rose Heilbron—whose husband, Nathaniel Burstein, was a physician and surgeon—immediately elicited from Firth that on all the men's clothing tested he had not found any bloodstains of the same group as Mrs Rimmer's, which was Group A. She then put it to him that in a presumptive test there are other substances which give a similar reaction to blood. He agreed but added—again an assumption—that if you found visible human bloodstains and presumptive stains on the same garment, "then that *would tend* to indicate the *possibility* of the presumptive areas also being of human origin" (Author's italics).

Heilbron, however, was not going to let this assumption go unchallenged. "Of course", she said, "but on the other hand it might not? It might be other stains. It is merely a matter of interpretation and opinion. It is not a fact of any sort?"

"No."

Later during Firth's cross-examination Heilbron exposed a deception, perhaps not deliberate but misleading all the same. An exchange had been going on for some time about presumptive blood tests, during which Firth stated he had cut out pieces of the cloth containing the stains and had placed pieces of cellophane over the areas he found to be both visible and presumptive. But replying to Heilbron, he admitted that the size of these "areas" was considerably enlarged due to the dilution tests he had applied. And this gave the jury the impression there was much more blood on the clothing, than was the case. After evading her question several times about the size of the actual stains—as opposed to the "treated areas"—he finally admitted that the stains were very much smaller.

When Sir Noel Goldie rose to cross-examine, he again dropped his papers and, out of sight of everyone for a few moments, fumbled around on the floor before finally collecting them. Despite this however, perhaps in the hope of reclaiming some dignity, he was uncharacteristically direct and concise in his questioning of Firth.

"First of all," he said, "we can eliminate the [Burns] shoes altogether I think. You very fairly said in the court below that you are not able to say positively that the *blood you found on the soles of the shoes was human blood?* (Author's italics). Goldie had apparently not heard or had forgotten Firth only minutes earlier telling the judge there was "nothing on the soles"! Nonetheless Firth told him, "I cannot say that it is even blood definitely."

"So we may eliminate Exhibit 32. You cannot even say," repeated Goldie, "that it was blood. Now I come to Exhibit 18 — the suit. Now Dr Manning told us — and my Lord will correct me if I am wrong — that as far as he could see, blood had been splashed all over the place, coming, so to speak, spurting upwards. Do you follow me?"

"Yes."

"That being so, would you not, with your vast experience *as a pathologist*, expect to find clothes almost saturated with blood?" (Author's italics).

After making some telling points, here was Goldie falling once again into confusion and inaccuracy. Firth was *not* a pathologist. But rather than correcting him, Firth was more concerned with contradicting Goldie, as the short-lived cordiality between them evaporated.

"No. by no means," he firmly replied. Somewhat taken aback, Goldie reminded him that Devlin and Burns were accused of committing such a brutal assault that the lady was almost spurting blood. "Do you really say that you would not expect the victim's blood on the clothing of these men?" When he replied that you *may* find it, "But it didn't make it absolutely definite that there would be the victim's blood on the assailant," Goldie, becoming flushed, said, "Forgive me, that was not my question. My question was, would you with your vast experience, expect to find the victim's blood on the person who was alleged to have made the assault?"

"In most cases, yes," he replied begrudgingly, "but not necessarily in all cases."

"Not necessarily in all cases," mimicked Goldie, then went on, "Assuming in this particular case that Dr Manning is correct in saying there was really blood all over the place…" Here the judge once again gratuitously intervened, telling Goldie, "This doctor saw it as well. He went to the place himself." But for once, an irritated, Goldie now stood his ground against Finnemore. "I beg your pardon," he said — this time without addressing him as "My Lord" — "He is a doctor of *science*. I was confining myself to the *medical* evidence." Then turning to Firth, "What I want to get at is, what reason can you suggest that on my client, let alone Miss Heilbron's, there was not one single trace of category-A blood." Basil Neild was immediately on his feet protesting that, "My learned friend must not say that." And predictably supporting prosecuting counsel, the judge told Goldie, "He [Firth] has not said that at all. What he said was that there was blood on their clothes but not enough to enable him to group it at all. It may have been group A or *it may have been anything*" (Author's italics).

By allowing "It may have been anything" the judge had by default confirmed Goldie's assertion that there was no evidence of the victim's blood being found on the men's clothing. But despite being correct Goldie, slavishly said, "I stand corrected." He then maintained he was not suggesting there was no blood on the men's clothing but that there was no blood of Mrs Rimmer's. Then addressing Firth he said, "I am suggesting to you that as far as you can say, there was no category-A blood?" But once again the pedantic Finnemore would not allow this perfectly valid and important question to be asked without incorrectly commenting. "I do not think he does say that. He said that there is no blood that he can identify *of any group*" (Author's italics).

Apart from Finnemore clouding the issue, it seemed that Goldie wasn't alone with a faulty memory and guilty of inaccuracies. In his eagerness to help the prosecution, had the learned judge forgotten that Firth had in fact "identified" both Group A on the victim's clothes and Group S on the pocket of Burns trousers? If, as Firth confirmed, he could not say conclusively whether the blood was Group A on the accused's clothing, then perhaps the jury should have been directed to disregard all of the blood evidence?

Goldie still wanted to know from Firth that in an assault of such severity — "and you saw the result of it" — if he would expect enough of the victim's blood on the assailant's clothes to be able to group it? The "expert" witness replied that he would, provided such clothing, "had not been touched in the meantime or received any subsequent treatment." Yet, replying to both Basil Neild and the judge earlier, he had stated that the organic solvent used in dry-cleaning did not remove bloodstains nor reduce their visibility. This clear contradiction however was not picked up by defence counsel or the judge.

Before concluding his testimony Firth admitted that the only small stain on the inside right pocket of Burns trousers was Group B—his own, and that there where no other groupable stains on his suit. Goldie then said he was going to call evidence later that Burns received a small cut on his left leg and a small cut on his hand whilst climbing through the broken window during the Sunblinds robbery. Firth then said that a small area of the leg stain had been cut out by him and not retained. Why this was so, when all the other—even presumptive areas—had been cut out, marked with cellophane patched and retained, was not explained. Nor was it asked. Firth did however agree that Burns small cut would be consistent with climbing though a broken window at Sunblinds. As for the blood reaction on the inside trouser pocket, he also agreed that this could have got there by Burns simply putting his cut hand in his pocket. Finally, Firth agreed with Goldie that the 14 stains he had marked with an "H" for human blood were not able to be grouped and could well have come from Burns nose during a fight.

CHAPTER TWENTY ONE
BALMER'S BOYS IN THE BOX

Fourth Day

Matilda told such dreadful lies.
It made one gasp and stretch one's eyes.

Hillaire Belloc

The first of "Balmer's Boys" to enter the witness box was Detective Constable Leslie Skinner, the officer who with Manchester's Detective Constable Lynch, had arrested Devlin at Granelli's Stretford Road milk bar. His rehearsed evidence was on the whole, the same as he had given at the committal court. Like his CID colleagues he had been instructed by Balmer not to offer anything helpful to the defence. So when Heilbron asked him if he had arrested Devlin, instead of readily agreeing he procrastinated until eventually agreeing that if a police officer detains somebody for murder it is in fact an arrest—but, he maintained, only "technically"!

When Heilbron said Lynch told Devlin he was taking him to Ormond Street Police Station for questioning about the Playhouse robbery, Skinner denied this, and although agreeing he was indeed taken there, said he didn't know if he was being taken for that purpose. Reminded of his lower court evidence where he had stated Devlin *was* being taken for questioning, he again prevaricated, and now stated that, it was Lynch and not he who had said that and now stated it was he who told Devlin he was being taken for questioning. Non-co-operation is one thing. But this was outright obstruction!

There now occurred a further pro-prosecution irregularity by the judge. Heilbron put it to Skinner that Devlin maintained nothing was mentioned about a Liverpool murder on the way to the police station. He denied this, saying that he had told Devlin outside the milk bar that he was, "detaining him regarding the murder of Beatrice Alice Rimmer." When Heilbron

255

suggested that at no time did he tell Devlin this, it was clearly a matter of unresolved dispute. Yet Finnemore intervened with a question which implicitly accepted Skinner's version by unequivocally stating, "When *you said* you were detaining him about the murder of Beatrice Alice Rimmer, did you say where it was?" (Author's italics).

"In Liverpool on the 19th of August my Lord."

Not only did the judge accept Skinner's version as fact, he also took the opportunity to remind him to add the location and date, which he had not previously mentioned![1]

Next in the witness box, was Detective Inspector William Lees. As he took the oath, swearing to tell the truth, the whole truth and nothing but the truth, a watching Balmer, being the accomplished actor he was, found it quite easy to maintain a straight face!

Lees' evidence was also more or less that which he gave in the lower court, including denials that any questions were asked of Devlin either when he was in the police car or when he made his statement in Liverpool. A great deal of time was taken by Basil Neild asking him detailed questions, the answers to which were largely irrelevant and could hardly be called evidence. Much was made by Neild, for example, about how and where the police had located Burns trousers and jacket. Given that none of the victim's blood was found on them, the purpose of these questions was unclear — unless, by having them officially entered in evidence as exhibits, Neild hoped somehow to infer that the clothing was factual evidence against Burns. Indeed, during Dr Firth's earlier evidence, when asked by Neild to indicate the tear on Burns trousers (which Goldie said was caused cutting his leg at the Sunblinds break-in) the forensic scientist said it was not a tear, it was the location of where he had cut out a small sample of the fabric for testing. This action had of course effectively removed any evidence of the tear and its support for Burns story.

In further replies to prosecuting counsel, Lees stated that in the police car on the way to Liverpool he was sitting alongside Wade, who was driving, and Devlin was seated in the back handcuffed between Richardson and Sturrock. He heard Devlin suddenly ask, "Have you seen the girls? What do they say?" He then immediately followed this with, "I was not in Liverpool

---

1.   This devious practice of Finnemore's would feature frequently during the defence case and his
     summing-up.

when the murder was done." Up till then, said Lees, nothing had been mentioned about any girls. "Sergeant Richardson then advised him in his own interests to say no more." But despite this advice Devlin, again unprompted, said, "The last time I was in Liverpool I stayed in Mount Pleasant and gave the name of Ford." The remainder of the journey, he added, was conducted in silence apart from Devlin asking for a cigarette.

It is remarkable that although Lees could quote verbatim what Devlin was supposed to have said, he later stated that he did not hear any remarks made by Sergeant Richardson to Devlin.

On arrival at Allerton Police Station, Lees said he cautioned Devlin and then took a statement at his dictation.

"What did he say in the statement?" asked Neild. Lees then read out his statement:

Edward Francis Devlin says, I was not in Liverpool at the time of the murder and I did not hear of a murder whilst I was there or since, until tonight, because I have not been reading the papers for the past couple of months. I have known June since last Whit Monday, but I did not see her again until I met her in Liverpool at the beginning of August 1951. She introduced me to a girl named Marie in the Rainbow Café. My mate Alfie Burns was with me and he paired off with Marie. Alfie got a room at an end house in a street off a main road. I don't know the name of the street but a nigger kept it. The room was on the first floor and the bathroom was at the top of the first flight of stairs. Alfie and Marie stayed at this house and I used to go there with June. At the finish up the two girls lived there for a week as far as I know. We took the girls round and we also took the two girls to a house in Manchester where a mate of mine lives. We went by train and we got in by Central Station, I remember. When we were in Liverpool we went *to the Continental Café and a Chinese Café*, which was not far from a wash baths where we had baths [Author's italics]. The last time I was in Liverpool was the 8th or the 9th of August. I remember when we were in Manchester we gave June our two Macs to mind. Mine had a cut, a little tear in it. I later went to June's house to get the Macs back, with Alfie and another geezer, but June said they were at the cleaners and I went back again and saw her mother, and while we were there a police car came around the corner and we had to make a run for it. I forgot to say that the name of my mate whose house we went with the girls in Manchester, was Norman Higgins.

Telling Lees to pause, Neild asked if at that point there was an amendment which was initialled by the prisoner, to which he agreed before continuing:

I am quite *definite* I have not been in Liverpool since the 9th of August (Author's italics). When in Liverpool I wore a fawn gabardine suit and the shirt I am wearing now, which is salmon colour with a scotch plaid collar and cuffs. I want to make it quite plain that when I said Marie and June stayed in the room in Liverpool for a week, we had taken them to Manchester and we had difficulty in finding digs for them, so we got a taxi for them and took them to the station to get the train to Liverpool. Alfie and me went to Liverpool a couple of days later, went to the house, knocked at the door and the nigger opened it. I went upstairs and no-one was there. June came in a moment or two later. While you are going around Liverpool it saves time to get taxis, and we took two or three during the couple of days we were in Liverpool. The last time I saw June was in Manchester about the 16th or 17th of August 1951. I have not seen her since. The last time I saw Marie was one Saturday or Sunday night about the 5th of August 1951 at Manchester, when we took them to the station to get the train to Liverpool. While we were in Liverpool, I gave June a blue shirt of mine to get washed. Round about the time of the murder I was doing a lot of screwing jobs in Manchester, in Hulme, Deansgate and other places. I know definitely I was in Manchester on the 23rd August because my mate Victor Le Vesconte was released from prison that day. I know I was screwing all the time from the 10th of August until the end of the month, so I was probably screwing a gaff on the 19th of August.

There followed further questions to the inspector to do with where amendments were made in the statement and initialled by Devlin, including the curious following exchange:

Neild: Was the last amendment to, 'I know definitely I was in Manchester…?'
Lees: The word *definitely* was spelled wrongly and he corrected it and initialled it.
Mr Justice Finnemore: It is spelled properly the first time and then altered. But it does not really matter.

Neild: It is a spelling mistake.

Finnemore: That does not matter except to show he was following it, perhaps.

This exchange was puzzling in several respects. Despite earlier stating that Devlin dictated the statement which he wrote down, Lees now appeared to be saying that Devlin had written it himself and was therefore responsible for the spelling mistake and correction. Yet the judge remarked that the word was spelled correctly the first time. That being the case, rather than dismissively saying it didn't really matter, perhaps the judge should have pursued why a correctly spelled word was scratched out and changed. One thing is certain, Balmer — who was present throughout the taking of the statement, and indeed asking questions — was virtually addicted to the adjective and adverb *definite* and *definitely* and seemed incapable of using any alternatives. Was this therefore a clumsy attempt to remove his "trademark"? This statement, and that of Burns and how they were really obtained, would later in the trial be the subject of intense questioning by the defence.

Although he had apparently named the Liverpool cafés he and Burns had visited, Devlin in truth did not know any of their names. These were provided by Balmer and included by Lees during the taking of his statement, which Devlin unquestioningly accepted. The inclusion of the Continental was crucial to Balmer's conspiracy, despite the two men never having been there.

Lees told Neild that Burns was interviewed on the 11th October at Strangeways Prison Manchester, the day after Devlin's arrest and that Balmer was again present, along with Detective Sergeant Richardson. When he told Burns he was investigating the murder of Mrs Rimmer on the 19th of August in Liverpool, Burns replied, "I have been worrying about it. I know you knocked Devlin." Interrupting, the judge asked, "'Knocked' means arrested, I suppose, does it?"

Burns then agreed to make a statement and, like Devlin, initialled various amendments, after it had been written. Lees then read out the statement as follows:

Alfred Burns says:

I didn't do the murder. I never knew there was a murder until this morning when I was told about it. Ted Devlin is my mate and June and Marie were girls we met in Liverpool, although Teddy knew June before that. It was through June we went to Liverpool. Marie was my girl and I was first introduced to her by June when I was with Ted Devlin in the *Rainbow Café* Liverpool [Author's italics]. I then took a room in No 2 Verulam Street , Liverpool. I paid a nigger 25s.od for it for the week. June and Ted came to the room once, the day after I rented it. That was the only time Ted and me were together there. I now remember that we went to Manchester the same day leaving the girls in the room. I think it was two or three days later that we came back for the girls but there was only June there. We took her to Manchester the same day. I must be wrong because we took both girls to Manchester, I think it was on the Sunday—the Sunday after the day we met them. I don't know the date but I can find out later. We came to Manchester with both girls once and we sent them back to Liverpool on their own. That's right, we sent them back on their own. On another occasion we took June to Manchester on her own. I only knew Marie for two or three days and the last time I was in Liverpool was 3 or 4 days after I met the girls in the Rainbow Café. We only went in two cafés in Liverpool as I know, one was the Rainbow and the other was by the Pier Head. I only gave June clothes to wash once at the most—and she didn't wash it. It was a yellow shirt. She put in a suitcase she had there and she took it to her house. I got the shirt back later from June, when her mother was with her. June also had my Mac. She was minding it for me and her mother told me and Devlin that they had gone to the cleaners. I mean that there was two Macs—mine and Ted's. I have not seen Marie or June since. I don't think we were in Liverpool any Sunday and I can prove later where I was on the 19th of August 1951. I now remember that I also gave June a pair of socks to wash at the same time as the shirt. She put them in the suitcase. I can't remember whether I gave her any handkerchiefs at the same time. I may have done but I don't remember. We only went in a taxi once while in Liverpool. And that was from the Pier Head to the street where we lived, I mean Verulam Street. I forget what name I gave but it wasn't my own. I might have given my own now that I come to think of it. I never told Marie what my name was. She didn't ask. That is all that I know.

Lees continued, "It was read over to him, he read it over then signed it.

Then he made an addition. He said, 'I would like to put in that the only time I was apart from Devlin was the day we got the room in Verulam Street. All the time, from the day we first met the girls and for the next two or three weeks, I was with Devlin all the time. I can't say where I was but my mother will be able to give me an idea'. He again signed that and signed the amendments."

As with Devlin, Burns did not know the names of the cafés or Verulam Street. Balmer had suggested these, which Lees included in his statement. Unlike Devlin however when the incriminating café visit to the Continental was suggested, Burns, as can be seen from his statement, was not so gullible and would not accept it, truthfully stating they had only visited two— "One was the Rainbow and the other was by the Pier Head" (the Lighthouse) of which he also obviously did not know the name.

The prosecution would lay emphasis on the minor discrepancies between Burns and Devlin's statements—for example how many taxis they took—in order to show that they were lying. But with imperfect memories, their accounts quite naturally diverged on some matters—unlike the accounts of the detectives which were carbon copies of each other and altogether *too* perfect!

When Heilbron rose to cross-examine, Lees was not to get such an easy ride, although she still had to overcome his many lies and imprecise replies. His posture in the witness box was a strategy taught by Balmer—his dictum being to always give vague, indirect answers such as, "I think" and, "to the best of my knowledge." You could then not be held to a specific answer or caught out as self-contradictory. You could also offset any accusations of deliberate lying by conceding you may have made a mistake. Thus, when asked when the police first saw McLoughlin, Lees replied, "the 20th September *I think*" (Author's italics).

Most of Lees answers were in this vein. Yet there was no uncertainty or hesitation when he wanted to make telling points against the accused. He nevertheless made several slip-ups under Heilbron's questioning. When asked the date of Bury's first statement, for example, he immediately replied, "the 4th October." And although he swore that Detective Sergeant Sturrock took it, Balmer would later at an inquiry state that only an oral statement was taken on that date and by a Manchester constable in his notebook, which was later torn up.

Asked the date of Milne's interview and statement, he immediately rattled it off as the 7th October. Similarly that Emery's statement was taken on the 14th October, Rubin's the 16th and McNeill's, the 30th. The inspector however did not see fit to tell Heilbron that Milne had made a second, expanded and more damning statement to himself on the 9th October. Neither did he mention that Bury had given a signed statement on the 8th October to Balmer. This non-divulgence was in keeping with another of Balmer's dictums: "Just answer the question. Don't volunteer anything."

Heilbron wanted to know how many convictions Crown witness Rubin had but Lees, back in imprecise mode, replied that he could not remember off hand. But when she reminded him that he had 12 convictions for larceny, malicious wounding, felonious receiving, assault occasioning actual bodily harm and wilful damage, etc., the inspector readily agreed — even though he could not remember seconds before! Out of the blue Heilbron then asked Lees who was in charge of the investigation, and when he replied, "Chief Superintendent Balmer", she commented, "And you were directly under him?" [2]

During further questioning Lees said he saw Devlin in a room at Bootle Street Police Headquarters, Manchester. But, disagreeing with Heilbron that there were a number of detectives present, he replied that there were just four present including Balmer. "Perhaps Devlin thought four was a 'number'", she sardonically remarked.

At this stage, Devlin, who was still suffering from the urinary infection, again asked to be excused from the dock. This time the street-wise Burns, seeing the chance of them both having a cigarette in the cells below, decided to join him by pretending he also needed to urinate. Thus Rose Heilbron told the judge, "My Lord, I gather the defendants would like a slight adjournment."

Resuming when the two men returned to the dock, Heilbron asked Lees if he remembered a confused Devlin at Bootle Street asking, "Look here, what am I being charged with?" and Detective Sergeant Richardson saying

2.   Given Balmer's primary role in the investigation, it is puzzling why Heilbron or Goldie did not request that he be called — particularly in view of evidence that he was present throughout the taking of the accuseds' statements.

"Murder"? No nothing like that was said in his presence, he replied.

"And Devlin said to the officer, 'You are kidding aren't you?' and Richardson said 'No'?"

"No such thing was said," insisted Lees.

"Devlin will say he said to you, 'He is not serious is he'? And that you said, 'You will find out whether he is serious or joking or not'. And that Devlin then said to nobody in particular, 'Who's supposed to have been murdered?'"

"No such conversation took place."

To emphasise Lees denial for the jury's benefit, the judge asked, "Nothing like it at all?"

"Nothing at all," repeated the inspector.

"And," said Heilbron, "one of the detectives said, 'There has been a murder in Liverpool and you know all about it'."

"No."

"And Devlin said there was no murder in Liverpool whilst he was there?"

"No."

"Nothing like that at all?"

"Nothing like that at all."

Lees was so hell bent on denying everything put to him that he had forgotten earlier telling the court that one of the first things Devlin had said was, "I was not in Liverpool when the murder was done." When Heilbron said Devlin was then charged with the murder. Lees pedantically phrased it differently. "That," she said, "is very like what I have just put to you," to which he then conceded, "Yes, it is very like that."

This was obstinacy for sheer obstinacy's sake, yet the judge, always quick to intervene on behalf of the prosecution, made no comment.

Determined not to give an inch to the defence, Lees continued to make denial after denial, even over matters which had no material effect on the case.

Referring to one conversation in the police car on the journey down the East Lancashire Road to Liverpool, Heilbron asked if he remembered Sergeant Richardson telling Devlin he knew all about Burns, Marie and June and they had all swung it on him and he should now tell them what he knew? He would, he said, have remembered a long conversation like that if it had taken place. "Is that your estimate of a long conversation?" she asked. "Well, it is not a very short one", he replied.

Here again, Finnemore intervened: "It would be a very improper thing for an officer to say if he *did* say that." Like a dutiful parrot, the chief inspector echoed, "It *would* be an improper thing for an officer to say, my Lord." Lees also said he did not hear Devlin in the car saying, "As God's my judge I do not know anything about it," nor Richardson saying, "Well God's not your fucking judge."

Most onlookers found it incredulous—that with five men cramped into a Vauxhall saloon car for over an hour—one of them, a senior detective, "trained to listen and observe"—as the judge would later comment—did not hear a single word that was spoken.

Questioned about other conversations between Richardson and Devlin on the car journey Lees either similarly denied everything outright or equivocated over others. His guarded and evasive replies continued when it came to whether Devlin's statement was the result of answers to questions put to him. Heilbron suggested this was the case and that the answers were written down. When Lees denied this she said, "Are you suggesting to members of the jury that this was sort of just reeled off by Devlin without any assistance, without any questions at all?" But with a blank expression, the inspector replied, "There were no questions put to him at all."

Apart from Lees implausible replies, it would be a gross dereliction of duty if during a murder enquiry, the police, after cautioning the suspect, did *not* ask the accused any questions. But surprisingly Heilbron did not turn the tables on Lees and accuse him of incompetence by putting this to him. To support her contention however that questions *were* asked, she quoted to the inspector from Devlin's statement: "'We went by train and we got in by Central Station'. Then there is a full stop. Then he says, 'When we were in Liverpool we went to the Continental Café, the Rainbow Café and a Chinese Café' and so on'. Did someone ask or did you ask, 'When you were in Liverpool where did you go'?"

"No."[3]

"Then a little later, lower down in the statement, 'The last time I was in Liverpool was the 8th or 9th of August'. Was he not asked, 'When was the

---

3.　The names of these cafés, including the Continental, were suggested by Balmer and Lees to Devlin, who whilst not knowing their names agreed they had been in three cafés, i.e. The Rainbow, the Lighthouse and the Golden Dragon.

last time you were in Liverpool'?"

"No."

Turning to the part where Devlin said that in Manchester they gave their macs to Bury, Heilbron asked if this was in reply to him being asked if he had ever given anything to Bury to mind. Again the answer was "No." Then, even though Heilbron had not seen Bury's statement she tellingly commented, "But of course," June had *already* made her statement, had she not?" to which he agreed. Asked again if he was sure he hadn't asked a question about the macs, Lees, contradicting himself, replied, "The only time *I spoke* to Devlin was when dates were *mentioned*" (Author's italics). Yet he had previously said that when Devlin mentioned the 8th and 9th August he had *not* put any questions to him.

Referring to the part which said, "I am quite definite I have not been in Liverpool since the 9th of August", Heilbron asked, "Are you quite sure he was not asked whether he had been in Liverpool since that date?" Yet despite just admitting to discussing the dates, Lees, again insisted no questions were asked.

Further questioned about Devlin stating what suit he was wearing whilst in Liverpool and that it must have been in reply to a question, Lees again said he was not asked about that because the police already knew which suit he was wearing. Heilbron however did not challenge him as to how, as opposed to an assumption, he *knew* this, nor did he offer to enlighten her. Nor did she ask why Devlin would need to describe in detail in his statement the shirt he was wearing which they could plainly see anyway.

Concluding her cross-examination, Heilbron pointedly asked if Superintendent Balmer was present during the taking of the statement. Yes he was. Did *he* ask Devlin any questions? "The only time Mr Balmer spoke", he replied piously, "was to ask Devlin if he would like a cup of tea after he had signed his statement." At this outrageous lie, Devlin in the dock shook his head in disgust and muttered, "Lying bastard!" As for Balmer, intently watching the proceedings, he did not bat an eyelid.

Apart from it being obvious—despite the inspector's denials—that Devlin's statement was indeed in response to questions, Heilbron did not query the uncharacteristic tone of his language: for example his unusually excellent terminology and concise syntax—"When in Liverpool...", etc. More importantly, she did not notice the linguistic Balmer trademark, "Definite", as in, "I am *quite definite* I have not been in Liverpool." But then, she was not aware that it was the superintendent who had asked all of the questions!

Cross-examining Lees, Sir Noel Goldie was surprisingly more effective this time than Rose Heilbron. Commencing deceptively with his usual quaint language, he asked Lees to confirm that Burns was an absconder from borstal and that he had been "a naughty boy" who had been arrested in Strangeways Prison. After establishing that Burns had never been convicted of any violent offence and noting that there was no Manchester police officer in the case, he then asked the inspector if he had made enquiries in Manchester as to the men's whereabouts on the night of August 19th. When Lees agreed he had, Goldie asked, "Am I right in saying that on that night a burglary was committed, a breaking-in at Sunblinds Ltd, 6 Great Jackson Street Manchester?" But before Lees could reply Basil Neild was on his feet protesting that this was hearsay. When the judge confirmed, "Pure hearsay it seems to me," Goldie robustly responded, "I am surely entitled to put to him (Lees) what my defence is? There is nobody here or coming from the Manchester police." If he wanted to prove it, said the judge, he would have to do so. "I will my Lord," he responded. "I am bound to put to the principal police officer in this case, when he says he has made enquiries, what the results of those enquiries are." But the judge said, quite wrongly, that Lees could only tell him what somebody else had told him. And interrupting Goldie whilst simultaneously putting words into the mouth of the witness, he added, "If you like to put it to him that your client was in some other place on the 19th August, he will say 'I know' or 'I don't know'." Goldie said he would have to be careful because he would not want it to be said later that he was taking the prosecution by surprise. Then turning to the witness he said, "Do not answer any of these questions unless my Lord gives permission." Those in the packed court were unsure whether this was Goldie's usual obsequiousness or a sarcastic response to Finnemore.

Continuing, he asked Lees, "Was a man called Campbell arrested for a burglary in Manchester, which took place on the night of 19th/20th of August?" At this simple question Finnemore commented, "Do you think he can answer that unless Mr Neild would like him to answer it?" This prompted many observers to wonder who was actually presiding over the proceedings—Mr

Justice Finnemore or the Crown prosecutor!

Encouraged by the judge's partiality, Neild commented, "My submission is that he cannot answer it." To which Finnemore agreed, stating, "He cannot in law. Certainly it is not evidence." When Goldie caved in after again bemoaning the difficulty of nobody from the Manchester police being present, the judge commented that there was nothing preventing him from calling someone from that force if he wanted to. His curious and seemingly contradictory response to this was, "Yes my Lord. Of course it is not for me to say who I am going to call. But I propose my Lord to call the burglar (Alan Campbell)."

Goldie elicited from Lees that Burns had denied throughout any involvement in the murder; had explained how they had met the "undesirable" girls and that he had given a full account of his movements in the three or four days in Liverpool. "For instance", he went on oblivious to his repetition of the offensive description, "he says he took a room in 2 Verulam Street, as we know he did. And *it is*, as he says, kept by a nigger?" [4]

"It is," replied the inspector, equally oblivious to the offensive term.

If Goldie wished to impress the jury with his client's frankness, he surely couldn't have used a more distasteful example than this!

Coming to the accused men's whereabouts on the 19th August, Goldie, dutifully prefacing his question with a warning not to answer it without the judge's permission, asked Lees if the police had made enquiries as to where the two men were on the murder night. The inspector replied that all possible enquiry had indeed been made. Had they been made in Manchester? Everywhere, said Lees.

"In Manchester?" Goldie again asked.

"Yes: all possible enquiries."

"All possible enquiries," repeated Goldie, "have been made as to where Burns was on the night of 19th/20th August?"

Finally forced to cease his equivocation, Lees replied, "Well, witnesses have spoken to where they where on the night of the 19th." This was still not a direct answer nor was it clear whether he was referring to defence witnesses

---

4. Nobody in court, including the judge and counsel were in the least perturbed at this description in 1952. Indeed the judge during his summing-up and Balmer (at the later inquiry) would freely repeat it.

or the tutored Crown witnesses. But Goldie did not pursue the matter, turning instead to the questions issue. In truth, no enquiries had been made to ascertain or confirm the men's true movements.

Eschewing Heilbron's earlier full-frontal attack about the statements Goldie, approaching from the flank, said, "Do not think I want to criticise the police in the slightest degree but I take it there must have been questions about this?" but Lees repeated there were no questions asked. Becoming a little bolder, defence counsel then said, "I am putting to you that this (Burns' statement) was taken down by question and answer?"

"No."

"Are you sure?"

"Quite definite about it", replied the inspector (Author's italics). Nobody seemed to notice that this was exactly the same phrase Devlin was supposed to have used in the statement that he had allegedly dictated himself!

Apart from mentioning that Emery the taxi driver had been asked questions, Goldie failed to comment on the bizarre procedure whereby every other witness in the case had been asked questions *except* the two men who were accused of the murder! He switched instead to a new line of questioning about the identity parades and about who had identified whom, apparently scoring points that Rubin identified Devlin, but not Burns and that McNeil had failed to identify either man. But this was an area of common agreement between prosecution and defence—there was no mileage in it.

Next in the witness box was Detective Sergeant Gordon Wade. Lying as Lees had done, he also denied any questions had been asked on the car journey to Liverpool or during the taking of both men's statements. Similar evidence and denials came from Detective Sergeants Sturrock and Richardson who followed him into the box. All three were in close harmony and word perfect. But then, their parts had been well choreographed and rehearsed!

Cross-examined by Rose Heilbron, Richardson was the personification of the Liverpool CID's prevailing philosophy—Give no quarter to the defence. Deny everything. We will be believed. We are the police![5] This was exemplified during an exchange between Heilbron and the detective sergeant, whose evidence was particularly pernicious. After denying he had made any

---

5.   Richardson succeeded Balmer as Head of the Liverpool CID and made the presentations at his retirement party.

comments about the girls to Devlin in the police car, Heilbron asked, "You knew all about Marie and June, did you not?

> **Richardson**: I knew *of* them.
>
> **Heilbron**: And you knew *all about* them, did you not?
>
> **Richardson**: I knew *of* them.
>
> **Heilbron**: You knew *about* them at that stage, did you not? I mean you knew they had made statements?
>
> **Richardson**: Oh yes.
>
> **Heilbron**: I am suggesting to you that you in fact told Devlin that you knew all about them?
>
> **Richardson**: No.

Richardson was adept at playing the role of the virtuous, idealistic, upstanding "rule-book" policeman of integrity, as illustrated by this further three-way exchange between Heilbron, himself and the judge:-

"Did you say to Devlin, 'If you don't tell me what you know to clear yourself you will get topped'?"

"I did not."

When Finnemore addressing nobody in particular, asked, "What does getting 'topped' mean?", Richardson volunteered with assumed prudery, "*I* know what the expression means my Lord. It is jargon usually used by men of undesirable character." He did not, however, similarly enlighten the judge that it along with insulting and derogatory terms like, 'Chinese Bit' or 'Nigger's Bit' was even more common parlance among police officers — especially in the Liverpool CID!

Briefly re-examined by Basil Neild, Richardson agreed that nothing much was said except for Devlin making the three alleged remarks about not being in Liverpool when the murder was done, asking about the girls and for a cigarette.

"Did I understand that you had advised him not to say anything," asked Neild.

"After his first remark I immediately cautioned him and advised him to say nothing."

"Did you think that was the fair thing to do?"

"I did."

When the judge commented, "It is your duty of course not to talk yourself under those circumstances," Richardson solemnly replied without the faintest trace of a smirk, "*Most important* my Lord." [6]

Neild then announced, "My Lord, that is the case for the Crown".

On their return to prison that evening, Devlin and Burns were again being processed through the dreary routine of Reception when a prison orderly sneered at them, "Fuckin hard cases eh? Killin' owld women. Murderin' bastards." At this, the agonising months of frustration and the daily tension of the trial exploded from within Burns who, without hesitation and before any officer could intervene punched him flush on the chin. "You fuckin Scouse prick," he roared at the man who was now picking himself up off the floor. "We're screwsmen not fuckin' murderers! We've never murdered *anyone!*" When the prisoner complained to the prison officer, he was told to "fuck off" and that he was out of order.

Unknown to the two men, the orderly, who was serving 18 months, was none other than Kiernan Oates—the same Kiernan Oates who had originally told Inspector Morris back in September last year that McLoughlin's friend "Ginger Dutton" was the murderer!

6. This was similar to the chief constable who, when it was reported a constable had hit a prisoner on the head with his truncheon said, "Impossible. The regulations clearly state prisoners can only be hit on the shoulders!"

CHAPTER TWENTY TWO
ROSE HEILBRON OPENS THE DEFENCE CASE

Wednesday 20th February 1952.

Have you ever seen a more cool, calculated, and calculating young woman of seventeen?

Rose Heilbron QC

Now it was the turn of the defence. On this, the fifth day of the trial, Heilbron rose to make her opening speech. Starting slowly but emphatically, she reminded the jury that it was the prosecution's task to prove the guilt of the two men rather than the defendants having to prove their innocence. And their task was not to decide who murdered Mrs Rimmer but whether Devlin and Burns did. She then told them that it mattered not what anyone else thought. It was their decision which counted, based alone on the evidence they would hear. By purposely stressing this she was indirectly giving notice to the judge for him to cease his constant interjections on behalf of the Crown which had been such an irritating feature so far. Lest Finnemore had missed this clear hint she pointedly told the jury, "*You* will decide. And it is a matter entirely for you, *and you alone*" (Author's italics).

Heilbron went on to warn about the inevitable prejudice, not only because of the expansive pre-trial press coverage but also in the knowledge of the jury's own prejudices, as respectable law-abiding property-owners against self-confessed criminals. They should not believe, she warned, because the police have arrested someone that they must be guilty, that the police wouldn't arrest an innocent person. "For instance you hear people saying, quite loosely, 'Oh they have got the man who killed so and so'. That is a very dangerous approach to take," she said.

After telling the jury that the prosecution case was riddled with contradictions and inconsistencies, and fully aware that the defence's deadliest enemy was Marie Milne, Heilbron embarked on a full scale attack both on her evidence and her character. Did they believe, she asked, the facade of the innocent, virginal 17-year-old she had adopted in the witness box. "This somewhat brazen girl…who had the audacity to admit she was quite prepared to rob though she would draw the line at violence? Who unashamedly you may think, admitted to having intercourse with one man, although she said only one man, the day after she had picked him up or had been picked up in an all-night café? The same girl, if her story is true, who admitted associating with thieves."

Here however Heilbron was in danger of turning the court into an inquisition of Milne's morals, and it was surprising Basil Neild did not object nor the judge censure her, as he quite frequently did over more innocuous statements.

Defence counsel suggested that if Milne's story was true she may have been protecting some other men. She had also admitted that Burns was, 'indifferent to her charms', so by telling lies against him was it perhaps a case of "Hell hath no fury like a woman scorned?"

"Could you really believe Milne," she went on, "who had the temerity, and I would suggest, impertinence, to alter her evidence in your face — that is the evidence of the knife threat?" This was important, she said, reminding them of the current inflammatory nightly newspaper headlines — "Marie Milne Threatened Twice With Knife". But they now knew different and that was why they should decide the case on the evidence alone.

When Milne was caught out in her conflicting story about where she was threatened with the knife, said Heilbron, "She didn't say her evidence in the committal court was a mistake, because it is a little difficult to be mistaken about such a vital incident like a threat to cut her up into little pieces. So to get out of it she suddenly decided that she was threatened twice. It is this sort of evidence on which the prosecution are asking you to convict these two men of murder." More tellingly, she then observed, "Of course the greatest liar is not necessarily the one who invents completely the whole story, but he or she who adapts, *who skilfully fits in the false with the true*, with the object of making it more difficult for you, members of the jury, to discover the deceit and to uncover the lies" (Author's italics).

Devlin's counsel had hit the nail firmly on the head! But she was directing her fire in the wrong direction, attributing to Milne a *modus operandi* and authorial powers of falsification she did not possess. The real author of the deceit and lies, the puppet-master whose *modus operandi* this really was was smugly sitting in the well of the court a mere few feet behind her. But whether he was able to appreciate Tennyson's apposite poem, 'The Grand-mother', is most doubtful.[1]

Coming to Milne's story of the alleged three visits to Cranborne Road on the 19th August, Heilbron was equally scathing. "Three visits to reconnoitre; one at 1.30, one at six o'clock and one at nine o'clock. Yet on none of these visits does she go near the house—she, who was to be one of the principal accomplices in this crime by holding the woman in conversation."

Continuing, she said that, according to Milne, she went up at 1.30 in a taxi to the street corner, then there was the "amazing visit at six o'clock. She is so scared she waits an hour and a half for these men, and when she doesn't find them she goes back to the Rialto. And you remember, she said she let them know she was annoyed that they had not turned up at Cranborne Road—*she, who was so scared of being cut up into little pieces"* (Author's italics). Then, said Heilbron, she went back again at nine o'clock and was told, what the jury may think was a preposterous story about what her role would be—to keep the woman talking at her front door and then try to get into the house to act as an obstacle between Mrs Rimmer and the front door.

"She was told to wait for five minutes so what does she do? She is so scared—did she look scared when she was giving her evidence? You can judge by the demeanour of witnesses, members of the jury; do you think she looked the type—so scared she waits for an hour and a half on the corner of Smithdown Road and Cranborne Road till ten thirty at night? Well, do you really swallow that? Do you believe that? Have you ever seen a more cool, calculated and calculating young woman of 17?"

After further attacks on Milne, including the matter of her telling June Bury she had to back her up in her statement, Rose Heilbron told the jury, "This young woman is quite unworthy of belief in a matter so grave as this and is the last person upon whose evidence you should rely."

Referring to McLoughlin's evidence, she reminded the jury of how he had

---

1. "A lie which is half the truth is ever the blackest of lies. A lie which is all a lie may be met and fought with outright. But a lie which is part of a truth is a harder matter to fight": Alfred Lord Tennyson, 1809-1892.

changed his story several times—first at the committal court saying it was
going dark when he and Devlin arrived at the rear of the Rimmer home and
now saying it was morning. Then changing the dates and occasions he met
Devlin and Burns. "He stated in his evidence here that he met Devlin (and
Burns) in the evening of the first day he met Devlin. (27th or 28th July). But
at the police court (committal) he said he met them six days later." Yet the
prosecution, she said, were asking the jury to rely on his evidence.

"They said he was a truthful person. But can you place any belief in a man
who changes his story so often—this man who admitted robbing his own
aunt?" And even on that matter, she went on, he said he did not know *when*
he robbed his aunt's house. "He said he robbed her before he met Devlin,
then he said he had robbed her after the meeting. He then said he robbed
her on two occasions." He said he told Devlin of his intention to rob his
Aunt's. "But when he came to give his evidence here, it transpires he had
already robbed his Aunt's." Then again, continued Heilbron, "He said that
on the night he met Devlin with Burns they went to the Pier Head after
leaving the Continental all- night café. But Bury in her evidence said he
was not there—'McLoughlin did not go with the men to the Pier Head. I
went with the men to the Pier Head, and Marie went too.' Members of the
jury, do you think there ever was such a liar as McLoughlin? Can you really
believe a word of what that man told you?"

Heilbron was doing her utmost to discredit McLoughlin as she had with
Milne and would do so with Bury. But had she been aware of their undisclosed signed statements, she would have proved that not only were all three
liars but would also have been able to demolish Balmer's whole fabricated
edifice. The trial would have been stopped in its tracks and the two men set
free. For the signed statements of all three clearly stated that they had first
met Devlin and Burns on the 9th or 10th of August!

In the absence of those statements however—even within the evidence
already given—neither Heilbron or Goldie thought to ask how Milne could
possibly have accompanied Devlin, Burns and Bury to the Pier Head on the
27th or the 28th July when, according to McLoughlin, or August 2nd, according
to Bury, she had not been introduced to them in the Rainbow Café until
the night of August 3rd/4th!

When it came to June Bury, she fared no better under Heilbron's piercing spotlight. "You will remember," she told the jury, "that a good deal of her evidence was a mass of contradictions." She was not going to go into detail, she said, because it would be too tedious. But the jury would remember how Bury would say one thing and then say another. An example of this — insofar as it affected her credibility — was when Bury had said that on her first meeting with Devlin at Whitsuntide, they had spent a week together but later admitted they had only spent one night together. "A mistake about a whole week?" And then, she continued, there was the "mistake" about the incident she had just been referring to with McLoughlin and the Continental. "First of all she said that meeting happened at the beginning of August, (on the 2nd, the same evening of the day she had first met Devlin and then Burns in the Dive). And secondly, you remember, she said Marie Milne was in the Continental with her when McLoughlin was there. She then said she only saw McLoughlin on one occasion, which was *after she came back from Manchester* (on the first occasion) and that she Devlin, Burns and Milne went to the Pier head but not with McLoughlin. She says the next morning they went to Canning Street. So she places the incident when McLoughlin was present on the evening before going to Canning Street. We know one thing is clear," she went on, "that this group of people arrived at 39 Canning Street on Saturday afternoon (August 4th). So according to her evidence that incident took place on the Friday evening. That is a week and one day later than McLoughlin puts it."[2]

Apart from making the point that either Bury or McLoughlin were lying, Heilbron missed the greater opportunity of demonstrating to the jury that it was obvious the true movements of Devlin, Burns, Bury and then Milne — between August 2nd and the 5th — had been fully accounted for and that this left no available evening on which they could possibly have been in the Continental with McLoughlin or Bury. That is to say; after first stating she went to the Continental with the accused men on the night of August 2nd, Bury agreed she was "mistaken" and admitted that she went that day to Manchester with the two men and returned in the early hours of August 4th, when she introduced Milne to Burns in the Rainbow. All four then went to

2. It would be pointed out at the subsequent inquiry by Devlin's junior counsel that Milne could not have been seen in the Continental by McLoughlin in late-July because she did not come into the picture until August 4th.

the Pier Head and Lighthouse Café and from there to Canning Street. That night Burns and Milne took the room at Verulam Street, and the following day (August 5th) all four went to Manchester by train. It was therefore clear that, far from being in the Continental on either the 2nd or the 3rd of August with Bury and McLoughlin—the two accused were on their way from Liverpool to Manchester with June Bury on the first occasion, where they stayed overnight, and on the second occasion—Sunday August 5th—with Bury and Milne in Norman Higgins Manchester flat.

Heilbron had already pointed out that Bury had lied about not going to Manchester with Devlin and Burns on the 2nd August—the night she and the two accused men were supposed to have met McLoughlin in the Continental—and only admitted it when challenged in cross-examination. She also lied, said Heilbron, about the Wednesday morning, the 8th August, when the two men returned to Verulam Street. "She agreed with me that she had been out all night. She said, 'It is not true what I said about that at the police court'. And she admitted telling a complete lie about the men's raincoats." The jury would remember, she said, that Bury was left with the two raincoats. "But for some reason, which she admitted to you, she told these two men what was a complete fabrication. She said they had been sent to the cleaners when she knew nothing of the sort had happened and that they were in fact at her mother's. That was a complete lie, wholly untrue."

Had Heilbron been aware that during the previous October (the 17th), Bury had made a statement to the Manchester police, naming a David Coyne as the killer, and had also told three girls at the hostel where she was living, that her-ex-boyfriend, Austin O'Toole, was responsible for the murder, she would have been clearly exposed as a pathological liar and the trial in all probability would have been halted there and then.

After asking the jury why they should rely on Bury's evidence in the face of such a catalogue of lies, Devlin's counsel, winding down her opening speech, asked the jury whether the evidence put forward by the prosecution was sufficient to convict the two men of murder. Referring to McLoughlin, Bury and Milne, she asked, "Could you ever find three more unsatisfactory and untrustworthy witnesses?" And, she added, "They were backed up by two men who were possibly worse and certainly no better. Rubin, with his many convictions, and McNeil, who went along to an identity parade in a murder case and picked out two entirely innocent men. He said he was nervous. A great pity," she mocked. "This poor nervous man who could deliberately pick out innocent men." The jury, she suggested, "may have been struck with horror at McNeil's actions, knowing as he must have, that *those* men may have found themselves in this dock charged with murder. Are you going to trust that man's recollection, trust the reliability of a man who would do a thing like that?"

Rubin, she said, was produced by the prosecution in order to say that the conversation with Devlin about Bury's "disease" in the Dive public house, must have been on the 18th August. "But Devlin will tell you that it was at a time before the 8th of August — the last time he was in Liverpool." Reminding the jury of Rubin's hesitancy when giving evidence, she said he was the man who could not remember, or was not too sure what arrangement he had with Bury; the man who was found in her bed and was apparently so intimate with her that he could use her bed whether or not she was in it."

Rather than indulging in these subtle hints that Rubin was possibly Bury's pimp, which she hoped the jury might find distasteful, Heilbron would have served the defence more productively by sticking to the facts — for example by reminding the jury that Rubin in his evidence had admitted that the police had suggested the date, August 4th, when Bury had left Canning Street with Devlin, and had at the committal hearing even admitted the police suggested the 18th August as the date of his confrontation with Devlin in the Dive.

Coming to the medical evidence, Devlin's counsel maintained that the bloodstains on his fawn gabardine suit — most of which were presumptive — were caused by him being in fist fights in Manchester before and after August 19th and she would be calling witnesses to testify to this. Moreover, the suit, which he admitted to wearing when in Liverpool, was in fact in the pawn shop from the 11th to the 23rd of August. She would also be calling witnesses to confirm this. Therefore, she said, the evidence of Dr Firth did not really help them.

Preparing the jury for Devlin's appearance in the witness box, Heilbron told them that he was an admitted thief who had convictions for larceny and housebreaking — although warehouse-breaking, she candidly remarked, seemed to be his forte! Indeed, they would hear that he had been involved in more crimes than he had been arrested for. But, she said,

... because a man is a thief does not mean he is a murderer. On the contrary, on the other side of the picture, there are many murderers who have in no wise been thieves, so the two do not necessarily go together.

The jury's sympathies would naturally be alienated from such a villain, she said, but asked them not to allow that to prejudice their fair hearing of the case. "He is not on trial here for his burglaries or warehouse-breaking; he is on trial for the murder of Mrs Rimmer—a very different matter." She then quickly ran through his record of four convictions:

1942, aged 12, probation for stealing (four loaves of bread).
1945, found on enclosed premises. Again put on probation.
1946, office-breaking. One month's detention in a remand home.
1950, six months' imprisonment for theft (boxes of tomatoes).

"That is his record," she said. "As records go, there have been many worse in this court. But he is going to go into the witness box and he will tell you that he has been doing a certain amount of warehouse-breaking during August last year."[3]

The most important of Devlin's movements, she said, were those on August 19th, and the jury would hear that he was committing a burglary on that night at Sunblinds Ltd in Manchester. There was no doubt that the warehouse was broken into that weekend and there would be evidence called to prove it. Unfortunately, she said, had it been a weekday and not a weekend there would have been no doubt as to the precise date. But Devlin and other witnesses would testify that it occurred on Sunday night, starting at 11 pm. And if the jury believed the burglary happened on that night and that Devlin was present from the time he said he was then that was the end of the case.[4] But, she reminded the jury, it was not for the defendant to prove his innocence. "In short, rather than Devlin satisfying you that he was at Sunblinds on the

---

3.   Heilbron might also have profitably explained to the jury of laymen that Devlin was going into the witness box voluntarily, knowingly subjecting himself to a gruelling cross-examination for hours by Basil Neild in order to establish his innocence.

4.   Heilbron was unaware of Frederick Downing's suppressed statement of 27th October corroborating Devlin's date and time of the break-in. Nor was she aware he and his wife Joan had been threatened with imprisonment for theft and receiving if they gave evidence for the defence.

murder night, the prosecution had to prove he was at 7 Cranborne Road." Therefore, she said, if they had a reasonable doubt about the matter — particularly in view of the unsatisfactory and often contradictory evidence of the Crown witnesses — they should acquit him.

Heilbron then dealt with the discrepancy between what the men had told Bury and Milne before putting them on the train for Liverpool on the night of Sunday 5th August. June Bury testified that the men, in Milne's presence, said they would see them in two or three days' time. But Milne said she did not hear this and that in fact Burns took her aside and told her he would see her in Liverpool on the 17th. "Yet they did indeed return to Verulam Street, not on the 17th, but on the morning of the 8th, as they said they would."

"Members of the jury, I am not going to go into detail because you will only hear it twice, but you will hear witnesses who say that Devlin was in Manchester on the 17th." She then proceeded to outline her client's movements right up to the Sunblinds break-in on Sunday night, the 19th August, including witnesses who had either been with him and Burns or who had seen them together in Manchester. People like Alice Ford, Henry Burns, Matilda Miller, Mabel Williams, Alice Shenton and the taxi driver, William Butler, who took the two men and Burns' relatives back to 6 Medlock Street in the early hours of the morning. But most importantly, she told the jury, would be the testimony of Alan Campbell who had been convicted of the offence. When Campbell came to give his evidence, she warned,

He will not come from the Witnesses Room, he will come through the dock from down below because he is serving a sentence of 18 months imprisonment for that Manchester warehouse-breaking which took place with Devlin and Burns on the night they are said to have murdered Mrs Rimmer in Liverpool.

Concluding her opening speech she told the jury,

In a very short while you will hear the other side of this story. And when you have heard it all, when the *whole* story has been unfolded before you, I will ask from you, and I will ask with considerable confidence, a verdict of not guilty.

CHAPTER TWENTY THREE
DEVLIN (AND THE COSH) IN THE WITNESS BOX

He might or might not have been innocent of the crime of which he was accused. But if he was charged with it, it was because he belonged to the classes amongst whom they looked for crime.

Sir Robert Lowe, Former Home Secretary

When Rose Heilbron announced, "I call Edward Francis Devlin", the diminutive, five foot seven inches, smartly dressed Mancunian left the dock and walked briskly across the well of the court to the witness box. But because the jury box was behind him all the jurors could see was his back, which prevented them observing his demeanour whilst giving his evidence. Facing on the opposite side of the courtroom was an identical box for the press. It is not known why this was not used for the jury, which would have made the trial more open and the witnesses more fully transparent.

Replying to his counsel, Devlin stated that he was born on March 21st 1929. His father died, aged 38, on May 3rd 1943, almost one year after his daughter Amy was killed by a bus on Stretford Road in the blackout. There were now six in his family: his mother, himself, older brother Leonard, older sister Eileen, younger brother Peter who was in the army, and younger sister Jean. He was at present unemployed but had been a general labourer. After serving in the army from April 1947 to May 1949, including a period in Nigeria, he had been discharged with a "good character". When his criminal record was put to him, he agreed his first and only prison sentence, was six months, imposed in July 1950 for stealing tomatoes from the wholesale market. In June 1951, at Manchester magistrates' court he was charged with larceny and committed for trial on August 1, but absconded whilst on bail and was on the run during August. He had absconded, he said, in order to locate witnesses in his defence. He was re-arrested on September 24th and on October 4th 1951 he was acquitted of the larceny charge at Manchester Quarter Sessions. If there had been any doubt about this acquittal he had the best witness anyone could have had—the judge, Sir Noel Goldie!

When asked if he knew George McLoughlin and if had met him in a café in late July, he replied, "I have never met McLoughlin in my life." Answering further questions from Heilbron, he stated he first came to Liverpool in the early hours of August 2nd. He did not know where Cranborne Road was and had never been there with McLoughlin or anybody else. He had never been convicted of any offence of violence. Asked when he first met June Bury, Devlin said in Manchester on Whit Monday. After spending the night together he arranged to see her later that day in Mary's Café on Stretford Road but he didn't turn up. When asked if he still fancied her after that occasion he replied, "Yes, I was rather keen to see her again." That was why he went to Liverpool in August to try and locate her. After asking some people, he finally located her in Canning Street where he had gone by taxi. They then went to the Dive where he introduced her to Burns. At closing time, 3 pm, all three then went to a café before travelling to Manchester by train. Why did they go to Manchester? asked Heilbron. Because, he said, they needed a change of clothing, also he explained rather cryptically, "To make arrangements with a certain man, Thomas Nicholson, for future reference, which I will explain to you later." For the benefit of the jury, Heilbron asked, "Future reference is something to do with a job [robbery]?"—to which he agreed.

They returned to Liverpool, he said, in the early hours of Saturday 4th of August. When asked if Bury had said anything about digs he replied, "We were going to stay in Manchester, and when we went back to Liverpool the first time, she suggested if we collected her clothes, she could probably find digs for us and she knew some girls which Alfred Burns could take his pick of." On their return at approximately four o'clock in the morning did they go to a café? asked Heilbron. "Yes", he said, they went to the Rainbow Café.

Here—apropos her earlier questioning of the detectives about the circumstances surrounding the men's statements—a more astute Heilbron could have productively asked Devlin if he knew the name of the Rainbow Café before being arrested or had he learned it from the police? His reply would have shown that the police had indeed suggested the café names to both men. But she never asked. And hadn't her client been instructed by Heilbron herself not to embellish his replies in the witness box?

Devlin said that when June Bury "brought this young lady upstairs" in the

Rainbow, another blonde girl came with her, whose name he didn't know, who started talking to both Bury and Milne. "We included her in the meal we bought." Then the girl told Marie that "he" was downstairs. "The girl told Milne that she had better wait upstairs until he had gone or until the café closed." Asked if Milne said who was downstairs, he said that she told them it was just some boy she knew and that she could handle it.

Answering further questions, he said that when the café closed at about 4 am he and Burns and the two girls then went down to the Pier Head and were there a couple of hours. Eventually they arrived at Canning Street, where they walked up and down the street whilst Bury and Milne were inside. When the girls emerged, Rubin appeared a few minutes later. He then related the incident between Bury and Rubin, after which they left and deposited Bury's suitcase in the left luggage at the station. They then went on the ferry boat over to New Brighton with the intention of looking for digs but in the end they didn't bother. When they returned they went to "a street near the Rialto where Burns and Milne got lodgings." When asked where he went he explained that he and Burns had made an arrangement that, "If they went to the rooms first it would save money."

"If they went where?" asked the judge.

"If they went to the room first, me and June would go there about nine o'clock and they would let us in so the four of us could occupy the room." The reason for this was that they wanted accommodation near to each other but there were no other rooms in the vicinity. He and Bury went to the pictures and then returned to the room at 9 pm, but getting no answer they went to a hotel in Mount Pleasant. He signed the register as "A Ford". What did Bury sign as, asked Heilbron. "I was very tired. I cannot remember whether she wrote in the book or not." The reason he could not remember was because Bury never signed the register. She didn't have to. Unknown to him, the owner, Dorothy Jones, was a friend of Bury's, who on the 13th September was given six months for running a brothel there.

The following morning he and Bury called at Verulam Street and he went with Burns across the main road (Upper Parliament Street) to a nearby public house (the Sefton in Bloom Street) for a drink. "When we were having a pint Alfie told me he didn't like Marie Milne, so we discussed a change-over and ..."

"Do you mean", interrupted Finnemore, "he was taking on June and you were taking on Marie Milne?"

"Yes, my Lord."

Asked by Heilbron if he had met anyone in that pub that he could remember, he replied, "Not in that particular beer house," adding that he *had* met someone in another pub.

After collecting the two girls from the room, he said, "The four of us went down to a beer house called the Dive." Despite him explaining all four went to the Dive, the judge wanted to know where the girls went. They waited on the corner, outside the pub, he replied, whilst he and Burns had a quick pint.

Continuing, he said Eskimo Joe was in the pub. Then Rubin came in with another man and asked to speak to him in the lavatory, where he told him June Bury had a disease. "Well", I said, 'I'm all right.' I thought he was just saying that so I would throw June Bury over."

In a further reply to his counsel, Devlin said a woman came up to Milne at the station and called her a "professional brass". The woman wanted to know why she wasn't at home and said her parents were going to kill her if she didn't come home. But Marie did not want to go home. "That is when, on the spur of the moment, we went to Manchester. It was through Marie that we went to Manchester that Sunday." He denied discussing on the train any "jobs" about an old woman or anybody else. Reminding him that Bury had admitted going on an abortive job with him and Burns on their first trip to Manchester, Heilbron asked him to confine himself to the second train journey when Milne was present? "Did you ask June or Marie to go on a job with you in Liverpool?" When he denied this, she asked if *any* job had been discussed, to which he again said "No." Seemingly reluctant, however, to accept his two denials, Finnemore persisted in asking him if he had discussed doing a job *anywhere*—"Whether Liverpool, Manchester or anywhere?" to which he replied, "None at all. No sir."

This, however, was only partly true. Devlin and Burns *had* discussed with Bury on that journey—when Milne was singing to herself—the earlier Rail Goods Depot abortive robbery on their first trip to Manchester on the 2nd August. But it was true they had not asked either woman to go on any jobs with them on the second train journey.

Giving an account at Heilbron's request, of his movements on arrival at

Manchester that Sunday, Devlin recounted going to the flat of a friend Norman Higgins, then the two girls going out for something to eat and bringing some food back for all of them. Then Burns and Bury said they were going out for a drink and he and Milne ended up in bed having sex, after she had told him she knew Burns didn't like her. Continuing, he said Burns and Bury arrived back at about ten pm after which he and Burns went out looking for Norman Higgins to ask if the girls could stay, but when they met Higgins, both he and his wife refused, and that was why they took the girls to the station to put them on the train to Liverpool

For some odd reason known only to himself, Mr Justice Finnemore wanted to know whether he and Milne were still in bed when Burns and Bury returned. They were, replied Devlin, but, they both got out of bed and he went down and opened the front door. At the railway station — "I can't remember if it was Exchange" — they made arrangements to see the girls in Liverpool in two or three days and gave them a few shillings to get some food to tide them over. Asked why he and Burns stayed in Manchester instead of going with the girls, he said they did not have much money and their intention was to do a job.

Replying to further questions from his counsel, he related how he and Burns duly returned to Verulam Street at about eight am on "either the 8th or the 9th of August," but he could not be sure. He then explained how June Bury arrived a few minutes later. When asked where Marie Milne was, Bury said she had "floated." She also told them, "I have been out all night with some blokes screwing."

"Does that mean a thieving expedition?" asked Heilbron, to which he agreed. He said he started shouting at her. She then started crying. When the judge asked, "What did you say?" he replied that he told her that as soon as he turned his back she has to go with other men, that she would always be the same and that she couldn't be left alone with other men. "She then told us that she had been arrested that night and the blokes had been arrested. She said she was in the police station all night."

Asked when this was, he said it was the night before and she told them she had just been let out of the police station. Commenting on this, the judge in an ostensible gesture of fairness to Bury, pointed out that none of this had been put to her in cross-examination. Heilbron however had a reasonable reply. "I'm afraid it could not my Lord because I did not know about it." This may have been a clever riposte to Finnemore but it nevertheless demonstrated either a slipshod preparation of her brief by Livermore or her own negligent lack of consultation with her client. Turning again to Devlin, she repeated, "She said she had just come out of the police station?"

"Yes, she said she had to appear at ten o'clock. She told me she didn't want to face it and would we take her to Manchester with us and she would not go with any other men."

On this third journey to Manchester with Bury, he said, they first went to Salford because with being on the run, they were not so well-known by the police there. Later Burns and June Bury went to the pictures and he went home to his mother's. But by prior arrangement he met them both at 10.30 pm with a man named Thomas Nicholson. This was the man, he said, with whom they robbed a bale of sheets from the Liverpool Road Goods Depot in Deansgate that night. "You had better tell us," interrupted the judge, "You stole it or Nicholson?" to which he replied that he and Burns had stolen it.

Further questioned by his counsel, he said he and Burns had left their macs with Bury whilst she was keeping watch on a street corner. A few days later on the 11th August they went looking for her to retrieve them and found her in an amusement arcade on Oxford Road. All three then went to her mother's house but Bury told them to wait on the corner. She returned to tell them her mother had sent their macs to the dry-cleaners. "We started shouting at her, asking why they should be in the cleaners when they were new except for a little tear in mine. Then her mother came up to us and we went into town with June." That, he said, was the last time he saw Bury. He did not see her after that occasion or tell her that he had an important job to do in Liverpool. When Heilbron quoted his statement where he said, "The last time I saw June Bury was in Manchester about the 16th or 17th of August." He replied, "That that date was suggested to me by…" But interrupting again, the judge asked, "Was the statement right or wrong, first of all?"

"It is wrong my Lord," he replied. "Actually I could not remember the exact date when I made that statement and Mr Balmer suggested that date to me."

How, Finnemore wanted to know, did the officer suggest it?

"Balmer said, "That would that be about the 16th or 17th you last saw her Ted'?" He knew there had been an interval between last seeing June Bury.

He could not remember fully so he agreed with Balmer about the 16th or 17th. "But since I have been able to think back I know it was the 11th when I last spoke to her. It was a Saturday." Still sitting impassively in court, Balmer slowly shook his head in mock sad resignation.

Did they go back to Bury's house on the Monday and get their macs asked Heilbron. "Yes. But we never did get them," he replied. "And we never saw June. We were talking to her mother when a police car came and we ran away."

Accounting for his movements between Monday 13th and Sunday 19th August, Devlin told his counsel that he and Burns never left Manchester between those dates. At her request he then outlined his movements from meeting Bury on the 2nd August, including taking Bury back to Manchester the first time; their early morning return on the 4th and meeting Milne at the Rainbow; the visit to the Lighthouse and later through Lewis's store, then to New Brighton to look for digs; the visit to 39 Canning Street and the Rubin episode; the booking of the Verulam Street room by Burns; his own stay with Bury at the Mount Pleasant hotel; the Sunday trip by all four of them to Manchester, then putting the girls on the train at about midnight; their return to Verulam Street on the morning of the 8th, meeting Bury there and taking her back to Manchester; the robbery at the Goods Depot that night and Bury keeping their macs.

Continuing, Devlin then related his movements on the 17th, 18th and 19th August, including Burns nephew's 5th birthday; meeting Alan Campbell on the Friday and reconnoitering Sunblinds; leaving Henry Burns' house in Cobden Street, Blackley, by taxi in the early hours for Medlock Street with Billingham his wife and baby; visiting Alice Ford's and his own sister's house at the Barracks Flats in Grenham Avenue on Sunday afternoon the 19th, robbing Sunblinds later that night at about 11.30 with Burns and Campbell; their unsuccessful search around Piccadilly for transport and finally enlisting the help of Joan Downing and her pram to remove the goods.[1]

This requested resume was a deliberate ploy by Heilbron to demonstrate to the jury Devlin's truthfulness. On the basis that a liar has to have a good memory, she was confident that his account would not waver from what he had now told the court to what he would say in cross-examination. Devlin's

---

1.   See *Chapter 1.*

narrative however was related in such a subdued tone that a testy Finnemore at one stage said, "You have told us several times, 'I shouted at June'. Try to shout at us will you. It is absolutely impossible to hear you at times."

Referring to the visit to his sister's flat, when she gave him money, Devlin said he had left Burns in Alice Ford's flat on the second floor and went to the pictures, meeting on the way a friend Sidney McDiarmid who was also going to the York Cinema and they both watched a boxing film called Joe Palooka. Afterwards he went to his mother's for something to eat and he met Burns by prior arrangement at 6.45. He then began to add, "Me mam told me…" but Finnemore, rudely interrupting, said, "Never mind what your mother said. Burns came to your house at 6.45?" And despite already stating he was at his mother's, Finnemore asked, "You were there, were you?" The only purpose of this constant repeating by the judge of questions already answered, seemed to be to try to trip up the witness and hopefully catch him out in a lie.

On the Saturday afternoon, said Devlin, he and Burns had arranged to meet Campbell in the "Mug Shop" but he wasn't there. They met him on the street in Deansgate then went to the Ship Inn, where they stayed till 10pm closing time. In the Ship they met John Ford and Anne Fitzgerald (who was now Mrs Ford). On the corner outside they saw the girls, Matilda Miller, her sister Margaret Miller, Mabel Williams, Elsie Roberts and Bernard Roberts.

When Devlin said he thought there may have been a chance of pairing off with two of the girls, the judge asked, "You tried to, did you?" No, he did not really try, he said But added he would have done if they'd got the chance. "But you wanted to?" insisted Finnemore. It seemed that not only Goldie was guilty of wasting the court's time asking irrelevant questions — even if Mr Justice Finnemore's appeared to have a more vicarious flavour!

Again replying to Heilbron, Devlin said they left the Sunblinds break-in until about 11 or 11.30 in order for the drinkers outside the few pubs in the vicinity to clear off. Then responding to various questions from his counsel and the judge he explained in detail how he Burns and Campbell had carried out the break-in. Included in this was how he smashed the "decent-sized" window with his fist covered by Campbell's raincoat and then picked out the broken pieces with a handkerchief around his hand. They left about 100 gabardine raincoats, eleven rolls of red cloth, seven rolls of gabardine and bundles of grey trousers in an enclosed compound whilst they went to look for a car or lorry driver to transport it. Being unsuccessful after a few hours, they went to Joan Downing's house, about 200 yards away and she helped them to cart away some of the property in her pram. Although they made two journeys they still left quite a lot of stuff behind, he said, because, "A bloke flashed a light on me and I spoke to him. He seemed to be a night watchman from an adjoining factory from what he said." Given that this encounter was crucial to the men's alibi, neither Heilbron nor the judge bothered to ask what the night watchman said to him.[2] When Devlin stated they had wasted a couple of hours in the middle of the job, finishing at about four am, the judge asked, "You were about five hours were you?" He also wanted to know *who* went to look for the transport. "The three of us my Lord," he replied.

The purpose of Finnemore's questions was that Devlin's answers would later be used to show any discrepancies between his, Burns and Campbell's accounts when they later gave evidence.

Staying several hours at the Downing's home, Devlin said all three men left at about 6.30 that morning and went to Burns home in Medlock Street. Later that afternoon he was with Campbell in City Road, when he was recognised and chased by a police car and Campbell was arrested. In relation to the fawn suit, he said he was wearing it in May last year when he was in a fight in a pub. There was, "A lot of blood on the shoulder and all over my clothing." It was sent to the cleaners at the beginning or the middle of May, he couldn't be sure. He last wore it on August 6th. After being chased by the police the day after the Sunblinds break-in, Devlin explained that, needing a change of clothing so the police would not recognise him, he asked his mother to get the fawn suit out of pawn and send it for express cleaning so it would be decent to wear. That was after the 20th, he said, about the 23rd or 24th August. He did not have that suit on the 19th of August. Replying to Heilbron, he said he had a fight with two Irishmen on Sunday 26th of August in Mary's Café in Stretford Road. There was some blood on one of the men's faces which got on to the same fawn suit.

---

2. This man, 73-year-old Daniel Norton, who was located and interviewed by Devlin's solicitor and later by Detective Sergeant Richardson, agreed speaking to a man carrying a bundle at the rear of Sunblinds Ltd at 4 am on the Monday morning. But he refused to sign the two statements. He was not called by the defence or the Crown.

Regarding his arrest, Devlin said Detective Constable Lynch told him he was being arrested for the Playhouse Theatre robbery the night before, which he *was* guilty of committing. He denied saying to Detective Sergeant. Richardson, "Have you seen the girls yet? What do they say?" And, "Have the girls been talking? Have you seen June and the Chinese bit?" He could have added that it was actually Richardson who had described Milne as "the Chinese bit" but instead heeded his counsel's warning not to attack the police and risk alienating the judge and jury.

As Heilbron concluded her examination, Burns' counsel, the ever eccentric Sir Noel Goldie, addressed the judge in such a melodramatic fashion that onlookers—not least the two accused—imagined he was preparing to reveal some sensational development. After telling the judge that he would respectfully ask for his direction on the right to cross-examine Devlin, he added, "I have gone into it very carefully, and my impression is that I have *not* that right. It is only when one accused gives evidence inculpating or exculpating the other accused that counsel has a right to cross-examine. Here of course, my defence being like my friend Miss Heilbron's, it cannot be said that this witness' evidence inculpates or exculpates my client." An apparently bemused Finnemore said, "Is there anything you want to ask?"

"No, my Lord."

Finnemore: "No? But if it is something in his evidence that you want him to explain…"

"No, I don't think so", interrupted Goldie, who had already answered his own pointless question! There was no apparent reason for this puerile performance, other than perhaps him thinking aloud about an academic question he might ask or perhaps an attempt to impress everyone with his legal expertise. Whatever the reason it was a frivolous waste of time and an unpardonable self-indulgence which lessened even further, opinion of him as an able and competent defence counsel.

CHAPTER TWENTY FOUR
DEATH OF JUROR'S MOTHER CAUSES POSTPONEMENT OF THE TRIAL

And many destructions played, in this ghastly masquerade.

Percy Byshe Shelley

When Basil Neild QC rose on behalf of the Crown, his cross-examination of Devlin—in the absence of any forensic or material evidence—would consist mainly of hypothesis, innuendo, "guilt-by association" and non-evidence. Most of his questions should not have been admissible. But then, Finnemore was the same judge who, the previous year, had condemned William Watkins to death by allowing the Crown to put in evidence a statement fiercely claimed by the defence to be inadmissible.

The forensically naïve Devlin would prove to be no match for Neild's clinically incisive approach as he gradually built up to the killer questions by a series of ostensibly innocuous ones. An example of this was how he gradually made the connection between the broken window at the Rimmer home and the means of access at Sunblinds, by getting Devlin to agree that housebreakers usually have the same *modus operandi*—in his case breaking windows to gain entry. Readily agreeing, Devlin truthfully but perhaps foolishly, replied, "Well each is supposed to do it very nearly the same."

Didn't Devlin also agree, he asked, that thieves adopt similar methods—in his case using young women to "keep douse"? "No," he didn't. Denying ever using the expression "keep douse", he and other Manchester villains always said either, "dog out" or "keep crow."

This use of "douse" was a small clue un-noticed by everyone, of Balmer's authorship of his witnesses' statements. He may have been a brilliant Liverpool detective, as some journalists wrongly believed, but he obviously knew nothing about the vernacular of Manchester thieves![1]

1. This was another of Balmer's verbals. As explained in the text, Manchester villains never used

Next came one of the first instances of Neild's non-evidence when asking, "Not only on the 9th August did you use a young woman to keep watch, but on the 19th you broke a window to get in (Sunblinds) did you not?" When Devlin agreed, he added, "And wrapped your fist in a handkerchief?"[2] "No," said Devlin, "a raincoat." But he agreed he had wrapped his hand in a handkerchief to remove the remaining bits of glass?

Here was an incongruous situation of the Crown refuting the men's alibi for the 19th, yet at the same time using it as evidence of *modus operandi!* This pattern of wanting his cake and eating it would be repeated numerous times during Neild's cross-examination, with only the odd weak objection from both defence counsel and entirely without censure from the judge.

Switching to another aspect, Neild again began his build up to what would be a devastating point against Devlin by asking him to tell the judge and the jury what he would have done if they had been disturbed by a watchman. When he replied he would have just gone away, this wasn't enough for Crown counsel. What if they had been inside the warehouse? What would they have done? "We would have tried to get away," he replied. "We would not use violence." But again this wasn't sufficient for Neild, who then asked if in addition to some of the stolen goods he had left a cosh behind at Sunblinds, what it was for? As he began to explain how and why they came to have the cosh, the judge interrupting, said, "You were asked what it was for *that night.*"

"Well," said Devlin, "we took it off a man who might have hit both me and Burns with it." But Neild insisted on knowing what it was *for.* "No particular reason," he replied. But intervening again, Finnemore demanded, "Why did you take it to the factory *that you say* you were breaking into?" (Author's italics).

Mindful that Neild's questions were hypothetical, Finnemore ensured he didn't repeat the mistake, by qualifying his own question with "that you say."

When Devlin replied that he could not give a reason, Sir Donald Finnemore, in his Boys Brigade commander's disciplinary mode, demanded, "Do not say you don't know! Could you not tell the jury why you took that

---

this Liverpool expression. They used "dog out" or "keep crow."
2. It was this knowledge which provided Balmer's script for Milne to include Devlin having a bloodstained handkerchief around his hand when she met them after the murder.

cosh to the factory?" He then ordered, "Take it in your hand."[3] The cosh was handed to Devlin but because he was not ordered to hand it back, he unconsciously began fiddling with it as he answered further questions. The spectacle however of him manipulating this horrific weapon whilst still being questioned, had a fatal effect on the jury. Onlookers were aghast at Devlin's apparently nonchalant and unfeeling attitude. It was as if the Sword of Damocles had become a hangman's noose slowly descending from the court ceiling! Yet it was the judge, who had deliberately put the young man in this iniquitous position of opprobrium.

Purposely leaving, for effect, Devlin absent-mindedly handling the cosh in the witness box whilst distracting him with more questions, Neild again asked why he took it with them on the 19th August. If the noose was already descending, then Devlin's next reply certainly helped to put it around his neck! Despite his earlier reply, he said, "Well, if a policeman had come and pulled his truncheon out to hit us with, we would have been able to retaliate if the need arose." He had been instructed by Heilbron to tell the truth at all times. And this may have been a truthful answer. But with Neild glowing and both Heilbron and Goldie frowning, the effect in the courtroom was devastating. Indeed, later in the cells one of the prison officers told him how foolish he had been and that he should have told Neild, "To stick the cosh where Paddy stuck his ninepence!"

A delighted Neild then asked, "Would you have hesitated to do that?" to which Devlin, naïvely heaping up his own funeral pyre, replied, "If he had hit me with his truncheon I would not have hesitated. Or if he had gone to hit me." Was that why he carried it that night? asked Neild. It was Burns, he said, who had carried it. But it was too late. The damage done to their case was fatal. It is more than likely that was the moment the jury had decided to convict them.

Basil Neild's hypothetical questions were a classic example of non-evidence and should never have been allowed by the judge — particularly since the Crown's case was that Devlin and Burns were never at Sunblinds on the 19th. It seemed the Crown did indeed want to have their cake and eat it: on

---

3.   This was similar to Lord Goddard inflaming the jury in the Craig and Bentley case the following year by brandishing a knuckleduster before them and inviting them to take it into the jury room — even though no such weapon was used.

the one hand totally refuting the men's alibi yet enlisting an object found at Sunblinds to prove their guilt!

When Devlin later stated that he had never used a knife or a cosh on anyone and never intended to do so, Finnemore reminded him, "You said you *did intend* to use it" (Author's italics). When he weakly replied, "Only if necessary," the judge chided, "Well don't say you never intended to use it."

If Neild's questions about an imagined situation of being discovered by a policeman were hypothetical then surely were Devlin's replies. It was therefore quite wrong of the judge to misrepresent these literally as Devlin "intending" to attack a police officer — and at a crime which the Crown maintained had not been committed by him!

Devlin went on to explain how they came into possession of the cosh; of how Mac, a big fellow did them out of the money and some of the bales of sheets on August 9th, and his threats of how he would deal with anyone who tried to get tough with him. They removed the cosh from his van, he said, in case he tried to use it on them. Only after this full explanation did Neild ask Devlin to hand him back the cosh, asking with the obvious implication, "You would call that a blunt instrument, would you not?" to which he replied, "It is, I suppose. I don't know." The inference, for the jury's benefit, loaded as it was with innuendo, was that Mrs Rimmer had been attacked by a blunt instrument. It didn't seem to matter that this particular blunt instrument, which contained no traces of blood, had been found at a warehouse in Manchester 30 miles away from Cranborne Road!

Asked if Sunblinds Ltd was broken into on the 18th of August? Devlin said not that he knew of. Neild then suggested that, if Devlin had added 24 hours to the truth, that would explain his story. "Yes, if that were true," he replied, "But we didn't do it on the Saturday. We did it on the Sunday night."

At Neild's request he then reiterated his movements on the 17th, 18th 19th and 20th of August. On Friday night, the 17th he stayed at 34 Leinster Street, his brother Leonard's house. Leonard was in hospital so his wife Annie let him stay at her house as she was temporarily staying with a friend at No. 14. On Saturday night the 18th he stayed with Burns' at his mother's house, 6 Medlock Street. And on the night of the 19th and early morning of the 20th, he stayed at the Downings, 38 Foster Street, leaving about 6.30 am with Burns and Campbell for Mrs Burns' house Asked if he had seen Mrs Burns the following morning. Yes he had. Had he seen Mrs Burns since the case started? Yes, he had seen her in court. He then pointed her out in the public gallery. This occasioned Sir Noel Goldie to intervene with one of his bizarre diversions. Addressing the judge—despite Devlin just picking her out—he said, "My Lord I understand Mrs Burns is in court?" to which Finnemore replied, "Yes. He has just picked her out." Then, "Would your Lordship kindly direct all witnesses for the defence to be kept outside the court," to which an increasingly exasperated Finnemore responded, "I directed it some days ago at your request Sir Noel. I am not going to direct it again." When Basil Neild explained the lady in question was Burns' mother, Goldie apologised, saying he thought it was the other Mrs Burns, her daughter-in-law. By this and numerous other confusing episodes, it was becoming evident that Sir Noel Goldie, despite his idiosyncratic behaviour and quaint turn of phrase, was worryingly incompetent—a grave deficiency considering he was defending a man on trial for his life.

When Neild observed that although Burns mother could presumably back up his evidence, she was not appearing as a witness, Devlin replied, "It is not my fault she is not a witness."[4] Remarking also on the absence of Joan Downing, he tellingly pointed out that both she and Mrs Burns could have greatly supported Devlin's story about the trips with the pram and sleeping in their houses on the nights 18th and 19th August.

When stating that he and Burns spent the early morning of the 20th after the break-in, at Downing' house, Devlin, not knowing the house number, described it as, "The third house from the end." This innocuous commonplace phrase would later be used against him to support the evidence that he had told Milne Mrs Rimmer's house was "the fourth house from the end."

Asked if Mr Downing was present at the house, Devlin explained he wasn't when they were at the house earlier making arrangements with his wife and telling her to wait up, which she did, whilst they looked around Piccadilly for transport. But later when they couldn't get transport and she helped remove the stolen goods to her house in her pram, her husband *was* there. The judge, however, asked if Joan Downing knew they were going to

---

4. A tired Mrs Burns had been apprehended during October after a hard day's work by Detective Sergeant Richardson and compelled to sign a muddled statement whilst sitting in a police car. When she later requested a copy of this the police refused on the advice of the DPP. The defence therefore thought it best not to put her in the witness box.

break into Sunblinds and if she was going to wait up. Despite already saying so, Devlin repeated, "Yes" But, he added, her husband did not know about it beforehand. Notwithstanding his earlier clear explanation, it seemed this unnecessary question was designed to test Devlin's veracity to the jury.

Still scoring points with matters which were not strictly evidence, Neild now asked if he usually described houses as three or four from the corner. "Well he repeated, "I do not know the number." Alluding to Cranborne Road, Neild asked, "Have you ever described a house as, 'four houses past the entry'?"

"I have never in my life described *that* house", replied Devlin.

Asked what he got the six months imprisonment for in 1950, Devlin explained that in the Potato Market a man asked him and a friend to help remove some boxes of tomatoes to his car down the street. He did not know they were stolen and was arrested on the spot. No, he did not appeal. But he did plead not guilty, he told Neild.

Questioned about his statement made to Inspector Lees, Devlin agreed it was true but he never gave it in detail because at the time he could not remember all the details. "It was just an outline of our time in Liverpool and that."

Responding to more questions, he denied knowing Liverpool "pretty well" and knowing where Paddington or Bill's Café was but admitted knowing the location of the Dive and 39 Canning Street. He did not know the Dive was near the Royal Court Theatre. During these quick-fire questions he admitted knowing the Rainbow and Lighthouse cafés but then erroneously admitted knowing the Continental. His confusion was apparent during Neild's next questions which were not specifically about the Continental. Asked if he agreed with McLoughlin that (the Continental) was where the lads knocked around, Devlin replied, "*That* was where there were some people lying about and sleeping on the floor" (Author's italics). From this exchange and what followed it was clear the witness and the prosecutor were talking at cross purposes and that Devlin was referring to the Pier Head and the Lighthouse, *not* the Continental in Chinatown. Did he agree with McLoughlin when he had said it was an odd crowd, mostly crooks? Devlin said it looked to him that, "they were just people stopping out all night because they had nowhere to go."

"How often had you been there?"

"The 2nd of August was the first time I had been to the Pier Head Café."

Neild now changed direction, asking if he knew Central Station and the Rialto and its surrounding area? Yes, he did. Did he know Wilkie's Club or the Somali Café? No. Neither did he know Tracey's pub in Hanover Street or the name of the department store (Lewis's). "The girls took us through a store on the Saturday before we went to New Brighton but whether it was Lewis's or Woolworths I do not know." They had just walked through the store, he said, but did not go into any cafeteria there. Nor did he know of any café called the Golden Dragon. When the judge asked if the Chinese restaurant was a café or a public house, it seemed that Goldie wasn't the only one failing to keep a firm grasp on the proceedings!

Denying that he had pointed to his fawn suit at the Liverpool police station and said, "You're wasting your time with that," he said he never saw the suit there. He also denied telling the police he had not been in any fight, because he had been in several fist fights. To further questions about the suit, he explained it had been both cleaned and pawned in May because there were bloodstains on it after a fight. He believed his mother pawned it but did not know the name of the pawn shop. He agreed it was again pawned four days after the murder also after being first cleaned. That was, he said, because although he had only worn it from the beginning of August up till about August 6th, his young brother Peter, who was home on Army leave had been wearing it. Because it was light coloured it got dirty quite quickly. That was also why it had to be cleaned beforehand, otherwise the pawn shop would not accept it. Asked if he had heard Mrs Wilson of Silver Knight Dry-cleaners say the jacket was crumpled as if a rough attempt had been made to wash it, he replied that he could not say whether it was or wasn't as he had only seen it *after* it came out of the pawn shop. He knew however, that *he* had not attempted to wash it. Intervening, the judge asked, "You are sure you never saw it when it came from the pawn shop before it went to the cleaners?" This question, whether deliberately or otherwise, was confusing: By, "when it *came from* the pawn shop," did he mean after the May pawning? If not then he had the sequence wrong. The express cleaners were part of the pawn shop and it had been well discussed that garments were cleaned *before* they were accepted for pawn.

When it was put to Devlin by Neild that he had been in prison just as McLoughlin had testified, it was yet another piece of non-evidence, which Devlin denied telling him anyway. Moreover, being in prison did not necessarily mean he had told McLoughlin of that fact.

Asked if he knew of any other source of knowledge McLoughlin could have had about him other than himself, Devlin replied that he seemed to know the area quite well. He could have planned it with someone else and, with the help of Bury and Milne, thrown the blame on himself and Burns. At this, Balmer wearing an aloof expression simply stared straight ahead.

When the accused man denied everything he was supposed to have said and done with McLoughlin, from the alleged meeting in Bill's Café to the alleged meeting at the Continental, Neild said, "Now I don't want you to guess or conjecture. Do you know of any reason why that witness should say that of you?" When Heilbron objected to the question, Finnemore said it merely gave him an opportunity to say if he knew of any reason. After further argument about the propriety of the question the judge finally asked Devlin, that, according to him, he was a complete stranger to McLoughlin, "and you a complete stranger to him?"

"Yes."

"And until you got to court you had never heard his name?"

"I never even knew he existed."

At one stage Neild, enquiring about Norman Higgins (who was not even a witness in the case) asked Devlin had he seen him in court, whereupon Heilbron said she could not understand the question and that her client was not in a position to see him. Finnemore however, once again siding with Neild, told her, "It is only a question of seeing him in fact. Nothing more than that." But this was not good enough for Heilbron, who rejoined, "In case the jury gets a misconceived idea of *that*, he is not in a position to see *anyone*, because he is kept in the cells."

Later questioned about his statement stating the last time he saw Bury was on the 16th or 17th August, Devlin reiterated that Balmer had suggested that date to him. By not responding to this assertion Neild was implicitly accepting the truth of what Devlin said about the head of the CID. Yet all of his subordinates had testified he took no part in taking the men's statements. But brushing Balmer's involvement aside, Neild asked, "Whatever the suggestion was, did you agree with it?" Devlin explained: "You see he was asking me questions what happened two months ago and I could not remember so I said, 'That would be about right.'"

Since this gave the lie to the judge's earlier comments on the rectitude of the police officers conduct whilst they were giving evidence, it is remarkable that he did not enquire further, or even comment, on Devlin's assertion that Balmer had played an active role in the interviews.

Asking Devlin about describing to Milne the layout of Mrs Rimmer's living room; the armchair and the two mirrors, Basil Neild passed him the photographs showing these and wanted to know how she would know this unless *he had told her.*

"It is impossible" he cried almost incredulously. "I never even knew this house existed." But Neild insisted, asking him if he knew of any way she could have got these details right if he had not told her. He could only reply that he did not know of any way she could have got them right. Shaking his head with puzzlement, he declared, "I just don't know."

Devlin's protestations were understandable: Marie Milne's evidence, and the prosecution case, was that it was *Burns* who was supposed to have told her about the mirrors and the armchair — not Devlin. Yet this fundamental error of Crown counsel went un-remarked upon by defence counsel and the judge. Nonetheless Balmer, still sitting impassively behind the lawyers, the architect of the story, the man who *did* know, allowed himself a wry grin.

Given that Bury had visited him in prison and brought him cigarettes, Neild asked Devlin if he knew of any reason why she was giving false evidence against him. But before replying, Goldie objected that it was not a proper question to put, adding, "Nobody can read anybody else's mind." But ever favourable to the Crown, Finnemore said, "But you see there may be some reason. If he knows of one he ought to have the chance of saying so. It does not go any further than that." But Goldie insisted it should not have been put in that way, stating, "The answer to, 'Do you know?' is: 'How can I?' Surely you cannot read someone else's mind."

When Neild, doubtless encouraged by the judge's support, repeated the question to Devlin, Goldie asked that his objection be recorded but was simply reminded by the judge that it would obviously be done as part of the trial transcript!

Minutes before Devlin's evidence was concluded, he made numerous denials, including not meeting Rubin in the Dive on August 18th and insisting it
was about 1 pm "dinner time on Sunday the 5th of August."

Briefly re-examining, Rose Heilbron wanted to know what June Bury had
to say during the January visit to him in prison? "She mumbled something,"
he said, "that she had given a false name to get into the prison and then told
me she was sorry she had put us in prison for four months, and that Marie
Milne had told her to back her story up, and that she would tell the truth
when she came to court. But apparently she has not."

"Did she say anything about her evidence at the police (committal) court
and anything about McLoughlin?"

"She said her evidence was untrue and that she did not even know
McLoughlin."

After a total of four and a half hours in the witness box, that concluded
Devlin's evidence.

Other defence witnesses following him included dock worker Samuel
Crehan from Baguley. He said he had lived all his life until last June at 40
Foster Street with his mother and sister. Replying to junior defence counsel, Mr Tarsh, he testified that at the end of April or early May last year, he
and his friend were in the house when Devlin knocked on the front door,
holding a handkerchief to his nose and there was quite a lot of blood on the
front of his coat and shirt. Devlin told him he had been in a fight and had
been knocking next door at the Downing's house but couldn't get an answer.

When Neild implied that Crehan was unemployed and was an associate
of Devlin's, he replied he was employed on the Manchester docks. He had
never been out of work but was on strike at the beginning of May 1951. He
denied he was a friend of Devlin's. On the contrary he stated that he went
to Devlin's home in Leinster Street the following day and complained to his
mother about him knocking on his door with blood all over him. And she
told him he was knocking for the Downings next door but nobody was in.

When Crehan's friend John Riley was called, he corroborated his evidence. Stating that he and Crehan were already in the house when Devlin
called. He added that he was wearing a fawn suit and bleeding heavily from
the nose. Riley was about to relate what Devlin said as he entered the house
but the judge, interrupting, told him, "Do not tell us what he said. What

did you notice?"

"He was bleeding from the nose and there was blood on his shirt and down his right side." When Riley stated that the suit shown *was like* the same suit, Finnemore, emphasised, "That is *the sort* of suit is it?" thus implying doubt to the jury as to whether it was indeed the same suit.

The next witness, Mrs Frances Connor, a friend of Devlin's mother, unlike the previous witness, *positively* identified the suit as "Teddy Devlin's fawn suit" and testified that she and Mrs Devlin took it to Appleton's pawn shop in Stretford Road on 4th May last year. She handed it to the pawnbroker Mr Morby whom she knew. There was blood on the coat and on the trousers. They received 30 shillings and the suit was first sent by the pawn shop to the cleaners. Implying collusion, as he would in questions to other defence witnesses, Neild asked if she was anxious to help Devlin. She replied, "I am only anxious to tell the truth."

The trial was then adjourned until 2.15 pm the following afternoon because a juror had to attend his mother's funeral in the morning. This was ostensibly an act of kindness by the judge, although Dr Firth commented to the *Liverpool Echo* that in his 30 years of giving evidence in the courts this was unprecedented. Many observers wondered was the judge simply acting compassionately or did he have an ulterior motive in releasing the juror? Was it mere coincidence that the two men were on trial for the murder of someone's *mother!*

The sensational headline carried that night by the *Liverpool Echo* was, DEVLIN: "I WOULD NOT HAVE HESITATED TO USE MY COSH."

CHAPTER TWENTY FIVE
ALAN CAMPBELL TESTIFIES IN SUPPORT OF THE ACCUSEDS' ALIBI

Sixth Day

I'm not ashamed of being poor.

Mrs Amy Devlin

When the court resumed on the sixth day, Appleton's pawn shop manager, Herbert Morby confirmed that Mrs Connor pawned the fawn suit in May. It was heavily bloodstained and was sent to their cleaners, Embassy Renovators. It was so heavily bloodstained that he remembered remarking, "Someone has committed a murder!" That remark, another piece of non-evidence, nonetheless provided a suitably dramatic and prejudicial headline for that evening's Liverpool and Manchester newspapers—even though it referred to an occasion four months before the murder!

Morby was followed by Devlin's mother Amy. Replying to Rose Heilbron she said she was a widow who had given up her job since the case began through having to visit her son in Walton Prison several times a week. She had never been in trouble with the police. Rather than ask for charity, she regularly used the local pawn shops when she was short. She agreed Mrs Connor and herself pawned the bloodstained suit in May 1951.

In August Devlin had changed into other clothes because the suit was too conspicuous given that he was on the run from the police. Her youngest son Peter had worn it until returning from army leave. She pawned the suit at Roylance's pawn shop in City Road the following morning August 11th because she had given Peter all the money she had whilst seeing him off on the train. The suit was redeemed on the 23rd August. On the same day she sent it to the Silver Knight Dry-cleaners in Upper Jackson Street to be cleaned so her oldest son Leonard could wear it when coming out of Manchester Royal Infirmary, where he had been a patient since 16th August. When she agreed she was well-known to Mr Armitage the manager of Roylances, Neild grinned knowingly at this remark. But she told him, "I'm not ashamed of being poor," to which he commented, "I'm not blaming you Mrs Devlin."

Cross-examined by Crown counsel, she stated that the suit was blood-stained when pawned in May but not when pawned on August 11th. Rather confusingly, Neild asked her if Leonard had left the suit at home when he went into hospital. If this was a trick question it was soon shot down when she replied that he could not have worn it as he was in hospital when it was in pawn and did not wear it until he was discharged in September.

The next witness, pawn shop manager Joseph Armitage, stated that a coat and trousers had been pawned by Mrs Devlin on the 11th August and this was confirmed by an entry in the shop's pledge book, handed to him by Heilbron. Replying to Neild, he agreed he could not remember whether it was a suit but it probably was. He knew the Devlin family quite well. Roylance's, he said, was about 40 yards from their home in Leinster Street He said he had seen Devlin wearing a light suit on several occasions but could not say for definite it was a fawn suit on every occasion. Getting more specific, Neild asked if he recognised Detective Sergeant Wade, who was sitting in the well of the court alongside Balmer. When he agreed, Neild read out a statement he had made to the officer on October 13th in which he said, "I remember the gent's gabardine suit belonging to the Devlin family of 26 Leinster Street. I can say that it has been pawned at my employers shop before August 16th but not between that date and October 13th. Between August 1st and Sept 25th I saw Edward Devlin wearing the same suit in the street on more than one occasion."

Apart from this statement confusing the issue and having an incriminatory slant — as most of the statements taken by the Liverpool detectives did — it was not evidence against Devlin, given that it had earlier been conclusively proved by production of the pledge book that the suit was in pawn between the 16th and 23rd August, which included the vital August 19th.

The pawn shop owner, Arthur Roylance had to be subpoenaed so was obviously an unwilling witness. Questioned briefly he was of no help to the defence since he did not deal personally with customers. Why Rose Heilbron went to the trouble of subpoenaing this man who had nothing of any value to offer — particularly when she failed to call vital witnesses like

Burns mother—is a mystery.

Next in the witness box on this sixth day of the trial was widow, Alice Ford, who lived at the Barracks Flats on Grenham Avenue. She said she could remember August 19th very well because Devlin and Burns called on her at about 1.30 pm after her house window had been broken by one of her children. She had seen the two men watching a Sunday League football match on The Green outside the flats. They had some dinner then at about 3.30 Devlin went to borrow some money off his sister Eileen Ackroyd, who lived downstairs. They didn't go to Eileen's for dinner in case the police raided her house. Devlin did not come back and Burns who had been watching the football out of her window left at about 4 pm. Continuing, she told Neild she remembered the date because it was the day after she left her job as a pub cleaner. She had also received a summons two days earlier, dated the 17th about another of her children who had got into trouble and she had asked the two men for advice. She agreed she was a sister-in-law of John Ford, a friend of the two men, and that she had been in trouble herself with the police on one occasion for receiving stolen property.

Without anything more substantial with which to attack the witness Neild, falling back on mere supposition, attempted to make the link that because her brother-in- law was a friend of the two accused she was telling lies to help them. She was not telling lies, she said, and he had not consorted with them since he had begun courting some months ago. Rejecting his further suggestion, she emphatically denied that he was currently on the run from borstal.

A succession of defence witnesses followed Alice Ford, including 18-year-old textile mill worker Matilda Miller, who confirmed Devlin's evidence about meeting him, Burns and Alan Campbell on the night of August 19th near the Ship public house. She remembered that night because she and her friend Mabel Williams had been to the York Cinema and watched a boxing film, after which they walked around Deansgate. They met the three men on the corner near the Ship and chatted awhile.

Sidney McDiarmid testified that he met Devlin on the corner of Leinster Street earlier that Sunday at about 4 pm. They both went to the York Cinema, where they watched a Bowery Boys film and a boxing one about Joe Palooka called *The Champ*. Replying to Neild, he said he knew Devlin but was not a friend. He just happened to be going to the pictures at the same time as him.

Next in the box was Anne Ford, who had married the men's friend John Ford a few months ago. Testifying that she and her husband went out at 8 pm on Sunday 19th of August, they first went to the Chester Inn then onto the Ship, where she saw Devlin, Burns and Campbell. They left at 10 pm with Campbell and Devlin and her husband followed with Burns. All five talked awhile until they reached the corner of Jackson Street when they parted, she and her husband going home. Replying to Neild, who was once again resorting to innuendo and vague "guilt by association", she agreed she knew the Burns and Devlin families and that her husband had been in borstal. She remembered the 19th because it was her birthday the day before.

Replying to Neild, she said she had been subpoenaed to appear and was not asked by anyone to remember the date, she just remembered it. She agreed she used to live at 3 Cornbrook Street because Joan Fitzgerald was her sister-in-law, and that she was living there when the two men were arrested on September 23rd.[1] "Teddy was on bail," she explained, "and Alfie Burns was on the run from borstal." No, her husband was not at present in borstal. But she frankly volunteered he had been in the past. She agreed she knew the accused "exceedingly well"—a question put to insinuate that she may be lying in their defence.

At one stage Neild asked if Devlin was wearing a fawn gabardine suit in September and when she said she didn't know what he was wearing, he demanded, "Why not?" This question, which was not pursued, did not seem to have any purpose other than to perhaps question her memory to the jury. Whether or not Devlin was wearing the fawn suit in September—an issue that had previously been thoroughly ventilated in court—was totally irrelevant. It seemed Goldie was not the only one guilty of asking pointless questions!

Despite her repeating she did not know what suit Devlin was wearing, the judge then asked, "What sort of suit? Do you remember? Dark or light? Do you remember *at all*?" To many in court this insistence, when she had twice said she could not remember, seemed to be bordering on harassment.

---

1. Joan Fitzgerald was jailed for two months on 6th February 1952 for child neglect but was brought to court under escort to give evidence for the Crown regarding Burns' jacket, left at her home.

But it didn't end there. Neild now wanted to know if she also knew what Burns was wearing. Replying forthrightly she told Finnemore and Neild, "No, I do not remember. I do not know what Burns was wearing either. I did not take any notice."

When Crown counsel later demanded to know whether she knew whether the licensee of the Ship Inn knew Devlin and Burns by their Christian names (another totally irrelevant question) and she replied that she didn't, Goldie was on his feet protesting: "How on earth can this witness say whether or not the licensee knows my client by his Christian name?" But coming to the defence of the Crown once again, Finnemore said, "Only if she has heard her use it." But, said Goldie, that was quite different from how Neild had put it. Neild then apologised and amended the question. But once again, a great deal of the court's time was being wasted on this and other equally peripheral matters which had no real bearing on the case and were certainly not evidence against the accused men.

The final petty points Neild scored occurred when he suggested that she remembered nothing about the 19th of August and that she and her new husband had previous convictions. Re-examining, Heilbron asked Anne Ford how many times she had been convicted. "Once," she replied. And the sentence? "Twelve months' probation." In the absence of proper evidence it seemed that prosecuting counsel had indeed been scraping the bottom of the barrel!

When the name, Alan Campbell was called by the clerk of Assize, a young man emerged into the dock from the cells below, causing Devlin to shift his chair to let him pass. As he entered the witness box, people in the crowded public gallery strained forward to catch a glimpse of this witness who they had heard so much about. Twenty-one-year-old Campbell, who had never been in trouble before, was serving 18 months for the robbery at Sunblinds. His otherwise smart appearance was marred by the very rough "back and sides" military-style haircut he had been forced to have the night before at Walton Prison, which made him look like a convict.

Replying to a series of questions from Heilbron, he confirmed that he was with Devlin and Burns on the robbery but although he was certain it was on a Sunday in August, he did not know the precise date. Despite this, Finnemore asked, "Do you know the dates at all?" to which he replied, "I have no idea what the dates were." But Heilbron told the court that she would prove the date by another witness she would later call (the Sunblinds owner).

Campbell verified meeting John and Anne Ford in the Ship pub. He did not know Matilda Miller's or her friend's name but recalled "bumping into" two girls after leaving the pub with Devlin and Burns who *did* know them. Replying to the judge, he agreed that was the *first* time the robbery was suggested to him by Burns. This answer—which was the purpose of the pointed question—would later be used to try and discredit the men's alibi.

After leaving the girls the three men, according to Campbell, left for Sunblinds near midnight. At Heilbron's invitation he then described how the robbery took place, essentially confirming Devlin's account, adding that they then went for Joan Downing who brought her large, coach-style pram to help remove the goods. He did not know of any other arrangements for moving the goods. They left some of the stuff outside the compound on a blitzed site next to the warehouse. He did not know what time they finished the job. He confirmed Devlin's account about staying at Downing's until the early hours of Monday morning and then going to Burns' mother's house. When Heilbron asked if he went to work on the Monday, the 20th, Basil Neild objected, stating that the witness had said he didn't know any *dates,* at which Heilbron conceded she was perhaps anticipating the evidence of her next witness, the warehouse's owner.

Continuing, Campbell said on the Monday afternoon he was with Devlin in City Road when a carload of detectives drew up. Devlin was wanted for skipping his bail so he ran away. He (Campbell) was taken to East Union Street Police Station but later released. When, later in October, the police interviewed him over the Sunblinds break-in he readily admitted the offence, telling them it was on a Sunday night and that it was with Devlin and Burns. At his trial in November (after Devlin and Burns were charged with the Rimmer murder) the judge directed that his accomplices could be named as "Teddy" and "Alfie" but their surnames should not be mentioned.

When asked by Heilbron if he had made *a* signed statement, he agreed. But by referring to only one statement, she clearly did not know he had signed a second statement later the same day to Detective Sergeant Richardson which was more vague and considerably less helpful to the alibi.

Sir Noel Goldie's questions either went over matters already established or were typically irrelevant. For example, he asked Campbell if Burns was with him on the robbery! He then randomly suggested — despite Neild's earlier acceptance that Devlin's had broken the window — that, "Burns picked up a brick or stone and broke a window?" to which an obviously confused Campbell agreed. This difference of accounts would later be exploited by both Neild in cross-examination and the judge in his summing-up.

If Basil Neild's insinuations and innuendo were not strictly evidence and should have been disallowed by the judge, then Finnemore should also have censured Sir Noel Goldie for his continually absurd questions which were contrary to the proper defence of Burns. Instead, apparently as irritated as everyone else by Goldie's bizarre conduct, he suddenly announced, "We will rise now, I think."

The proceedings were then adjourned until the following day.

CHAPTER TWENTY SIX
WHERE ARE ALAN CAMPBELL'S STATEMENT AND HIS INDICTMENT?

Friday 22nd February.

You need people like me so you can point the finger and say 'That's the bad guy'.

Al Pacino, Scarface

As Alan Campbell resumed his place in the witness box on this seventh day of the trial, Basil Neild, rising to cross-examine, first exploited the witness' agreement with Goldie, by having Campbell repeat that it was Burns, not Devlin, who broke the window with a brick and not with his fist wrapped in a raincoat.

When they reached Downing's home, said Campbell, Fred Downing was in the kitchen with a little boy. Joan Downing then arrived and Burns asked her to go with them. She took her pram and all four returned to Sunblinds. They then loaded the pram with 20 to 30 gabardine coats and parcels of trousers but left a lot of stuff behind outside the compound. Asked if he knew the date he said he could not remember but agreed he pleaded guilty to the indictment which stated the 18th August.

Now came one of the most insidious aspects of the case. For although the *charge sheet* imprecisely but clearly said that he broke in 'between 1.30 pm on the 18th and 7.30 am on the 20th of August', Neild asked, "And did the *indictment* read that you, '*On the 18th August* broke and entered this warehouse?'" Always unsure of the dates, Campbell agreed (Author's italics).

It is not known who changed the dates between Campbell being charged in October and the date on the indictment at his trial in November, or how this had occurred. But it is not difficult to realise why and to whose benefit it was. What *is* known is that after his original statement to Manchester's Detective Constable Hancock after being charged by him, a second statement was taken the same day by Detective Sergeant Richardson of Liverpool CID. This was the practice of "Balmer's Boys" with many of the defence witnesses' statements in order to make them less favourable to the accused. The result of this change to the 18th would later be seized on by Neild and the judge in his summing-up, to virtually destroy Devlin and Burns' alibi.

Despite this inexplicable alteration, Campbell nonetheless insisted, as he had done in both statements, that although the 18th August was a Saturday he was certain they did the robbery on a Sunday night. It was clear from further exchanges that, his general confusion aside, Alan Campbell was a most suggestible young man. Asked if anyone had mentioned the 19th to him, he replied that the police did so. But this was not the answer Neild wanted, who then asked if Burns mother had done so. He at first said he could not remember but then, under repeated questioning, agreed she had suggested he was with her son and Devlin when they did the robbery on the 19th.

Pointing to the cosh, "Exhibit 37", Neild asked if he had seen either man with it on the 19th. No he hadn't. Had he seen them with it on *any* night? No he hadn't. Again intervening, the judge pressed him, "Think, will you." But he replied, "No sir. I have never seen it before."

Re-examined by Rose Heilbron, Campbell again stated that although he could not remember the actual date he was certain the robbery took place on a Sunday night in August. Here Mr Justice Finnemore, increasingly adopting the role of prosecutor, said, "You do appreciate do you, that you pleaded guilty to doing it on a Saturday the *18th November*. You understand that do you?" (Author's italics). When Campbell replied, "Yes but it was a Sunday", nobody seemed to notice that the judge had cited the wrong month.

It was indicative of the intimidating attitude of Finnemore to the defence that Heilbron then had to ask him if he would *allow* her to ask her own witness one further question. "Yes, what is it?" he sternly asked.

"I would like to ask if he knew what day the 18th was? Because he did not know what day the 19th was."

"Yes."

She then asked, "Did you know when you were pleading to the 18th what day it was?"

"No," he replied.

The next witness for the defence, Ronald Kessler, the owner of Sunblinds

Ltd, stated his premises had been broken into on three separate occasions. The first was on 13th July, the second on the night/early morning of Friday the 17th and 18th August and the third between 1.30 pm on Saturday 18th and 7-30 am Monday the 20th.[1] Regarding the weekend break-in he did not tell the police any specific date simply because he did not know. On the first two break-ins different methods of access were used. But on the weekend break-in, he confirmed the defence account of which protective wire was cut and which particular window was smashed. He also agreed that some of the stolen property was left on the blitzed site outside the warehouse, which the public had access to. If the break-in had occurred on the Saturday night, he agreed that the stolen goods left behind would have been available to anyone passing by all Sunday, day and night, but these goods were recovered intact on the Monday morning.

It was the police who found the cosh on the blitzed site among the property. It was not found on his premises. Asked by Heilbron if the police regularly patrolled the area, Kessler said, "I should imagine so, yes — I hope so."

"So if the goods had lain there all day Sunday either the police would have discovered them or they may been pilfered by members of the public?"
"Yes."

In further replies he said he had never suggested to the police or anyone else a *particular* night over that weekend when the break-in occurred. At this stage Finnemore inadvertently let the cat out of the bag vis-à-vis the changed indictment, when he stated, "The original charge was between the 18th and 20th." But when Heilbron pointed out that Neild had specifically suggested Saturday the 18th, he replied, "*It was put in that form* but the full indictment was 'between the 1.30 on the 18th and 7.30 on the 20th'" (Author's italics). When Neild said he himself had been reading from the indictment, the judge hastily backtracked and said he was sorry and that Neild was quite right, adding, "It does say simply 'On the 18th day of August'. *It was the original police charge sheet* I was thinking about. They put the *general date*. But when the indictment was drawn — *to which this man pleaded guilty* — It

---

1.   Three other men, Connor, Payne and Lucas, were responsible for the Aug 17th break-in. Before the Crown's last-minute assertion that Devlin and Burns could have commenced the robbery on the 18th and completed it on the 19th, Connor, then serving four years for another robbery, offered to give evidence for the defence but was not called.

simply said 'on the 18th'" (Author's italics).

This exchange revealed vitally important matters which clearly showed that not only the prosecution but the judge were doing verbal somersaults in order to explain the changed date which denied the men's alibi. Firstly it betrayed Finnemore's knowledge of the wording of the original charge sheet. And despite observing, in relation to the 18th, "it was put in that form", he stated it was only a "general date" on the charge sheet! "General date" is however a contradiction in terms? It also showed that he missed no opportunity to include the fact that Campbell had pleaded guilty to the 18th (even though Campbell had maintained throughout it was a Sunday).

These were remarkably vague and contradictory observations coming from a High Court judge who was expected to be precise about the police and prosecution's adherence to the Judges' Rules. It also showed that he was not in the least concerned as to how a charge sheet merely stating a weekend period, was somehow changed to a specifically dated indictment by the time it got to trial, and which just happened to deny Devlin and Burns their alibi

When Heilbron asked Kessler to clarify that the remaining stolen goods must indeed have been left in public view on the blitzed site side of the barbed wire, Finnemore admonished, "He has said so four times Miss Heilbron." But when emphasising telling points *against the accused*, this was precisely the sort of thing he himself was guilty of throughout the trial.

Sir Noel Goldie had no questions for Kessler yet there were many he could have profitably asked in order to confirm the truth of Burns' story when he would later appear in the witness box.

During his cross-examination of Kessler, Neild, in the absence of anything substantial to refute, resorted to a series of questions about how many and what type of materials were stolen and what was recovered, even going into the amounts and sizes of some of the rolls and parcels of trousers which were left on the blitzed site. In this he was supported by interventions from the judge repeating the same questions. If, however, you insist on asking trivial, irrelevant questions you are sooner or later going to trip yourself up and look absurd. This is what occurred when debating the difference between rainproof and waterproof material during the following exchange:

Neild: You mentioned three pieces of red material?

Kessler: It is a *raincoat* material but not waterproof.

Finnemore: There was some *rainproof* material?

Neild then raised another matter of non-evidence but intended as a black mark against the accused men. Asking Kessler if he had been visited by anyone enquiring about the date of the weekend break-in, he agreed he had by two men, one of whom he had seen in the witness room (Burns brother-in-law Edward Billingham) and a young soldier he had not seen since (Devlin's younger brother Peter). The sinister effect of this was however extinguished when Kessler stated that both men openly explained who they were and simply wanted to confirm that his warehouse was broken into over the weekend of 18th/20th August. Getting no mileage out of this, Neild then asked him to describe the roll of red material known as duck cloth used for making blinds. But this again was non-evidence, with Kessler explaining that that particular material had been stolen on the previous break-in, not on the weekend in question.

When the witness withdrew Heilbron, suspecting more than confusion about the altered indictment, caught both Neild and Finnemore off guard by suddenly asking the latter for Campbell's statement to be produced. Apologising for not requesting this during Campbell's evidence, Heilbron said that in view of the confusion over the wording of the indictment she would like to see his statement which was put to him by the judge when reminding him he had pleaded guilty to doing the robbery on the 18th. Interjecting, Basil Neild said it was not a formal statement but a *notebook* and was made an exhibit. But when this was questioned by the judge, he admitted, "My Lord, I am wrong about that. I have not put in that *statement*" (Author's italics). When Heilbron then repeated her request for Campbell's statement, the judge disingenuously asked, "About what?"

"About this murder my Lord," she replied, pointing out that Campbell in evidence had said he had made a statement to the police in answer to the charge and the circumstances of the robbery. Astonishingly, Neild said, "My learned friend knows quite well that the prosecution cannot allow that, my Lord."

The matter of the difference between charge sheet and indictment was a crucial issue but Heilbron surprisingly conceded that if Neild objected to producing the statement she would not press it. Not satisfied with this surrender however, Neild pompously declared that she must not put it that way; that she knew very well that the prosecution was under no duty to provide it, adding, "I do not wish to hold anything back but the rules should be observed." In a brazen attempt to change the subject, Neild then asked if Sidney McDiarmid could be recalled as he had forgotten to ask him a certain question. When Heilbron and Goldie objected on the grounds that Neild had already cross-examined him, the judge overruled them, stating, "We had better have him (McDiarmid) back."

Neild's diversion appeared to have succeeded until Sir Noel Goldie asked, "Does your Lordship rule against Miss Heilbron's request for Campbell's statement?"

Astonishingly, like Neild, the judge cynically swept away this crucial issue, stating, "Oh yes. It is not really a matter of law at all, it is a matter of discretion." Precisely whose discretion, he did not say. If it was his then this was surely a gross dereliction of his duty. And if it was the Crown's then surely he should have over-ruled it?

The judge had refused the defence sight of a statement (and attached charge sheet) that could well have proved the accused men's alibi, whilst allowing the Crown to recall a minor witness as a diversion. Many in court that day must have been bemused by the vagaries of the law and wondered whatever had happened to justice.

When McDiarmid was recalled, Neild's questions were solely about his minor "criminal" convictions for drunkenness, which had nothing at all to do with the guilt or innocence of Devlin and Burns but were simply another petty example of non-evidence by smear. It did however successfully serve its *real* purpose — to divert attention way from the much more important question of who changed Campbell's indictment and why. This matter was subsequently allowed by the judge to remain unexplained.

Although the manager of the York Cinema verified that the Joe Palooka and Bowery Boys films were only shown on the Sunday, the judge commented, again in favour of the prosecution, that he had said the boxing film was "The Knockout" whereas Devlin had said "The Champ". In fact, despite the judge's petty distinction, there were two Joe Palooka films with both names in distribution at the time.

Henry Burns, Alfred's elder brother, called by Devlin's junior defence counsel Mr Tarsh, said he was a window cleaner and had never been in trouble with the police. His five-year-old son Henry's birthday was last August 17th, at which Devlin and Burns were present. After arriving home from work he went for a drink with the two men and returned home with them at 9.30 because Friday night was "Ladies Night" and his wife usually went out with her friends, one of whom was Alice Shenton who was at the house and who did later go out with her.

Continuing, he said the following night, the 18th, he met the two men at about 8.30 in the Wellington Inn by prior arrangement. His brother-in-law Edward Billingham was also there and all four visited several public houses. Although he clearly stated they all went back to his house at 11 pm, the judge asked, "They went to your home that night, did they at 11 o'clock?" There seemed no other purpose to this question, like many others from the judge, other than to try and trip up the witness.

Between 1.30 am and 1.45 am, said Burns, he telephoned for a taxi and waited for it on the corner of Upper Cobden Street. When he said he then directed the driver to his house, the judge pointlessly asked him which house, to which he replied "My own house." Again pointlessly remarking, "I thought they were in your house?" seemed to be another attempt at confusing the witness. Refusing to be distracted by Finnemore's interventions, however, the witness then stated that Devlin, Burns, his brother-in–law and wife (his sister Marie) and their baby left in the taxi for his mother's house at Medlock Street, and he paid the fare of fifteen shillings in advance. He did not see his brother until 8.30 the following Monday morning at his mother's house. Devlin and Campbell were also there. The reason he travelled from Blackely was that he had mislaid his driving licence which he had been showing to his brother on the Saturday night and wondered if he had inadvertently kept it. He was then, he said, with his brother all that day. Up till what time, the judge wanted to know. "Till about 8.30 or 9 pm, he replied.

"What about Devlin and Campbell?" They, he said, left them at about 1pm.

Sir Noel Goldie once again had no questions.

During his cross-examination, since Henry Burns had no criminal record to be reproached about, Basil Neild's strategy consisted almost entirely of trying to trip him up in order to expose him to the jury as having a faulty memory if not actually lying. When the witness — replying to Neild who said his brother was arrested on the 11th October — said he had no idea when he was arrested, he was asked why not? Replying that he thought he was told the day after, the judge upbraided him, "Why say you had no idea if you were told it the day afterwards?" Because, he replied, he did not know the *date* he was arrested. Not satisfied with this Finnemore asked, "You do not know the date now?" to which he replied, "I know now because I have just been told." This was one of the rare occasions when Finnemore's officious interventions backfired on him!

After repeatedly asking him the date of his brother's arrest, Neild then insinuatingly pointed out that although he could remember the 17th, 18th and 20th of August, he could not remember the date his brother was arrested on a murder charge. Burns replied that those dates stood out in his memory because he was not that close to his brother and they normally did not see much of each other. Replying to further questions he said he knew his brother was in borstal and had been on the run since, "I think about the 19th", meaning July.

Now was the opportunity Neild had been waiting for. "Did you know he came home on leave on the *19th of April?*" he innocuously asked (Author's italics).

"Yes."

"You know that?"

"Yes," he replied, falling into Crown counsel's trap.

"I'm sorry," said Neild, "I said 'April' *by mistake* and you quite agreed to it, did you not? [Author's italics]. But actually it was July." But Henry Burns had a valid answer. Unlike his brother, he explained, he did not live with his mother and had never lived with her since he was a baby. "I do not know the comings and goings of my family very much", he added, "because I do not associate with them to that extent." It was however no "mistake" by Neild. Although defence counsel had warned Devlin and Burns that Neild was a clever advocate and might try to trip them up, they had unfortunately not warned their defence witnesses.

Despite Henry Burns reasonable reply Finnemore could not resist intervening once again as he chided, "If you do not accept a date, say you do not know. It was put to you he was on leave in April, and that was the wrong date but you agreed. Do not agree if you do not know, say you do not know." This reinforcement of Neild's minor victory for the jury's benefit was yet again reinforced by Neild himself. "You do not know. Is that it?" to which he meekly replied, "I do not know." With both Neild and the judge persisting in the matter of Alfred Burns borstal leave date, Neild, like a dog with a bone, and despite the witness agreeing it must have been July, again asked him if he knew the date! He said he had only seen his brother once, before August at his house in Blackley, but Neild wanted to know precisely *where* in the house. When he replied that he couldn't say, the judge asked "Have you no idea?

"No idea."

He was then reprimanded by Finnemore for stating he remembered seeing his brother on the three August dates and now, although he was at his house the previous month, he could not remember the actual date.

The only thing of any value to emerge from these repetitive joint attacks on the witness by prosecuting counsel and the judge was that Basil Neild's junior counsel was perhaps being rendered superfluous to requirements! The final volley of absurd questions directed at the witness by both Finnemore and Neild, which had no bearing whatever on the guilt of the accused, was exemplified by Neild—desperate to trip him up and attack his credibility—asking if he could remember how many children were at his son Henry's fifth birthday party a year earlier, and if not why not?!

Next in the witness box, Henry's wife Marie, despite confirming her husband's and Devlin's accounts, was subjected by Crown counsel to the same sort of persistently trivial and irrelevant questioning. But when she differed from her husband by saying she had seen Devlin with her-brother-in-law *more than once* at her house about two years ago—although qualifying this by stating her husband was at work on those occasions—this would later be used by Neild and the judge to infer to the jury that one of them was lying. And when she said she did not know when Burns was arrested but thought it might have been September, Neild asked if she knew the date. She didn't know. But this did not stop him from then asking if she knew the actual day!

This sort of nit-picking, designed purely to confuse and discredit defence witnesses, was a poor substitute for actual evidence. But the judge not only allowed, but actually encouraged it.

When the witness withdrew, Rose Heilbron again raised the issue of Campbell's statement. Having so far been denied sight of it, she tried another approach, asking if he could be recalled simply to ascertain if it had been stated in writing that he had committed the robbery on the 18th. To this simple request about this important issue, Finnemore disingenuously asked her, "What is the point?" During his evidence, she said, she had omitted asking him that question. Obviating the need to recall Campbell and determined to bury the issue of his statement, Neild suggested that the shorthand writer could give that information. Equally determined not to have the statement produced, the judge tried to obfuscate the matter by quoting what Campbell had *said* in evidence—"I told the police, when I was arrested, it was on a Sunday. I told the police Devlin and Burns done it with me."

But when Heilbron insisted she did not ask him if that was in a *written* statement, Finnemore, knowing full well that prisoners statements were usually dictated, misleadingly remarked, "He would not write it himself."

"Of course not", she responded. That was not what she meant. "But to the police my Lord. Could that matter be put to him again?" But the obdurate judge would not have it. "He says that is what he *told* them (Author's italics). You will not get it further than that will you?" This comment completely ignored Heilbron's specific request—to know if it was *written* down. The judge was deliberately refusing to accept her distinction between what Campbell had said in evidence and what was attributed to him in writing by the police.

After further argument Neild intervened, stating that Heilbron was simply using a different tactic to obtain sight of Campbell's statement. He was, he said, willing to help the court but he did not see the point of recalling Campbell. The judge, again avoiding the issue, said he was prepared to remind the jury later of what Campbell had *said*. But he did not think it made it, "any stronger or better or weaker that some police officer wrote it down." The tenacious Heilbron however would not let go, insisting that there was no mention in the given evidence that it had been written down. But, surprisingly she then said that if the prosecution would agree it *was* written down she would not insist on re-calling Campbell, explaining she had simply wanted Campbell to verify that it was. Neild did not take up the invitation and Finnemore, unmoveable as ever, repeated what Campbell had *said*, stating the matter would be left in abeyance and he would consider it later. Still deliberately missing the point, however, he added, "But it is quite plain he *told* us that." Determined to have the last word however, Heilbron insisted, "But it only goes so far. It does not show how."

Rather than supporting his colleague, Sir Noel Goldie then said, "May I make it clear that my note and my learned junior's note is that the police interviewed Campbell and he said, 'I *said* a Sunday'" (Author's italics). Predictably this gratuitous comment—which still ignored Campbell's written statement—did not help to resolve the issue. But it did undermine Heilbron and apparently supported the prosecution and the judge. And Finnemore was doubtless grateful for Goldie's intervention. "Certainly," he said. "That is my note as well, *which is more important*" (Author's italics).

Astonishingly, not only was the judge and prosecuting counsel condoning the suppression of vital evidence which supported the accused men's alibi, but also one of their defence counsel! All of them had asserted that a contemporaneous note of what a witness *said* was "more important" than a signed statement given to, and counter-signed, by the police![2]

Despite Heilbron's repeated requests, Campbell's original statement given to Detective Sergeant Hancock, which also included details of the charge, never was produced. It is therefore difficult to accept that both Basil Neild and the judge—who by his comments had obviously seen it—were unaware of its importance and of the damaging effect it would have had on the prosecution case. Was this why they so fiercely resisted it being admitted in evidence?

2.   In addition to this suppressed statement taken by Manchester Detective Constable Hancock, Heilbron and Goldie were unaware of a second more inconclusive statement taken later the same day by Liverpool Detective Sergeant Richardson.

CHAPTER TWENTY SEVEN

BURNS' EXAMINATION-IN-CHIEF BY JUNIOR COUNSEL

In the end Truth will out.

Sir Ludovic Kennedy

Before Alfred Burns was called there were two further defence witnesses: Marie Burns' neighbour Alice Shenton, and private hire taxi driver William Butler.

Factory machinist, Alice Shenton of 10 Cobden Street confirmed Henry and Marie Burns evidence about the accused men being at Cobden Street on the 17th August. Because she was short-sighted and hard of hearing, junior counsel Mr Tarsh had to stand beside her at the witness box. Mrs Shenton, who had never been in trouble with the police, stated that Marie Burns was her friend who looked after her seven-year-old son whilst she was at work. And when she arrived home from work at five o'clock on the 17th August she went to pick him up.

"As you were going along to *your house at 6 Cobden Street,*" asked Tarsh, "did you see anybody who you later knew?" (Author's italics).

"Yes," she replied, "the two men that are accused of murder."

Asked if they were the same men who were in the dock, she could not see properly. But leaving the witness box and approaching the dock, she pointed, "Yes those two there; Teddy Devlin and Alfred Burns."

Rose Heilbron was annoyed at her junior who, despite Mrs Shenton telling him she lived at number 10 Cobden Street had wrongly stated her house as number 6. She therefore determined to conduct the re-examination herself. This witness was too important to be questioned in such a sloppy fashion!

Continuing, Mrs Shenton said she followed the two men into the house. Up until then she did not know them but Marie Burns introduced Alfred as Henry's brother. She did not know who his friend was until Marie told her later on that night. "I said to her 'who was the other one with Henry's brother?' and she said, 'That was Teddy Devlin.'"

Having picked up her son she then returned at 7 pm to make sure that Marie was still going with her for their usual Friday night out. This was because she thought Henry might be going out with his brother and Devlin. In the event the men did go out but promised to return at 9.30 so that she and Marie could have the last hour out. The men kept their promise and two women left for the pub at about 9.35.

All that Neild's brief cross-examination could elicit was that Mrs Shenton also knew the birthday dates of Henry Burns other two children, that she had known Alfred Burns mother for some time and she had visited her once only with a request from Joseph Norton, Burns' solicitor, to get in touch with him.

In Heilbron's re-examination, Mrs Shenton stated she could not only remember the date because of young Henry Burns' fifth birthday but also because she was looking forward to another neighbour Mrs Broadhurst coming home from a holiday in Rhyl the following day with her own little boy because he was her son's playmate and she always brought a present home for him.

Confirming the details of the taxi fare from 6 Cobden Street, Blackley to Medlock Street, Deansgate, private hire driver William Butler testified that one of the men in the group sat next to him in the front and said how fast the car was. The man also mentioned another taxi driver, Ginger Davis, who they both knew. When Heilbron asked if he remembered that it was the early hours of August 19th, Neild protested that it was a leading question. But replying to her, Butler agreed he had a record book of all his journeys from which he read out the precise details, including the date, time and price of the fare. A man was waiting on the corner of Moston Lane and Cobden Street and directed him to the house, he said. He now knew the man was Henry Burns after recognising him earlier in the Witnesses Room. The passengers were three men a woman and a baby. Asked if he could recognise any of them now in the courtroom, he began looking behind at the jury box. At this, although Heilbron told him they would not be there, the judge could not help intervening. "Would you recognise them again, do you think?" to which he replied he did not think so. Countering Finnemore's negatively suggestive question however, Heilbron more positively, asked if she might ask the witness *if he did* recognise the two men (Author's italics). Then asking Devlin and Burns to stand up she said, "Would you look at the two men in the dock. If you do not recognise them, say so. But if you do, say so." Pointing to Devlin, the witness said, "I think I recognise this one."

Goldie, for a change, actually had a question for this witness. But even then, it flopped! Despite Butler clearly pointing to Devlin for the whole court to see, Goldie said, "Let us be quite clear. When you said you recognised the man in the dock which of the two was it?" But Neild, ignoring this absurd question, seized on a more important issue. "He said he *thought* he recognised him." But when Goldie persisted, "Which was it you thought you recognised?" the taxi driver again clearly pointed to Devlin, at which Goldie declared what everyone bar himself seemed to know, "That is Devlin."

Cross-examined by Neild, who was vaguely attempting to imply some collusion, Butler said he did not know Henry Burns and had never been to his house before nor to Medlock Street. Suggesting that since Butler agreed he had not been asked about the taxi journey until three months after the murder, Neild said it mustn't have been easy for him to remember the details. He agreed, but said he didn't have to remember because it was in the record book. That ended his cross-examination.

Briefly replying to Heilbron, Butler agreed that (unlike Crown witness McNeil) he had had no opportunity until today of finding out whether he could recognise the two accused men. He further stated he had not been asked by the police to give a statement.

After the judge agreed to Goldie's request that Butler's record book be made an exhibit, Heilbron told him as far as Devlin was concerned, "My Lord, that is the evidence for the defence, *subject to that one point about Campbell's statement*" (Author's italics).[1]

Goldie asserted that in view of the evidence called by his learned friend Heilbron, he was dispensing with his opening speech and was calling no witnesses other than Alfred Burns. Therefore he claimed, he should have the last word in the closing speeches. But Neild objected, pointing out that Goldie had "adopted" Heilbron's witnesses so should not have the last

---

[1]. Campbell never was re-called and the court never had sight of his two statements. Nonetheless the judge would emphasise in his summing-up that Campbell had pleaded guilty to the indictment which stated the 18th.

word. The judge simply said he would determine the matter later. Despite this convoluted legal argument however, instigated by Goldie, he then left it to his junior Mr Nance, to examine his own client—the second most important defence witness!

When Burns walked smartly across the well of the court and entered the witness box, people in the crowded public gallery craned their necks to get a glimpse of the young man whose head they had so far only seen the back of. Many were surprised to see how young and boyish-looking he actually was.

Keeping his answers brief, Burns, apart from broadly corroborating Devlin's, and the other defence witnesses' accounts of their movements from the 2nd to the 20th of August, admitted he had seven previous convictions for house and office breaking and breaching probation orders but had never been convicted of violence. Replying to questions from Nance and the judge, he said he and Devlin left Liverpool with Bury later on the 2nd August, the same day as they had arrived. After staying at a house in Stretford Road, they returned to Liverpool on the night of the 3rd or early morning of the 4th. He did not know the name of the café they then went to but it was near the city centre and the police told him it was called the Rainbow. Despite this reply however, the judge said, "Never mind what the police said. Do you know where it was or what its name was?"

"I could not tell you," he replied. But not content with this answer, Finnemore insisted, "You really mean you do not know the name of the café at all?" to which he casually replied, "No idea."

Apparently taking over the role of prosecutor, the judge began asking him more questions, most of which he had already answered. For example what time they went into the Rainbow Café? Where was it located? Which rail station did they arrive at? Was the café near the station? And the most fatuous of all—since Burns had already said it was in the early hours—whether it was light or dark when they arrived in Liverpool. But these questions were also devious: following his usual practice Finnemore was clearly trying to catch Burns out in order to discredit him to the jury. However, these constant interruptions, time-wasting questions and undue pressurising of Burns—for no other purpose than to try and catch him out in a lie—were regarded by Joseph Norton, Burns' solicitor, as unforgivable. But this hostility towards the defence would be as nothing compared to the coarse "ganging up" by

Finnemore and Neild during Burns cross-examination.

Regarding the Rubin/Bury incident of August 4th, Burns said he had told Bury not to be frightened and to simply tell Rubin who she wanted to go with, him or Devlin. When she said "Teddy", Rubin just shrugged and walked away. This innocuous incident however would later be distorted by Basil Neild into a sinister confrontation.

Continuing his evidence Burns, this time avoiding the N-word, replying to Nance, said "I paid the coloured gentleman 25 shillings for the room at Verulam Street."—an amended description which more cultured people like Sir Noel Goldie and Sir Donald Finnemore failed to follow in their closing speech and summing-up!

Asked if he had had a meal anywhere before taking the room, Burns at first said "No," then said, "Wait a minute. Yes it was a Chinese Café. Or at least Chinese people worked in it." But he had no idea where it was. The following day, they went to the Dive where they met Eskimo Joe shortly before Rubin came in at about 11 am and asked to speak to Devlin who then went with him to the lavatory. Devlin later told him what the conversation with Rubin was about. Although the judge was fully aware of Devlin's testimony about the girls waiting outside the Dive, he asked Burns *where* they were, who mistakenly said they had been left at Verulam Street.[2]

After a short adjournment Burns, replying to Nance, said after the Dive they collected Bury and Milne and all four went to Manchester. When he said he did not know for certain which rail station but that they probably travelled from Central Liverpool to Central Manchester, the judge interposed, "Are you not certain? The jury might like to know. Do you really mean that you do not know which station you went to?"

"I could not tell you the station," he replied, "I just assume it was Central."

Apart from the judge, most onlookers wondered why it was so important for the jury to know which station they travelled to and from—it being two weeks before the murder and having nothing to do with the evidence. It seemed totally irrelevant. Unless, of course, it was intended to faze and rattle the witness.

Answering further questions from Mr Nance, Burns said they put the girls

2. A confused Burns was referring to their return to Verulam Street to pick up the girls after visiting the Sefton pub across the road.

on the train at Exchange Station at about midnight on Sunday the 5th of August, telling them they would see them again in Liverpool in about three or four days' time. He never saw Milne again until his committal hearing appearance. He did not tell her he would see her again outside the Rialto on the 17th of August. Indeed, he did not want to know her anymore.

Continuing, he said that about 9 am on the 8th August they returned to Verulam Street, shortly after which Bury appeared and told them she'd been out all night after being picked up by the police for, "screwing with some blokes". Milne was not there. Bury said she had "floated". He then recounted how they took Bury back to Manchester because she did not want to attend court later that morning, and how they robbed the Liverpool Road Rail Goods Depot that night whilst she minded their raincoats. After getting a 15 cwt truck to remove the bale of sheets they returned to Liverpool Road but Bury had gone, with their macs. He then explained how they tried to get their macs back. He had not seen her since Monday the 13th of August when he and Devlin had to run away from the police near her mother's house. He did not see her on the 16th or 17th of August and did not tell her they were going to Liverpool on some business. They had not been in Liverpool since the 8th of August and he did not know McLoughlin or McNeil.

Replying to further questions, Burns verified the accounts of his brother and his wife, Matilda Miller, Alice Ford, Ann Ford Alice Shenton and the taxi driver Butler.

Referring to the Friday night, Burns said that when they left his brother's house he and Devlin went to Mary's Café on Stretford Road where they met Alan Campbell and asked him to come on the job with them on Sunday. Replying to the judge, he said they had been thinking about doing the job for a few days. "What did you want Campbell for? Any particular reason?" asked a pertinacious and apparently obtuse Finnemore. And when Burns replied, "To go with us." He asked, "For what reason?"!

"To break into the place," said Burns.

Nance wanted to know why three were needed, to which he gave the obvious reply, "You can move more gear. It is a quicker job." Between 11 pm and midnight on that Friday night, he said, all three went to Sunblinds but decided to postpone the job till Sunday because a man was walking up and down outside. "We thought he was one of those vigilantes, who walk about taking care of property."

When Nance said that although they only went to have a look at the job, somebody else actually broke in that same night, he replied, "Yes, it seems like it". But again, despite his earlier reply, the judge asked if *he* had broken into Sunblinds on the Friday night.

At various stages, despite the judge's repeated urging, Burns truthfully admitted he could not remember certain matters, such as where he slept on certain dates and the Friday night in particular. He agreed he had heard Devlin in evidence saying they stayed at his (Devlin's) brother's but he could not remember. This however did not satisfy Finnemore, who told him to tell the jury what he meant by "cannot remember".

"Do you mean you do not know the name or where it was in Manchester or what?"

But when Burns repeated he just could not remember on that particular night, the judge insisted, "You have no idea?"

"No idea at all."

Further questioned by the judge, Burns said he did not know whether it was Maine Road he visited on Saturday the 18th with his brother-in-law as it was the first time he had been to a football match. But he knew it was Manchester City v. Wolverhampton Wanderers and there was no score.[3]

When asked by Nance if he had recognised Butler the taxi driver when he gave evidence earlier, Burns could have helped his own case considerably by saying he did so—particularly since Butler had recognised Devlin in the dock. Yet he truthfully stated he had not recognised him. But he did remember having a conversation with the driver about how the car quickly picked up speed and about a chap named Ginger Davis.

Burns further told Nance that they stayed in his mother's house on the Saturday night and on the 19th went to Devlin's home but he soon left and they both met up at Joan Downing's house in Foster Street at lunchtime. He then recounted the visit to the home of Alice Ford at the Barracks Flats and Devlin visiting his sister Eileen on the ground floor. Learning his friend had gone to his mother's, he followed but was told he had gone to the York Cinema, so he followed him there, where the film was, "The Knockout" or

---

3. Burns, not being a football fan, the teams names and scores were later ascertained by his
    solicitor, Joseph Norton.

something like that, and a Bowery Boys film.

He did not find Devlin at the cinema but they later met up at Leinster Street and went to the "Mug Shop" looking for Campbell. They finally met him in Castlefields and all three went to the Ship Inn where they stayed till closing time.

When Nance unnecessarily raised the matter of the cosh, Sir Noel Goldie, interrupted his junior counsel, not to silence him but to irrelevantly comment that he had forgotten its Exhibit number! The judge assured him it was numbered and not to worry. But he said he would like to have the number, to which the judge impatiently answered, "Thirty Seven"!

Why defence counsel should be so keen to concentrate the jury's minds on such a hideous weapon was mystifying. Jumping on this bandwagon, however, the judge now wanted to know who carried the cosh, what made Devlin hand it to Burns, and why he had been carrying it? When Burns' replied it was not his cosh and they had taken it to give back to Mac the owner (because they anticipated seeing him after the robbery to help remove the goods in his truck) the judge so confused him that he agreed he could not remember who had taken the cosh.

Finnemore's line of questioning wasn't as innocuous as it appeared. Although the jury had witnessed Devlin's naïve witness box admission of his willingness to use the cosh, there had been no such admission by, or imputation against, Burns so far. Thus, by the judge conveying to the jury that it was Burns who also carried the weapon, the clear implication was that he too would have been prepared to use it. To this end, once again taking over the cross-examination, he asked Burns if he really would have hesitated to use the cosh, to which he forcefully replied, pointing to the weapon, "I would not have used *that* thing." Neild rejoined, "Not even if a policeman's truncheon had been used?" But in contrast to Devlin's earlier self-incriminating reply, Burns replied, "I do not see why that would have been necessary." Many people in court however wondered what relevance the cosh had, since not only was it never suggested that it was the murder weapon but the Crown's case was that Devlin and Burns did *not* commit the robbery at Sunblinds Ltd. where it was found!

The remainder of Burns examination consisted of his junior counsel getting him to successfully corroborate the evidence of Devlin, Kessler, the warehouse owner and the other defence witnesses—despite the judge's frequent interventions trying to blow holes in his testimony.

Coming to his statement to the police, Burns replying to both Nance and the judge, testified that it was made in response to questions asked by Superintendent Balmer who had, among other matters, asked him about, the washing he had asked Bury to do, and how many taxis they took whilst in Liverpool. After he had signed the statement and it said, "I would like to put in that the only time I was apart from Devlin was the night we got the rooms in Verulam Street…" and "I can't say where I was but my mother will be able to give me an idea," Burns said, "I did not put that in, Mr Balmer put that in." [4]

"But you signed it and initialled it," said Finnemore. "Yes," he agreed. He thought it was right at the time but had since discovered there was one night, the 16th, August when he and Devlin *were* apart.

Recounting the occasion of his arrest, Burns said that the first thing Balmer said was, "Hello Alfie, you know what I want you for." He said he had no idea and thought he was referring to "some screwing jobs in Liverpool" because Balmer did not say at the outset why he wanted to see him. Balmer asked him where and when he was in Liverpool and who he was with. He told him, "Two girls and Teddy Devlin." Balmer then said all three had made statements implicating him. He did not say, "I have been worrying about it. I know you knocked Devlin." Fellow prisoners in Strangeways had said Devlin had been arrested for murder but he just thought it was a bluff by the Manchester Police to get him to admit to some robberies. He did not know Devlin had been actually arrested for murder by the Liverpool police.

This concluded Burns' examination-in-chief by junior defence counsel, Frank Nance, whose directness and plain speaking was in sharp contrast to the tortuously grandiloquent style of Sir Noel Goldie. The proceedings were then adjourned until Monday the 25th February, which would be the 8th day of the trial.

As the men were escorted down to the cells, Devlin's sister Eileen and Burns' sister Marion dashed out of the courtroom and went downstairs to see them before they left for Walton Prison. Midway down the stone steps they rattled on the barred gate until a prison officer appeared, and asked if

---

4. See his statement: *Chapter 21.*

they could see their brothers. After several minutes, the two men appeared
with two prison officers and a chief officer. But when Eileen and Marion tried
to hand them newspapers and tobacco they were told this was not allowed.
Eileen protested that they were not yet convicted and should be allowed to
receive them. But the chief officer said that may be true but the men were
now on trial so they would have to take them on their next prison visit. This
was a cold-hearted, purely bureaucratic decision. As of yet unconvicted, there
was no reason why the men could not have received them.

Over that weekend, the prison medical officer continued his scrupulous
daily observation log on the two men, which he had been making since
their arrival in October. Diligently recording their weight, general health
and attitudes, he wrote of Burns, "Still devious, cocky and arrogant." And
of Devlin, "Still implausibly protesting his innocence."[5]

---

5.   Prison Commission files.

CHAPTER TWENTY EIGHT
"IF I WERE YOU BURNS I SHOULD TRY NOT TO BE CLEVER" — JUDGE

Monday 25th February.

Prosecution is a bigger word than marmalade.

Alfred Burns

In the absence of any concrete evidence with which to confront or challenge Burns, Crown counsel Basil Neild's cross-examination consisted almost entirely of, suggestiveness, innuendo, hypotheses and provocation of the witness. Yet, only rarely did defence counsel object or the judge intervene. All in all, this uneducated 21-year-old who'd left school at 14 not only held his own against the learned Queens Counsel but often outshone him. Burns was to discover, however, that his ordeal in the witness box was to be quite different and totally more mundane than the glamorous combat he had envisaged in the letters to his friend John Ford. He did however adhere strictly to the advice of his counsel, keeping his replies brief and cogent, refusing to be put out of his stride by seemingly innocuous, irrelevant and misleading questions, and remaining courteous in the face of both Neild's gruelling cross-examination and the judge's constant distracting interventions.

Despite none of the victim's blood group being found on Burns' clothing, Crown counsel began by minutely going through the largely irrelevant issue of where and when Inspector Lees took possession of the brown pin-striped suit he wore during August in Liverpool. The purpose of this was clearly to unsettle him in the hope he might slip up in replies to more important questions later.

Asked whether he, Devlin and Campbell had gone to Sunblinds on the night of Friday 17th of August to reconnoitre or to actually break in, Burns said he intended breaking-in on that night and only postponed it because a man was walking by, "pretending to be whistling for his dog or something."

When Neild asked why he said "pretending", he replied to laughter in the public gallery, "Well it took him an awful long time to find it."

Quoting the evidence of Kessler the warehouse owner, Neild implied that the accused had done the job on the 17th, but Heilbron pointed out that the prosecution's case was that the men were in Liverpool on that night and couldn't be in two places at the same time. The judge however told her that Crown counsel, "was only testing his [Burns'] memory"—doubtless a euphemism for trying to trip him up!

Neild had first implied the job was done on the Friday yet we now had Mr Justice Finnemore reminding Burns that Campbell had testified the first he knew of the job was on the Sunday night. But Burns replied that Campbell was wrong, saying he may have forgotten. There then followed a pedantic argument, instigated by Neild and supported by the judge, about the difference between reconnoitring a job and actually breaking-in. It was only settled by Burns—to whom the difference was merely a matter of words. "Naturally," he told the judge, "the way we look at it, going to look and going to break in is the same."

Attempting to demonstrate to the jury the similarity between Burns "casing the joint" before the break-in at Sunblinds and the same *modus operandi* employed in the robbery of the Rimmer home, Neild seemed to have forgotten that McLoughlin had never alleged that Burns was present during the reconnaissance of 7 Cranborne Road! Clearly realising he had made a *faux pas,* Neild, suddenly changing tack, said to Burns, "You were in the Dive in Liverpool on Saturday the 18th August at about 1 pm, and you were spoken to by Rubin about June Bury having a disease." Shaking his head emphatically, Burns denied this. In his haste to spring something on him out of the blue, Neild now repeated the *faux pas,* once again mis-stating the facts. The Crown's own evidence was that it was Devlin who had spoken to Rubin in the pub's lavatory. Yet once again defence counsel and the judge let it pass without comment.

When Burns insisted that the meeting with Rubin occurred on Sunday the 5th August, Neild began a dialogue on what time Liverpool public houses opened on Sundays. Burns said he thought it was 11 am. Yet although he did not know the true time, which was 12 noon, Neild continued to argue the point for some minutes.

The exchanges which followed clearly showed Neild trying to confuse the witness. Insisting that the Dive meeting was on the 18th, he put it to Burns that afterwards they all went to the Golden Dragon Chinese Café in Leece Street. Burns admitted going to a Chinese Café but not on the 18th, and truthfully described its interior layout, even though he didn't know its name. Allowing for Burns meeting his brother on the evening of the 18th in Manchester, Neild suggested that he could have easily been back there in an hour on the train. But when the judge also observed that if he was in the Golden Dragon until 4.30 he still could have been in Manchester by 6 pm, Burns challengingly replied that Neild had not said that. "He did!" Finnemore angrily retorted. "And it was perfectly possible," to which Burns then reluctantly agreed.

Neild then misleadingly stated, "I am asking you about Saturday the 18th. *You have just said you were in the café* and then you said it would be about an hour to Manchester and then you said that was the day you spent with your brother. I put it to you, *as has been sworn to by other witnesses,* that you were in the Golden Dragon on that day talking with Marie Milne" (Author's italics).

This was not only misleading but also a gross distortion. Burns had *not* said he was in the Golden Dragon on the 18th but had simply agreed that *if he was* he *could* have been in Manchester within an hour. And no "other witnesses" apart from Milne, had "sworn" he was there.

Neild then appeared to undermine his own argument by reminding Burns he had said he was at a football match on the afternoon of the 18th with his brother-in-law Edward Billingham and later at a party with him and his wife (Burns' sister). Despite Neild's and the judge's hypotheses — about him being in the Golden Dragon before leaving for Manchester — if he was at the football match he could not have been in the Liverpool Café at 4.30 or any other time. Apparently realising this illogicality, Neild changed tack again, asking who Billingham was. When Burns again stated he was his brother-in-law, Neild wanted to know where he was, since he had not been called as a witness.

"Do you know about him?" asked Neild, to which Burns asked what he meant.

"Has he been convicted?"

"I know he got into trouble one night."

When Neild said he was going to ask him "What sort of trouble?", Sir Noel Goldie objected that surely Neild was not entitled to ask one man about the criminal record of another man who was not even a witness.[1] But stating that it was material to the case, Neild asked Burns if the police had tried to arrest him and Devlin and had failed, to which he replied, "Not in regard to this [the murder charge]. I was on the run from borstal and Teddy was running from bail." And did *someone* help them to avoid arrest? No, said Burns, nobody helped them. Neild's clear implication was that Billingham had prevented the arrest of the two men during a police raid on a Manchester pub.

Later, asked about the last time Burns had seen his mother apart from Sunday morning the 19th August, Burns replied, "Last Saturday." Although this was not important, Neild attempting to correct him, said, "You mean Friday when the court was sitting?" But turning the tables on Neild, he replied, "I mean Saturday when she visited me in prison."

Neild's seemingly puerile questions continued, provoking exchanges between himself, the judge and Burns, who finally lost his composure—which was possibly the reason for the questions in the first place. One particularly trivial question concerned Burns and Devlin's friend, Thomas Nicholson, a peripheral figure, who had returned almost immediately to Manchester after their arrival in Liverpool on August 2nd and had not even been a witness. Who was he? Neild wanted to know.

"A fellow we know," answered Burns.

"Who is he?" repeated Neild.

"Who is he? He's a bloke named Nicholson. We know him."

"What is he?" asked Neild.

"What is he?" asked a puzzled Burns.

"Do not repeat the question," ordered the judge, "Just answer it."

"A human being," said a genuinely confused Burns.

"Answer the question!" snapped the judge.

"He is asking me ridiculous questions my Lord," he pleaded.

Ignoring his plea, Finnemore, as if admonishing one of his recalcitrant

---

1. Neild was aware that Billingham, who subsequently received a short prison sentence for a pub affray involving Devlin and Burns when they escaped from the police, was currently on remand in custody.

Boys Brigade charges, warned, "If I were you Burns I should not try to be clever. You know quite well what you are being asked. Tell the jury what you know about Nicholson." Burns then replied, "Very little my Lord." But prolonging this totally irrelevant matter, Neild said, "Burns, when I asked you what he is, why say, a human being?"

"Because you asked me two or three times."

"Yes, and I am going to ask you again. *What* is Nicholson?" (Author's italics).

"I cannot understand you," he almost pleaded. When Neild said he would try and help him, and asked Nicholson's occupation (which he may have more intelligently asked in the first place) Burns said he did not know. Yet despite this, Crown counsel asked if he had one. When Burns replied that as far as he knew Nicholson worked but he did not know where or what at, Neild asked why he should "resent these questions?" To most onlookers it wasn't so much Burns resenting the questions or "trying to be clever" as being bullied and confused by them. Yet throughout this unedifying charade, Goldie, Burns counsel, remained silent.

Finally leaving the time-wasting issue of Nicholson, Crown counsel then asked Burns where he was on the 1st August—again an entirely irrelevant question, in the absence of any concrete evidence about that date with which to confront him. In this vein he returned to the issue of the cosh to try and elicit from Burns a propensity for, or willingness to use, violence. But insisting he had never used weapons, he replied that he only ever fought with his fists, and only one-to-one. Ignoring this however, Neild asked if Rubin had not accepted the situation with June Bury and Devlin on August 4th, would he and Devlin have attacked him. "No", he emphatically replied. That day he had simply told June Bury not to be afraid and to tell Rubin who she wanted to go with. If Rubin had held her against her wishes then he supposed it may have come to a fight—"But a fair one, not two on to one." Replying to a further question, Burns, to his own detriment, candidly said, "I am only telling the truth. Just because I have never used violence it does not mean to say I would not."

Regarding the cosh, Neild gratuitously remarked that it was a blunt instrument, even though there was never any suggestion that it was the murder weapon. Adding to this "guilt by implication", Mr Justice Finnemore, who

338 Murderers or Martyrs

was handling the cosh, then prejudicially commented for the obvious benefit of the jury, "It is used for hitting people on the head, is it not?" To which Burns frankly replied, "That is the usual purpose, yes sir."

These damning questions and inferences by Crown counsel should really never have been allowed since they were not material evidence of anything. But then, the judge, the only person who could have stopped them was equally culpable in employing them! One of the many examples of this was when Burns explained that he had taken the cosh that night to return it to Mac so they could borrow his van, and Finnemore, with an incredulous expression, exclaimed, "Do you really mean that?"

Notwithstanding the considerable help provided by the judge's supplementary questions, Neild was clearly losing the cross-examination battle in the face of Burns clear cut unambiguous yes and no answers and the lack of any material evidence to challenge him with. Indeed learned counsel seemed to be losing his grip on his own case when, in one exchange, during which Burns said Eskimo Joe was with them in the Dive on the afternoon of 2nd August, he claimed—contrary to his own witnesses' evidence—that the crime had been planned in the Dive pub before Burns had even met McLoughlin—and not with McLoughlin but with Eskimo Joe!

"In the Dive what happened is this," said Neild, "that you Devlin and Joe planned it?"

"No," he replied, "I was just there talking to this fellow Joe and Teddy was talking to June Bury." In order to rationalise this scenario Neild was now implying, but not actually claiming, that Eskimo Joe was really McLoughlin.

When Burns frankly stated that he "fancied" warehouse or shopbreaking to housebreaking, he was asked if Devlin fancied housebreaking. This was hardly a fair question but once again defence counsel did not object. When he said he did not know what Devlin fancied, Nield asked why not? Why was it different from the other housebreakings they had committed?

"Besides knowing nothing about this housebreaking you are talking about," said Burns, "I just do not fancy housebreaking as a means of getting money." This straightforward reply forced Nield to move on to the well-ventilated matter of the brief relationship between the two men and Bury and Milne. But these non-contentious questions were easily parried by the accused man.

When Burns said that on Saturday the 4th August he and Devlin went into a department store and bought toothpaste but didn't know the name of the store or the Liverpool railway stations, the judge commented unbelievingly, "You must have some idea must you not?"

"Well my Lord," he replied, "while I was in Liverpool I did not take any notice of *anywhere*." But insisted Finnemore, "It is difficult is it not to go into a big store without ever seeing its name or wondering about its name at any stage?" They were passing and just went in to get toothpaste, and that was the only occasion they were in the store, he replied.

Either Burns or both Liverpool born defence counsel, may have explained that three-quarters of the building was a mere steel skeleton clad in scaffolding. And if the judge had been as familiar with the Lewis's store as he expected this Mancunian to be, he would have known that there was no sign outside the store, extensively damaged during the May 1941 Blitz, due to the ongoing rebuilding work following its near total destruction.

In further replies to prosecuting counsel, Burns said he had never been in the store's cafeteria and had never before seen Kenneth McNeil until the identity parade after his arrest. He was not in Liverpool on the 17th August when McNeil was supposed to have seen him. He did not meet Marie Milne outside the Rialto on the 17th, and had never arranged to do so. Nor was he in the Golden Dragon on that date. He had never seen Devlin with a red-handled spring knife or ever seen him threaten Milne with a knife.

Asked if Milne's evidence about him telling her to go to the house four doors past the entry and knock on the door where the old woman lived all alone was all wrong, Burns replied, "All wrong."

"It was going to be on Sunday the 19th," said Neild, "when it was getting dark. All wrong?"

"All wrong."

"She was to try and get behind the door between the door and the woman. Is that all wrong Burns?"

"All wrong," he repeated, determined not to be rattled by Crown counsel.

And what about the two mirrors and the chair by the fireside? As far as he was concerned, said Burns, it was all wrong. He did not know anything about it.

Handing him a bundle of police photographs, Neild asked Burns to look at the privet bush in the backyard which McLoughlin had described, an exterior photograph of the house showing it four doors from the back entry and one of the living room. "Now look at photograph No. 82", he said, "Is there a mirror over the sideboard and one over the fireplace?" Burns agreed with the contents of the photos but said they had nothing to do with him. He had never been to the house and had never told Milne anything about the mirrors.

In an attempt to shock and get a reaction from Burns, Crown counsel then handed him a series of photographs of Mrs Rimmer's body lying in the blood-spattered hallway. "Are you saying you have never seen anything like that before Burns?" he taunted. If he had intended to unsettle Burns he had miscalculated: He simply replied, "I have never seen anything like that. I do not know anything about it."

Asked about the taking of his statement, Burns, replying to the judge, said he did not make a statement as such. He was asked questions by Superintendent Balmer and Inspector Lees wrote down his answers then told him to sign it. It seemed right at the time, he said, because he could not remember details. But now it did not seem right. At this Balmer, still sitting in the well of the court, was seen to slowly shake his head in mock disbelief.

Burns denied telling Balmer he knew *they* had "knocked Devlin" for murder. He had heard this in prison, he said, but thought it was the Manchester Police who had arrested him in order to get him to confess to other crimes. Neither had he said to the police, "I have been worrying about it." The police did not take his clothes immediately but later whilst he was in Walton Prison. And he did not say there couldn't be any blood on them. He knew there would be blood on the suit he was wearing in Walton because he had cut his knee a few days before.

Explaining why he thought the murder charge against Devlin was a police bluff, Burns decided to give the court a lesson on how the police try to entrap criminals. "This is the way they actually work," he told Neild. "They suggest something serious like a murder has happened. They know quite well the job was done on that night and they have an idea you have done it, so they try to frighten you into saying 'Oh I was not there. I was doing such and such a job'. Do you understand me?"

Burns knew this from his own experience. Indeed it had happened to him when he had lied to Manchester Police that he was in Liverpool for three weeks in order to avoid blame for the Manchester murder—although he *hadn't* been doing another job. But now, carried away by his vanity to impress the court with his "professional" knowledge, he was unwittingly support-ing the prosecution case—for that is precisely what the Crown was saying his and Devlin's defence was—claiming to be somewhere else on August 19th. Distorting what he had said, the judge asked if Burns was saying that the police, thinking Devlin may have committed offences *on the 19th August* decided to arrest him for murder in order for him to confess to burglaries (Author's italics). But Burns, avoiding the trap, replied, "I did not know it was the 19th."

As the bombardment of questions from both Neild and the judge was renewed, Burns denied he had used a brick at Sunblinds (the same method as the Rimmer home break-in) but had used his fist whilst Devlin had held Campbell's mac against the window, adding that this was his usual method of breaking-in. "Is *that* what happened at Cranborne Road?" asked Neild. But neatly side-stepping the pitfall, he replied, "I know nothing about that."

Returning once again to the issue of the cosh, Neild was determined to portray Burns as a man of violence, asking him if it was a weapon. "Of course it is," he replied. And when he repeated that he was going to return it to Mac because they wanted to use his van, the judge, implicitly refuting this explanation, said, "Do you really mean that?" Unable to rattle Burns any further, Basil Neild ended his cross-examination and Sir Noel Goldie rose to re-examine.

CHAPTER TWENTY NINE
GOLDIE QC ACTING MORE LIKE THE PROSECUTOR

Full of wise saws and modern instances;
And so he plays his part.

Shakespeare. As You Like It.

Pre-fixing almost every question with, "Now let us get this quite clear", the first thing Goldie unnecessarily asked, despite Burns previous replies to the contrary, was if the cosh belonged to him? "Well it is not mine," corrected Burns, "I was the last one to have it before the police."

When Goldie indicated he did not know whether Campbell had been arrested on the night of the murder, before Burns could reply, the judge intervened with a resume of the events following the Sunblinds break-in, including that Campbell was arrested the following afternoon. Revealing his ineptitude, Goldie unashamedly said, "I am so grateful my Lord. There is such a mass of detail in this case." The judge however was quite wrong. When Devlin and Campbell were chased by the police on the 20th of August, Devlin (who they were after for jumping bail), escaped and they let Campbell go.

Despite Burns' earlier evidence about preferring other break-ins to house-breaking and his stated repudiation of violence, Goldie, oblivious to the jury's natural feelings as homeowners, carelessly asked, "In all your *housebreakings* have you ever used violence?" (Author's italics). No he hadn't, he replied. Stating that Crown counsel had "now conferred on George McLoughlin the persona of Eskimo Joe," Goldie asked Burns if he had ever met McLoughlin. He had not, he replied, nor did he know Joe's surname. The police had suggested Joe was in fact McLoughlin, he said, but he had never met or seen McLoughlin until the identity parade.

Emphasising for the jury's benefit that Burns was totally unfamiliar with Liverpool and that none of his offences had been committed there, Goldie asked in his quaint fashion, "Had you ever before had the pleasure of meeting these distinguished Liverpool policemen?"

"No."

Asking how long he had known Devlin, Goldie interrupted him before he could reply, which brought a rebuke from the judge to let him answer. "I am very sorry my Lord," said Goldie, before continuing his superfluous and irrelevant line of questioning, which included asking Burns if he had previously visited New Brighton as a child, "to play on the sands!" When Burns agreed he knew Verulam Street, Goldie irrelevantly commented that it was on a slight hill, to which he dismissively said he didn't know and wasn't interested.

Replying further to his counsel, Burns re-iterated that he did not know Liverpool, apart from the area around the Dive. He did not know where Princes Park or Sefton Park or Cranborne Road or the Rialto Cinema were. Not content with these answers however, Goldie then asked, "If I may say so, apart from a few of these extraordinary all-night places and public houses frequented by the underworld, you have no knowledge of anywhere outside the city centre?"

"That is right," replied Burns.

Notwithstanding Burns agreement, the images evoked by his counsel of Burns involvement in a shady, mythical underworld, damaged rather than helped his client's status to the jury, implying him to be, as it did, a professional criminal at home in a sinister milieu.

Apart from regularly rebuking or correcting him, the judge also now had to curb Goldie's exaggerated language when he referred to the alleged conversation on the train when Burns discussed committing, "this ghastly offence."

"There was no suggestion of a ghastly offence," he reminded Goldie. "It was nothing more than housebreaking at that time." His response was, "My Lord I am sorry. One is liable to be carried away by one's misplaced *enthusiasm*" (Author's italics). Then to Burns, "What I ought to have said was, was this terribly serious offence of breaking into the old lady's house or any such thing ever mentioned?" to which he replied,"No."

Many people in court, including probably the judge, wondered why Sir Noel Goldie should feel so "enthusiastic" about such a grave duty he was there to perform. Or was he perhaps unconsciously referring to his own peculiar penchant for frivolity and melodramatic language?

Asked by Goldie if burglars usually told girls they had just met what jobs they were planning, and if it wasn't wiser to, "keep your mouths shut?" Burns replied that they didn't even tell their best friends what jobs they were planning. So far, Burns counsel was doing more harm than help to his defence—even more so when he decided to narrate the events leading up to the men's return to Verulam Street on the 8th August.

"Am I right in saying this, that you went back to this house, *kept by a nigger* as you put it, where you paid 25s.0d for a week's lodging? Is that right?" (Author's italics). This gratuitous question and insulting description was totally unnecessary. The court was already well aware of their return visit. Moreover, the word "nigger" may have been in Burns' statement, taken by Balmer (It was one of Balmer's own descriptions of black people).[1] But in his *evidence* Burns had referred to "a coloured gentleman". It was therefore typically inept and injurious for Goldie to attribute that particularly offensive word to him.

Later, when in typical fashion Goldie confused the Liverpool Road Goods Depot robbery with that of Sunblinds, Burns, after correcting him then grinned at his mistake, which brought the rebuke from his counsel, "Don't smile Burns. This is serious."

Shortly afterwards Goldie was again corrected by both Burns and the judge regarding the men's attempts to recruit a lorry driver to remove the Sunblinds goods. Referring to the Whitworth Street/Piccadilly area he asked, "I understood you to say that from there you were going to try and—to use un-forensic language—pinch a lorry in order to remove the stuff from *Liverpool Road*. Is that right?" (Author's italics). Burns first explained that they were not going to "pinch" a lorry but to enlist the help of a lorry or van driver like Mac. Secondly that attempt was in relation to August 19th, not August 8th when they had removed the Liverpool Road bale of sheets by car. This explanation was reinforced by the judge: "No, what he said Sir Noel, was that he was going to offer a lorry driver a few pounds to come and do it for them. And Devlin also said that."

It seemed that now even the judge was doing a better job of defending Burns!

Without any trace of embarrassment however, Goldie told the judge he

---

1.   At the later Gerrard Inquiry held in camera, Balmer, unaware that its proceedings would later be published, unabashedly referred to "the nigger clubs" in Upper Parliament Street, Toxteth.

was much obliged. Then oblivious to the judge's explanation, he asked Burns if he was going to offer a lorry driver some money to remove the goods? The undeterred Goldie then asked if the lorry drivers slept in their cabs? And — despite Burns' earlier replies that he did not know where the Rialto was — Goldie asked if he had ever been in the Rialto Cinema or the Rialto Café. Moreover it had never been alleged throughout the trial that he had been in either, nor the existence of such a café ever mentioned. Replying to a more relevant and specific question from his counsel, Burns stated that the only names of Liverpool cafés and pubs he knew were the Lighthouse Café at the Pier Head and the Dive.

Nearing the conclusion of Burns evidence — during which Mr Justice Finnemore had elicited more favourable replies than his own counsel — the judge disarmingly suggested that Burns always took off his jacket before having one of his "fair fights". But Burns didn't fall for it. "Not always," he replied. If he always took off his coat before having a fight then as he — and the judge knew full well — there would be no reason for blood to be on his jacket as he claimed!

During his resumed questioning, Goldie was as ineffectual as ever when asking Burns to confirm that the Dive meeting with Rubin was not on the 18th but on the 8th or 9th. When Burns, corrected that it was on Sunday the 5th, Goldie's usual obsequiousness towards the judge, extended even to his own client as he told him he was "much obliged."

Referring to the taking of Burns' statement, Goldie's approach was a classic case of "willing to wound but afraid to strike" against the Liverpool police. After first stating he was not criticising the police, he asked Burns, "I am not attacking the police at all and I don't want the jury to think I am. But did they naturally ask you questions?" Burns, who had already told the court this, agreed. "And you did not make a running statement but it was in reply to questions?" Before Burns could answer, the judge intervened with another diversion, asking him where he was first interviewed and if it was specifically about the Liverpool murder? "No," he replied, mistakenly referring to prison conversations. "Someone just said, 'Devlin has done it this time'. Or something like that." Telling him he was not talking about that, the judge asked whether Inspector Lees had first mentioned Mrs Rimmer's murder? "No," he replied, "Balmer just said, 'Hello Alfie you know what I want you for' and I said I didn't."

Returning to the statement, Goldie went through extracts of it, asking if they were in response to questions. Burns replied that Balmer asked him if he'd been in a café in Liverpool and when he said yes, "…he put down 'Rainbow Café'." Again quoting from his statement, Goldie asked if he had told the police he had only been in two cafés whilst in Liverpool — "the Rainbow and another one down by the Pier Head?"

"That is what the superintendent said," he replied. "I just said 'more than likely'."

Before concluding his evidence Burns was again asked by the judge if he had had many fights, "Fair fights with other men?"

"Quite a lot," he replied.

When Burns again stated that he did not *always* take off his coat, Finnemore insisted, "You do, do you not?" But, depriving him of his required answer, Burns explained, "If a bloke starts a fight without any previous conversation then I obviously don't have a chance to take off my coat."

If Burns had unequivocally agreed that he *always* took his coat off before a fight then the jury might be convinced that the bloodstains on his jacket, however minute, however presumptive, could only have come from Mrs Rimmer!

Burns' evidence ended at 12-30 on the eighth day after a total of five hours in the witness box. Despite being constantly undermined by his own counsel and incessantly distracted by the judge, he had given a good account of himself.

CHAPTER THIRTY
HEILBRON'S CLOSING SPEECH FOR DEVLIN

Liars should have good memories.

Rose Heilbron QC

After the lunch adjournment, Rose Heilbron, before commencing her closing speech on behalf of Devlin, once again asked the judge if the matter of Campbell's statement could be cleared up. He replied that she should leave it for now and that he would remind the jury later and thought that no doubt she would too. In the event Campbell's statement was never produced.

Addressing the jury, Heilbron told them she was not asking for a verdict based on either compassion or prejudice but on the evidence, upon which, she said, it would be very dangerous for them to convict. She first pointed out that Milne, who had supposedly waited on the corner of Cranborne Road for one-and-a-half hours, had not actually seen the men entering or leaving Mrs Rimmer's home. Here, she said, according to the Crown were two professional thieves, who enter the house whilst Mrs Rimmer is not there, stay for over an hour, without stealing anything and then leave without any trace of their ever being there. Regarding McLoughlin's evidence, she asked the jury if he could really be believed. "This man who had changed his story several times." His evidence, she went on, about the meeting with Devlin and subsequent conversations with both men were complete and utter lies. In the committal court he said it was just going dark when he went with Devlin to "case" the Rimmer home, then changed it at the trial to the morning when he said it was just going dull.

Continuing, she said that on the only night possible he said that after leaving the Continental Café he went with the men and Bury to the Pier Head but Bury was emphatic he was not with them. Indeed, as Heilbron had proved during Bury's cross-examination there was no available night when even Bury could have gone with them to the Pier Head from the Continental.

Accounting for McLoughlin's identification of Devlin and Burns at the

349

ID parade, Heilbron suggested that he may have remembered their faces
from seeing them in one of the all-night cafés which they *agreed* they had
visited — "The *Continental,* the Rainbow and the Lighthouse" (Author's
italics). Unfortunately she had mistakenly included the Continental, which
both had never "agreed" visiting. She was very lucky that Neild during his
closing speech did not use this to hoist her by her own petard!

What Heilbron did not know, however, was that McLoughlin was able to
identify them so readily because he had first been shown their mugshots by
detectives. Farragher and Wade at Walton Prison on October 5th and several
times subsequently by Balmer.

"Having seen him", she continued to address the jury, "can you justifiably
believe a word he says?"

Coming to Bury, her evidence about meeting the men in the Continental
Café with McLoughlin was confused at best and at worst untrue. "There is
an old adage that liars should have good memories," she went on. "And if
you have a liar with a bad memory you may get the sort of evidence presented to you in this case by some of the prosecution witnesses, including
Bury." Regarding Marie Milne's evidence of arranging to meet Burns on the
17th August, why, asked Heilbron, would he have to take her aside to make
a special arrangement, when they had agreed to meet at Verulam Street in
a few days time –particularly as it was agreed by all concerned that he no
longer fancied her? Her evidence was a "complete fabrication". Indeed it was.
But Heilbron was not to know that it was Balmer's fabrication, not Milne's!

Did the jury really believe that after committing such a grave crime, the
two men would be hanging around at the Rialto corner for Milne to show
up? "Surely," she said, "they would have hurried back to Manchester as fast
as they could?" But even allowing for this improbability, Milne in her own
evidence stated that they were in no particular hurry but, "Just walked away
towards the city centre." The jury would have found it even more incredible
if Heilbron had been able to tell them that in her *undisclosed* statement of
9th October taken by Lees, Milne had said that before leaving she had taken
the two men to the South China Café for a meal![1] Defence counsel then
launched her second attack on Milne's character.

"This 17–year-old", she mocked; "this innocent girl who had had nothing

_____

1.   Merseyside Police Files.

to do with a man before that night, yet who without any shame tells you she was picked up in the Rainbow all-night café and slept with Burns, a man she'd only just met; this girl, supposedly having previously nothing to do with men, who on the Sunday night in Manchester then also slept with Devlin. Do you get a picture of her as frightened timid and scared or tough and brazen and unashamed?"

According to June Bury, another disreputable woman, said Heilbron, Milne asked her to back up her story but Milne denied this so one of them was lying. Then, linking McNeil's evidence to Bury's and Milne's, she said it was curious that Bury knew McNeil but he and Milne said they did not know each other, yet Bury said they did. "Can you really believe *any* of them?" she asked.

Moving on, counsel pointed to the evidence of Alice Shenton — "an unimpeachable witness unshaken during Mr Neild's cross-examination" — who had corroborated Henry Burns' and his wife's evidence that the accused men were in their house at their son's birthday on August17[th].

Of the alibi, she said whatever the confusion about his involvement, Campbell had maintained throughout that the Sunblinds robbery with Devlin and Burns occurred on a Sunday night. There was no evidence whatever that he was in the company of the accused men on the Saturday night when the Crown alleged it had happened. Heilbron went on to suggest that the so-called arrangement between Burns and Milne to meet on the 17th — which the men and even Bury denied took place — was patently untrue and designed by Milne to fit in with her alleged meeting with the men on that date. It further served the purpose of introducing McNeil in to the scenario, whose evidence would corroborate Milne's story.

Bury had stated in evidence that McNeil and Milne knew each other so Heilbron wanted to know why they both denied this. It was a rhetorical question. But the answer was contained in Balmer's script! Firstly, if they'd admitted knowing each other, the jury might have wondered why, when she and the two men met McNeil outside Lewis's, she should immediately leave them. There had been no evidence that the accused men knew or had previously met McNeil, so why should they then spend that Friday evening with a complete stranger? Secondly, if Milne and McNeil had admitted knowing each other, the defence may well have alleged collusion between them. On the whole much better to keep it simple and lie that they did not know each other!

Condemning McNeil, she told the jury this was the man who said he had spent the whole evening of 17th of August with Devlin and Burns yet who admitted picking out two innocent men on the identity parades, knowing it was in connection with a murder. "Did he care what happened to those men?" she asked. He had also testified, she said, that he had previously seen the accused men in Lewis's cafeteria but later during cross-examination admitted that he either took lunch in the staff canteen or in the Lime Street Milk Bar.

If the defence had bothered to inquire it would have discovered that Lewis's staff were not allowed to eat in the main cafeteria—especially scruffily dressed porters!

"Again I ask you," said Heilbron, "are you going to rely on the evidence of that man McNeil? Are you *really*? Do you think it would be safe?"

As for the mirrors and armchair in the Rimmer living room allegedly described to Milne by Burns, Heilbron suggested that maybe Milne had been in the house before: But what *purpose* would such information serve to the break-in? Such matters as furnishings, etc., she said, "were more what a woman would notice; a *man* would normally not be interested in, remember, or even think about such things." But here she was quite wrong: Balmer *had* thought of it –and he was a "man"! And his "purpose" was to give authenticity to Milne's evidence—as he had when priming her about how much Burns allegedly paid Emery the taxi driver.

Returning to the alleged arrangement to meet Milne on the 17th, Heilbron pointed out that it would not have made sense for Burns to arrange this. He had paid rent on the Verulam Street bedsit on the 4th for one week only so why would he wait till the 17th before returning. "Wasn't the men's evidence –confirmed by Bury—much more credible when they said they would see them in a few days time, which is what they actually did?"

Referring to McLoughlin's evidence that the Rimmer break-in was postponed for two weekends because Devlin and Burns wanted to be seen around Manchester, Heilbron asked the jury to reject it out of hand as not even worth considering. "These two men," she exclaimed, "who were actually on the run at the time from the Manchester Police to whom they were well-known. Do you really believe that?!"

Coming to the disputed date of the meeting in the Dive with Rubin—who she described as, "a man with 12 convictions for all sorts of nasty offences like wounding and housebreaking"—Heilbron reminded the jury that after stating it was the 18th, "he had admitted under cross-examination that he wasn't sure of the date of the conversation about Bury's "disease." He must also have held a natural grievance against Devlin for "stealing his girl from under his very nose" she added. She, however, failed to make the more important point, that he had also stated the *police had suggested* the 18th to him.

Before concluding, defence counsel again told the jury that the accused men, who had allegedly told McLoughlin Mrs Rimmer had "plenty of dough", were, according to the Crown, in the house for almost an hour and a half yet did not disturb anything or steal anything. And, she postulated, even if after searching the house and finding nothing, they had waited to waylay Mrs Rimmer, why didn't they rob her handbag, which contained five pounds, yet was untouched? With undeniable logic she said, "It just does not make sense."

Recalling Milne's testimony when she said after the murder, "I could not see because it was dark but their shoes looked muddy," Heilbron asked the jury if they understood what that meant. "Does that not mean, 'I could not see but I am going to say they looked muddy' because that is another bit of fabrication? She could not see but she tells you she was able to see small stains on these men's coats and shirts and so on. How much weight can you attach to the evidence of a woman who answers like that?"

Regarding the alleged conversation between the men about, "to hell with the old woman", and taking "the little bitch Marie with us", Heilbron commented that they did not in fact take her anywhere except walk with her down Upper Parliament Street. And although she also mentioned Devlin's alleged remark, "Will the old woman live?" Heilbron missed the significance of this particular piece of Balmer's "verbals". That is to say, Devlin asking would she live would prove both men were not only at the murder scene but were uncertain whether or not she was dead. And this would neatly coincide with the pathologist's report stating death occurred some hours after the attack—which Balmer had received weeks earlier!

Despite being repeatedly fobbed off by the judge over Campbell's statement, Heilbron, realising its vital importance, now returned to it in depth.

The jury may remember, she said, Campbell's evidence stating that when he and Devlin were chased by the police and Devlin got away, it was a Monday, "The day *after* we done the robbery". And at his trial for the Sunblinds robbery in November the judge ordered that Devlin's and Burns' names should not be mentioned. She may have added that if the police did *not* *believe* they had been involved, why had the judge ordered their names not to be mentioned — unless it was intended to charge them should they be acquitted of the murder charge?

Continuing, Heilbron, recalling Neild producing the indictment, said that an indictment was the same as the charge. "Yet the indictment apparently said the 18th. But it does not say 'Saturday the 18th', it just says '18th of August'." Now implicitly challenging the judge's earlier comment, she reminded the court

> It was suggested to Campbell 'You pleaded guilty to this indictment on the 18th' Members of the jury do you think that when he was pleading guilty to that indictment he knew what day it was, or even cared? He had said it was a Sunday and he has said that all along but he did not know the date. How could he know whether it was the 18th, the 19th or the 20th? But there was no statement stating, 'I did it on a Saturday night'.

Heilbron didn't know how close she came to the truth when she said "You may wonder where the police got that information (of the 18th) from. You may think it was *their own working out,* because they did not get it from Campbell, and they did not get it from Mr Kessler (Author's italics). *He* said he did not know what date it was. As far as he was concerned it was between the 18th and the 20th."

Heilbron had made the best argument she could on this issue. But she was sorely handicapped by the non-disclosure of Campbell's original combined statement and charge sheet which clearly stated, "…between 1.30 pm on Saturday 18th August and 8 am on Monday 20th August." Had she had sight of it she could have proved the dates had been deliberately changed on the indictment.[2]

Coming to Kessler's evidence, she reminded the jury he had agreed that when called by the police on Monday morning quite a lot of the stolen property was laying in the open and accessible to the public. If the break-in had occurred on the Saturday night, the goods would have been lying out in the open all day Sunday and Sunday night. Yet it had not only not been looted but its presence had not even been reported to the police. If the defence had made proper enquiries she might also have added that according to weather reports it had rained all night Saturday and Sunday daytime, yet the recovered clothing was bone dry![3]

The matter of fingerprints was not raised by defence counsel to the jury, yet, although it had never been alleged that they wore gloves or any hand protection, none of the accused men's were found anywhere in the Rimmer home. She also failed to point out how two men from Manchester could possibly know, according to McLoughlin's evidence, that the occasional visitor to Mrs Rimmer's house was "a relative". Or was this simply Balmer's script over-egging the pudding?

The jury only had Milne's and McNeil's word for what happened on the 17th outside Lewis's, said defence counsel. One had changed her story several times and the other had picked out two innocent men at identity parades. Yet the defence had produced five witnesses that the accused were in Manchester that day and night for Burns' nephew's fifth birthday—one of them an unimpeachable Alice Shenton, who was neither a friend nor relative of either of the accused men. And on the following night, the 18th, several witnesses, including an independent taxi driver, William Butler, had corroborated the men's story of being picked up at Henry Burns' home and taken to 6 Medlock Street. If, as the evidence showed they did not arrive home till 2.30 am, asked Heilbron, how on earth could they have been breaking into Sunblinds as the Crown alleged? And Campbell, who had never been in trouble before and had never previously stayed out all night: where was he? It was common ground, she said, that he had broken into Sunblinds with Devlin and Burns. And there was no suggestion he was with them at Henry Burns' home, nor on the taxi journey home. "So was he just hanging around at 2.30 in the morning on the off chance they might show up?"

Heilbron asserted that Emery's Liverpool taxi was hired to go to the

---

3. Burns' friend John Ford had, at Burns request, obtained these reports from Manchester Meteorological Office after the trial.

hospital—the true destination which he had finally agreed at the committal proceedings. Otherwise, she asked, why would the accused travel with Milne to Cranborne Road at 1.30 pm and then arrange to meet her again at 6 pm at the same place? They had planned apparently to do the job when it got dark. But it was August and it wasn't dark at 6 pm. Describing Milne's entire story as, "incredible and fantastic", she exclaimed, "It doesn't make sense."

Whilst it may not have made sense to defence counsel, these "purposeless" visits certainly did so to Superintendent Balmer. The men were maintaining, as they did throughout, that they were not in Liverpool after the 8th. He also knew they had witnesses to support where they were on the afternoon of the 19th (e.g. Alice Ford, Sidney McDiarmid). So, creating three visits ensured they were in Liverpool all day and night. And although the second and third visits were pure fiction, the first visit could arguably be corroborated with the germ of truth from the taxi driver. Marie Milne's alleged visit to the cinema was also a variation of this strategy—after all there were only so many visits to *cafés* in Milne's evidence that the jury would believe!

At this juncture Mr Justice Finnemore politely asked Heilbron if it would be a good time to adjourn and the proceedings were discontinued till the following day. In the cells below a prison officer told the two men, "You'll both get chucked on this. It's a nap. Rosie's the best in the business."

"I fuckin' hope so," said a worried Devlin.

"She didn't get Kelly chucked though, did she?" said a cautious Burns, "and she had *two* chances."

"That's different," he replied. "*He* was guilty as fuck." [4]

---

4. A reference to Heilbron's unsuccessful defence of George Kelly in his two 1950 Cameo trials—but who was exonerated in 2003.

CHAPTER THIRTY ONE
"HE MAY BE A THIEF ... "

Tuesday 26th February

A lie is halfway around the world before the truth has got its boots on.

Mark Twain

Concluding her closing speech, Rose Heilbron summarised the reasons why June Bury could not possibly have been in the Continental Café with Devlin and Burns on any of the nights she had claimed. Thus there was, she said, no corroboration of McLoughlin's evidence of the meeting there. Indeed, apart from Bury stating it was McLoughlin who had suggested the Rimmer robbery (on the non-existent occasion), she had also contradicted his evidence of going with her and Devlin and Burns to the Pier Head.

And if Marie Milne was so scared after the knife threats—first one, then two—why wait, asked Heilbron, one-and-a-half hours at night whilst they robbed the Rimmer home. Nobody was preventing her from leaving and she had admitted the men did not know where she lived. Then regarding the implication that the men had arrived at the Rialto via Princes Park or Sefton Park because their shoes were muddy, Heilbron made the valid point that to do so they would have had to cross Smithdown Road, where Milne was waiting on the corner, but she had not seen them and that main road was quiet at that time on a Sunday night. And above all, did the jury really believe the coincidence of her seeing them casually loitering around the Rialto after just committing a brutal murder?

"Does this woman have any credence at all?" she pleaded.

Finally referring to the cosh and the implication made by the Crown, she stressed to the jury that although Neild had emphasised it was a blunt instrument and Dr Manning had said some of the victim's wounds had been caused with a blunt weapon, they must not assume for one moment that it

357

was the murder weapon. It had been scrupulously examined for blood and fibres, etc. and nothing was found. Moreover, she added, both the prosecution and defence were agreed it was found at the Manchester warehouse. "There was no way that it was ever in Liverpool on the 19th August, just as Devlin and Burns themselves were not there."

In a veiled attack on the police evidence, she commented on the fact that all four of them in the police car with Devlin had told the same story. "But remember this," she warned, "because a man is a police officer he has no more right to be believed than any other man in this court. He is not infallible. He can make mistakes and can forget." The police, she said, would have the jury believe that during the journey lasting one and a quarter hours there was no conversation between themselves and Devlin, apart from Devlin's three self-incriminating remarks about a cigarette, the girls and complaining about the handcuffs. But none of the officers replied to Devlin or even spoke. "This was indeed a journey of four silent men," she mocked. "Do you believe that, members of the jury?"

Moving on, Heilbron similarly criticised the taking of the men's statements, telling the jury it was fanciful for the police to insist no questions were asked during the one-and-a-half hours it took to obtain Devlin's. This line of questioning enabled her to come to Superintendent Balmer and make the crucial point of his absence from the witness box. Devlin and Burns had said Balmer was asking the questions during the taking of the statements, "But Chief Superintendent Balmer was not called to refute that." From her revealing cross-examination of him in the Cameo trial, she probably realised why he was not called. Inviting the jury to take the men's statements into the jury room when they left to reach a verdict, she asked them to seriously consider who was telling the truth, the police or Devlin and Burns—whose version was "quite incredible?"

Reminding the jury that the various pieces of cellophane, put on Devlin's suit by Dr Firth during his forensic tests, were much larger than the actual size of the alleged bloodstains, she emphasised that none of Mrs Rimmer's group were found. But when she also reminded them of Firth's evidence that the bloodstains were four or five months old when examined in October, the judge, interrupting her, said, "I think he said not more than four months Miss Heilbron." But as the case was nearing its end, she wasn't having any more of the judge's constant and often inaccurate interventions. "I put to him four or five months and I thought he agreed," she forcibly told Finnemore. Suitably corrected, he contradicted himself, reluctantly saying, "We will take it at five months." Then not wishing to lose face altogether, he added, "We will get the shorthand note if necessary but we will take it at four *or* five months" (Author's italics).

Mr Justice Finnemore's insistence however, was not as pedantic as it seemed. Devlin had told the court that the bloodstains came from a fight at the end of April or early May. From May to October is *six* months. The judge's rather insidious and biased implication was that the bloodstains could not have come from the fight, "four or five months ago!" But this of course ignored the fact he had been in fights after May.

Conceding her client's criminal record, Heilbron told the jury that, "He may be a thief. But he's not a murderer." He had seven convictions, she said, and had candidly admitted more offences. The jury, she said, should not however be influenced by that. "If you could do so," she said, "then just look at the records of some of the prosecution witnesses: McLoughlin 40 convictions: Rubin 12 convictions." And, she said, at least three of them—McLoughlin, Bury and Milne—were also accomplices.

The jury may ask, said Heilbron, why McLoughlin, Bury and Milne should blame innocent men? But they only had to look in this very case, she said. "Why did McNeil blame innocent men? For he did so. That is the sort of thing that these sort of people do. Judge them not by your standards but by theirs." Notwithstanding the truth of this claim, Heilbron was not to know, no more than Crown counsel, that these witnesses were telling lies because they had all been falsely embroiled and threatened with being charged with serious offences if they did not do so. McLoughlin whose story was clearly confused had had to be told several times to speak up; a nervous June Bury was obviously reluctant to give evidence and was similarly of muted voice—indeed at one stage in the witness box she almost fainted—and McNeil also gave his evidence quietly with a cowed expression. This was because they and Marie Milne—despite her brash demeanour in the box—were not so much wicked as afraid of Balmer's convincing threats.

Calling it a case full of doubt, confusion and contradictions, Heilbron concluded by telling the jury it would be too dangerous, too uncertain and too unsafe to convict on the evidence which had been presented. Her final plea was that, "The only verdict which is consistent with the evidence, consistent with justice and conscience, is one of not guilty." As she resumed her seat, Sir Noel Goldie gave her a light fatherly pat on the back.

Rising to his feet, Basil Neild informed the jury that the order of events would now be that when he had finished speaking on behalf of the Crown, Sir Noel Goldie would address them for Burns and the judge would then sum up. Although this information was essential for the jury, it was really the judge's role to inform them of this.

In an attempt to explain McLoughlin giving different dates from when he met Devlin and Burns, Neild said witnesses' evidence often slightly altered between what they said in the magistrates' court and at the trial and that the jury should reach their verdict "based on the evidence'. But *which* evidence he did not say. McLoughlin and the other Crown witnesses—whose discrepancies he was also excusing in advance—had sworn on oath at the committal court that their evidence was the truth, yet they had also sworn in the witness box that their different evidence was also the truth. Moreover, whilst slight discrepancies between trial and committal may be understandable, there were fundamental differences between the suppressed statements of McLoughlin, Bury and Milne and their evidence at both courts, of which the jury was of course unaware.

Dismissing the men's defence as a "manufactured alibi", Crown counsel said, "This is either murder or it is not. And it is murder by both these men or by neither of them."

It was now that Neild introduced a completely new and extraordinary theory. Still refuting the defence claim that the Sunblinds robbery occurred on the 19th, he asked the jury to transpose the events to 24 hours previously to the night of the 18th. The men, he said, could have committed both the Manchester robbery *and* the murder of Mrs Rimmer. The accused he said were going to and from Liverpool at that time, which was only an hour's travelling distance from Manchester. "There is nothing impossible," he said, "in breaking into that warehouse on the 18th, partially completing the job, returning on the 19th, and in the early hours of the 20th [after the murder] to finish the job and to provide an alibi."

This was pure speculation. Not only did this come completely out of the blue, which the accused had not been given an opportunity to answer, it simply did not make sense. If Neild's scenario was true why would they partially complete the job? Where was the evidence of their whereabouts between leaving the partially broken into warehouse that night and meeting Milne by the Rialto in Liverpool at 1.30 the next day? The prosecution could not account for that period but the defence had produced witnesses stating the men were in Manchester on the night of the 18th and afternoon of the 19th. Neild moreover did not explain *how* they got to Liverpool and back to Manchester when there was no public transport at that time of night. If he was correct, it also meant Campbell, who Neild asserted had pleaded guilty to robbing Sunblinds on the 18th, must have been with them in Liverpool—something the Crown had never suggested. But Neild had thought of this. Whilst maintaining Campbell was with Devlin and Burns at the robbery on the 18th, he rejected Heilbron's assertion that it was "common ground" that the three men were together at Sunblinds. The clear implication was that Campbell was not involved in the second part of the break-in.

This theory of Neild's—which by no stretch of the imagination could be called evidence—was nonetheless allowed by the judge and not objected to by the defence.[1] If however the court had been aware of Frederick Downing's statement, which specifically stated the men arrived at his house with his wife and the stolen goods 11.30 pm on Sunday the 19th, Neild's theory would have been exposed as the pure nonsense it was.

As for the "manufactured alibi", Neild never explained how Devlin and Burns had colluded with each other in order to construct it or how it was otherwise possible—given that they had been isolated from each other since their arrests, and that all their prison visits and letters had not only been closely supervised and censored but also copied to the police and Home Office. Neither did he explain how they were able to collude with Campbell, who was not only arrested in October whilst they were in prison, but pleaded guilty, saying the men were with him. This was therefore simply wild speculation rather than evidence.

When he referred to McNeil as "carrying on the prosecution's case on the 17th"—almost as if it were a relay race involving Milne and McNeil—Neild

---

1. This matter was only complained about at the men's appeal, where Lord Goddard said the defence could have raised it at trial.

probably never realised that this was Balmer's invention and intention, designed precisely to provide corroboration for Milne's story of the meeting outside Lewis's. But still sitting in his usual seat behind the lawyers' benches, the superintendent remained impassive.

Despite earlier asking the jury to excuse the Crown witnesses changing their stories, Neild made much of Henry Burns wrongly agreeing with him when he had "mistakenly said his brother was on leave from 19th April, rather than 19th July. He also implied he and his wife were lying when pointing to the discrepancy between the former stating the accused men only visited once but his wife saying three times. This was of course true. But he omitted that he had not asked Molly if her husband had been present on the other two occasions. Had he done so, he would have been told Henry was then at work so would not have remembered those visits. Yet again, neither defence counsel nor the judge picked up on this.[2]

Crown counsel then went on to imply intimidation of Campbell by Burns' mother, when she had told him that the date of the Sunblinds break-in was the 19th August. The truth however was that when she had spoken to Campbell before his arrest and he said he couldn't remember the exact date, she reminded him of what her son had told her. Once again, Neild had to resort to scoring points like these in the absence of any concrete evidence.

Dealing with Saturday the 18th August, Neild said the story of the party at Henry Burns' home that night, even the taxi journey home with the Billingham's in the early hours might well be true. But it didn't prevent the "prisoners" from being in the Dive at 1 pm earlier that day meeting Rubin and then going for a meal with Milne, as she had said, to the Golden Dragon. Then after conceding that Burns went to a football match with Billingham, he contradictorily maintained that leaving Milne in Liverpool at 4.30 pm, the accused men could still have met up with Billingham at 6pm. More supposition. But Crown counsel failed to explain how Burns was at the football match with Billingham well before 4.30 pm? Surely the men's story was either *all* false or *all* true? But wanting his cake and eating it as usual, Neild was selectively and illogically indulging in "pick n' mix"! Once again there was no intervention from defence counsel or the judge.

Questioning Heilbron's use of the word "suggested" in relation to Milne's

2.   It was left to Alfred Burns to make this important point after the trial to his solicitor, Norton.

evidence, Neild said she hadn't suggested anything but had given evidence on oath. "*She may not be right* but she has given her evidence on oath," he claimed (Author's italics). This curious statement seemed to the more erudite onlookers to be a subconscious slip by Crown counsel that Milne had perhaps committed perjury or an admission at least that she was mistaken.

Whether it was because he had so little material evidence to go on, Neild seemed increasingly to be not only scraping the bottom of the barrel but also becoming very careless about the accuracy of his comments. For example, he simplistically stated that, "Milne...was taken on *a reconnoitring visit* on the Sunday. And *that* is the case" (Author's italics). Since her implausible evidence was that she had made *three* visits on the Sunday, this comment was clearly intended to minimise the implausibility of her evidence.

Continuing, he maintained that at 10.30 Devlin and Burns left Milne and "...then hurried back to Manchester which they could have reached at about 2 or 3 am." Had such wild speculation come from the defence it would doubtless have provoked an interjection from the judge, who remained silent. But defence counsel, and even the judge, would have unhesitatingly intervened had they been aware of Milne's 9th October statement about going to the South China Café, where she had knocked the owner up and shared a meal of corned beef and chips with the two men!

In his haste to expose a discrepancy between the evidence of Campbell and the accused men, Neild wrongly quoted the former as saying, "It was on the Sunday that the first mention of breaking into *the house* ever happened" (Author's italics). Campbell had not referred to any "house", yet defence counsel and the judge once again let this prejudicial statement pass without objection or comment.

Crown counsel then dismissively said, "So much for the alibi for Friday the 17th." Did he not remember or had he conveniently forgotten all the other witnesses who had stated the accused men were in Manchester on that night?

Refuting the men's story about staying at Joan Downing's, after she had helped to remove the stolen goods in her perambulator, and then going to Burns' mother's on the morning of the 20th, Neild said the only person who could speak to that morning apart from Burns' mother was Joan Downing. He then commented that it was curious why Mrs Burns hadn't been called by the defence. But more importantly he never mentioned why *he* hadn't called Mrs Downing to refute the alibi. Was he afraid that, despite being coerced by Balmer to sign a statement saying she was not with them, she might nonetheless crack under cross-examination? Was he also aware of her husband's statement confirming his wife's involvement?

It is clear the defence must have learned that Mrs Downing would be of no use to them. But she *would* have been able to confirm the Crown's refutation of the alibi. Indeed, according to Joan Downing in her statement to the author, she attended the trial, on Balmer's instructions, on two consecutive days, "just in case you are called." And was paid a total of £40.

At one stage, Neild led himself into a blind alley. It was when quoting Kessler, the warehouse owner's evidence as saying the break-in occurred between 1 pm on the 18th and 8 am on the 20th. Suddenly realising he was undermining his own assertion that it was the 18th, he digressed onto the amount of property stolen, stating that it could not have been transported on a perambulator. Devlin, Burns and Campbell had however stated all along that they left the majority of the property behind. Yet Neild went on to make the astonishing claim that — despite Kessler's evidence that some of the property was later found outside the compound — "No part of that was left on the waste ground or anywhere else. It was removed." Even more astonishingly neither defence counsel objected to this blatant misrepresentation!

Mentioning witnesses who the defence may have called but did not, Neild named in addition to Burns' mother, Edward Billingham and once again Joan Downing of whom he said, "You would reasonably have expected to see her, this woman who helped in the crime. But you have not seen her." He then added rather curiously, "and she can speak to other times of course." Neild never explained what he meant by this remark. But was he daring the defence to call Joan Downing in the knowledge that she had already made a statement to the police denying any involvement?

Stating that "the hole" in Burns trousers was not consistent with a shard of glass cutting his knee whilst breaking-in to the warehouse, Neild omitted to mention that the forensic scientist Dr Firth had stated he had cut out pieces of the trousers for blood analysis.

Crown counsel asked the jury to reject the alibi, that it was not a genuine case of the men being elsewhere at the time of the murder. "It is a false alibi," he said, "which has been advanced in order to escape the guilt which is theirs." Reminding them of McLoughlin's evidence, that the job was post-poned for a fortnight in order for Devlin to be seen around in Manchester, he added, "This was the ground being laid for the alibi."

Basil Neild may have been a renowned Queens Counsel but if he believed two villains on the run from a city's police would return to the same city in order "to be seen around", his knowledge of basic criminal psychology was sorely deficient!

Continuing, Neild dealt at length with the bloodstains on the men's clothing but since none of Mrs Rimmer's blood was found, it was a purely academic exercise and was not evidence against the men. Yet, throwing doubt on the evidence of defence witnesses Crehan and Riley, who had seen the bloodstains on Devlin after his fight in early May, Neild insisted that the blood was from a nose bleed, but that the spots Dr Firth had found were more likely to have come from wielding a bloodstained weapon. He then rather recklessly told the jury that they need not bother with groupings. "It is no good saying, 'Well the blood cannot be grouped and it cannot be prop-erly analysed' and so on. There is no doubt at all that there is human blood on both those garments." And, he went on, if they accepted the prosecu-tion evidence, those garments were worn in Liverpool on the 19th of August.

Once again, despite counsel's language, none of this was evidence proving guilt. The issue of which suits the men had been wearing was, like the blood evidence, inconclusive and of considerable doubt according to the evidence given by the many witnesses. And to wantonly tell the jury that the blood group findings did not matter was unpardonable. It was even more unfor-givable that neither the judge nor defence counsel said a word.

Just before the court adjourned for a short break, Mr Justice Finnemore made another intervention, this time *ostensibly* on behalf of one of the accused men. "There is one point I did look up regarding what Burns said about his suit," he commented. "He said he wore it in Liverpool once only, on the 8th August: otherwise not." He did not however indicate which suit he was refer-ring to. Nor did he tell the jury: that Burns had said in evidence he was not wearing the brown-pin-striped suit at all in Liverpool after the 2nd August.

When the hearing resumed Basil Neild told the jury that the defence case had not only challenged the veracity of the witnesses, McLoughlin, Bury and Milne but the police as well. "We are all challenged," he declaimed.

"Is this really a conspiracy by people to convict the persons who have not committed this offence?"

How little did defence counsel realise how near he had come to the truth!

He then told the jury they could decide to accept the evidence of self-admitted accomplices, McLoughlin and Milne if they wished. There was *nothing in law* preventing them. It was merely the custom and practice in the courts to warn of the dangers of accepting the uncorroborated evidence of accomplices. This advice which was the proper function of the judge which he would repeat in his summing-up anyway, gave the green light for the jury to accept Milne's uncorroborated evidence of the crucial periods when she was allegedly alone with the men.

Recounting when Devlin was supposed to have said in the police car, "Have you seen June and the Chinese bit," Neild asked the jury, "You have seen her. Isn't that a *reasonable* description?" (Author's italics). Coming from learned counsel, a presumably cultured gentleman, quite apart from this comment being — like the references to the Verulam Street landlord — insulting and racist, one might ask, so what? Devlin freely admitted he knew both women. And his alleged remark was in any case a police invention proving nothing.

Dealing with the other corroborative witnesses to the wider story, Neild cited Rubin's evidence of the 18th August meeting but failed to mention that he had admitted the police had suggested dates to him. As for McNeil, his evidence, said Neild, was most important. He had seen the men in Lewis's cafeteria when the accused had denied being in Liverpool after the 8th August.

It is amazing that Neild was allowed to get away with these comments. By not stating the dates when McNeil had seen them in the cafeteria, it could equally have been *before* the 8th. Moreover, this witness' evidence, like most of Milne's, was uncorroborated. And finally, this was the "important" witness who after allegedly spending a whole evening with Devlin and Burns, had failed to pick them out on ID parades!

Attempting to show that McLoughlin, "This wretched creature, coming from gaol, speaking low, in a quiet voice," was telling the truth, Neild quoted his evidence, 'I saw a privet bush in the backyard on that day.' We look at the photograph and there is the privet bush."

The first answer to that was that McLoughlin could have seen the privet bush on *any* day. It proved nothing . And the second answer was that he had been shown photographs of the backyard by Balmer, who incidentally, allowed himself a brief smile at a distinguished top lawyer unknowingly endorsing his conspiracy!

Balmer allowed himself another self-satisfied grin when Crown counsel, asked how McLoughlin could have known that Devlin had been in prison and that Burns was a borstal absconder unless he had been told? "And *who* could have told him save these two, who he said told him."

Continuing, Neild asked the jury, what, "McLoughlin, this miserable specimen from prison had to *gain* by telling lies (Author's italics). Or has he not much to lose? Having heard this case and having seen *that* weapon (indicating the cosh) have you any hesitation in realising what might happen to a squealer?" With due respect to Neild that was the wrong question. What should have been asked was, "What does he have to *fear*?" And what he had to fear after signing Balmer's statement and incriminating himself, was up to 15 years' imprisonment on charges of conspiracy to murder and accessory before the fact. And why mention the cosh? It wasn't even alleged they had it with them in Liverpool or had ever attacked anyone with it.

Counsel's excuse for McNeil not picking out Devlin and Burns—that he was nervous—did not really hold up. If he was so nervous, he did not have to pick *anybody* out, much less two innocent men. It indicated however what pressure he was under to pick *somebody* out!—an important point Sir Noel Goldie would later raise to devastating effect.

When reiterating the alleged meeting with Rubin in the Dive, Neild repeatedly referred to the 17th August rather than the 18th. But nobody apparently thought it serious enough to correct him. Citing as proof however that Rubin's date was the correct one, Neild reminded the jury that the two men had changed over girl friends in Manchester on the 5th August. Did they think Burns would have exchanged Milne for Bury if he had known at the time of the conversation about her "disease"? This would have been a telling point if it were not the fact that Burns had simply told Devlin he didn't fancy Milne (without telling him the reason) and that there had been no evidence of Burns having intercourse with Bury—at the pictures the sex was limited to masturbation![3]

---

3. See *Chapter 1*.

Coming to the taxi driver Emery: Neild conceded that *he* could not remember the precise date of the journey to Smithdown Road and could not identify Devlin and Burns. Yet he told the jury that he was a corroborative witness to the "general story", whatever that meant! Pointing out that Bury had visited Devlin in prison, had taken him cigarettes and was indeed still fond of him, Neild asked why would she give false evidence against him. "Isn't she striving hard to help him? Didn't she say to him on the prison visit 'I don't know McLoughlin'? She is trying to help him… *short of lying about what actually happened.* And she is an acceptable witness" (Author's italics). This assessment was quite correct up to a point. She was indeed a reluctant witness and was still fond of Devlin. But her testimony was not given because, "short of lying" she simply had to tell the truth. On the contrary, it was because she had been threatened that *telling the truth* would mean not seeing her child again and spending several years in prison for the Berry Street shop burglary, the Liverpool Road Goods Depot robbery and absconding from bail.

As proof that Marie Milne's story was true, Crown counsel reminded the jury what she had said about four doors from the back entry, the two mirrors in the kitchen and the armchair by the fire. "And when you see these photographs," he went on, "all these matters are correct. They are all there. And you ask yourselves 'How did she know?' And the answer is she was told—and told by these two prisoners." Undeniable in its logic, it was a very powerful statement, which must have heavily influenced the jury—particularly as juries did not believe the police could be corrupt or even tell lies! But in truth, like McLoughlin's privet bush, it was yet another of Balmer's scripted episodes... with the help of crime scene photographs!

There was no logical reason why Marie Milne should give false evidence against Burns, said Neild. "She was friendly with him, had even slept with him." But in fairness to the distinguished Queens Counsel, he had never been threatened with his family being broken up, himself being put away in a home and his father being deported!

Later, when referring to the arrests, Neild stated that the defence had intimated the police were "party to this wicked plan." Of course they had not claimed any such thing, apart from suggesting that the men's statements had been taken by question and answer. Indeed, Sir Noel Goldie would later forcefully reject that proposition.

Despite initially conceding that it was not evidence against either man, Neild nonetheless reminded the jury of Devlin's words that he wouldn't have hesitated to use the cosh. And, he asked, did they really believe Burns when he said he had taken the cosh in order to return it to its owner? Not only were these prejudicial comments not evidence, but—considering where the cosh was actually found—why mention it at all? And Devlin had *not* said he would have used a cosh without hesitation. He had said only if he was first hit with a truncheon by a policeman. Indeed would not a policeman have done the same thing if struck with a cosh?!

Concluding the case for the prosecution, Basil Neild repeated his implausible thesis that Devlin and Burns had committed the Sunblinds robbery on the 18th and that the alibi was a manufactured one.

"The jury", he said, "may feel, and the evidence points to it, that these men broke and entered Mr Kessler's warehouse *during the 18*[th]. And they had returned as McLoughlin said, in order to be seen about Manchester." In his submission, he said, "those are *the facts*" (Author's italics).[4]

Firstly they were *not* "facts" but mere supposition. Secondly, the assertion that they "returned on the 19th and early hours of the 20th to complete the job." was clearly absurd. Moreover his linking of McLoughlin's evidence to support this new theory was equally illogical. McLoughlin had said the men wanted to be seen in Manchester *a fortnight before* the 19th, which was the reason for the postponement of the Rimmer robbery. Nonetheless, in winding up, Neild claimed that it was, "now proved beyond any real doubt, that those who had planned and perpetrated this crime [the murder] were the two prisoners in the dock, and justice required a verdict of guilty."

---

4. This eleventh hour switch would be one of the grounds of the subsequent appeals. See note 1 above.

CHAPTER THIRTY TWO
GOLDIE AND THE RELEVANCE OF GEORGE BERNARD SHAW'S "JOAN OF ARC"

The old lady was on the floor and the blood was flying upwards.

Sir Noel Goldie QC

When Sir Noel Goldie began his closing speech on behalf of Burns such was his reluctance to attack the police that, emphatically refuting any allegations of a police conspiracy, he appeared at times to be more prosecutor than defender. It was however not only his florid indignation in favour of the Liverpool City Police which harmed his client but also the obscure references to classic literature, which must have left some of the less esoteric jury members, thinking, "What on earth is he talking about?"

Stating he was also speaking on behalf of Rose Heilbron, he said that neither of them had suggested a conspiracy by the police. Referring to Basil Neild's relatively mild comments, he declared it was a disgraceful thing to suggest. "I spew it out of my mouth, if I may use un-forensic language. The Liverpool Police and Manchester Police have only done their duty in this case. And although it is my duty to show you where mistakes have been made, I will be no party to any counsel who suggests that there was any wicked conspiracy of the Liverpool Police." But, he added, "There *was* a conspiracy in which the police were *not* concerned." This was an inference that Milne had conspired with two other men.

He then went on to praise his "younger sister counsel who had largely conducted the defence because Devlin had appeared first on the indictment." When he said he himself had played an "inferior part", Burns whispered to Devlin, "You can fuckin' say that again"!

Stating that Heilbron had presented the defence case exhaustively and in great detail and that the judge would also do so in his summing-up, he was going to deal only with what he termed the "danger points". The jury, he

371

said, had three choices: If they believed the prosecution case, the verdict was guilty. If they believed the defence the verdict was not guilty. But there was a third: if they held a reasonable doubt, then the verdict should still be not guilty. He then used a literary analogy in an attempt to explain the definition of reasonable doubt. To bemused expressions among the all male jury, he asked if any of them had read or seen George Bernard Shaw's play *St. Joan*? And did they remember the trial scene where—"the longest speech made on any English stage is entrusted to the Inquisitor. And do you remember how the curtain falls with the two words by Warwick—'I wonder'? That is the finest illustration I know in English literature of a reasonable doubt." He then added that if any of them were, like Warwick, left "wondering", then there must be a verdict of not guilty.

During the last 100 years, he said, a jury had never had a more difficult or doubtful case to consider. They were therefore entitled to ask, "Why are you trained lawyers asking us to determine the case?" Because, he said, lawyers simply pick out selective points but a jury of 12 ordinary people used their commonsense to ascertain the truth. "And I am appealing to your common-sense to return a verdict of not guilty."

Up to this point it was a "commonsense" explanation but he then returned to English literature asking if they recalled G K Chesterton's essay on jury service. Almost certainly they hadn't, as indicated by their bemused expressions! It may however have been a good thing they were not familiar with Chesterton's *The Twelve Men,* for it was every bit as verbose and abstruse as Goldie's oratorical style!

Defence counsel made a telling point when he said the whole of the prosecution case was that the only thing planned at the Rimmer home was not a murder but a robbery. Yet nothing had been stolen—not even the gas meter's contents and nothing had been disturbed.[1] The attack on Mrs Rimmer was more the work of a homicidal maniac, he said. Asking how two Manchester men should be expected to know the suburbs of Liverpool, he spoke in characteristic melodramatic language about the "appalling underworld of Liverpool and Manchester which would make the ordinary man sick on the floor with it."

"They had to go down there," he said, "into the underworld, not of Eskimo

---

1.   Although he was not aware of it, neither was a five pound note taken from her handbag.

Joe but of McLoughlin and two youthful prostitutes, for that is all they are."

He then embarked on a lengthy social commentary about the undesirability of such places as all-night cafés, suggesting they should be licensed like pubs, before returning to the points at issue like the "blood evidence". Although praising both Dr Manning and Dr Firth for their "fairness and honesty", he pointed out the contradictions in their evidence: Manning had said there was blood everywhere, even up the walls, yet Firth had said the accused men would not necessarily have blood on their clothing. "According to Manning," he said, "the whole place was spouting with blood. The old lady was on the floor and the blood was flying upwards." Surely, he went on, Dr Firth could have told them it was not only human blood but that it was Mrs Rimmer's. "Yet there was not a scintilla of blood Group A found on the men's clothes." Then, recalling the judge's leading question to Burns about whether he took off his coat when fighting, the ex-public schoolboy Goldie said, "Some of us remember the Fives Court at the public schools when we settled disputes with our friends in a bloody if not bloodthirsty way. But you do not take your coat off in a public house when you are having a Donnybrook Fair with an Irishman."[2] The the upper-class Sir Noel Goldie, as folksy and whimsical as he tried to be, utterly failed throughout in these various attempts to establish a rapport with this lower-middle class jury, who were now left expressionless.

Carried away once again with his own florid rhetoric, Goldie was not concentrating when referring to June Bury's lifestyle he declared, "What a comment on June. Sixteen-and-a-half, I think." To which the judge, by now used to his gaffes, tiresomely corrected him with two words, "Twenty-one". But instead of letting the matter pass he humiliatingly apologised to the judge and pleaded to the jury, "In a case of this complexity if I make the slightest slip on fact do forgive me. It is not done intentionally. I know my Lord will correct me and I am sure you will. But in the mass of details in this case and the great responsibility, there comes a time when your brain is not working as well as a fortnight ago. So do forgive me if I make a slip." This grovelling comment ensured not only his failure to strike any rapport with the jury but—finally perceived as incompetent—he had now lost their respect and any authority he may have had.

---

2.   Euphemism for a brawl, named after Dublin's traditional Donnybrook Fair.

His exuberant language notwithstanding, Goldie seemed to becoming increasingly nervous of being corrected or censured by the judge by qualifying his statements with such pre-fixes as, "My Lord will correct me if I am wrong." Indeed he was so apprehensive that when he described McLoughlin as, "being in it up to his neck", he actually censured *himself* thus: "I ought not to say that. I got carried away. I mean he was an accomplice, we will put it that way." But, he went on, McLoughlin was the one who knew all about the privets. "This man who had already robbed his auntie's in the same road. He knew all about *what there was inside the Rimmer house* in a way a man from Manchester could not possibly know, because he had reconnoitred all around the place" (Author's italics). Nobody bothered to point out to Goldie that it was Marie Milne not McLoughlin who had described the interior of the house!

Again wrongly stating that McLoughlin had said they originally planned to do the job over the weekend of August 4th, the judge once again had to correct him: "He never said that. He said, 'Over *the* weekend'." Continuing his address, Goldie heaped scorn on Marie Milne's evidence concerning the 19th August, suggesting that she may indeed have journeyed by taxi but it was with two other men not Devlin and Burns. And it was to the hospital not to reconnoitre Cranborne Road. Then, referring to all three alleged visits that day and night, he asked the jury, "In real life, in the thrillers which some of you read, have you ever heard of a more amazing reconnoitring expedition than that?" Describing Milne's story as incredible, he then catalogued most of the events already covered by Rose Heilbron. But when he was in full oratorical flight, the judge asked if it would be convenient to take a short break, to which he agreed—this time with more annoyance than deference.

When the court resumed, amid all his blundering, Goldie did however make a very important point—albeit subsequently disregarded by the jury—when he said, "Remember this, Milne's evidence does not prove in the slightest that the accused men were actually at 7 Cranborne Road that night." This was of course true since there was no corroboration of that part of her evidence. Indeed the same applied to the most damning parts of her evidence when she was allegedly alone with the two men. Balmer however was obviously aware of this potential deficiency, which is why he scripted the "handover" from Milne to McNeil outside Lewis's on the 17th.

Although he said he was going to deal with the 17th and 18th August, Goldie nonetheless then began explaining the alternative routes from Cranborne Road to the Rialto in order to refute Milne's story of the men coming through the park on the 19th, the lost knife and their muddy shoes, etc. Unfortunately he gave the wrong details, which again did not impress the jury. He, Crown counsel and the jury all had maps of the area yet he described one route as "Going up Smithown Road to Tunnel Road and then by some way down to Granby Street and to the Rialto." It was clear however from the map that this route was in the opposite direction to the Rialto!

Mentioning that it was a clear August night with no rain, counsel wondered where the story of the muddy shoes came from — particularly since it was too dark for Milne to observe this. "Members of the jury," he said, this is a murder trial not a thriller. Can you believe evidence like that?" A good point, which probably made Balmer regret not sticking to his original script (contained in Milne's statement) of her observing the men's shoes and clothing stains *inside the South China Café!*

Despite the ebbing away of his credibility and esteem, the highlight of Goldie's closing speech came when he dramatically declared that far from the men's alibi being manufactured, it had actually been proved to be true... and by no less a person that Basil Neild himself!

Pointing to the cosh lying on the table below the judge's bench, he said that the use of such things were common among criminals, even though they should not be. But even the prosecution agreed it was found at Sunblinds in Manchester *not* at 7 Cranborne Road, Liverpool. Then, once more adopting his eccentric use of language, he told the jury that on the night of the 19th August, "*We* were breaking into this Sunblinds place with Campbell" (Author's italics). It was open, he said, for the Crown to deal with that in two ways. But Neild had not said Devlin and Burns were not there or that Campbell was a first class liar. "So what did my learned friend do? Carried away by his sense of misplaced duty and the chance to waggle that thing at Burns and say, 'Is that the sort of thing you care to use?' I don't for one moment say he did that. I say that was one way of dealing with the case. But in fact the *first question* he asked Burns was, 'Is this your cosh?'" (Author's italics)

Neild was immediately on his feet protesting that he never said that. A fumbling Goldie asked the judge for the record stating, "My recollection was…" But interrupting, Neild said it was not his "first" question. "It certainly was not *that*", agreed the judge. "I am much obliged my Lord," said Goldie. "I ought not to have said "first." Not only was Goldie's incompetence demeaning but the jury, witnessing this spectacle of trivial semantics between men of high learning, could have been forgiven for forgetting the real issue here—that two men were on trial for their very lives.

When Burns agreed it was his cosh, *whenever* Neild asked the question, said Goldie, that reply proved beyond a shadow of doubt that Campbell was telling the truth, when he said Devlin and Burns committed the robbery with him. "Burns said, '*That is my cosh*' (Author's italics). Never mind, 'I am going to hit a policeman over the head or anyone else who disturbs me', he said. 'I left that cosh in those premises on that Sunday night', and to that extent the alibi is established, not by any evidence I have called but by the fair and proper cross-examination of my learned friend, who proved—I hope to your satisfaction—that Burns in the course of that exploit left behind that cosh."

The only problem with Goldie's otherwise plausible explanation, was that Burns had never said, "That is my cosh". He said it belonged to the van driver Mac, to whom he was returning it. Moreover, it was Devlin and not Burns who had said what he would do with the cosh if attacked by a police officer.

After rambling irrelevantly through the underworld of the all-night cafés, "Where nobody ever slept, and lived rough, but not under haystacks as they did in the old days"—defence counsel in support of the alibi reminded the jury of Mrs Alice Shenton's evidence. She had testified that both Burns and Devlin were at Henry and Molly Burns' house on the 17th. "Even learned counsel agreed she was a truthful witness. So where on earth does the story come from about them meeting Milne in the Golden Dragon, and McNeil later, outside Lewis's and drinking with him for three hours in Tracey's pub?"

Continuing, he said that it was not a manufactured alibi. It was true of the 17th. And Neild had no evidence with which to contradict it. This assertion of course ignored Milne's and McNeil's evidence of events on the 17th.

Although, according to Goldie, Burns visit to the football match with brother-in-law Eddie Billingham on the 18th was subsequently verified by the police, they had only verified that he was correct about the names of the two teams and the goal-less draw. But if untrue, how could Burns have obtained this information, given that this was the first football match he had ever attended, and that the strict conditions he had been kept under since his arrest would have made it impossible to receive this information from anyone?

William Butler the taxi driver, like Emery the Crown's taxi driver, was a reliable witness, said Goldie. Moreover, he had his written log to *prove* the journey took place with Burns and Devlin at 2 am on the morning of the 19th with Billingham, his wife and child. Burns and Butler had even discussed a mutual acquaintance who Burns had been in borstal with. And he had identified Devlin from the dock. If nothing else, he said, it disposed of the Crown's 11th hour theory that they were breaking into Sunblinds on the night of the 18th. "Is that a manufactured alibi, members of the jury?" And on the Sunday afternoon, when the accused men were supposed to be riding in taxis and buses and trams back and forth to Smithdown Road for no discernible reason, said Goldie, the jury had heard the defence witnesses who said they were at the Barracks Flats watching an amateur football match and Devlin had gone to the pictures. "Don't you think the police must have checked that and found it to be true?"

Like Heilbron before him, Goldie never realised how near he came to the actual conspiracy against his client and Devlin when he raised the issue of Campbell's indictment. "Very often," he explained, "indictments usually allege that so-and-so on or between certain dates so-and-so. But," he went on without any suspicion of dirty work, "it so happened on this particular charge to which Campbell had pleaded guilty—and all honour to him—that he had been *charged* with committing the offence specifically on the 18th August" (Author's italics). Goldie was of course wrong, the *original* charge sheet had *not* specified the 18th. But oblivious to the crucial issue of the altered date, he, again like Heilbron, naturally concentrated on whether Campbell would really have been thinking about what actual *day* it was. He had already admitted the offence and that it was in August, said Goldie, so what did the date matter?

One of the major weaknesses in the defence case was the fact that Campbell had pleaded guilty to the 18th. Rose Heilbron in her closing speech had voiced her curiosity about this. But both defence and Crown counsel, and later the judge, would all accept the indictment as gospel. Heilbron had unsuccessfully requested production of Campbell's statement (even though she was unaware of his further statement to Detective Sergeant Richardson). But it is tragic that none of them asked to see the original charge sheet.

After repeating that as far as a conspiracy by the Liverpool Police was concerned, "There was nothing of the kind", Sir Noel Goldie concluded his closing speech to the jury thus:

> I am not inviting you to shirk your duty. Consequences have nothing at all to do with this. But I am saying to you with the utmost confidence that it would be most dangerous in accordance with your oaths, to convict on the evidence that has been called before you. I now pass to you the responsibility which myself and my learned friend have been carrying for the last fortnight. And I ask you in all seriousness to do what I know you will; that is to examine the evidence in this case with the most scrupulous care. And provided you do so, I ask with the utmost confidence for a verdict of not guilty at your hands.

The proceedings were then adjourned to 10.30 the next morning.

Sir Noel Goldie's and — to a lesser extent — Rose Heilbron's cross-examination of the witnesses had been more conspicuous by the questions they did not ask rather than those they did. But given the massive amount of documentary and other evidence which had been withheld from them, perhaps this was inevitable.

Down in the cells, Burns was fuming at his counsel's performance, calling him all the stupid bastards under the sun. "I could have done fuckin' better myself," he cried. One of the escort prison officers begrudgingly said, "I must admit, he didn't do you any favours Alf." A weary Devlin, sitting quietly on the bench, commented that he was sick and tired of the constant lies and the whole affair, adding, "I just hope the judge isn't against us tomorrow."

CHAPTER THIRTY THREE
SUMMING-UP, VERDICT AND SENTENCE

Wednesday 27th February 1952.

The conduct of the trial and direction of the jury must be judged according to the standards we would now apply under the Criminal Justice Act 1968.

Lord Chief Justice Bingham (2001: The Bentley Appeal)

On this final day of the trial, crowds — to whom murder trials were much more entertaining than the cinema or the wireless — had been queuing to get into court from as early as 2 am. At 9.30 one man who jumped the long queue and was hectored by several women would not budge until three men attacked him and dragged him away.

At 10 am a luxurious Daimler car arrived at the northern end of St George's Hall carrying Mr Justice Finnemore in all his red-robed splendour. Flanked by several police officers and the Lord Lieutenant of Lancashire, he ceremoniously proceeded into the William Brown Street entrance. Half an hour earlier, un-noticed because of the fracas among the crowds, Devlin and Burns had also arrived at the northern end. But theirs was not so dignified an occasion. In a grey van with small barred opaque windows, they were quickly driven down the cobblestoned ramp at the side of the entrance, into a tunnel and to the dungeon-like cells in the bowels of the building.

During his summing–up, Mr Justice Finnemore frequently referred to and quoted from "the evidence" but most of his comments, like those of prosecuting counsel, were often conjecture and pure speculation. In fairness, however, he, like the prosecution and defence, was unaware of the mass of undisclosed evidence — except Alan Campbell's statement and charge sheet!

Opening, he told the jury the Crown's case was that the accused's motive was robbery and that they had been surprised by the return of Mrs Rimmer. He significantly failed however to explain why they had been "surprised" when the Crown's case was that they had already been in the house for one-and-a-half-hours and that nothing had been stolen.

Similar omissions were to be a hallmark of his four hour address to the jury. His adroit style throughout was ostensibly sympathetic to the defence but making the prosecution points much more forcefully and favourably — often in the process being erroneous and factually wrong. He was quite inaccurate for example in telling the jury that Bury had made her statement on the 4th October and Milne on the 7th. This effectively demolished, he said, the defence point about Milne telling Bury she had to back her story up and everything else which flowed from that. The truth of course was that Milne's first statement was on the 7th, Bury's first *written* statement on the 8th and Milne's expanded one on the 9th. But Balmer, sitting in his usual place, was quite happy to let the judge, however unintentionally, mislead the jury.

Casting further doubt on the men's defence, Finnemore also pointed out that at the committal court Bury had given her evidence *before* Milne — a point which was immaterial in view of the sequence of their statements. Reiterating Milne's version of events on the night of August 19th, Finnemore told the jury that it was supported by McLoughlin, Bury, Rubin, McNeil and Emery. This was of course patently untrue. None of them were in the company of Milne, Devlin and Burns during Sunday the 19th, nor were they anywhere near the scene of the crime at that time.

When telling the jury they would have to decide who was telling the truth between the Crown and defence witnesses, he referred to the "case for the prosecution" but simply to "the defence *setting up* an alibi" (Author's italics). This was perhaps a subconscious indication of his pro-prosecution thinking. And when he said that the alibi did not cover *all* the material times, it is difficult to know what more evidence the numerous defence witnesses covering the 17th, 18th and 19th of August could have provided.

In a veiled attempt to mitigate the changed evidence of McLoughlin (seeing the men a week later then seeing them the same night); Bury (about being in the Continental with Devlin and Burns) and Milne (about the two knife threats), which he intimated could be "honest mistakes", Finnemore said they shouldn't be expected to remember verbatim their evidence from the committal court. Indeed, he went on, it would be more suspicious if they *did* remember every word. This was undeniably true. But these discrepancies were not mere mistakes, they were fundamentally crucial and cast grave doubt on the Crown's case. Moreover, had Mr Justice Finnemore been aware of the discrepancies between their signed *statements* and their *evidence* at both hearings, even he could not have excused them.

Mentioning that Bury in evidence had agreed she spent one night at Whitsuntide with Devlin in Manchester, he omitted to mention her original testimony that she had stayed with him for a week. He was again incorrect when, regarding the evening of 8th August, he said, "They took her back to Manchester *and she then went back to Liverpool*" (Author's italics). She never said she went back to Liverpool, she said she never saw them again until the 16th or 17th in Manchester. He also omitted altogether the fact that she did indeed keep watch and minded their macs at the Liverpool Road Goods Depot robbery. This sort of misdirection, including such vagueness as telling a lay jury it was up to them to decide if Bury was an accomplice, only served to make them even more confused in what was already a very complicated case.

Despite stressing that Bury had taken no part in the planning or execution of the crime, Finnemore nonetheless described her evidence as "important" and that she could corroborate the evidence of the other witnesses — "Because they were preparing *this* house-breaking in Liverpool and she was being asked to take part in it" (Author's italics). But he conspicuously failed to also remind the jury that she had at first stated that nothing more than just "doing a job" had been mentioned on the train journey. Describing her as "Miss June Bury", Finnemore referred to her morals, like Milne's, as merely "not beyond reproach", gratuitously adding, "Not that those men in the dock are in a position to throw any stones."

The jury, he said, would have to ask themselves why Bury, "given that she had been in some trouble herself", would go into the witness box and give false evidence against Devlin of whom she said she was still fond? The simple answer, known only to Balmer, was cause and effect! It was precisely because she had been, *and still was*, in trouble, that she had reluctantly done so!

Later Finnemore misquoted Devlin as saying, "Of course *we* would have used the cosh" (Author's italics). Devlin had said, "I" not "We". Indeed Burns, when asked if *he* would have used a cosh — even if attacked with a police-man's truncheon — had clearly stated that he did not think it would have been necessary. Yet after conceding that the cosh could not be the murder weapon, the judge by some perverse syllogism then concluded that, "It cannot now be said that these men would not use violence." This passage which also branded Burns as violent, was spuriously based on the Canning Street incident when he had told Bury not to be afraid of Rubin. Yet in other circumstances—for example at one of his Boys Brigade summer camps—Sir Donald Finnemore would probably have instructed his young charges that such reassurance to a lady in a tense situation was in fact a very good example of old-fashioned chivalry!

Dealing with the issue of accomplices and the various reasons why they may have given false evidence, the judge probably never realised how near he came to the truth when he said, "He (McLoughlin) may even hope to escape punishment altogether *if he helps to convict somebody else*" (Author's italics). Listening intently, Balmer must have wondered if the judge was actually psychic!

Avoiding any mention of Bury's actual involvement on the evening of the 8th August in the Liverpool Road Goods Depot robbery, Finnemore simply said that "after that *episode*" she—like Milne on her return to Liverpool—"had gone back home." Yet he then said that although she had refused to take part in *this particular* housebreaking—he wasn't even sure she knew where the Liverpool robbery was going to be. This, by any measure was selective summing-up.

Having reminded the jury of "what sort of men the accused are" he warned not to convict them because of that. But there was one matter, he said, which they could not put out of their minds. The defence had said that no matter how bad they were, the accused men had no convictions for violence. "Well, members of the jury," he said stretching out his right hand and picking up the cosh, "during Devlin's cross-examination *this* was produced.[3] Perhaps it shocked you when you first saw it. Now you know that on one occasion they took this with them when they were going to, 'do a job'. Oh yes, Burns said he wouldn't think of using a thing like that, with which you hit people on the head. His fists were good enough. They never meant to use it but to give it to the man they had taken it from who they

---

3.   This gratuitous and prejudicial gesture was only equalled by Lord Goddard wielding a knuckle-duster in the Craig and Bentley trial a year later.

might meet for the use of his car." Devlin, he went on, was different. "Of course *we* would have used it but not on a woman, not on a civilian. But if a policeman had drawn his truncheon, then of course *I* would have used it" (Author's italics).

Care to qualify the "we" to an "I", did not alter the fact that these prejudicial and inflammatory comments should never have been made. There was no evidence that the cosh had ever been used to attack *anyone*. Indeed its presence at Sunblinds proved they were telling the truth. Burns had denied ever using a cosh and Devlin had never mentioned a woman, nor said, "Of course *we* would have used it."

Anxious however to portray Burns as a violent man, Finnemore again told the jury to remember what *he* had said about dealing with Rubin if necessary. "And there is no doubt that is what he said he *would have* done" (Author's italics). Knowing the cosh had been in the men's possession, could the jury really accept that they would not have used violence? "If this very horrible weapon is any sort of guide," he continued, "is it not so surprising that Marie Milne thought they were men who, if she crossed their desires, she might be frightened of—and properly frightened?" These damaging comments totally ignored the fact that they never had the cosh when in Milne's company. But it was the sort of conjecture and prejudicial non-evidence employed by the Crown throughout the trial, to which the judge was now deplorably adding his own considerable weight.

Cleverly covering himself however against future accusations of prejudice, Finnemore then told the jury—despite what he had just said—that they should not convict them because they had bad characters. "Convict them only if the evidence satisfies you they are guilty of this crime." But just as a little objectivity and fairness was emerging, he pointed again to the cosh on his bench and said, "But in view of *this*, I don't think you can say that these are two men who would not use violence or force."

Regarding McLoughlin's evidence, the judge reiterated that on the evening of the day he first met Devlin, he also met Burns in the Continental Café, where June Bury was. But he failed to add that McLoughlin had previously stated it was a week later. Nor did he remind the jury that June Bury had been forced to admit that there was no evening from the 2nd to the 8th of August when she could possibly have been at the Continental. But most importantly—even if McLoughlin's story was true—he did not remind them that Bury in her evidence had stated it was *he* who had suggested the Rimmer robbery.

Devlin and Burns, said the judge, had protested they did not even know McLoughlin, had never met him in their lives. So the jury may wish to know how he on two separate identity parades, "arranged you may think with considerable fairness by the police, could pick out each man without any trouble or difficulty." They may also ask *why* he would do this if it were not true? "The second question was if they had never spoken to him, how did he recognise them? It is very extraordinary," he went on, "that McLoughlin should pick the two men whom June Bury and Marie Milne gave evidence about. But according to them they were not in Liverpool much."

This was a most compelling argument, the logic of which was inescapable. But despite the profoundly damning effect it must have had on the jury, it was not irrefutable. Neither they nor the judge were aware of the repeated showing to McLoughlin of the men's photographs and of his prolonged tuition. The judge then made a most prescient comment about McLoughlin, telling the jury whether it was helping, "this weak specimen in any way to tell such a story. I do not know and probably you do not know what he can *hope to get from it* (Author's italics). But there it is". Given that Mr Justice Finnemore had no inkling of a conspiracy, Balmer, who *did* know, must have thought that the learned judge was most definitely psychic!

Like Sir Noel Goldie, the judge did not seem to have a firm grasp of events as his summing-up became increasingly marked with, "I think", "I suppose" and "I'm not sure." This was particularly evident when dealing with crucial dates, as when he stated at one stage, "I think it is the 8th, I am not sure. But it really doesn't very much matter."

Giving a resume of Bury's involvement, he was, whether by accident or in his desire to help the prosecution, incorrect in several respects. Despite being disproved by Rose Heilbron, he stated that Bury went to various cafés with the men on the night of the 2nd August. Only later did he partly rectify this by merely mentioning in passing that, "there was some discrepancy about that." But he crucially omitted to remind the jury that Bury had finally admitted to going to Manchester with the men that night.

After stating that Devlin and Burns had *agreed with Bury's story* apart from discussing jobs with her and McLoughlin in the Continental, he then did a *volte-face*, wrongly asserting that the defence claimed *all* of it was untrue! And when he stated that all of Bury's evidence was very important, it clearly wasn't—given that it did not provide any *direct* evidence against the accused men.

Referring to the morning of August 8th when the men returned to Verulam Street to find Bury alone, who told them she had been out all night, he said, "It was only their word that she told them she had been out, screwing or something of that sort, had been *taken by the police,* spent the night in the police station, had just been released and was to be back at 10 am" (Author's italics).

Apart from having no idea of how she had *actually* been "taken" by the police (or rather a detective), he suggested Devlin and Burns had fabricated this story. "It was a little unfortunate that when Miss June Bury was in the box, no one suggested a word of that to her as being a true story." Heilbron had said she knew nothing about it, he said, "And we heard nothing more about it. You may therefore wonder if it was not an embellishment put on by the two men without any foundation." Anyway, he went on, none of that story was ever put to June Bury in the witness box. A credible response to this, which the judge again failed to mention, was when Rose Heilbron suggested to Bury that she had been in some trouble with the police and she snapped back that it had nothing to do with the case. And he, Finnemore—unlike his upbraiding of Burns for calling Neild's questions ridiculous—had let her insolence pass without comment. Other responses could reasonably have been—what purpose would it serve Devlin and Burns to have made up this story? And what opportunity did they have since their arrests to concoct it? It was however, a valid criticism of Heilbron that, since Devlin had informed her of it, she had not pursued the matter with Bury in the witness box.

Regarding Bury being arrested in the early hours of August 8th, it was significant that, although Devlin and Burns had testified to this (the truth of which is confirmed in the police files) the judge nevertheless implied that they had made up the story. Yet when earlier relating events after the Liverpool Road Goods Depot robbery—and with only Bury's word to go on—he told the jury that she, "quite properly went home." In truth she had not gone home. She had taken their raincoats, gone to a Piccadilly Coffee

Stall and met a man who took her to collect her suitcase from Exchange Station and then took her home. And the man had told Devlin and Burns on the 10th August, that he had also been with her that morning in an Oxford Road Amusement Arcade.

Coming to the alleged conversation between Devlin and Rubin, in the Dive on the 18th of August, Finnemore commented quite tellingly (albeit unintentionally), that the Crown had not produced any evidence of the men's whereabouts between that time and 1.30 pm the following day when Milne allegedly met them by the Rialto. This raises the question that if there had been a proper and thorough police investigation, the Crown — since they refuted the alibi — would have been able to say where the men where between those times. This was doubly important because the defence had asserted the men were in Manchester on both the Saturday and the Sunday and had produced several witnesses to prove this. But the judge did not explain this. Moreover, although Milne had stated that Devlin had told her he and Rubin had "a sort of a fight" in the Dive, there was no evidence from Rubin about a fight and no corroborative evidence Devlin had ever said such a thing to her. Indeed her account of what Devlin said should really have been inadmissible.

Moving on, the judge gave Milne's evidence the ultimate credibility as if it were proven fact, telling the jury, "You will remember they went by taxi to Smithdown Road, you may think it was Mr Emery's taxi. There was two shillings on the clock and Burns paid him two shillings and sixpence." But after conceding that Emery was not sure it was Sunday the 19th, he astonishingly told the jury that Emery had corroborated Milne's evidence. Only as an incidental afterthought did he comment that the taxi driver could only say he took Milne and two young chaps.

In his zealous support of the prosecution Mr Justice Finnemore seemed to be drifting further and further away from fairness, objectivity and truth. A further example being his stating, "The defence was a denial of *everything* to do with this trial" (Author's italics). Had he forgotten his own earlier comments, when telling the jury that Devlin and Burns had *agreed* with Bury and Milne's story up to the 8th of August?

Following this damagingly untruthful statement, he then told the jury they should totally discount Milne being mistaken but must simply decide whether she was telling the truth or lying. "It is just true or it is a complete lie," he added. "There is no half-way house." He did not however warn the jury that they only had Milne's word that Burns told her on the night of August 5th at the station, he would see her again on the 17th. Nor did he remind them this was contradicted not only by the accused men but also June Bury, who had agreed they promised to see them in a few days time—which in fact they did. On this issue the weight of evidence was clearly in the defence's favour—three witnesses against one—but Finnemore completely failed to mention this most important point.

Regarding McNeil, the judge again said that he had seen the accused men in the Continental Café at odd times. "But forget about that," he said, "But McNeil said he certainly saw them in Lewis's cafeteria between the 16th and 21st August."

Despite telling the jury to forget about the Continental, doubtless because there was no corroboration, there was equally no corroboration he had seen them in the cafeteria. But Milne could at least corroborate his story of meeting them *outside* Lewis's on the 17th. As for deliberately picking out innocent men at the identity parades, the judge repeated McNeil's excuse that he was nervous and, minimising its gravity, simply remarked, "It was a very wrong thing to do."

Dealing with the blood evidence, Finnemore made a strangely paradoxical statement. After admitting that Dr Firth had been unable to group the bloodstains on the men's clothing, he then said that it was *not quite right* that Mrs Rimmer's blood had *not* been found on their suits. "*It is right* to say there was no blood which could be shown to be her blood or anybody else's" (Author's italics). One can only guess what the jury must have thought about this seemingly self-contradictory statement. Apart from anything else, this was surely taking the already spurious circumstantial evidence to extremes?

Staying with the subject of bloodstains, the judge again made one of his extraordinary leaps to illogical conclusions. Telling the jury that Devlin *had* worn the fawn gabardine suit in August (despite some dispute about this), he said it had *many* visible and *presumptive traces* of human blood. "If that is right," he said, "it is consistent with the fact, if it be a fact, that he was one of the people who attacked this lady and got his clothes splattered with *some* drops of blood". But how un-groupable and presumptive bloodstains—"many traces" one moment "some drops" the next—could possibly be evidence against Devlin, only Mr Justice Finnemore applying his bizarre logic, knew!

Faced with the incontrovertible evidence of Devlin's suit being pawned on the 11th August and not redeemed until the 23rd, the judge, seemingly reluctant to accept this, said, "Quite plainly *some suit* was taken on the 11th because we have seen the ticket, if it was the *same suit*" (Author's italics). Then to drive home his point he told the jury, "You have to consider whether that is the suit or not."

After the lunch adjournment, Finnemore asked the jury if they wished him to complete his summing up today, in which case they would have to be sequestered until they had reached a verdict. Or would they rather he broke off at about 4 pm and continue the following morning (which would obviously give more time for them to deliberate). After they had briefly conferred the foreman said, "My Lord the sense the jury is that we would prefer to sit on and finish tonight."

Finnemore's apparently innocuous question was not as considerate at it appeared. By mentioning sequestration he rightly guessed that the jury would not willingly choose to be kept away from their homes all night, and therefore would not be taking long in reaching their verdict. Balmer also knew this and from his experience he knew a quick verdict usually meant guilty!

During an exhaustive account of Devlin's evidence, the judge on several occasions, reminded the jury that they only had his word or in some instances only his and Burns', making comments like, "That is what Devlin says," etc. For example, *only* Devlin had confirmed Burns account of meeting him after the Saturday football match at Maine Road. Yet when reiterating Milne's evidence he made no such qualifications, giving the impression that what *she* said was factual and true.

Referring to the morning of the 19th August, the judge made the telling point that, since Burns mother had not given evidence, there was only their word that they stayed at her home. He then made a curious statement which was even more telling. Burns he said, would not stay at Devlin's house too long because it was near a police station so they arranged to meet at Mrs Joan Downing's house. "Who again, you have not seen, *perhaps understandably, as she took part*, or is alleged to have taken part, in receiving the stolen property on the Sunday night" (Author's italics).

It was not clear why it was "understandable" that the jury had not seen Joan Downing, considering that the judge had said she had "taken part", before correcting himself. Nor did he ask why she wasn't called, or why it was not commented on whether this vital witness had been charged with "taking part." Was he privy to the fact she had made a statement, albeit under duress, denying she was with them at Sunblinds? And was this also why the defence did not call her? Whatever the reason, Balmer was doubtless greatly relieved when Finnemore quickly moved on to the men's visit "according to them" to Alice Ford's at the Barracks Flats!

The judge's further misrepresentations of the defence evidence included repeating that Devlin said in relation to the cosh, "*We* would have been able to retaliate with it on a police officer" (Author's italics). Devlin of course had only said what *he* would hypothetically do so. But then he *was* anxious to portray Burns as a violent man!

Again, either by accident or design, the learned judge related comments made by the van driver Mac to Devlin in such an un-punctuated manner as to make them appear to be Devlin's. Quoting Devlin regarding the cosh he said, "'I kept it on my person'. Then he told you they had some trouble with the man from whom they got it. *He* said 'If anyone got tough with me I would use this'. And he wanted to have a go with this man but apparently that passed off peacefully" (Author's italics). As if this gross distortion were not bad enough he then added, misquoting Devlin, "We had the cosh in our possession from the 15th August. I agree it is a blunt weapon."

Later, exploiting a mere one hour discrepancy between Campbell's and Burns evidence regarding the time they took looking for transport, he told the jury that they may have to consider whether that had really happened or not. And, as with most of the defence witnesses, he said the jury would have to make up their minds whether Alice Ford was telling the truth about the men's visit to her flat on the Sunday afternoon. The implication was clearly not to believe her, particularly when he quite unnecessarily remarked, "*She said she had been in trouble for receiving stolen property* but she agrees they were at her house on the Sunday afternoon" (Author's italics). Then, Sidney McDiarmid who went to the York Cinema with Devlin on the Sunday afternoon: "He was also a man of not very good character. He has been convicted of housebreaking and a good many times for disorderly behaviour, *which is the same sort of thing"* (Author's italics). Disorderly behaviour is a misdemeanour and *not* the same as housebreaking, which was a felony. But this was the sort of "balanced" imbalance typical of the judge's summing-up!

Coming to Ann Ford, another defence witness, who had testified to the accused men being in the Ship Inn on the 19th, Finnemore did not miss the opportunity of reminding the jury that her new husband had been in borstal and that she was the sister or sister-in-law of Joan Fitzgerald who, he implied, had tried to conceal Burns clothing from the police at her Cornbrook Street home. These and other imputations against the defence witnesses, as against his apparent endorsement of the Crown's case, was totally unwarranted and had no bearing whatever on the guilt or otherwise of Devlin and Burns.

Commenting that Ann Ford had said she had spoken to Devlin's mother about the case, Finnemore then magically transmuted Mrs Devlin into Mrs Burns by again wrongly recalling that, "Mrs Burns went round to *see people* about this date" (Author's italics). Mrs Burns had spoken *only* to Alan Campbell about the 19th of August.

Adopting the Crown's changed scenario that the men could have done both the murder and the robbery on the 18th/19th, the judge again wrongly said Milne had testified to Devlin and Burns saying after the murder that they had to "hurry back to Manchester". Yet she had actually said they just walked away toward the city centre. But now hearing even the judge's validation of his false scenario, Balmer must have congratulated himself for suppressing her signed statement in which she said, far from hurrying back to Manchester they went with her for a meal at the South China Café.

Finnemore's conjecture, like Basil Neild's, did not include Campbell being with them in Liverpool — probably because of the inescapable fact of his conviction for robbing the Manchester warehouse! Indeed he then emphasised to the jury that, "Campbell had pleaded guilty to an indictment charging him with doing it on Saturday the 18th."

Regarding Devlin's evidence about a night watchman from an adjoining factory shining his torch and speaking to him, the judge said, "It was astonishing, *if this was true*, that seeing several men pushing a pram full of stolen goods in the middle of the night, he did not interfere or take any action" (Author's italics). The obvious inference here was that Devlin was lying.[4] But Finnemore was unaware that the night watchman, who did not give evidence and was not subpoenaed, had refused to sign two different statements he had made in January to Livermore and the police, broadly confirming Devlin's story.

Dealing with Burns sister-in-law's evidence about his and Devlin's visits to her home, the judge also cast doubt on her testimony, disparagingly telling the jury it was "rather odd" that apart from the two visits on the 17th and 18th she had not seen *Devlin* for two years. Again he wrongly stated that she knew "*Devlin* had been home from borstal since July" (Author's italics).

Referring to Mrs Alice Shenton, he said the jury might think she was different from the other defence witnesses because she was not a family member—"although she *was* a friend of the family." This mildly prejudicial comment was followed by him sarcastically stating, "She only remembers the 17th because it was *her* child's birthday. You might think there were quite a lot of birthdays" (Author's italics).

If Rose Heilbron could not prevent the judge's prejudice and sarcasm she could at least correct him on his facts. "My Lord," she politely said, "I think it was young Henry Burns fifth birthday." After apologising for the error however, he again wrongly misrepresented Mrs Shenton's testimony, stating, "She had never seen this Alfred Burns in her life before." It was of course *Devlin* who she did not know and who she asked Molly Burns about.

As Goldie had said, Alice Shenton was an impeccable witness with no criminal record and no relationship to the accused men. But this did not stop the judge's expressed doubts about her evidence, telling the jury to remember she was deaf and short-sighted and had had to get close to the dock in order to identify the two prisoners.

Passing quickly over the indisputable evidence from taxi driver Butler regarding the 15 shillings journey in the early hours of the 19th, he reminded the jury that there was only the evidence of the two accused as to what happened after arriving at Medlock Street—the clear implication being that they could have then travelled to Liverpool for the 1 pm meeting with Marie Milne—despite the evidence of Alice Ford and McDiarmid that they were at the Barracks Flats and the York Cinema that afternoon.

---

4. Devlin's evidence about this was mentioned in Balmer's report of 5th April 1952 (See Appeal chapter) and verified by Mr Gerrard QC at the inquiry.

The jury, said Finnemore, must weigh up the evidence and ask themselves if some of the defence witnesses were mistaken over dates. "Or if they were purposely giving the wrong dates in order to try and establish this alibi to try and save these two men *from the consequences of their crime*" (Author's italics). Although Heilbron had earlier found it necessary to correct the judge on the minor point of a child's birthday, she and Goldie, shamefully remained silent in the face of this and other blatantly prejudicial comments. It had not yet been proven according to law that the two men had committed any crime.[5]

Telling the jury that Burns had said he had cut his leg climbing into Sunblinds, Finnemore remarked that it was rather odd there had been no tear in his trousers. He did not however remind them that Burns had said it was only like a pin prick from a small shard of glass, which would not necessarily leave a visible tear. Nor that Dr Firth had cut out several pieces of the trousers, where he thought there were bloodstains, and covered them with larger cellophane patches.

Dealing with the issues surrounding the arrests and the accused men's statements the judge's sophistry really came to the fore. Detective Skinner, he related, said that when he arrested Devlin he immediately told him it was for the Rimmer murder. But Devlin denied this, saying Detective Lynch had mentioned the Playhouse robbery and that is what he thought he was being arrested for. But police officers, said the judge, are trained to observe and record, so who did they believe? Similarly casting doubt on Burns evidence, he asked the jury to note that although he had said he did not know the names of any of the Liverpool cafés, in his statement he had mentioned the Rainbow Café three times. "Three times," he emphasised. He did not likewise remind them of Burns' explanation that Balmer had suggested the café's name to him. Nor that he had similarly suggested to Devlin the 16th as the date he had last seen Bury in Manchester.

The jury were asked if they believed the car journey to Liverpool had been conducted in silence, which Devlin denied. But, said Finnemore, "It was the right and proper thing for police officers to do, and was, among other things, for the prisoner's own protection in case he said something to incriminate himself." At this naïve observation Balmer self-righteously nodded his head.

5.   This was similar to Lord Goddard's reference to the "murder" of PC Miles whilst the trial of Craig and Bentley was ongoing before any murder had been proven.

Equally naïvely, the judge, commenting that Burns had denied saying, "I have been worrying about it. I know you knocked Devlin", said it was rather "astonishing" Burns should think that the murder charge against Devlin was a trick in order to get him to admit other jobs and that, "It threw a rather strange light on this case." He did not explain why it should be "astonishing" and "strange". After all, the entire court was fully aware that Devlin and Burns were "professional criminals". And wasn't that the way such people viewed the police?

Capitalising on Goldie's dramatically worded rejection of a Liverpool police conspiracy, the judge said he did not know whether Burns denials of the police evidence justified the word "conspiracy". "But of course Sir Noel Goldie would not for a moment dream of suggesting that, but that is what Burns said." Continuing in this disingenuous manner, he said, "It may be that it throws a sort of light on the mind of Burns and the way he looks at things. *But do not pay too much attention if it does not help you*" (Author's italics).

Burns, who had denied making certain incriminating comments to the police and simply said his statement was taken in response to questions, had never alleged a conspiracy. But this matter, "which the jury should not pay too much attention to", was nevertheless a good opportunity for the judge to remind the jury that even defence counsel had rejected the possibility of a police conspiracy!

At this stage the judge said, "Members of the jury that is the evidence in this case, that is the whole of this case." But Goldie rising to his feet corrected him. "Your Lordship said 'the whole of the case'. But Your Lordship has omitted Burns statement." A discomfited Finnemore told him he was very much obliged.

Doubtless pleased with himself for finally wrong-footing the judge, Goldie did not think, nor was he sophisticated enough, to realise that by allowing the judge to commit this sin of omission, he would have had excellent grounds for a successful appeal!

Going quickly through Burns statement, the only points Finnemore emphasised were those where it contradicted the police evidence or was self-damning. An example of this was when he quoted Burns as stating, "June and Marie were girls we met in Liverpool," adding, "I do not think we had any explanation as to how they came into his statement." He *had* been given an explanation by both Burns and Devlin but he and Basil Neild had already rubbished the idea of questions being asked by the police during their statements!

Quoting Burns saying he was introduced to Milne by June Bury— "when I was with Ted in the Rainbow Café," he again stressed, "Notice the number of times he mentions the Rainbow Café, because he told you he did not know its name." But once again he did not mention Burns' explanation for this.

Concluding his summing-up Finnemore told the jury they must decide whether they believed the Crown or defence witnesses. Both could not be right. It was not a case of mistaken evidence. One side or the other was deliberately lying. Stating that "the prisoners" had had the good fortune to be represented by two counsel, he added, "It is I am sure, as comforting to you as it is to me, when you know that every point that could possibly be taken and every argument that could possibly put forward on their behalf has been so."

During this speech Balmer had lowered his head thoughtfully scratching his temple. And when the judge reassuringly added, "You need not have any feeling at the back of your minds *that perhaps something has been overlooked. It has not*" (Author's italics) his lowered head made it quite easy to hide a beaming smile!

Apart from the accused men's defence being a *right* rather than "good fortune", yes it had been fully put… insofar as what was known. But of course what was *not* known to the jury were:

- Inspector Reade's suppressed report about nobody climbing through the broken window;

- the interrogation of Thomas Rimmer and his mother's damning letter from the grave; the vital corroborative alibi evidence of un-called Burns' mother and brother-in-law Eddie Billingham;

- the suppressed statements of Sydney Fairbrother, Alan Campbell, Bury and Milne, Fred and Joan Downing;

- Bury's statement accusing David Coyne; McLoughlin's original accusation against Ginger Dutton;

- the showing of Devlin and Burns photographs to McLoughlin before the ID parades and Alan Campbell's original charge sheet.

Before the jury retired the judge "thought it desirable" that they should take with them the men's suits, "on which the places where the blood is are marked. You already have the [crime scene] photographs and the prisoners' statements." Given that there was no direct evidence of Mrs Rimmer's blood being on either man's suit, and that the photographs of Mrs Rimmer's body lying in the blood-splattered hallway proved absolutely nothing against them, it is difficult to avoid the conclusion that these were provided simply to inflame the jury against the accused men.

As the jury were filing out, Goldie requested that they be also given taxi driver, William Butler's journey book, which conclusively proved the men's Manchester journey from Henry Burns' house in the early hours of August 19th.

"Yes of course, Sir Noel," he politely replied.

This apparently innocent omission of Finnemore's was typical of his whole conduct of the trial: giving the appearance of fairness and balance whilst quietly and consistently putting the boot into the defence!

It was 4.15 pm when the jury left the courtroom Most of the crowd in the public gallery, afraid of losing their places stayed where they where, including Henry Burns, Devlin's sister Eileen and his aunt Mrs Swann. The widowed mothers of the two men found the tension too unbearable and waited anxiously in the Witnesses' Room. Down below in the large holding cell, Devlin and Burns anxiously lit up cigarettes and asked for mugs of tea. But these were refused because, the prison officer said, "The jury could be back any minute."

"Fuckin-ell," said Burns, "don't say that!" He knew only too well what a jury's quick return usually meant. "I'll tell you what," said the principal officer ominously, "if none of the jury look at you when they come back, you'll know you've had your chips."

"Oh, thanks very much!" said Devlin.

In the stone-floored crowded passageway outside No.1 Court the group of Balmer, Morris, Lees, Wade and Richardson could be seen smoking and laughing as they shared a joke among themselves. Suddenly the court usher appeared announcing that the jury were coming back. It was exactly 5.30 pm. The police officers and others in the passageway, including reporters, solicitors and barristers, immediately made their way back into court, and as the jury took their seats the hub of lively conversation in the public gallery quickly died down as the judge resumed his seat on the high bench, flanked by the High Sheriff and the Under Sheriff of Lancashire.

Down below in the cells, when the two accused men were told the jury were back, Devlin groaned apprehensively, "Oh No!" But Burns reassuringly lightly remarked, "Don't worry Ted, the Pantomime's over now!"

"Get up those stairs sharpish," ordered the principal officer.

When they entered the dock escorted by three prison officers, both men immediately looked across at the jury, who all wore solemn expressions, each one ominously refusing to look directly at the two prisoners. Replying to Ian Macauley, the clerk of the court, the foreman said they were all agreed on their verdict.

"Do you find Edward Francis Devlin guilty or not guilty?"

"Guilty."

"Do you find Alfred Burns guilty or not guilty?"

"Guilty."

"And that is the verdict of you all?"

"Yes."

The clerk's next words were interrupted by groans in the public gallery and a woman, shouting, "Oh no! Never!" who was quickly escorted outside by a police officer.

"Edward Francis Devlin and Alfred Burns," the clerk continued, "you have severally been convicted of murder on the verdict of the jury. Have you or either of you anything to say why the court should not pass sentence of death upon you according to law?"

Sitting immediately below the two men in the dock, Balmer at last allowed himself a fully unabashed triumphant smile as a stunned Devlin clasped the dock rail. Addressing the judge he said,

My Lord I would like to stress a couple of points, which makes the police not infallible to tell lies. When I was arrested they took me in custody on a pretence of doing a theatre which had been broken into. The men that had broken into that theatre — they [police] told deliberate lies to me because the men who broke into that theatre was innocent. I had done the job at 12 o'clock. They turned round and told me they had seen me there at two in the morning. Everything I have said in this court is true. I have not told one lie.

Devlin's allusion to the infallibility of the police was not about being framed for the Rimmer murder but the fact that Skinner and Lynch had deceived him that he was being arrested for the Playhouse robbery. The innocent man was Victor Le Vesconte, who was indeed innocent and had been in bed drunk at the time of the robbery committed by Devlin, John Ford and Joseph Kirwan. But Le Vesconte was given 12 months, Kirwan two years and Ford not proceeded with.

After the court ushers had ordered silence in the public gallery, Burns then addressed the court in a loud, clear determined voice. His declaration was more forceful more reasoned and more apropos to their dire situation. "I have something to say," he began, "as far as the evidence is concerned I think it has been quite a fair trial. But as far as the judge is concerned, I think he gave a very prejudiced view of the case." Then turning to the sheepish-looking 12-man jury, he said,

I cannot understand how you managed to bring in a verdict of guilty considering the evidence. I think it is a very unfair verdict for you to bring in. We have told the truth and nothing but the truth. We have nothing to fear, and I can go to the Appeal Court and everything will come out in a true light. There is definitely prejudice against us.

At this another female spectator burst into tears. She too was escorted from the court by police officers and the ushers had to shout for silence whilst the sentences were passed.

Neither man had made the faintest insinuation about a possible police conspiracy, of which of course they were completely oblivious.[6]

---

6.   Devlin did suspect a conspiracy but between Milne, Rubin and McNeil. With grim irony the

With the black cap placed on his head and ignoring Burns' accusation of prejudice, the judge solemnly pronounced, "Edward Francis Devlin and Alfred Burns, after a very careful trial you have been found guilty by the jury of murder, and as you know there is only one sentence according to our law for that offence, and that is that each of you will be taken from this place to a lawful prison and thence to a place of execution, and you will there suffer death by hanging, and your bodies buried in the precincts of the prison in which you were last confined before your execution. And may the Lord have mercy on your souls."

The deadly combination of unbelievable wickedness by the police, judicial prejudice, staggering legal bias and incompetence, and the vagaries of British justice had finally ensured the condemnation of the two young men.

---

person he wrote to from the condemned cell, pleading with him to investigate his theory, was none other than Superintendent Balmer. Note: With grim irony the judge who sentenced them to death, died himself aged 85 on the same date they were executed — 25th April 1974.

CHAPTER THIRTY FOUR
HOW "EXPERT" IS THE EXPERT WITNESS EVIDENCE?

Facts are what get in the way of the truth.

Iris Bentley, sister of Derek Bentley, hanged 1953

The evidence of the expert witnesses like forensic scientist James B Firth and pathologist George Manning were automatically taken as gospel by juries and this case was no different. They were always prestigiously described as "Home Office pathologist, scientist", etc., which gave them an unwarranted aura of official scientific impartiality and medical objectivity. But in truth they were private consultants engaged by the police mainly because they could be relied upon to give evidence favourable to the prosecution.

The Director of Durham University's Forensic Research Centre, Dr Zakaria Erzinclioglu, stated in an article in the *Daily Telegraph*, 17th December 2000,

> I know the kind of pressure the police bring to force you into a certain kind of investigation and there can be financial pressure for special witnesses to say certain things because their livelihood depends on it... New and unhealthy pressures have been brought to bear on forensic scientists because of the pressure on police to secure convictions.

Given the uncertain nature and lack of impartiality in Manning's and Firth's evidence it is surprising that neither Rose Heilbron nor Sir Noel Goldie did not think of calling their own experts to counter it. But perhaps this was not possible representing the men under legal aid as they did.

Apart from Norman Birkett's success against Professor Bernard Spilsbury in the 1934 Mancini case (see *Chapter 9*), numerous "expert" witnesses have been proven to be incompetent, self-contradictory or just plain wrong. Firth for example, whom it was pointed out by Goldie, was not medically qualified, was (as we saw in that earlier chapter) severely criticised by defence counsel at the 1947 Rowland trial regarding his conclusions about the same issue of blood spatter, "which were wholly inconsistent with the medical evidence."[1] And, as previously shown, pathologist Dr Manning wavered under cross-examination and amended his evidence about the time of Mrs Rimmer's death. Moreover, in Manning's case, his professional expertise must be questioned if (according to Balmer's memoirs) rather than making his own objective assessment, he could be persuaded by Balmer that two weapons were used.[2] However, Richard Shepherd, a distinguished pathologist has stated that wounds such as those sustained by Mrs Rimmer could have been caused with *one* (double-edged) weapon, e.g. a claw hammer.[3] To support this view it is most unlikely that two assailants would attack her with two different weapons on the same (left hand side) of the head which is where all the wounds were inflicted.

In a Parliamentary debate on the judiciary in January 1957, the Labour MP and solicitor, Leslie Hale (author of *Hanged In Error*, Penguin 1961), had this to say on the subject of expert witnesses:-

> Some experts said that if a lethal dose of arsenic is administered it is effective in 48 hours whilst others have said it takes six or seven days. Yet these experts speak the words of oracles and their views are accepted as dogma... Judges say 'Here is this distinguished Home Office expert... He must be a man of absolutely no prejudice... He was asked to examine this matter on behalf of the Crown and he came to it as an expert free from bias. You should have regard to what he says'. Once Sir Bernard Spilsbury had gone into the witness box as to what the post-mortem disclosed, there was no one who could contradict him.[4]

Mr Hale's views were borne out years later in the cases of solicitor Sally Clark and Angela Cannings—both convicted of murdering their babies on the "expert" evidence of the discredited paediatrician, Professor Sir Roy Meadow, who had simply *invented* the condition Munchausen Syndrome By Proxy (MSBP), which was responsible for their convictions and who were ultimately exonerated by the Court of Appeal. Likewise, the Birmingham

1.   *The Trial of Walter Rowland*, Henry Cecil (David and Charles 1975).
2.   The Balmer Memoirs, *Liverpool Echo*, Dec. 1967.
3.   In correspondence with the author.
4.   *Hansard* (New Evidence), 29th January 1957.

Six, Guildford Four, Maguire family, Judith Ward, Stefan Kiszko and Barry George all had their convictions quashed after being convicted of murder on discredited "expert" forensic evidence.

Barry George was convicted of murdering television presenter Jill Dando on the flimsiest of forensic evidence. At his second, successful, appeal however, forensic scientist, Dr Robin Keeley, admitted that his evidence at the trial and first appeal had been quite wrong. If the death penalty had still been in existence this admission would have been far too late for Barry George. Other erroneous diagnoses and calculations by "experts" include that previously mentioned, by the supposedly infallible Sir Bernard Spilsbury at the Toni Mancini trial. And the following was stated (in the book, *Born To Be Killers,* Time Warner 2005) about one of the child killers of baby James Bulger in 1993: "The opinion of the psychiatrists is that Jon Venables is no longer a threat to the community". Yet, in 2010, Venables had his licence revoked and was recalled to prison for possessing child pornography.

Again, at the successful 1992 appeal of Judith Ward, sentenced to life imprisonment in 1974 for the M62 bombings, all the agencies of the prosecution (three police forces, the Director of Public Prosecution's personnel, psychiatrists and forensic scientists) were castigated for denying her a fair trial by the suppression and falsification of evidence. But it was the government forensic scientists who came in for the most severe criticism. Douglas Higgs and Walter Elliot, were condemned for providing evidence in support of the prosecution and suppressing that favourable to the defence. The appeal judgment said that both men had knowledge of relevant facts which they had suppressed. Lord Justice Glidewell pointed out that not only did they provide jaundiced evidence individually but that they "acted in concert in withholding material evidence."

In further condemnation of these "experts", the court observed that,

The cause of the injustice here stems from the fact that the forensic scientists regarded their task as being to help the police. They became partisan. It is the clear duty of Government scientists to assist in a neutral and impartial way in criminal investigations. We reject Higgs account as being a deliberate falsehood, Elliot was also a party to concealment of the results. Also Berryman's [a third scientist] evidence was untrue.

Again, senior forensic scientist Sir Frank Skuse was severely criticised over his flawed evidence and incompetence in the successful Stefan Kiszko, Birmingham Six and Maguire Seven appeals.

In the context of the non-disclosure of the reports of Inspector Reade and Mr Allen of the Home Offices, that nobody had climbed through the broken window in the Rimmer backyard, Lord Denning (in the case of *Dallison v Cafferey* 1964) said, "If one knows of a credible witness who can speak to material facts which tend to show the prisoner to be innocent, then that witness must either be called or their statement made available to the defence." Their reports were of course, *not* made available to the defence (or probably even the prosecution). But more crucially, one wonders what Lord Denning would have thought about the police intimidation and bribery of Fred and Joan Downing and the suppression of their statements. Perhaps the most convincing criticism of the "expert witness" however, comes from Dr Sandra Lean in her masterful work, *No Smoke!— The Shocking Truth About British Justice* (Checkpoint Press, 2008). It is worth quoting at length. After commenting that some expert forensic witnesses (now employed privately by the Home Office) do not have any qualifications and whose competence, even honesty, cannot be assessed, she goes on to say,

> If their evidence is satisfactory for the purposes of those who pay them, they are likely to be consulted for future cases. If on the other hand, their findings are not satisfactory for the purposes of those who are paying for their services it is highly unlikely that they will be consulted again. How do we (therefore) square the concept of 'independent and impartial' findings with the knowledge that the financial survival of the investigating expert is dependent on those findings meeting a pre-determined outcome?

As to the reputation and standing of expert witnesses, none was more awe-inspiring to juries than the renowned pathologist Sir Bernard Spilsbury (1877-1947). Yet defence counsel J D Cassels KC (later Mr Justice Cassels) once challengingly told a jury, "It will be a sorry day for the administration of justice in this land if we are to be thrust into such a position that because Sir Bernard Spilsbury expressed an opinion, it is impossible to question it."

In the trial of Devlin and Burns, amid all the confusing detail and obfuscation there was no real or tangible evidence—blood or other-wise—against the two men other than suspicion, prejudice and innuendo. Indeed there was contradiction between the two "experts." Despite Dr Manning testifying that there were massive amounts of blood at the crime scene, including spatter on the walls and front door, Firth insisted that the killers would not necessarily have had blood on their clothes. Was this implausible, pro-prosecution statement in order to justify the lack of any traces of Mrs Rimmer's blood group on either man's clothing? Their explanations of how blood traces had got onto their suits through pub fights were corroborated by several witnesses yet the jury preferred to believe the "expert" witness.

It is not good enough to say, as Dr Firth said, that the small stains he could *not* group *could* have been Mrs Rimmer's. That is not evidence. They equally *could* have been anybody's from her blood group or not from her blood group at all. And the judge should never have allowed it to be admitted. But, as we have seen in the William Watkins trial the previous year, Mr Justice Finnemore had a bad habit of admitting inadmissible evidence.

CHAPTER THIRTY FIVE

THE APPEAL AND "JUSTICE-IN-A-JIFFY" GODDARD

Next came Fraud, and he had on, like Lord Eldon, an ermine gown.

Percy Bysshe Shelley, The Mask of Anarchy

On the 31st March Devlin and Burns appeared in the Court of Criminal Appeal at the Royal Courts of Justice in London's Strand. The outcome of their appeals was a foregone conclusion, not only because of the fearsome reputation of the pro-hanging Lord Chief Justice, Lord Goddard (known in legal circles as "The Tiger") towards appellants but also through Balmer having written to the Home Office that *he thought* Burns would kill Crown witnesses if he was freed.[1]

Travelling to London the previous day both men were housed separately overnight in Wandsworth Prison. Although no longer able to do or say anything to help themselves, they were still not allowed to be together.

Goddard's fellow appeal judges, Mr Justice Ormerod and Mr Justice Parker (later to succeed Goddard as Lord Chief Justice) as was usual in his court, neither said nor were allowed to say much. The diabolical Goddard, who on a day five years later would dismiss six appeals in one hour — earning him the added sobriquet "Justice-in-a-Jiffy" — opened the proceedings in his usual intolerant and prejudicial fashion by telling Basil Neild, "We need not trouble you Mr Neild" and then proceeded to fulfil what should have rightfully been the Crown's function of outlining the circumstances of the case. This remark alone was a clear indication that he had made up his mind the appellants would hang.[2]

During his diatribe — a foretaste of his conduct as the trial judge in the Craig and Bentley case a year later — he described both men as, "professional

1. Merseyside Police files.
2. The introduction of the Criminal Justice Act 1948, which abolished the barbaric punishment of the cat o' nine tails and suspended the death penalty, was described by Goddard as a "Gangsters Charter".

criminals and scoundrels, who by their own admission had been committing factory breakings or shopbreakings at the time the prosecution alleged they were murdering this unhappy old lady. They were," he went on, "the type that carried about with them as wicked a weapon as a cosh."

Telling the court that the trial had lasted ten days, out of which eight were given to evidence, he congratulated Mr Justice Finnemore, as he always did his fellow judges, on conducting a fair trial despite being unwell.

The Lord Chief Justice incorrectly stated that the main issue was that the men,

> ... had come over from Manchester to Liverpool on *the evening of the 19th August* to carry out the burglary at this *old woman's* house, which they had plotted, some days or weeks earlier, she being an elderly lady who lived alone and believed by these scoundrels to have money in her possession, and they thought of course that she would be an easy victim (Author's italics).

The Crown's evidence of course was that the accused men came over to Liverpool at 1.30 in the afternoon, not in the evening. And by no stretch of the imagination could Mrs Rimmer at 52-years-of-age be described as an "old woman"—a term obviously used to excite prejudice against the appellants from the outset. Even from these limited opening remarks, the dangers of such a bombastic ill-informed judge usurping the function of prosecuting counsel were readily apparent. Ironically, however, by asserting that the men "by their own admission" were carrying out break-ins "at the time of the murder, he was unwittingly supporting the defence evidence. For if they were committing a factory break-in at the time of the murder (although not shopbreaking as he earlier incorrectly stated) then how could they be committing the murder?! It also appeared that he was ignorant as to whether they had plotted the Rimmer burglary "days *or* weeks before" yet this was a matter of crucial importance during the trial, as was the prosecution's contention that the two men had been in Liverpool since the 17th August. As for the "wicked weapon": they may have carried a cosh on the night of the Sunblinds break-in but there was no evidence that it had ever been used to attack *anybody*. And it had been established at their trial, despite the Crown's and the judge's inferences, that neither of these "two professional criminals" had ever been convicted of violence.

As the hearing progressed Lord Goddard would continue to show himself as both fool and knave. After again praising Finnemore's conduct of the trial, the Lord Chief Justice went into some detail of the evidence — mainly that of the prosecution. Stating that, "McLoughlin could not take part in the robbery because he had been arrested and was in prison at the time", he omitted to reveal that McLoughlin had been convicted of breaking into his own aunt's house in the same road as Mrs Rimmer. Instead, he implied that the 19-year-old criminal — with three times as many convictions as Devlin and Burns put together — was of the decent, old fashioned villain type. He may have been a robber, said Goddard, but when he discovered a murder had been committed on the job he was to be on, then he, "as usually happens in the experience of this court, decided to give evidence for the prosecution." Nobody, he said, knew the exact date of the break-in at the Sunblinds warehouse and that "was a difficulty from the defence point of view." Indeed it was. But this admission completely ignored the fact that the indictment against Campbell — *after* Devlin and Burns had been charged with the murder — had been changed specifically to the 18th, thus depriving them of their alibi.

Coming to the evidence of McLoughlin and Milne, he stated that if the jury believed them, especially Milne, then on their evidence alone there was an overwhelming case against the two men. In an apparent contradiction in terms, and despite no evidence given at the trial that the men had, "*agreed to meet Milne after the murder*", he stated that this was indeed the case, but doubted whether the meeting took place willingly or by *duress* of Milne!

Frequently utilising the word "obviously" he then went on to give Milne's testimony a totally unwarranted credibility. Describing her alleged meeting with Devlin and Burns after the murder he said, "They were in an *obviously* agitated state when one of these men — Burns I think — had *obviously* cut his hand or damaged his hand in some way." Firstly there was nothing "obvious" about their alleged agitated state and it was Devlin not Burns who was supposed to have had a handkerchief on his hand

Meanwhile, he continued (and here he was forced to concede *if* that evidence was true), "the old lady was lying with *no fewer than 20 wounds*, some inflicted with a blunt instrument, some inflicted with a cutting instrument.

She was lying there dead and her body was not found till her son went to her house the next evening" (Author's italics). This was again incorrect, the forensic evidence being of 15 wounds. It is one thing to begrudgingly prefix a damning statement with the caveat, "if that evidence was true", but quite another not to give equal mention to the emphatic denials of Devlin and Burns, which he conspicuously failed to do.

The Lord Chief Justice then went on to state that although June Bury had taken no part in the crime and had not been an accomplice, her evidence nevertheless supported Marie Milne's evidence, "and supported it very, very strongly." Was he unaware of Bury being exposed as a liar at the trial? Or did he purposely overlook it? Not once did the highest judge in the land ever mention that the entire prosecution case was wholly circumstantial, and that there was not an ounce of direct material or forensic evidence against the appellants. As he continued with his own distorted version of events, it seemed as if the presence of counsel and his fellow judges was superfluous. He was holding centre stage. And he made it *obvious* it was his court!

When Rose Heilbron stood to address the court she revealed new evidence which in any other court would have resulted in the convictions being quashed. But after experiencing his opening diatribe full of venom against the prisoners, together with his obduracy and blatant denial of justice in the Cameo appeal two years earlier, she was most apprehensive—justifiably as it transpired.

The new evidence, said Heilbron, was that 15-year-old Elizabeth Rooke, a resident at a Liverpool girls hostel had contacted Devlin's solicitor after the trial and gave a statement that last October, shortly before the committal proceedings, June Bury had told her and two older girls that Devlin and Burns were not the murderers but that it was a boyfriend of hers named "Austy" (later identified as Austin O'Toole) to whom she was pregnant. Somewhat predictably however, Goddard, as he did in the Rowland and other cases, would not entertain this vital new evidence and refused to allow her to read out the girl's statement—although he and his fellow judges nonetheless accepted copies handed to them.

"It is not a matter for this court," he announced. "We are not here to re-try cases. If necessary the matter can be submitted to those whose duty it is to advise the Crown on these matters. It is not something this court can go into." In other words she would have to raise it with the Home Secretary.[3] This decision was based on his oft-quoted ruling that, "We cannot usurp the verdict of a jury". But that is precisely what the court did in the 1931 case of Herbert Wallace for the murder of his wife, when it quashed the jury's guilty verdict on the grounds that it was "perverse" and flew in the face of the evidence. Moreover, considering his assertion that they were not there to re-try cases, Goddard was thus far actually "re-trying" the case... but on behalf of the prosecution!

Could she then, asked an undaunted Heilbron, call the witness to give oral evidence? But ignoring her request, and minimising the importance of Rooke's evidence, he confusingly observed, "The case had depended much more on the evidence *of another witness, June Bury,* than the evidence of another young woman (Author's italics). This remark demonstrated the Lord Chief Justice's woeful grasp of the case, by being either unable or unwilling to differentiate between Marie Milne and the evidence of "another young woman" (Bury)!

Refusing to be diverted or confused however, even if Goddard was, Heilbron said Elizabeth Rooke's statement could not be put to Bury at trial because it wasn't then known to the defence. Had it been, she said with massive understatement, it may have had an effect on the course of the trial. Conscious of his dismissal of the Rowland appeal, she added it was not a case of somebody else saying, "I did that murder" (as David Ware did in that case). Rather was it a major prosecution witness saying somebody else did the murder. But ignoring this important distinction, Goddard simply repeated that it was not for the court to allow *any* application for fresh evidence to be called.[4] Visibly annoyed, Heilbron struggled to maintain her composure as she resignedly told him she had made her application and would not waste any more of the court's time but would now deal with the judge's misdirection of the jury.

Having disarmed Heilbron of her main weapon, Goddard wanted to know if the remainder of her case was because the judge in his summing-up

---

3.   There was no statute preventing the Court of Criminal Appeal hearing new evidence. It was merely a convention adopted over the years by that court.

4.   The Court of Criminal Appeal, with Goddard presiding, did in fact allow fresh evidence from two minor witnesses in the Rowland case, whilst refusing to allow the signed statement of or hear in person the man who had confessed to the murder.

did not put every point to the jury. If she had said yes, she knew what his stock answer would be—that judges could not be expected to deal with *every* defence point. But avoiding this trap she said her complaint was that in general Finnemore did not put the defence case "fairly and squarely" to the jury in a number of vital matters. Now appearing to agree with her, he said the defence was that the accused were in Manchester *at the time the murder* was *committed* (Author's italics). But not accepting this, Heilbron said, "The defence was that they were in Manchester *on the 19*th" (Author's italics). She was making this distinction, she said because, although Campbell was charged with committing the Sunblind's robbery on the 18th, he had insisted it was on a Sunday and the accused men had also claimed throughout it was on Sunday.

Heilbron went on to complain that the judge had compounded the Crown's last minute change of tack in his summing-up by telling the jury, *"Could these men have been concerned in the murder and have gone back to Manchester and taken part in the warehouse breaking?"* (Author's italics).

"It was," she said, "a most important deviation from the Crown's original case that the robbery was carried out on the 18th. The accused men and Campbell had had no opportunity to refute or even respond to this last minute allegation. Moreover, Finnemore—despite suggesting this alternative scenario to the jury whilst still reminding them that Campbell had pleaded guilty to doing it on the 18th—did *not* tell the jury that the Sunblinds break-in *might* have been done on the19th, as the defence had maintained. Furthermore, it seemed that at the eleventh hour the Crown had accepted the men *were* in Manchester, even though they could have already committed the Liverpool murder. "Apart from confusing the jury it must have had a great influence on them," she said. In other words, the prosecution had wanted to have their cake and eat it.

Up until the Crown changing direction at the last minute by saying the men could have done both the murder and the robbery, it had been a relatively simple matter for the jury to decide, said Heilbron. "The jury would think, 'That is their alibi but the Crown say it's untrue. It's simple. There's no complication'. But with the Crown later suggesting that both the murder and the resumed robbery were perhaps on the 19th, it cut the ground from under the appellants' feet and prevented them from dealing with that aspect."

If they had been given that opportunity, she said, they would have been able to say how they got from Liverpool to Manchester and to the warehouse at that time of night when they had no private transport and the trains having stopped at 11 pm. But all they and Campbell were cross-examined about was that the warehouse breaking took place on the 18th."

Before Heilbron could move on to Mr Justice Finnemore's summing-up of Marie Milne's evidence, Goddard insisted on dealing with her previous observations. His court may not have been the place to hear *new* evidence but he did not mind dealing at length with the *old* evidence if there was a chance of excusing a fellow judge's behaviour. By stating the men might have done the murder then got back to Sunblind's to complete the robbery, he said, the trial judge was actually putting to the jury the *whole of the alibi…* and asking them to decide if it was true or not! Protesting against this absurd explanation, Heilbron repeated that the Crown's last minute change of direction and the judge's summing-up, was suggesting a new theory whilst the Crown had maintained up till then that the alibi was false.

Heilbron again clashed with the Lord Chief Justice, when he misinterpreted another aspect of the summing-up by stating that he (Finnemore) had been inviting the jury to decide simply whether Devlin and Burns met up with Campbell on the Saturday night or the Sunday night. No, she insisted, the judge was telling the jury that the alibi may be right but they could still have committed the murder. "I doubt," she said, "whether the jury would have appreciated the refinements of that argument. It was putting into their minds something entirely different from the Crown's case throughout the trial." But this important aspect, according to Goddard, was merely a small passage in the summing-up which as a whole ran to a hundred pages of print. Heilbron may have justifiably replied, "So what? It's quality that matters not quantity!" But instead, she reiterated the basic unfairness of two different theories being put to the jury, the second of which the accused men had no opportunity to respond to.

In a rare intervention, Mr Justice Parker absurdly stated that the trial judge was actually helping the defence by, "disposing of the evidence of the Crown." But that could be interpreted in two ways, said Heilbron: one that the judge was disposing of the Crown's suggestion and the other that juries were not used to listening to summings-up and had therefore forgotten the

Crown's original case! "My view," interjected Goddard before Heilbron had fully stated her grounds, "is that there was clearly no misdirection." But apart from this opinion being premature, he hadn't even asked Ormerod and Parker what their views were.

Among Heilbron's further complaints of misdirection, incompetence or unfairness by Finnemore, were that he did not deal sufficiently with the improbability of two admitted thieves breaking into a house, remaining there for an-hour-and-half and not stealing anything nor causing any disturbance or damage. "There was no evidence that so much as a drawer was opened," she said. "It looked as though whoever was responsible had just got into the house when confronted by Mrs Rimmer as soon as she opened the front door. It was a very vital point in the defence case but there is not one word in the summing-up referring to that." She may have added that, although nobody had ever alleged the men wore gloves or any other hand covering, none of their fingerprints were found at the scene. But obdurately dismissive or failing to see the logic of her point, Lord Goddard insisted that it could hardly be said that the judge did not give an adequate summing-up. "I have said over and over again that a judge is not bound to put every point of the defence and prosecution to the jury." He then illogically declared, "The defence here is an alibi. It does not matter whether anything was stolen or whether anybody panicked or not!"

Still refusing to be intimidated however, as defence counsel usually were by Goddard, Heilbron pointed out that nothing was mentioned by the judge about the credibility of Marie Milne's evidence of waiting one-and-a-half hours on two occasions on the same day and night. Or that she had given three different versions of where she was threatened with the knife by Devlin. But blithely ignoring these specific shortcomings, Goddard again told her she could not say the judge did not put the defence case. Agreeing he had done so "broadly speaking", her complaint was that he did not point out to the jury the more significant points, such as the evidence of Alice Shenton: that she was a witness to be relied upon and whose evidence was significant as far as the men's alibi was concerned.

Referring to the important evidence of warehouse owner Kessler, who was not sure which night the break-in occurred, and the significance of that in relation to the alibi, Heilbron said the judge did not mention this to the jury, yet it was a very crucial matter of corroboration. "He was," she continued, "an independent witness whose evidence linked up with the evidence of Burns that the clothing was thrown over the fence after the break-in. Kessler had said it was unlikely it would have remained in such a public place all day and night Sunday until the Monday morning. Yet none of this was mentioned in the judge's summing-up."

When Goddard commented that there was no doubt the break-in had occurred but that the prosecution maintained that when Devlin and Burns were supposed to be breaking in they were in fact murdering Mrs Rimmer, Heilbron told him, "None of us at the trial got that impression. The impression we got was that the prosecution were saying the break-in occurred on the 18th."

Corrected once again but determined to have the last word, the Lord Chief Justice rejoined that it *may have been* the 18th or the 19th. "All these were questions were for the jury. The question of whether or not the alibi was to be believed was essentially a matter for them." This observation—which in a *fair trial* would of course be true—completely missed the point. Would this already biased jury—unaware of vital evidence such as the Downing's being threatened and their statements suppressed or the forensic report about the broken window contradicting Thomas Rimmer's evidence—have rejected the alibi had they known the truth?

Even though she was unaware of the suppressed evidence herself, Heilbron told the court that in a trial lasting so long, the jury required careful guidance on the arguments for and against. But Mr Justice Finnemore, although dealing adequately with the prosecution case, failed to deal likewise with the defence case. "In my submission," she said, "the judge dealt with the prosecution case in a different manner from that of the defence. He was very careful to point out where defence witnesses had tripped up. He was not so careful in pointing out the contradictions in the prosecution evidence." In a number of instances, she said, he put the evidence incorrectly of one or two Crown witnesses who clearly gave mistaken or untruthful evidence in regard to several matters. For example June Bury had said she was in the Continental Café with Devlin and Burns when they met McLoughlin, yet she admitted during cross-examination that she could not have been there as there was no available date for her to be so. Her evidence amounted to nothing, said

Heilbron, yet the judge allowed it to be used as corroboration. She might also have reminded Goddard that McLoughlin had changed his evidence on several points between the committal and trial and even during the trial.

When Heilbron accused the judge of mis-stating certain facts, Goddard, rather than accept this genuine point, blandly replied that if defence counsel had considered them important enough, he thought they, "…should have pulled him up at once and corrected him." There was of course an element of truth in this. Goldie, and Heilbron to a lesser extent, had been altogether too deferential to Mr Justice Finnmeore to the detriment of their clients

Excusing June Bury's contradictory evidence and Milne's changed versions of the knife threats, Goddard said that the men were arrested in October, "… And then *some months later, in January or February*, these young girls were called upon to give evidence, it was not surprising they found themselves in some difficulty in remembering dates and the number of cafés they visited" (Author's italics). This comment not only ignored the fact that their statements were given in October and their committal evidence in November, but also showed that the Lord Chief Justice of England, presiding over an appeal in a murder case, did not even know which month the trial took place (Fool). But he knowingly and deliberately excused the lies of Bury and Milne, knowing their depositions (if not their actual statements) had been taken at the committal court, not "some months later" but less than a month after the men's arrests (Knave).

Despite defence counsel's objections being precisely about the judge's summing up, he then extraordinarily commented that, "It was not for the judge to tell the jury whether they could believe her (Bury) or not. Any question of discrepancies should have been dealt with by counsel in their speeches!" In fairness however, he like everyone else in the case, was not aware both girls had been repeatedly coached by Balmer.

Continuing, Heilbron further complained that the judge did not remind the jury of Bury's admission in evidence that she was capable of inventing the story. Nor did he point out the conflict of the Crown evidence of Bury testifying that Milne asked her to back her story up and Milne denying it. Goddard's arrogantly flippant response to this was, "What is a judge supposed to say? Is he expected to make a speech for the defence?"

When Sir Noel Goldie rose to plead on behalf of Burns, he was predictably at sixes and sevens. After naïvely and unnecessarily fully quoting Burns' pre-sentence statement from the dock about the judge's prejudice, which was bound to inflame Goddard and his fellow judges, he then said *he* was not accusing the judge or the jury of prejudice. "But the circumstances of the crime must have created prejudice throughout the City of Liverpool. The murder," he went on, "was committed within a few hundred yards of another sensational murder which the Lord Chief Justice would remember.[5] At this point, an exasperated Lord Goddard interrupted him. "What is the point of all of this? I don't know whether there was prejudice or not. The jury were not challenged. If you felt there was strong feeling in Liverpool you could have applied to have the case held elsewhere." Ignoring this criticism of his own irresponsibility, Goldie made the purely academic point that where there was prejudice throughout a city it was essential that very full direction should be given to the jury on the question of reasonable doubt. Despite his earlier rejection of a police conspiracy however, it now seemed he was at least willing to accuse a Liverpool *jury* of prejudice!

Goldie submitted that the evidence, taken as a whole, should have created a strong reasonable doubt and Mr Justice Finnemore did not give the jury adequate direction on that. Exemplifying his point he then quoted the judge when telling the jury, "That is all the defence has to do." This in so many words, he maintained, was telling the jury that at a certain stage the onus passed to the defence, which must have created doubts in the minds of the jury. Enlightened by Ormerod and Parker that the judge had merely been telling the jury that if they believed the defence they should acquit, Goldie insisted, "Those words were a serious misdirection," i.e. the defence does not *have to* do anything. The onus of proof is always on the prosecution. It may have been a technical point but it was nevertheless a valid one.

Mr Justice Parker said the judge had put the matter of reasonable doubt at great length. Yes, agreed Goldie, but only in one passage at the very beginning of a long summing-up. Interjecting almost out of habit, Goddard said, "Does it matter whether it comes at the beginning or the end?" But Goldie said his point was that, although the judge dealt with the question at the beginning, by the final stages of his summing-up he had vitiated it.

---

5.   This was a reference to the 1949 Cameo Cinema murders in nearby Webster Road for which George Kelly was hanged in 1950. Goddard had also dismissed Kelly's appeal.

Goldie then went on to deal with the issue of the cosh, stating that most of the men's alibi had been proved, albeit unwittingly by Crown counsel Basil Neild himself. For despite Devlin having been lured into his garish display in the witness box, imputing a violent nature, the Crown had accepted that the cosh had indeed been found where the men said they had left it at Sunblind's Ltd. Moreover it had been forensically examined and there were no traces of blood or any other marks on it. The judge, he said, did not fully bring out the significance of those facts to the jury.

But by-passing the logic of Goldie's argument, as far as Lord Goddard was concerned, the only importance attached to the cosh was that, "It showed that they *were prepared* to use violence if necessary" (Author's italics). Coming from the Lord Chief Justice, a man of years of experience in the law, this observation was unforgivable. He was fully aware that what they were "prepared to do" was not evidence against them.

Focusing again quite unnecessarily on the cosh, and reminding the court that Mr Justice Finnemore was "horrified" at the sight of it, Goldie then gratuitously described it in detail. Wittingly or not, nothing could have been more designed—as it had with the jury—to inflame the Court of Criminal Appeal. He said however that he was dealing with the cosh because Basil Neild had said at the trial that the sort of people who carry such implements were the sort who use violence. But he (Neild) should have conceded that the discovery of the cosh at Sunblind's was direct tangible evidence that they were indeed there. This may have been true, but the point of the men's appeals—which Goldie seemed to have forgotten—was the trial judge's alleged misdirection of the jury, not that Crown counsel should act for the defence!

When the matter of *when* the Sunblind's break-in took place was raised by Goddard, Mr Justice Ormerod said the trial judge had dealt with it at some length. It was of course true that Finnemore had asked the jury to speculate about the actual time it occurred *insofar as what was known*. But had Frederick Downing's statement (taken by Detective Constable Hancock of Manchester Police) not been suppressed by the Liverpool CID, this vital matter would have been resolved there and then, for Downing had clearly stated Devlin and Burns, accompanied by his wife, arrived at his home with some of the stolen property at about 11.30 pm on August the 19th. And they could not have travelled from Liverpool to Manchester in half an hour. Indeed Goldie stressed the "extraordinary probability" of the men's alibi being true. According to the Crown's evidence, he said, the men were last seen in Liverpool at 11 pm, at least a mile from the nearest railway station. And, "It was extraordinary that they should come to Liverpool from Manchester, break into a house, stay there for one and a half hours and steal nothing."

Declaring that he and his brother judges were not a jury, Goddard, refusing to accept Goldie's sensible point, then amazingly said, "*We* are not concerned whether these men broke into the [Rimmer] house or not!" It was enough, he said, that the trial judge had taken three pages to tell the jury about the question of doubt.

In conclusion, Goldie asked the court to reverse the jury's verdict, adding that the case was full of the most incredible discrepancies and contradictions. And that the judge, although giving a full summing-up, did not sufficiently emphasise these.

Before delivering the court's ruling, Goddard embarked on a lengthy, but irrational speech in which he was at pains to minimise the importance of the disallowed new evidence from Elizabeth Rooke and two others. "We were asked at the outset," he said, "to allow a further witness to be called — a child of 15 — to say that before the arrests, or before the police court [committal] proceedings, the witness June Bury said something about somebody else being responsible for the murder. We are asked to hear this child come and say something about what June Bury was supposed to have said.[6] That is not a matter which this court can go into." As part of his trivialisation of this important evidence, Goddard did not mention that — as contained in Rooke's statement — two other women had also heard Bury's confession.

During his resumé of mainly the Crown's case, he said the jury had accepted June Bury's evidence as true. "She was evidently an unsatisfactory type of young woman. I do not know if she was a prostitute but she had been spending her nights with these men in low class cafés in the Pier Head district of Liverpool." He then extraordinarily declared, "Although she took no part in this breaking and entering, her evidence supported Marie Milne's evidence." This was of course incorrect: *nobody* had supported the

---

6. This was a gross simplification of the facts. Two older female residents at the hostel had corroborated the "child's" statement about Bury naming Austin O'Toole as the killer.

most damning parts of Milne's evidence when she was allegedly alone with Devlin and Burns.

When Goddard commented that the taxi driver, Emery, had corroborated Milne's evidence about the taxi fare of two-shillings-and-sixpence, Balmer, its author, allowed himself an almost imperceptible self-satisfied grin.

"There was other evidence," said Goddard, which he wasn't going to go into, "But if the evidence of McLoughlin and Milne were accepted by the jury—which it was, then there was overwhelming evidence of the men's guilt."

Despite the specific complaints of defence counsel, he went on to say that the judge had gone through the evidence *item by item*. "The jury did not believe the alibi, for after a trial of ten days, they took just over an hour to return their guilty verdicts."

Continuing, he said,

> Various attacks have been made upon the learned judge's summing-up: that he did not stress this or that point, that he did not mention this matter or that matter. This court has said so many times that it is no part of a judge's duty to go through the evidence microscopically. Why should he? It is not as if he has not put the case accurately for the defence. The judge put the case in great detail, as he thought right, and the jury did not have any doubt.

Concluding this patently biased and contradictory speech and rejecting the defence claims of misdirection, he went on, "On the judge's *proper* direction and review of the evidence, the jury were *justified* in coming to the verdict they did" (Author's italics).

Given the total absence of any material or forensic evidence against the two men, and the proven lies of Crown witnesses, this assessment was bad enough, but incredibly he then added,

> Whether or not someone has committed perjury or whether some other person is guilty of the murder, is not for this court to go into without a jury. It is a perfectly impossible situation and it is not for this court to do so. I can only say the evidence against these two men was overwhelming. And that is why the jury rejected their alibi defence.

Listening to this distorted interpretation of justice, everyone in court that day must have wondered what on earth *was* the purpose of the Court of Criminal Appeal?

Repeating that the court would not hear the new evidence, Goddard said, "It might be a matter for the Home Secretary in certain events." Then without any prior consultation with his two fellow judges, he pronounced "This appeal is dismissed. Take them down."

As they were led away to resume their agony 200 miles away in the condemned cells at Walton Prison, a cynical Burns turned to Devlin and said resignedly, "What did I tell you Ted. All fuckin' cut and dried before it even started!"

Despite Lord Goddard hiding behind the supreme sanctity of a jury's verdict there was in fact no legal impediment to the Court of Criminal Appeal reversing it—as it had in the Wallace case. There was no statute or legal ruling preventing the court from hearing new evidence which had emerged since the original trial. Indeed, in the Walter Rowland appeal five years earlier, the then Attorney General, Sir Hartley Shawcross MP, KC, had specifically complained about this mere *convention* adopted by Lord Goddard not to hear new evidence. In a letter of 21st February 1947 to the then Home Secretary, James Chuter Ede, he wrote:

I regard the judgement of the Court of Criminal Appeal as unsatisfactory both as to the practical grounds given for refusing to hear the fresh evidence (which grounds would have presented themselves equally to the trial, which would… have undoubtedly had to receive had it been available at the time).

As to the reliance placed on previous decisions [of the Appeal Court] suggesting that fresh evidence will only be admitted in exceptional cases, I think that it is unfortunate that the Court of Criminal Appeal did not appreciate that the appearance of justice would be better served by hearing this evidence in public rather than not hearing it at all.

The Attorney General's letter continued that although he himself could find no *point of law* whereby he could issue his fiat for Rowland's case to go to the House of Lords, he nonetheless said, regarding his rejected appeal,

I think that the true view of the judgement in its legal aspect is that the [Appeal] Court was not saying that its own previous decisions had fettered its discretion so that it could only receive fresh evidence in exceptional cases, but that the cases in which it was necessary or expedient in the interests of justice that fresh evidence should be called before it, were in fact exceptional cases. I am bound to say this is a benevolent construction to put upon their language, and it is unfortunate that some of its previous decisions do tend to put a gloss on the statute, since it is the clear statutory duty of the Court to hear fresh evidence in any case … whether exceptional or not, when it is in the interest of justice to do so. There is undoubtedly public anxiety about it. I ought to add that the case itself has given me some anxiety.

As Rose Heilbron had earlier stated, the only difference between her fresh evidence and that referred to by the Attorney General, was that in the Rowland case, another man had confessed to the murder and in the present case a chief Crown witness (June Bury) had told three people that someone other than Devlin and Burns was the killer. Needless to say, nothing was done by the legal and political establishment. The Court of Criminal Appeal continued to refuse to hear new evidence or order re-trials until the passing of the Criminal Justice Act 1968.

Leaving the Law Courts, Heilbron immediately visited the Attorney General, Sir Lionel Heald, requesting him to ask the Home Secretary to set up a public inquiry into the new evidence. This resulted — as in the case of Rowland — in the setting up of an inquiry which would be held in private by Mr Albert Gerrard QC at Liverpool's Municipal Annexe building.

On the 5th April, Burns wrote to his mother apologising for his pessimistic attitude during her visit. Then in remarkably restrained language, he said, "But after listening to the way Goddard conducted (sic), that trial and his whole outlook concerning it, I did not feel very happy. I am ok now though." Regarding a petition he had written to the Home Secretary, he then perceptively questioned his solicitor Norton's thinking, who had told him to delay his petition until the outcome of the Gerrard Inquiry was known. "He must think we are going to be in the same predicament after the inquiry as we are now," he said, "and it will be too late then. Anyway I hope it [the inquiry] is conducted with an eye for the truth and not just to keep the public quiet."

Referring to the night watchman who saw them at Sunblind's, he said, "He can't be much of a man if he hangs back when he has the opportunity of helping two innocent men out of a filthy frame-up like the one we've been convicted on."

On the very same day as Burns' letter, Balmer recorded in an internal police report for the Home Office that the night watchman in question, 73 year-old Daniel Norton, had been approached by Devlin's solicitor Harry Livermore on the 24th January, when he gave a statement verifying that he had seen a man outside Sunblind's in the early hours of the 20th of August with a woman who was pushing a pram.[7] He had said "Alright" to the man and the man muttered something back. Norton was informed a few days later by a local bobby on the beat, that Sunblind's had been robbed that weekend. The watchman however not only refused to sign the statement, said the report, but went to Manchester CID and told them about Livermore's visit. Informed of this, Liverpool detectives Richardson and Wade visited him the same day and took a second statement. In this, Norton contradicted his earlier statement, saying that the man who he spoke to was carrying a bundle of something on his shoulders and the woman did not have a pram. He said he did not know when the incident had occurred but it must have been much later than August. Although pleased with the watchman's partial recantation of his earlier statement, Richardson and Wade were not so pleased when he also refused to sign their statement.

Since these incidents occurred before the trial on the 12th February, and accepting the watchman's refusal to sign the statement, the defence, although unaware of his second statement to the police, could nonetheless have subpoenaed him to give evidence, which they failed to do — particularly in view of Mr Justice Finnemore's suggestion to the jury that Devlin's account may be untrue.[8]

---

7.   Balmer's report. 5th April 1952, Merseyside Police files.
8.   After suggesting various explanations for Norton's statements, it was accepted by the Gerrard Inquiry that the meeting at 4 am on the 20th August between Devlin and the watchman had indeed taken place.

CHAPTER THIRTY SIX
A ONE-MAN PRIVATE INQUIRY IS ORDERED

The Gerrard Inquiry

Where judicial reluctance to overturn a verdict or admit to a miscarriage of justice is most marked, is in the findings of those Inquiries set up by the Home Office and conducted by a judge or a senior QC.

Sir Ludovic Kennedy

The Gerrard Inquiry, held in the city's Dale Street Building, lasted from the 4th to the 9th April and was resumed on the 18th when the missing Kenneth McNeil was located. It was reported in the *Liverpool Echo* that he was a seaman who had been away on a trawler, which was untrue.

Attendance at the inquiry was not compulsory and witnesses were not required to give evidence on oath. The defence lawyers were not allowed to examine or cross-examine witnesses who included Bury, McLoughlin, Rubin, McNeil, Norton, the night watchman, Austin O'Toole, and Detective Inspector's Farragher and Lees. Their boss, Balmer, who had shrewdly avoided giving evidence at the trial, attended every day but not to help the inquiry — although in the event he was unexpectedly called to give evidence. His main reason for attending however was to keep a watching brief on June Bury in case she changed her story. Fortunately for him she didn't!

Shortly before the opening of the inquiry, Bury had been in contact with Devlin's married sister Eileen Ackroyd and his aunt Mrs Swann, and had told them that Kenneth McNeil had come to Manchester the day after the murder and asked her to get his bloodstained clothes cleaned. She also told them that Balmer had not only threatened her into giving false evidence but had also bought her nylons and paid for her hair to be permed before the trial. This information was conveyed to Devlin on a prison visit by the two women, and was duly recorded by the supervising prison officer, who forwarded a report to the governor who, according to his usual practice, in turn copied it to the Home Office and Liverpool Police.[1]

On seeing this, Balmer acting quickly, visited Bury at her mother's Manchester home and threatened that unless she made a statement denying this she could get ten years for perjury. He also told her that when she was called to the inquiry she would be told that it had been agreed with the Director of Public Prosecutions that she, like all the other witnesses, could now tell the truth without any fear of being charged with perjury.[2] But he warned that this exemption only applied to the murder case: if she did tell the truth it would not stop him from also charging her with the Berry Street tobacconists and Liverpool Road Goods Depot robberies, the theft of Devlin and Burns raincoats and absconding from bail. The result was a statement denying she had said anything to Devlin's sister and Aunt about threats and nylons and perms from Balmer or about McNeil and a bloodstained coat.[3] She also agreed to deny at the inquiry ever having told Elizabeth Rooke and the other two women that Austy O'Toole was the murderer and that she had been expecting his child.

Following a request from both defence counsel that any police assistance to the inquiry should not be from the Liverpool City Police, Detective Superintendent Harold Hawkyard of Scotland Yard was appointed to assist Gerrard. As a detective constable in the Metropolitan Police in 1928, Hawkyard was accused by defence counsel in the PC Gutteridge murder case of colluding with other detectives in the falsification of evidence concerning Browne and Kennedy's statements.[4]

Although the inquiry's terms of reference were to see if there was any truth in Bury's statement to Elizabeth Rooke and two other women that a soldier named Austin O'Toole was responsible for the murder and that she was expecting his child, Gerrard widened it to investigate allegations that Devlin had confessed to the prison's deputy governor to giving false evidence at the trial and had told a fellow prisoner that the alibi was false.

---

1. Devlin castigated his relatives for not getting Bury to put it in writing, which she had refused to do.
2. This controversial decision by the DPP, Sir Theobald Mathew, was subsequently the subject of much heated legal debate in the House of Lords.
3. Balmer's internal report. Merseyside Police files.
4. Frederick Guy Browne and William Kennedy were both executed for the murder of PC Gutteridge.

The fellow prisoner, Peter Cockcroft, who like the lying Robert Graham in the Cameo case was from Preston, had already left prison. Charged with breaking and entering a jewellers and remanded to Lancaster Prison he was transferred to Liverpool's Walton Gaol and deposited "for medical reasons" in the prison hospital — the precise location of Devlin! Despite such a serious charge necessitating trial at a higher court because magistrates could not impose a sufficiently heavy sentence, he was on the 29ᵗʰ February released on two years probation!

Cockcroft told the inquiry that Devlin had told him on exercise that he had not committed the Sunblind's robbery but had got all the details from the man who had. In the event he was believed by Gerrard, who said he was convinced it was a truthful account—although he said Devlin had probably been simply boasting! Despite this ambiguity—which became a hallmark of the inquiry—Gerrard had accepted that, although Alan Campbell had been in Walton in the main prison since December 17ᵗʰ, there had been no opportunity for Devlin in the hospital wing to have met or talked to him.

During his subsequent interview with Devlin in the condemned cell, Gerrard initially would not give Cockcroft's name. Indeed, he was referred to throughout the inquiry as "Mr X". Devlin was therefore at a distinct disadvantage and repeatedly said the incident did not happen. "I cannot really comment on these allegations if I don't know who has made them," he said. All I can say is that I have never had such a conversation, and that the only person I have talked to on exercise is a prisoner named McCready." When Gerrard then decided to tell him Cockcroft's name, he protested that he did not know anyone of that name.

It is incredible that Gerrard should believe for one moment that a condemned man, who had pleaded his innocence throughout committal, trial and appeal, would suddenly confess to a complete stranger — even if only "boasting". But this naïveté or disingenuousness was a recurrent feature of Mr Gerrard's conduct of the inquiry. For instance, he accepted that Bury had indeed told Elizabeth Rooke and the other two young women, Joan Porter and Dorothy Doyle, about O'Toole being the murderer and the father of her unborn child but he concluded that she had then been lying. When however she told the inquiry that O'Toole had not committed the murder and was not the father of her child, and that her trial evidence against Devlin and Burns was true, he said she was being truthful because, he commented in his report, "Her demeanour changed during that part of her evidence." In other words, Bury was lying but also telling the truth!

The reason for Bury's reluctance as a witness during the trial was partly revealed when her mother Kathleen Bury gave evidence to the inquiry, stating that she had often asked her daughter why she didn't tell the truth and she had said she was frightened. She also said June had told her she had just agreed with everything Marie Milne said, that her own statement was wrong and that she didn't believe "Teddy" had committed the murder. Amazingly, the defence lawyers did not ask her to elaborate on this or ask *who* her daughter was frightened of. Neither did Gerrard, who quickly moved on to another aspect.

This lack of follow-up occurred frequently during the inquiry, as did Gerrard's regular interventions whenever an important answer was about to be given. The lawyers, Norton and Livermore, were handicapped from the outset by the restrictions imposed, which made them hesitant to ask simple, much less searching questions. But as the inquiry progressed, counsel — mainly Heilbron, Goldie and Frank Nance — who were not present every day — began to put more and more questions directly to the witnesses despite the restrictions.

When Bury told the tribunal she had ceased to be fond of Devlin because she'd had a new boyfriend since Christmas, she refused to name him, saying that he had nothing to do with the murder case and had not appeared as a witness. In that case, asked Heilbron, why did she visit Devlin in prison in January, taking him cigarettes, and complain to a prison officer because she wasn't allowed to kiss him? It was because his brother Peter had asked her to, she replied. But this was another of her lies: the police had warned all the Devlin and Burns families not to approach her. It was she who had called on Devlin's sister at her Barracks Flats home, to tell her about McNeil, his bloodstained coat and Balmer's gifts.

When Stanley Rubin was called, he was brought from Birmingham's Winson Green Prison, where he was serving 18 months. The day after the murder trial had ended he had viciously attacked an elderly man, Robert Fisher, in the Dive public house for calling him a "copper's nark."

Rubin said he did not know McLoughlin but knew McNeil from the

Continental as someone who often worked there in the kitchen. He had never visited McLoughlin in prison. These replies related to a submitted theory of Devlin's that Rubin, McNeil and Marie Milne had somehow contrived with McLoughlin to commit the Rimmer robbery.

During the inquiry more lies by McLoughlin and Balmer were exposed. Mr Nance, Goldie's junior, pointed out that McLoughlin could not have seen Marie Milne in the Continental on the 2nd August, as he had said, because it was common ground that she did not come into the picture until the 4th in the Rainbow Café. Rather than concede this however, Gerrard obfuscated and somehow managed to have Nance believe it was Bury who McLoughlin was referring to. This was despite McLoughlin describing Milne and then identifying her from a photograph shown to him by Gerrard himself!

Balmer was called to explain an incident just before the appeal when Joseph Norton telephoned him to ask if June Bury– as she had told Elizabeth Rooke and the two girls—had been pregnant the previous October/November. Norton had told the inquiry that Balmer had told him she was and that he could guess who the father was. Balmer however, not hesitating to besmirch the defence lawyer's integrity, denied this.

During his questioning Balmer made a fatal slip when he said that on October 4th when she was located in Manchester, Bury had told him, "I'm no squealer. Go and see Marie Milne, she was on the job with them." How, asked Rose Heilbron, could Bury have told him this, since the murder was committed on the 19th August and the Crown's case was that she never returned to Liverpool after the 8th August? Suddenly faced with this incontrovertible fact and despite stating several times that he was sure of this, he suddenly backtracked, saying that he thought Bury had used "words to that effect." But before she could follow up the chairman once again moved on to another matter.

A similar situation occurred with McNeil, who was asked before answering questions if he was sure. Yes he was sure Bury was pregnant at the Assizes, then moments later did a complete about turn when questioned by Heilbron. But Gerrard either let this and other contradictions pass without comment or made various excuses for the witnesses' uncertainty.

It emerged during his questioning that McNeil had given a signed statement to Balmer on November 1st when he was brought back to Liverpool from Newcastle-under-Lyme. Yet nobody had ever seen it and it was never included in the list of Crown witnesses' statements. He continued lying when he said he had never left Liverpool from November 1st until the February trial. But the defence were unaware of the "be warned" message from Balmer just before the trial, ordering him back to Liverpool from his Birmingham job at the Grand Hotel!

Every time Balmer was caught out, he amended his answers with the phrases, "I got the impression", "to the best of my recollection" or excused his vague replies by pleading he didn't have his notebook with him. Asked whether Bury and Milne could have colluded with each other over their statements, Balmer lied that they were not only not in the same room at the time but were not even in the same city. After Milne's statement of the 7th, he said, Bury was seen the next day in Manchester and said, "I see you got Marie alright." She then made her statement. Not only did this contradict Milne's trial admission that she and Bury had indeed been together in the same Allerton Police Station room, it also exposed Balmer's predilection for creative dialogue. For when asked how Bury knew he had picked up Milne, he was left speechless for several moments before weakly mumbling, "I don't know." Like Inspector Lees, he also failed to mention Milne's statement of 9th October.

Later, asked by Superintendent Hawkyard if there had been any press reporting of Bury being interviewed on October 4th, the bad liar Balmer's memory again let him down. First replying, "No", he then said, "I'm not sure about that." Then without any compunction he added, "But it was known in the nigger clubs — Wilkie's and Johnny's. And all the girls knew. All the prostitutes off the town knew."[5] This grossly offensive comment went un-remarked upon by the chairman.

Asked by Gerrard if he knew the source of the press reports, which appeared after the appeal, about the successful investigation (in which he was praised), this elected member of the Press Club who frequently planted stories, replied with a straight face, "No, I haven't the faintest idea."

Cockcroft told the inquiry that Devlin was all smiles when telling him on exercise how he had got the story about the Sunblind's robbery from the man who done it. Answering both Gerrard and Sir Noel Goldie, he first

---

5.   Gerrard Inquiry Report, p.163.

said Burns was never mentioned but immediately then said he and Devlin had discussed Burns quite a lot. Considering the confused account he gave, if he was a plant by Balmer then he wasn't a very good one! According to him, Devlin had the cosh on him when he was arrested for the murder. And the man (Campbell) who allegedly told Devlin all about the robbery had got two years not 18 months. But although he "remembered" certain true facts—such as the judge falling ill early on and the trial being postponed, and Devlin's description of the cosh, " a long rubber one"—all of which he could not possibly have known unless he had been primed—he could not even remember Devlin's first name!

It had been clearly demonstrated that Campbell—who had been transferred in December to Walton at the request of the defence for ease of access—could not have had any contact whatever with Devlin. It was also established that Devlin and Burns had given statements to their lawyers regarding their alibi as early as October 17th, long before the committal, the trial and before Campbell was even arrested. Yet despite the numerous glaring inconsistencies in Cockcroft's story, and without his being subjected to cross-examination, Gerrard concluded that he was telling the truth!

When Austin O'Toole was questioned, he said he went to London in July 1951 because he was AWOL from the army. He never came back to Liverpool because all the police knew him from around Lime Street. He was now serving a sentence at HM Borstal Usk in Wales, which had been imposed at the London Sessions in December 1951 for burglary at the Green Street, Mayfair home of Sir Richard Foley-Phillips, a rich homosexual, where he had previously lived. He had later lived with an uncle at Caxton Road, Shepherds Bush.

Enquiries made by Scotland Yard revealed that he was a regular customer at Austin Reed's in Shaftesbury Avenue, where the homosexual, who had an account there, would buy him coats, suits and shirts, etc. Although it was ascertained that O'Toole was bought a suit there on the 20th August, police investigations failed to ascertain where he was on the 19th. In view of Bury's accusations to the hostel girls that he was the murderer, there was no actual proof that he was in London on *that* date. "But," decided Gerrard, "he *probably was* in London on the 19th" (Author's italics).

The 20-year-old, a nephew of one time European lightweight champion

Alf Howard, said he had known June Bury since he was 15 or 16. Asked when he had last seen her, "It was in July in the Rainbow," he said. "She was there with another bloke. She was wanting to talk to me but I told her where to go." Asked by Superintendent Hawkyard who the other man was, he didn't know, adding, "She was always with so many." Gerrard concluded that O'Toole, "had given his evidence very frankly and was in no way connected with the murder." Similarly, McLoughlin, Rubin and McNeill were later described by Gerrard as persons of truthfulness.

Apart from the lying Cockcroft story, the most damaging allegation against Devlin was made by Alfred Sheed, the prison's deputy governor, who stated that Devlin had admitted giving false evidence at the murder trial. In a sworn statement, Sheed said during a visit to Devlin in the condemned cell, at 7.20 pm on March 28, he said, "If I win my appeal on Monday will I be arrested by the police?" When asked why, said Sheed, he said, "At the trial we admitted doing a job at Manchester, but it was all false evidence. Of course we did not do the job." Sheed said he was so surprised he asked Devlin to repeat what he had just said, which he did. He left the cell and at once made a report, sending it to both the Prison Commissioners and the Under Secretary of State at the Home Office. Although agreeing two prison officers were present, Sheed said when he asked them later, they said they had not heard the full conversation.

With the agreement of the defence lawyers, Gerrard said he would visit Walton to interview Devlin and that Sheed would be present. The following day Gerrard duly carried out the promised interview, not in a neutral visiting room but in the condemned cell, where a shocked Devlin frequently became confused answering questions.

With Sheed present, Gerrard put his allegations to Devlin, to which he immediately protested, "That is wrong sir." The words, "Of course we didn't do the job," were, he said, referring to the Liverpool murder. He explained that when he said that to Sheed he meant that they did the job in Manchester of the 19th. "I then said, 'the evidence against us is all false' meaning the murder. We never done the job, the murder of Mrs Rimmer. He has misinterpreted my words sir."

Agreeing that Sheed had asked him to repeat his words, a stressed Devlin said, "He says — what did he say? No, I just says, 'I suppose I expect to be arrested for the job I have done in Manchester' but not for Mrs Rimmer, not for the murder which I *was* arrested for." Gerrard then put to Devlin the Cockcroft allegation, that he had learned details of the Sunblind's robbery from another man (Campbell) and had never been at the break-in himself.

In the event, although maintaining that Cockcroft's story was true (but that it was simply a case of Devlin bragging), Gerrard decided to give Devlin the benefit of doubt regarding Sheed's allegations, patronisingly stating that it was due "to the way in which uneducated people's unpunctuated speech sometimes distorts their meaning." This enabled the prison establishment to emerge unscathed whilst adding insult to Devlin's diabolical injury.

As anybody reading Devlin's letters would see at a glance, he was far from "uneducated". More importantly, why would a man who had protested his innocence during seven long months of incarceration and deprivation, suddenly confess to no less a figure than the prison's deputy governor? But this simple logic apparently did not occur to the *educated* Albert Dennis Gerrard QC.

Before the inquiry was reconvened on the 18th April, a desperate Devlin on April 11th wrote three letters. One, to the Home Secretary, tried to explain Sheed's misinterpretation of what he had told him. Included in the letter was the following:

Sir, I thought it would be much better to write direct to you ... and hope sir, you realise how easy it was for the Deputy Governor to misunderstand me. Sir, I would with your permission like to put evidence before you, which sir should prove to you without any doubt, that I robbed on Sunday night the 19th of August, the Sunblinds Ltd in Jackson Street, Hulme, Manchester with Alfred Burns and Alan Campbell. Sir, I can name the people whose house we took it to, the wife of the tenant actually went to the warehouse with us and wheeled on her carriage some of the property to her own house. The same woman less than 24 hours later, wheeled from her house, the carriage with 25 Gaberdine coats to a woman who is a funeral director, who Burns and myself had made arrangements with to buy at a said price. I accompanied her to the undertaker's. Burns and Campbell had gone a different way to it. When we met them Burns and myself took the stuff into the undertaker's while the young woman and Campbell waited on the street corner. Just after that I was with Campbell when the police chased us... I can also produce to you the person who we sold the bulk of the stuff to. I also sold a few coats to individualists (sic), who I can bring with the coats I sold them. Sir, I conclude this statement hoping I have proved in your mind what I have said is the truth… and that Alfred Burns and myself are both innocent of the murder of Mrs Rimmer.

Your Obedient Servant,

Edward F. Devlin.

PS: I have not brought this evidence up before because it hurts me to be a Judas.

The second letter was to a friend, Frank Ward, about Cockcroft's allegations against him. In this letter he wrote,

I have been fully occupied battling against further false evidence against me. It's enough to make one wonder whether the local Law is responsible for this frame-up. The latest development is a certain prisoner, who he is I don't know, told the inquiry that one day he was walking on exercise with me and I told him all the evidence for the defence was false. He has probably been paid by somebody to make that untrue statement. I have written to the Home Secretary objecting to that fresh false evidence and I have told him in my letter I will produce evidence to prove I was in Manchester when the woman Mrs Rimmer was killed. So Frank, with the help of God I should be home sometime next week. I am glad to hear you backed Teal in the National (which Devlin had tipped). In my opinion it was a certainty, it has proved itself to be the finest horse ever….And to think one of its (previous) owners was going to have it shot because he could do nothing with it. Then he changed his mind and sold it for thirty five pounds. I bet he's doing his nut now! How is Betty, tell her she'd better get a job for I am going to give her the privilege of buying all the beer Burns and myself can drink. Remember we will be very thirsty and will need all the money she can earn to quench it.

Your Old Pal Ted.

Although Devlin had hinted at a police frame up, the third letter he wrote that day in all innocence and expectation was ironically to none other than Detective Chief Superintendent Balmer! Oblivious to Balmer's intricate conspiracy which had put him in the condemned cell fighting for his life, his letter pleaded with him to take action to free himself and Burns.

> Sir, I hope when you receive this letter you will take the trouble to read it, and for the sake of justice investigate this man McNeil. If you was to take the trouble to study our case properly you would realise that A. Burns and myself are both innocent.

The letter continued,

> It should also become obvious to you how McLoughlin came to know so much about the crime. In my opinion it was him, McNeil and Marie Milne who at first planned the job. But before it took place, he got arrested and Rubin took his place... I feel sure that if you was to take the trouble to interview June Bury she would break down and tell you the truth. Before the trial she went to various people in my district and told them that McNeil came to Manchester on the 20th or 21st of August and gave her a coat to be cleaned which was full of blood. Then, from what I can gather, he took her back to Liverpool to Marie Milne's and Rubin, and it was then she was instructed what to say when the time came. Sir, I plead with you to take notice and act on what I say.

Knowing the truth, Balmer predictably did not respond to the letter but forwarded copies to the Home Office and the inquiry chairman. He then drove to Manchester and warned Bury to keep her mouth shut in future.

At the resumption of the inquiry Kenneth McNeil had been located and lied that he had just returned from a sea trip on a trawler. Dark haired, he denied he had ever dyed it red or ginger. Gerrard and Heilbron even rustled it, with Heilbron commenting, "His eyebrows are fair!"

Among his denials was going to Manchester a day or two after the murder and handing June Bury bloodstained clothing. Rubin, who McNeill agreed knowing, had earlier stated that he (McNeil) was a cook and a dishwasher at the Continental Café. But McNeil denied this saying he had simply helped out on occasion, "Clearing the tables and such like." Asked if June Bury, who he agreed knowing, was pregnant last Autumn and at the trial, he agreed that during the trial in the Witnesses' Room she had "looked fat" and they had joked about it. After first denying he knew Marie Milne, he then agreed that he did know her from the Continental, "but not to speak to."

His answers to further questions were vague, often stating that he could not be sure which town he was in at any given time. Indeed, he later told the inquiry both that he had never left Liverpool between 1ˢᵗ November and the trial and that he had been working in Birmingham during that period! Gerrard excused this, telling the defence lawyers that it wasn't so surprising given the itinerant life this "rolling stone" led.

Asked by Heilbron where he was living during July and August, including the week he worked at Lewis's, the "itinerant" replied that he had lived with the O'Toole family in the Vauxhall Gardens tenement block, and that he was a friend of Tommy O'Toole and his brothers Austin and Albert. Hearing this, the defence teams made no attempt to make any connection between June Bury accusing at different times, both McNeil and Austin O'Toole of the murder.

Concluding the inquiry, Gerrard replying to Burns solicitor Norton, said his report would be issued as a government white paper. Meanwhile he sent an interim report to the Home Office. Upon receipt, the Permanent Under-Secretary, Sir Frank Newsam, appended a note to it, expressing his disquiet that the police had shown photographs to McLoughlin before the ID parades. Gerrard however dismissed this criticism stating that he was more anxious to ascertain the truth or otherwise of Elizabeth Rooke's statement about June Bury blaming somebody else for the murder.

During the inquiry, Joseph Norton had visited Burns to see if he wanted any questions asked on his behalf. But on the orders of the Home Office and prison governor, the entire consultation was recorded by a civilian clerk, Daniel Cumella, whose wife was a city magistrate. His report, forwarded to the Home Office, included his observation of Norton telling his client that he could not say much and that Burns should not say much to him in case he incriminated himself. This blatant violation of the sacred lawyer client relationship ensured that even to the very end there was no peace or privacy for the two condemned men.

The final Gerrard Inquiry Report was published on the 22ⁿᵈ April, three days before the date fixed for the executions. It concluded that there had been no miscarriage of justice.

CHAPTER THIRTY SEVEN
LAST MINUTE PLEADING IN VAIN

Many a heart is aching, if you could read them all...

After The Ball. Charles K Harris, 1892

These are just some of the hundreds of letters and telegrams sent to the Queen and the Home Secretary, pleading for reprieves for the two condemned men. All were answered with the same official terse letter—sometimes several days after the execution. This plea was sent by the men's mothers:-

22nd April 1952.

From:

26 Leinster Street, off City Road Hulme.
6 Medlock Street, off Liverpool Road, Deansgate.

May it please your Majesty,

We, your humble servants, two working class widowed mothers, respectfully beg to draw your attention urgently to the plight of our sons, Edward Francis Devlin and Alfred Burns, who are due to die on Friday morning. The sentence upon them, which was confirmed today, is a terrible blow to us, and as a last resort we are appealing to your Gracious Majesty's clemency and mercy to intervene and save the lives of our sons.

We as their mothers believe in their innocence, and we feel that your Gracious Majesty as a mother, appreciates the terrible anxiety and sorrow which has come to us. A petition signed by six thousand people has been sent to your minister, the Home Secretary, but we feel ourselves that we must make this direct appeal to your Gracious Majesty. If in your mercy your Gracious Majesty feels it is possible to remove the threat of death from our boys, we would be eternally grateful.

We remain with the profoundest veneration, your Majesty's most faithful and devoted servants,

Amy Linda Devlin (Mrs)

Ellen Burns (Mrs).

This letter was received at Buckingham Palace and forwarded to the Home Office. It was date-stamped 26th April, the day after the execution.

Other letters and telegrams from members of the public included the following:

To The Home Secretary.

To hang two working class boys under present day conditions is not justice, it is brutal. I am sure that in your youth you have always known security and were quite untouched by conditions such as these boys must have known since childhood. An eye for an eye is revenge. I hope tomorrow when these boys are being hanged you will think of them and their distracted mothers.

Madge Allison, Altrincham. 23rd April.

To The Queen.

Your gracious Majesty,

As a mother with a son the same age as these two boys, little more than children, due to be hung on Friday for a murder I feel sure they have never done, they declared their innocence all the way through the trial. Think how their mothers must feel, if this were your son. Isn't it awful. Please will you stop the execution. They were not in Liverpool that night, it's mistaken identity, I am sure. They say they were in Manchester and I do believe them. They have decided to hang the wrong ones. You have such a kind heart, I know. So please intervene and stop it.

And for the sake of these poor mothers, I beg of you, don't let innocent boys be hung. There is little time to go now.

Yours respectfully Mrs. Larking. London. SW15. 22nd April.

To the Queen.

My most gracious Majesty,

I am writing to you on behalf of the two boys who are about to be executed at Liverpool on Friday. I am deeply sorry for them two boys also their loved ones they are leaving behind. I ask of you one favour. Do you think you can do anything for them to try and save the lives of these two boys from a terrible death. I am a complete stranger to them but have followed the trial right through. In my opinion they are innocent. I do not call this justice if these two boys die. I know you love Prince Charles and dear Princess Anne. And their mothers love these two boys. I am sure they must be broken-hearted. So for the mothers I beg of you to help them, and I know you will try. Time is very short for them. So my gracious Queen I beg of you to give this your immediate attention.

Thanking you, our most gracious Queen. Long may you reign.

I remain, your most obedient servant,

Mrs Claire Judd. Manchester. 22nd April.

PS I hope Prince Charles and Princess Anne are keeping well. I think they are two beautiful children.

To The Home Secretary.

I wish to make an appeal on behalf of Edward Devlin and Alfred Burns. In the first place I am appealing because of their youth. And there is little doubt they did not realise the seriousness of their crime nor what the consequences would be. They have already gone through a terrible ordeal, which is a lesson they won't likely forget. Secondly I would appeal because of the parents who must be suffering great anguish. If these lads are executed they must still suffer, although quite innocent. So I would humbly pray you to earnestly consider the matter and mercifully grant a reprieve.

Yours very sincerely, E W Haggerty. Sidcup, Kent. 23rd April.

Dear Home Secretary,

The Gerrard Report on the Wavertree murder deals at one point with the evidence of a night watchman at a factory near Sunblinds where the two condemned men say they were committing a robbery on the night of the murder. Mr Gerrard states that he accepts that the watchman spoke to a man on the night of 19th/20th August. And he is also willing to accept that this man was Devlin. Nevertheless he concludes that there has been no miscarriage of justice. The apparent contradiction here is very disturbing. Is there not a danger of a grave error being made here? I feel that in Devlin's case you should use your powers for mercy and grant him a reprieve. There will be widespread agreement with such action.

Yours truly, Kenneth Howse. Essex. 23rd April.

To the Home Secretary.

Dear Sir, God advise you.

May I respectfully and earnestly appeal for your clemency and prudence in the case of the condemned men, Devlin and Burns, to advise Her Majesty to extend a reprieve. I have merely a casual interest in the matter, but even that disturbs me because of the uncertainty which exists. Therefore permit me please, in order that I should be in time, to write to you in your ministerial capacity. May I tell you what relief was felt when the humane Sir Joynson Hicks reprieved the Brighton murderers because of the certain element of doubt in that case, "which made it undesirable to inflict the irrevocable penalty." Sir, you have already established yourself a reputation for clemency and scrupulous consideration. Please extend a reprieve to those two young, though strayed, lives.

Yours very respectfully, Hayden Morgan. Swansea. 23rd April.

To the Home Secretary.

Dear sir,

I have no personal interest in the case of Devlin and Burns. But I feel led to address this personal appeal to you asking you to exercise the prerogative of mercy on their behalf. They may or may not be guilty of the crime for which they were sentenced, but I do feel the environment in which they lived is as much to blame for their present position as they themselves. I pass Leinster Street on my way to my place of business. It is a slum area with no beauty to assist the people who live there, to lead the kind of lives we would desire. Whilst in no way condoning the terrible crime which has occurred, I beg you not to increase the death toll by allowing these two young men to be executed.

Yours sincerely, Norman Wood, Swinton, Manchester. 23rd April.

To Home Secretary.

Dear sir,

In view of the possibility of a miscarriage of justice, in spite of the finding of the Gerrard Inquiry, I earnestly request you to recommend that the two condemned men be reprieved.

Yours respectfully, Mrs G Giddings. Hertfordshire. 23rd April.

To Home Secretary.

Dear Sir,

May I appeal to your good self for the well-being of the two Manchester lads, They are the victims of environment. Of that there is no doubt whatever. I was born in Hulme and of course know the locality. There are different areas in it.

I was lucky being born in a fairly respectable part. But for the grace of God go I. So, Sir David, please extend the hand of human kindness and reprieve them.

Yours sincerely, Walter Holt. Manchester. 23rd April.

To Home Secretary.

Dear Sir,

I feel so uneasy in my mind about the fate of the two young men whose lives hang in the balance that, after reading every scrap of the evidence, the trial and ultimate findings of the judge and jury, I feel strongly, as do all my friends and family that these two very unfortunate fellows ought to be given the full benefit of the doubt, or doubts, and acquitted. We do not think for one moment that they did it. Please give them your full consideration and mercy. Do not make the horrible mistake of your predecessor, Strachey, whom I loathe, when he allowed two young servicemen for one doubtful — My hatred for that man is everlasting. I cannot bear to think about that case without a feeling of strong revulsion towards the man who could have saved two English boys. Or was it three? There was no doubt one of those boys fired a shot. But in this case of Edward Devlin and Alfred Burns there is too much doubt and the risk is too great. Innocent young men may be hanged and the real killer go free. Please do not take this chance. They are both too young to die needlessly. God help you to decide. Amen.

Mrs Thurlbeck. North Shields. 23rd April.

To the Home Secretary.

Dear Sir, I write to ask if you will kindly consider a reprieve for Edward Devlin and Alfred Burns under sentence of death.

Pastor Arthur H Bird. Rotherham. 3rd April.

To the Home Secretary.

Dear sir,

I hope it is not out of place to write to you about the cases of Alfred Burns and Edward Devlin. I have read in the papers that the final decision about their reprieve is in your hands. I cannot be content until I have put in my plea that they should not be hanged. I am a teacher taking a further course of study. We are taught as students about the causes of delinquency, about how great a part environment and upbringing play in the moral development of children. These two young men are not much more than children and, according to the newspapers, even the police who have known them since childhood, place the blame for their conduct on environment and the bombing. I feel sure there are many, especially among teachers, who feel as I do about this case but are hesitant to write, wondering whether the petition of one person could make any difference.

Yours faithfully, Monah Latimer, Bury Lancs. 2nd April.

Telegrams:

To the Home Secretary.

Kindly commute death sentence on Devlin & Burns. No reliable evidence of guilt. English law gives benefit of doubt—Mrs Fanny O'Riordan. Margate 24.4.52.

Priority. Home Secretary, House of Commons.

Reprieve Devlin and Burns.

God. Watford 23.4.52.

To the Home Secretary.

I called on Good Friday to see Mrs Devlin as myself in 1950 went to prison on an innocent charge. Also went to a mental home as a sane man. I am the only man in England today who has experienced what an innocent man has gone through.

I think these two boys who are due to be executed are innocent. And by the will of God I think also it would be bad for England if innocent men were hung.

F Lightwood. Manchester. 23.4.52.

The following is the duplicated response by a senior Home Office civil servant, sent to all the correspondents, including the men's mothers. It is almost certain that neither the Queen nor the Home Secretary, Sir David Maxwell Fyfe, even had sight of, much less read, their letters and telegrams. The replies to the men's distraught mothers were actually dated after the executions had taken place:-

Dear Sir/Madam,

I am directed to inform you that your letter/telegram on behalf of Francis Devlin and Alfred Burns has been referred to the Secretary of State for the Home Department who, by Her Majesty's command, gave it careful consideration, but regrets that he failed to discover any sufficient ground to justify him in advising the Queen to interfere with the due course of the law.

Your Obedient Servant, Sir William Murrie.

In a House of Lords debate on the 14th July 1972, regarding the contentious cases of Derek Bentley and James Hanratty, Lord Goodman said,

The parents have suffered the appalling tragedy of seeing the circumstances in which their sons died. I do not know the parents and I have not met any of the people concerned. But it is quite clear from the record of what has happened since, that they have devoted themselves unsparingly to seeking to procure a declaration of the innocence of their children and a declaration that the verdicts were wrong.

Unfortunately, the unworldly, widowed mothers of Devlin and Burns had neither the influence, nor financial resources to pursue the question of their sons innocence. Thus, for years they suffered in silence till their own deaths.

Last minute efforts to save the men's lives also included a 6,000 name public petition, passionate pleas to the Home Secretary by Sir Noel Goldie, Rose Heilbron and MP Sydney Silverman (who was also a legal partner of Harry Livermore), and a seven page carefully argued memorandum from solicitors, Joseph Norton and Harry Livermore. All stated how dangerous it would be to exact the supreme penalty in a case so full of doubt.

The memorandum, due to the shortage of time had to be dictated by telephone to London solicitors and then rushed to the Home Office the day before the executions. It began by stating its purpose was not to dispute the Gerrard Inquiry's findings but that sufficient evidence had emerged since the trial which, although perhaps insufficient to establish a miscarriage of justice, nonetheless created serious doubts as to the desirability of exacting the supreme penalty. It then made the following points:

1. The Gerrard Inquiry had accepted that Devlin and Burns were engaged on the Sunblind's break-in on the night of August 19th/20th. It was important to note that throughout the trial the prosecution had contended that:

2. The accused had not committed the Sunblinds break-in at all.

  (a) If they had done so it was committed on the night of the 18th/19th.

  (b) It was not until the evidence had closed that Basil Neild in his closing address to the jury, suggested for the first time the theory that the accused committed the murder on the night of the 19th/20th August and then proceeded to Manchester where they committed the warehouse robbery. It was strongly submitted that during the evidence if the minds of the jury had been directed solely to the issue that the accused had committed the murder and the robbery the same night and had not been confused by the two earlier alternatives they may well have taken a different view, as they would then have had to consider the probability or improbability of the two men getting back to Manchester. It pointed out that there was no public transport available to the accused after 10.45 pm, the time Marie Milne stated she left them.

(c)   Apart from the defence having no opportunity to call evidence to dispute the theory of the two crimes being committed on the same night, it further pointed out that at no time — given the press publicity the case attracted — had any individual come forward to say the men obtained a lift by road to Manchester. Had the issue been reduced during the evidence to this last minute scenario the jury would never have accepted so unlikely and incredible a theory.

3. The nature of the defence made it inevitable that the jury should know of the bad characters of the accused. Their associates were of the same general type, or were relatives whose evidence would have been regarded as suspect. Except in two cases it was easily possible for the jury, because of the general bad character and suspicion, to disregard the alibi evidence, and because the accused were of the type the jury despised. This, again was prejudicial to a fair unbiased trial by the jury. It may well be the bad characters of the accused turned the scale against them.

4. The main prosecution witnesses other than the scientific and police, were of very questionable character. It was submitted that Marie Milne was undoubtedly lying on a number of points, e.g. the story of the threats with the knife (see the conflicting versions given by her at the committal proceedings and at the trial). And then saying to June Bury that she must back her up.

In general the story told by her of the events of Sunday 19th of August, the day of the murder, was improbable to the extent to make definite certainty of its truth impossible.

From her story, it appears that these two practised housebreakers spent one hour in the house, 7 Cranborne Road without stealing or disturbing anything. It could not be a question of panic because the murder was not committed until after 10.

pm, and the accused left her to break into the house at about 9.pm, after arranging that she should knock on the door in five minutes time.

5. On the 6th February 1952, the Deputy Director of Public prosecutions sent the solicitors a list of the names and addresses of witnesses from whom statements had been taken but whom they had decided not to call. But the name of Walter Whittle was not included. (Mr Whittle had given a statement to the police that he saw and spoke to a man who was behaving suspiciously at a Smithdown Road bus shelter at the time of the murder). Mr Gerrard had stated at the inquiry that it was unfortunate that Whittle's evidence had not been disclosed to the defence. It is impossible to say what effect his evidence may have had on the jury. But taken in conjunction with the alibi evidence as it now stands, it might have created such doubt in the jury's minds as to lead them to a different conclusion.

6. Attention is drawn to the evidence given at the inquiry by Mr Cockcroft and the conclusions drawn by Mr Gerrard therefrom. To put the matter beyond doubt it is confirmed that solicitors for the accused proved at the inquiry that Devlin and Burns had made statements as early as 17th October 1951 particularising the events of the warehouse breaking on the 19th August. It was further evinced at the inquiry that Alan Campbell was only brought to Walton Prison on the 17th December, two months after the men's statements which, handed to Mr Gerrard.

7. Perhaps the most important feature is the conflicting evidence of June Bury between the trial and the inquiry. Mr Gerrard had apparently no hesitation in deciding that June Bury was lying to the three girls in the hostel about O'Toole being the murderer and other matters. And it is submitted that her whole course of conduct since the trial clearly indicates her addiction to inventiveness and falsehood. Had her total unreliability as a truthful witness been fully apparent to the judge and jury at the trial, as it was subsequently revealed at the inquiry, it is conceivable that the learned judge might not have directed the jury to attach the same degree of weight to her evidence as he did.

He had warned the jury that it was unsafe to convict on the un-corroborated evidence of accomplices McLoughlin and Milne but pointed out that June Bury was not an accomplice and that if they accepted her evidence then that was corroboration of the accomplices' evidence. But had the jury known of June Bury's disposition to invent and lie as extensively as has now been revealed, can it be said that that knowledge would not have materially affected the jury's decision?

We feel justified in submitting that there is a sufficient element of doubt to make it unsafe indeed to exact the extreme penalty.

It is contended that the evidence submitted to the Gerrard Inquiry tends to support the accused men's consistent protestations of innocence—particularly as it now appears to be accepted that they did in fact commit the warehouse breaking on the same night as the murder.

We submit that the theory that the men first committed the murder in Liverpool and then by some means other than public transport got to Manchester in time to commit the warehouse robbery—which from its very nature undoubtedly took a few hours—is impracticable and fantastic in the extreme and is not borne out in any degree by the evidence in the case.

We respectfully submit that in a capital case, if any element of doubt exists—even if not constituting a miscarriage of justice—it should nevertheless suffice to prevent the extreme penalty from being inflicted. We therefore respectfully submit to the Home Secretary that the foregoing matters are of such a nature and importance, that the sentence should be reviewed with a view to its commutation.

Signed;

Joseph Norton.

Harry Livermore. 23rd April 1952.

In view of the subsequent discovery of undisclosed evidence the most grimly prophetic observation in the memorandum—and perhaps the greatest argument against capital punishment—was the sentence, "It is not inconceivable that further evidence may arise in the future to support the innocence of the accused. And particularly so since the prosecution witnesses were mainly drawn from the criminal classes whose veracity is notoriously unreliable".

The memorandum was of course perfectly correct when it pointed out that if the jury had been aware of how much of a profligate liar June Bury really was, it may indeed have affected its verdict. But how much more powerful the lawyers pleas would have been had they been able to present the mass of evidence which had been deliberately suppressed. Never mind reprieve, the two men would have been immediately freed.

Although he said he had fully considered the contents of the memorandum and all the other passionate pleas for clemency, Sir David Maxwell Fyfe nonetheless refused to reprieve the condemned men.

Burns and Devlin themselves wrote many letters from their adjacent condemned cells where they had languished for eight weeks in circumstances where the lights never went out and where each was constantly watched 24 hours a day by pairs of rotating prison officers. These painful letters are remarkable for their stoicism, the grim humour of Burns, and the anguish and desperation of Devlin.

On the eve of execution, Burns wrote eight letters: to his solicitor Joseph Norton, family members and his friend John Ford and even, most thoughtfully, to Devlin's mother.

His last letter to Norton ran thus:

Dear Mr Norton,

I thought I would write this letter to convey my heartfelt thanks for all you have done for me. I should also like to thank Miss Heilbron, Sir Noel, Mr Nance and Mr Tarsh. There is no doubt, we could not have had a better team fighting our case.

If it had not been for the corrupt police force and prejudiced people concerned in this case, Ted and I would now be free. The only trouble with this country is that the public will allow anything to happen. Our innocence has been proved, and when we have been murdered and the truth comes out, all you will hear is, 'Poor boys' and, 'I always said those young men did not commit that murder'. It really is a sickening business.

Well I will close now. My family and friends know I am innocent, that is all that matters. I pray that God will punish all those who had a willing hand in this murdering of Ted and myself.

Once again, thank you for all you have done.

Yours sincerely,

Alfred Burns.

Burns also wrote on the eve of his execution the following to his brother-in-law Eddie Billingham:-

Dear Eddie,

Just after your visit yesterday the Governor came and told me about my reprieve being refused. He was very nice about it. I suppose it is a distasteful duty imparting such news to a condemned man; although I am something of a fatalist concerning such a matter. It is God's will that I hang, although I am innocent of the crime of which I have been found guilty.

Some day the truth will be known to everybody. It is such a pity that so many people had to suffer because of trash like Milne, Bury and Co. Why those people should have framed us … I don't know; we have never done Bury any harm and McLoughlin does not even know us…

Eddie do one favour for me, never let my mother live on her own. She is getting on now and she will soon need someone to look after her. Also never let Marie and the kid have any worries if they can be prevented. Young Brian is a lovely kid Ed, it did me the world of good seeing him yesterday. I am only sorry that was my last chance. Just think I went out without my last ambition to make some beer baron a millionaire. Still, you can carry on where I left off!

I don't know who you will use now as an excuse to get out more often, unless you get a job as a travelling salesman…"

All the Best.
Your old pal Alfie

His last letter to his friend John Ford included the following:

Dear John,

I hope this letter finds you suffering under your tyrannical wife. I can see you now, bowed shoulders, head in hand saying, 'Why didn't I listen to Alf'!

… Say John, I don't know where Ted will be by the time you get this letter. I'll be in heaven but Ted? Well you know what kind of a bloke he's been during his life.

Norton sent me a letter which I received yesterday. He mentioned his intention of sending a memorandum to the Home Secretary telling him the reasons we should be reprieved. I'd already sent a nine-page petition myself.

…I told you a couple of weeks ago what the result of the inquiry would be. They definitely know we are innocent but it would have cost them too much money to admit it. Make sure that this case is never dropped John. Even though it will do Ted and I no good, it will clear our name and make my Mam feel better. If you could have seen the letter my Mam sent me John, she is taking it hard.

That filthy trash that framed us must have minds like sewers, and there (sic) parents can't be any better.… What was done about that business concerning Balmer, exactly nothing. Believe me Johnnie, the police can get away with any-thing.[1]

I don't know how you are managing without me. Who directs you when you are uncertain, who can you tell your troubles to? Still if you are in any difficulties go to a spiritualist.

Ted as far as I know, is taking it well. We both go at the same time, so we will soon see who can move the quickest if there are any women in sight. It knocked me sick when you and my Mam left me today. I'm alright mind; it's just the thoughts of all the good times we've had in the past. Still, it is God's will that we go this way.

You really looked well today John. I shouldn't be surprised if it was the mar-riage business that has done you favours. Well John I will close now. Take care of yourself. Visit my Mam now and again. And give my regards to anyone that wants them.

---

1. June Bury had told Devlin's sister and aunt that Balmer had bought her nylons and a perm and had threatened her with ten years for perjury if she changed her evidence at both the trial and the Gerrard Inquiry.

Goodbye for now,
Your old Pal, Alf.

PS: Tell Ron that I will be in charge of all pink elephants from now on: so if he gets DTs it will be me tormenting him.

To Devlin's mother he wrote:-

Dear Mrs Devlin,

Just a few lines hoping they do not find you too unhappy; you know Ted would not want you to dwell on what has happened. It would not have been such a terrible thing if you and my mother had not known the facts of the case. It is just that the people we love must know that we have been murdered. God must have a reason for this, though I pray that the truth comes out soon and that all concerned in the death of Ted and myself will suffer. I will not keep on the subject as it only makes me feel bad.

So young Pete is doing 28 days. I had to laugh when I heard about it; although he would have been better off had he gone to Germany. Still, no one can blame him for going absent, after all Ted is his favourite brother. There is a book in my cell here, the title of it is "Papist Pie." Well this book is on Catholic religion and it explains everything concerning Catholicism: another day or so and I would have changed my religion.

I will close now.

I'm afraid I have always been hopeless at letter writing.

Give my regards to all the family,
Yours sincerely, Alf.

Devlin also wrote poignant letters to his mother, John Ford, sister Eileen, older brother Leonard and to Mary Bibby, the girl he had proposed to on one of his last visits. In this last letter to his mother, the Roman Catholic Devlin wrote:

For my sake Mam don't worry. The cross Our Lord has given you to bear has been very hard and I am now very sorry for not being the son I should have been. But at least I have the consolation that you and all my family know that I am innocent. Someday all of us will be together in the next world, so don't get upset—you will only hurt me if you do. You will understand how sorry I am for all the worry and trouble I've caused you in the past. Don't worry Mam, if we die we shall die as martyrs not murderers. I am trusting in God. I am now waiting for the priest to come and give me Communion, so don't think our God has forsaken me.

On the eve of his execution he wrote to Mary Bibby:

Dear Mary,

...tell your mother and father I hold no grievance against them for wanting their daughter to find somebody better than me. You can't blame them if you look at it sensibly. They must have thought with me being a thief that I would be in and out of gaol all my life, and they didn't want to think they had neglected their duty towards you by not trying to prevent you from marrying a gaolbird...I hope you will find someone who will cherish you all your life. I want you to remember me as you found me, and always remember that I was innocent of this crime...

His last letter to Ford, included the following:-

...John, it just makes one wonder how many innocent men have gone to the gallows in this present-day England of ours.

With his morale, which had sustained him since his arrest, now crumbling, Alfred Burns, still retaining traces of his grim humour, wrote this last letter to his mother, part of which *The People* Sunday newspaper published two days after his execution:

Dear Mam,

Just a few lines hoping they find you in the best of health. There is one thing I want you to do and that is forget what has happened.

Maybe everything has turned out for the best. I don't think I could have gone absolutely straight: so at least I will not cause you any more worry. *

The truth about this business will come out someday. We had our innocence proved at the trial but it was of no avail. (sic) As far as I am concerned, I don't worry, as death is only after all, a stepping stone. But when I think of the worry those people have caused you, I hope God will never let them have another moment's rest. Perhaps the jury did not know (which in my opinion is impossible to believe) but they not only helped those murderers to get away with one murder, they actually helped them to commit another two.

Well dearest, I will not dwell on the subject too much as it only brings bitter thoughts. As long as I know that you know I'm innocent that is all that really matters.

From what Marie tells me, little Brian is a wonderful kid. It seems he prefers you to anybody else—even when I was at home that was the case.

I can hear old Ted's voice through the door. He stands up to it pretty well, but I think it hits him harder than it does me. I feel really sorry for him in fact. Still, I'm better off now than some people. Look at poor John Ford. I knew him when he was happy and carefree. But since December 29th (his wedding) he's been wandering around in a daze.

I made a New Year resolution, to stop smoking and drinking after Friday!

By the way Mam don't forget to have all my stuff returned from the Law. And if anything is ruined by them, get their equivalent in money.

Today I was seriously thinking of changing my religion to RC. I have been reading a book on Catholicism, and your religious way of thinking is much more serious than C of E. Still, it all has the same meaning. Take no notice of that piece that I crossed out. (underlined above *) I was not sure if you would be too upset at what has happened and I put that in to make you think it might have been all for the best.

There is one thing Mam—I shall be able to make my peace with God. We are innocent of this wicked crime for which we have been convicted, so God must have a reason for taking us. He has taken far better people than Ted and I could ever have been. I know you will see it my way Mam, and I know you will pray for us.

Well dearest, I will close now. Look after yourself,

Your loving son, Alf.

PS: Don't forget to pray for Ted and myself.

Burns' letter to his sister-in-law, Henry's wife "Molly." is also a remarkable example of his fortitude in the face of such horrific circumstances.

Dear Molly,

I received your more than welcome letter. This is the last, in fact the only, chance of answering it. By the time you receive this I shall be being referred to as the late Alf.

When I heard the verdict of the Home Secretary I said to myself, 'Right again Alf as usual.' They could not afford to let us go. The very same thing happened to Rowland in '49.

Well it's no use me dwelling on the subject. I done so much writing, talking and listening about our case that I have almost got a one track mind.

Norton came to see me last night. I think I have had the wrong opinion of that man. In the past I have said that he has not done everything possible. I now know I have been wrong. Anyway I shall write and thank him for his help. I also want to thank you Molly. It is a pity you were not believed when you were obviously telling the truth. Will you also thank Alice Shenton for me.

I will close now. Give my love to the kids.

Your affectionate BIL, Alf.

PS: Don't forget to pray for me and Ted.

For the next two Sundays, *The People* continued to publish some of their last letters including the following from Devlin to his aunt, Mrs Swann and her husband:

The few words I am about to write, I want you both to realise, although I can't find fitting words, the sincerity I put behind the three words 'I thank you' for the firm faith in me and the kindness you have done me. And I know I can leave this

world knowing that you two, with the help of all my family, will leave no stone
unturned until mine and Alfie's innocence has been proved.

I will be looking forward for the time when my innocence is allowed by Our
Lord to be proved to the world.

God bless you all,

From your ever-loving nephew Teddy.

To his sister Eileen, who had given evidence for him at the trial and the
Gerrard Inquiry, Devlin finally wrote:

My dear Eileen and Eddie,

No doubt you will realise how hard it is for me to write but I know in the words
I say, you will understand my feelings towards you and what you have done for
me in the past and present.

I can leave this world with the knowledge that all who belong to me, know
without any doubt that I am innocent, and that all my family and relations will
thank Our Lord for giving me the opportunity of repenting for the sins I have
committed. For he foresaw the way I was heading. And to prevent me from being
separated from you all in the next world he has allowed this miscarriage of justice
to occur. So always have faith and then he will let us all be together in the next
world. Goodbye Eileen and Eddie and good luck till we meet again. Always look
after Mama. She has always done her best for us. I only wish I had the chance
to make up for the way I treated her.

I will once again say Goodbye and God bless all of you.

From your ever-loving Brother and Brother-in-law Teddy, xxxxxxxxxxxxx [2]

Next morning at 9 am both men were hanged side-by-side. The post-execution report on Devlin stated, "Some tearing of soft tissue of neck." [3]

---

2.   The original provided by his niece Jean Ackroyd.
3.   Prison Commission files.

A CCRC referral on behalf of Ruth Ellis who was hanged in 1955, was also rejected by the Court of Appeal in December 2003 as frivolous and time-wasting.

At her trial which lasted 14 minutes, Ellis had pleaded guilty, openly telling the court she had intended to kill when she had shot her boyfriend five times. Dismissing the appeal, Lord Justice Kay again criticised the CCRC for wasting the court's time with a referral, "Which was entirely without merit."

Having been publicly chastised for referring hopeless or frivolous cases, the CCRC's pendulum has now swung to the other extreme, causing its reluctance to refer more substantial cases even where it is virtually certain that a miscarriage of justice occurred.

In a 2004 interview, Tony Foster, a member of the CCRC since 1997, is quoted as saying among other things, "We have to use our *investigative techniques* to the full to find things out" (Author's italics). The CCRC does indeed have wide powers to carry out its own investigations into applicants' claims. Yet when in response to the Commission's provisional Statement of Reasons, I submitted further fresh evidence in the form of an affidavit from Joan Downing, stating she and her husband had been forced by the Liverpool police to change her statement and had been financially rewarded by them, this was again rejected. Rather than use its "investigative techniques" by independently interviewing her, they unbelievably dismissed her affidavit and tape-recorded statement on the spurious and contradictory grounds that her memory after 60 years could not be relied upon. But then contradictorily stated, "She did not describe how the break-in took place and had not described how the stolen gabardines had smelled!!" Apart from the absolute absurdity of this statement, they had not even remembered that Joan Downing had only come into the picture *after* the men had broken in so would not be able to describe the break-in.

Given its ludicrous dismissal of Joan Downing's statement, it is a great pity the Commission itself did not use these "investigative powers" to interview her before rejecting her vital 2011 affidavit which had corroborated her deceased husband's statement of 60 years earlier..

The terms of reference of the CCRC, together with its apparent re-interpretation of its role whereby it attempts to second-guess what the Court of Appeal would do, seem to make it now virtually impossible for an application however meritorious, to clear its hurdles. What also makes this more difficult is that it appears to demand—unlike the Court of Appeal itself—that new evidence be accepted only if proven beyond a reasonable doubt rather than on a balance of probabilities. This is the same onus of proof required before a jury can convict. But neither the CCRC nor the Court of Appeal is a jury!

As Dr Sandra Lean rightly says in her brilliant work, *No Smoke: The Shocking Truth About British Justice*:

> It is bad enough that miscarriages of justice occur in the first place, but it is absolutely tragic that, having occurred, they are virtually impossible to have recognised and overturned. It is almost as if it doesn't matter how much evidence to the contrary is found, the authorities cling tenaciously to the original findings, using some of the most ludicrous and unbelievable justifications for their actions.[5]

Dr Lean is perfectly correct in her analysis as the case of Devlin and Burns graphically illustrates. Examples of this absurdity and bureaucratic obduracy include the CCRC's final preposterous decision that the new evidence—including the revelations at the Gerrard Inquiry of Crown witnesses' lies and its acceptance that Devlin and Burns *did* break-in to Sunblinds on the 19th of August; the undisclosed statements of Frederick Downing and Sydney Fairbrother; the police coercion of Joan Downing; the undisclosed forensic reports on the broken window; Marie Milne's undisclosed October 9th statement saying she went with Devlin and Burns to a café *after* the murder; McLoughlin's undisclosed original accusation against "Ginger" Dutton; the discrepancies between his, Bury's and Milne's undisclosed statements and their trial evidence; the showing to McLoughlin of the accused men's photographs before the ID parade and the 2011 statement of Joan Downing—all *may* have been known to defence counsel who, for their own reasons decided not to use them!

That the CCRC could hold this view with a straight face beggars belief. Sir Noel Goldie QC and Rose Heilbron QC were the crème-de-la-crème of the legal profession at the time. Indeed Heilbron later became a High Court judge, as did Basil Neild QC. Neild who acted for the Crown, was a man, of the utmost integrity. It is not remotely conceivable that he could

---

5.   *No Smoke: The Shocking Truth About British Justice* (Checkpoint Press, 2008).

have prosecuted with such sincerity and conviction if he had been aware of this mass of undisclosed evidence.

Apart from denying justice to Devlin and Burns, by its decision not to refer this case and its comments about defence counsel's possible knowledge of the undisclosed statements, the CCRC has implicitly smeared their professional reputations.

With the government slashing expenditure across the whole public service spectrum erroneous decisions of the CCRC are perhaps now and in the future more likely. This, together with the insurmountable criteria by which it now decides whether to refer a case, will further saddle applicants with an impossible standard of proof, when for all practical purposes and in the interests of justice, the criteria should simply be: "Did the applicant receive a fair trial?" If that basic test had been applied by the Commission, there is no doubt this case would, and should, have been referred to the Court of Appeal. And there is even less doubt that that Court would have quashed the men's convictions. In this regard perhaps the observations of an 83-year-old reformed criminal might be of some value. Joe Kirwan, a close friend of Devlin and Burns, who turned his back on crime 60 years ago, recently wrote.

> Organizations such as the CCRC and IPCC [Independent Police Complaints Commission] which came into existence as a result of high profile miscarriages of justice, also exist to protect the legal and judiciary [sic] systems from irresponsible complaints. It was never going to be easy to reverse judgements which may have adverse effects on reputations and where allegations of manufacturing evidence exist.[6]

Despite its claims of progress, British Justice does not seem to have moved on much since the trial of Devlin and Burns. If the Commission's arguably perverse decision is anything to go by, and capital punishment was still in force, they still would have been hanged today. To that extent it can be rightly concluded that by its refusal to refer the case to the Court of Appeal — with its full knowledge of all the suppressed evidence — the CCRC sadly has just as much of Devlin and Burns blood on its hands as the state did in its ignorance 60 years ago.

---

6.   In a letter to the author, November 2011.

INDEX

H

The Cardiff Five
Innocent Beyond Any Doubt
by Satish Sekar, Foreword by Michael Mansfield QC

Satish Sekar shows how a miscarriage of justice destroyed families, divided communities and undermined confidence in the criminal justice system. The Cardiff Five case is the first example in the UK of a homicide in which the original suspects were vindicated by the conviction of the true killer in the DNA age. By then, they had shared 16 years in prison for a crime they did not commit.

A wake-up call for British justice.

'One of the most important books ever written about criminal justice': Michael Mansfield QC

'As the local MP I came to respect and admire Satish Sekar's thoroughness and persistence': Alun Michael

'No-one is better suited to explaining and unravelling the complexities': Duncan Campbell

'Tireless work and extraordinary insight': Bob Woffinden

www.WatersidePress.co.uk/C5

The Cameo Conspiracy
A Shocking True Story of Murder and Injustice
by George Skelly

The true story of Liverpool's
Cameo Cinema murders vividly
demonstrates the need to guard
against police corruption and
legal manipulation.

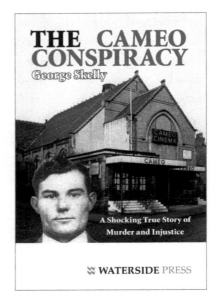

George Kelly was hanged in
1950 for shooting dead two men
early in 1949: the manager of
the Cameo Cinema, Wavertree
and his assistant. Undeniably
from the wrong side of the tracks
and involved in petty crimes of
the post-Second World War era,
Kelly and his co-accused Charles
Connolly (who went to prison
for ten years) found themselves
expertly 'fitted-up' as riff-raff in a
Kafkaesque nightmare.

'George Skelly writes from the heart': John Schlesinger

'One man's hunt for the truth': *Liverpool Echo*

'Skelly is a good writer': Norman Mailer

'A truly brilliant book': John Howley

www.WatersidePress.co.uk/cameo

Lightning Source UK Ltd.
Milton Keynes UK
UKHW020654040221
378229UK00001B/5

9 781904 380801